ENDORSEMENTS

Growing Up With Tanzania is more than a personal story;
it is also that of the birth of a nation and a vision.
Rich with anecdotes and an amazing cast of real life characters,
this thrilling memoir is an aesthetically satisfying mix of
memory, musings, meditations and mathematics.
People in all walks of life, young and old, must read it.
They will never look at numbers the same way.

Ngũgĩ wa Thiong'o

Eminent African Novelist, Poet, Playwright, Activist, Scholar
Distinguished Professor of English and Comparative Literature
University of California, Irvine.

✛ ✛ ✛ ✛ ✛ ✛ ✛

Growing Up With Tanzania is a refreshingly detailed memoir
that sees Karim Hirji's evolution from 'life in a brown cocoon'
into a world citizen in a process moulded by societal dialectics,
exemplary icons, devoted teachers and mathematics.
Brimming with love for his country, yet also reflecting his
profound pain at its current malaise, it is tempered with
solutions which stand to benefit nations beyond his own.

Zarina Patel

Kenyan Author, Activist
Manging Editor, *AwaaZ Magazine*

Growing Up With Tanzania

Growing Up With Tanzania

Memories, Musings and Maths

✤
✤ ✤ ✤ ✤ ✤ ✤ ✤
✤

Karim F Hirji

MKUKI NA NYOTA
DAR—ES—SALAAM

Mkuki na Nyota Publishers
P. O. Box 4246
Dar es Salaam, Tanzania
www.mkukinanyota.com

Copyright © Karim F Hirji 2014

ISBN: 978-9987-08-223-0

Cover Design: Mkuki B Bgoya

Visit www.mkukinanyota.com for information about and
purchase of Mkuki na Nyota books. You will also find
featured authors, interviews, and news about other
publisher/author events. Sign up for our e-news letter
for updates on new releases and other announcements.

International Distributor:
African Books Collective
www.africanbookscollective.com

To

Amer Mohamed El-Batashi, Isaac Marande,
Nassoro Mitawa, Abdallah Madenge,
Abdul Karim Mohamed, Ram Jogi,
Said Alawi, Juma Balozi, Abdallah Abbasi

and

Mr Calvin Brooks & Mr Fred Isaya

and

Elias Kisamo, Navroz Lakhani,
Amilo Pipi, Nazir Virji

Say what you know,
do what you must,
come what may.

Sofya Kovalevskaya

Contents

Acronyms

AKBS	:	Aga Khan Boys School
DTC	:	Dar es Salaam Technical College
ESR	:	Education for Self-Reliance
HQ	:	Head Quarters
IPS	:	Indian Public School
JK	:	Jamaat Khana
JKT	:	*Jeshi la Kujenga Taifa*
NGO	:	Non-Governmental Organization
NHC	:	National Housing Corporation
RM	:	Recreational Mathematics
SES	:	Socio-Economic Status
TANU	:	Tanganyika African National Union
TSh	:	Tanzania Shillings
UDSM	:	University of Dar es Salaam

Preface

To live in mankind is far more
than to live in a name.
                    Vachel Lindsay

❖ ❖ ❖ ❖ ❖ ❖ ❖

I WAS BORN INTO a tumultuous time. The people of Tanzania had begun to decisively confront colonial rule. Small and substantial struggles were unfolding everywhere. Though the British rulers attempted to derail the process by means subtle and sordid, the people's resolve did not diminish. All expectations confounded, our nation triumphantly attained *Uhuru* (political independence) on 9 December 1961. It was a peaceful, dignified transition, thanks in no small part to the wise stewardship of Julius K Nyerere. Two years later, the feudal regime of the Sultan of Zanzibar was dispatched to the dustbin of history, and the two neighbors joined hands to form the United Republic of Tanzania.

Over the next decade, the new nation began to consolidate itself. The colonizers had failed abysmally to improve the life of the common person, placed barriers against sustainable socio-economic progress, and divided us along race, religious and economic lines. We had a few rocky moments at the beginning. Eventually, our people bonded together to confront the major challenges before them. Projects in agriculture, health, education, industry, communications and culture took off. They were later synthesized into a socialistic policy aimed at promoting social equality, accountable leadership, and self-reliant development. In external affairs, Tanzania emerged as a stellar champion for the elimination of racist and colonial rule, and was globally perceived as such. It was an energetic decade of multiple achievements in which the generally engaged populace was in a forward looking, upbeat mood.

Personal and Social

These decades of epochal change in the nation were at the same time the first two decades of my life. As I look back, I find a host of narratives worthy of an audience. The upbringing, schooling, games, foibles and tribulations of my cohort are light years apart from what my grandchildren encounter today. When we meet them, which sadly is not that often, they insatiably seek childhood stories from *Babu* (grandpa) and *Nani* (grandma). This book drew its initial motivation from the wonder they display at what we tell them; it is firstly an extended answer to Emma, Samir and their cohort.

But I see that the major transitions in my life reflected, to one degree or another, the state of the nation, and the changes it experienced. While the nation was ensnared by a racially restrictive social order, I was confined within a brown coloured cocoon. As it emerged from that order, my social horizon expanded, and my communal and national agendas began to harmonize. As it struggled to stand on its own, so did I. As its education system expanded, my educational vistas grew. As one enlightened teacher inspired the whole nation, so a set of marvellous teachers moulded my life. When the call to serve the nation came, I was ready. It was a plunge into a rough and tough though simultaneously delightful and mind-numbing existence. As the hopes and dreams of the new nation consolidated, my desires took shape. From a colonial subject saluting the British, Indian and Ismaili flags, I evolved into a fervent Tanzanian whose heartbeat resonated with the tunes of *Mungu Ibariki Afrika* (God Bless Africa).

That story needs to be told too. This book embeds my personal journey within the evolution of the society at large. As I trace my path from Newala to Lindi to Dar es Salaam, Kibaha and Ruvu, I recall my family, friends, teachers and schools, picture my surroundings, describe my adventures, note my religious and secular activities, and allude to the movies, books and songs that mesmerized me. Simultaneously, I elucidate the uplifting and the disquieting aspects of my life, and reflect on race relations, morality, education, nationalism and politics. And, in the process, I convey my understanding of how the local and national socio-political environments affected the trajectory of my life.

Contents

The book has three parts: recollection (memories), reflection (musings) and a meditation on the spirals of life. The first eight chapters comprising Part I essentially follow the stages in my formal education. A special emphasis is placed on my education in maths. I do that because it later became the central pillar of my professional life. The bulk of the life events I relate occurred before July 1968, that is, just before I began my university level studies. However, when called for, I venture beyond that time frame, especially in Part III.

In Part II, I reflect on education related matters arising in Part I. They include my informal learning within the family environment, how race and education interacted over time, the ups and downs of the national education policy, and the teaching of maths in school. That exercise leads me to ruminate on personal and social responsibility, and present my views on educational reform in Tanzania.

In Part III, I inquire about the places, people, images and ideas I was associated with in my formative years. How have those places changed? How did those people navigate through these fifty odd years? How does the outlook of my cohort differ from that of the youth of today? What messages do those transformations convey? Addressing such questions finds me floating along diverse spirals of personal and societal change, and, in a nostalgic mood, connecting with individuals, social groups and institutions on the mental and real planes.

This memoir has an atypical feature: All chapters end with a section that contains elementary but eye-opening material linked to my education in maths. These minuets show the beauty of a major love of my life – mathematics – and offer my views on how it was being taught in my days, and on how it should be taught. The title lines of these sections are set apart by the symbol ❖; the reader who so desires may skip them without loss of continuity.

For sources and related matters, see Acknowledgments and Notes.

Expectations

No one who writes for public consumption stands above society in a perfectly neutral frame of mind. Deep down, each author, of fiction or non-fiction literary work, projects a message. He or she seeks to influence people or events, small or consequential, out there. Stated or not, by design or subconsciously, an expectation of one sort or another is embedded in each literary product of the human brain.

I come clean to declare that my expectations are threefold. First, I expect that these personally oriented but socially rooted tales of my youth, and my commentaries, will appeal to you at some level. Some parts may elicit a smile; some may sour your mood. Some may enlighten; some may leave you with a frown. On balance, I hope they will engage and entertain, and make you reflect on why our lives were and are the way they were and are.

My second expectation has to do with the fact that the relationship between races and communities is a central theme of this book. I would like to make it clear that it does not project the perspective of any race or community. Neither do I aim to denigrate any social group. On the contrary, I seek to promote understanding and cooperation between races, communities and religions. But I hold that such an outcome can be attained and sustained only by an open and frank discourse in which respect for the truth is a guiding principle. Having tried to adhere to this principle as much as I could, I expect that this book will play a positive role in promoting such understanding and cooperation.

And finally I have a broad expectation of you, my dear reader. In light of the undeniable fact that our planet is mired in social and environmental conflicts and hazards, I earnestly seek to draw you into a gentle conversation about how all of us can better function as free and dedicated members of a unified, mutually respectful, dignified human family. If I am able to do that even to a small degree, my labours will have more than served their purpose.

Part I

Memories

Part I narrates my life story from birth (June 1949) to age 19 years (June 1968) and links it with the concurrent social and political transformations in Tanzania. As the nation went from colonial rule to a decade of freedom, I went from early family life and primary education in Lindi to upper primary and technical education in Dar es Salaam. Two eventful years at a boarding high school in Kibaha preceded a five month gruelling stay at the Ruvu National Service Camp.

In that partly rugged life terrain, I encountered numerous twists and turns of the personal and social kind. While life brimmed with fun and learning, it also posed daunting challenges of living within and confronting racial barriers. By the end of that period, my teachers, friends and the social environment had combined to mold me into a religiously devout, patriotic Tanzanian whose principal goal in life was to plunge into the intricacies of advanced mathematics.

— 1 —

Lindi Life

Minor things can become moments of great revelation when encountered for the first time.

Margot Fonteyn

I GUESS I WAS eight years old. School was over. On a rough, dusty road, a crowded bus was sending us to Nachingwea. It being months since we had seen Father, my brothers and I were excited. He usually had nice things for us. My mind was on the set of marbles he had promised, the mango trees I would climb and the birds my hand catapult would target. Yet the long, bumpy ride was anything but thrilling. I was stiff and hungry. I whined and complained. How long was I to be squashed up? "Look at the milestones," said Mother. Etched on these uniform cement blocks were numbers in multiples of ten. Each time one came along, I strained my eyes. If it passed too quickly, my grumpiness intensified. And if I caught the number, I was happy or not depending on what it was.

Our lives are peppered with signposts of varied hue and import. Some resemble highway milestones. Others appear irregularly and in assorted guises. Some are one-of-a-kind events; others recur. Yet they too bestow joy or sorrow. Recall your first day at school: Were you excited, not at ease or outright scared?

Our early milestones – first word and step – usually occur with our family. But our family life may be constrained by rigid social barriers that limit what we experience. This was the case for me. I had a spectrum of experiences as a child. Most I enjoyed; a few I did not. But they took place within the confines of a small, racially distinct community that was economically, culturally and socially isolated from ninety nine percent of my country folk. It was as if I lived in a mini-universe separated from the mega-universe by a force field, and was impervious to its presence.

Background

I let out my first cry in Newala, a small town in the southern part of mainland Tanzania near the border with Mozambique. Probably unnerved by the cold arena I was suddenly thrust into, I made my first error in life. I should have smiled brightly. For, under the caring eyes of the two persons whose DNA I inherited, many joyful days lay ahead.

We were Ismaili, a sect of the Shia wing of Islam. Sir Sultan Mohamed Shah, better known as Aga Khan III, was our *Imam* (spiritual leader). Originating from colonial India, we were one of the immigrant groups collectively called Asians. That migration had been spurred by crop failure, dire conditions in the villages and social conflict. Our *Imam* advised our grandparents to move to Africa. His close ties to the British empire influenced many to land first in Zanzibar. The main period of their arrival was the first four decades of the twentieth century. By the year 1958, Asians constituted about one percent of the nine million people in mainland Tanzania. Among them, the nearly 30,000 Ismailis were the dominant group, both numerically and in terms of presence in the trading, professional, education, health and other sectors.

The Ismaili presence in southern Tanzania can be traced back to the 1860s. Their first prayer house in the area was built in Kilwa in 1880. With other Asians, they later spread out inland to establish small trading outposts. Despite obstacles like poor access to clean water, health hazards like malaria, rough roads and deficient housing, these pioneers managed to set up viable small businesses in many interior places. Some of these outposts evolved into larger towns (Dharas 1973).

At least one of my four grandparents was born in Zanzibar; the others disembarked at the island around 1890. My father (Fatehali Hirji) and mother (Sakarbai Kassam) were born in Zanzibar in 1921 and 1920, respectively. In the late 1920s, my paternal grandfather left the island to set up a small *duka* (shop) in Dar es Salaam.

Our *Imam* issued an edict in 1945 exhorting us to settle in the south. Each family had access to a loan of TSh 5,000 with flexible repayment terms. It sufficed to set up a small shop or business. His visit to Lindi in 1946 added emphasis to his words. The early 1950s saw other avenues for economic advancement open up. Housing and commercial loans on generous terms from community institutions were now regularly available. The colonial authorities provided plots for houses, shops, prayer houses and schools. While life was decidedly difficult, and our parents slogged daily from dawn to dusk to maintain a minimally decent existence, these were the conducive aspects of the historic conditions under which they came to make a home for themselves in Lindi and its interior areas.

Aga Khan III was a global statesman and one of the wealthiest persons in the world. His politics over a life time mostly reflected the agenda of the British empire. Thus, in India and Africa, he urged his followers to be loyal subjects of the Crown. The advice to set up shop in the south likely had the nod of the British rulers who were instituting a massive ground nuts production scheme in central and southern Tanzania. It came with an influx of colonial officials, company employees and their families. The Asians were to be the middlemen for the European firms, and were as well expected to establish the service infrastructure for colonial rule, thereby enabling the European way of life to operate without too many glitches.

The poorly conceived scheme failed in a matter of years. The bulk of the Europeans left, but the Asians stayed behind. Ground nuts or not, their presence was vital for the import-export structure to take root, expand geographically and flourish financially.

The South

Father had five living brothers and one sister. He attended the Aga Khan Boys School in Dar es Salaam, but neglected his studies, frequently missing classes to roam about town with friends. He dropped out in primary Standard 4 or 5. By that time he had learned to read and write in Gujarati. Unfortunately, what he wrote was barely readable. His English always remained rudimentary. He conversed in Swahili to the extent needed to deal with servants, vegetable sellers, customers and public officials.

Mother went further, reaching secondary Form II. Unfortunately, her mother's death put a stop to her education. For a few years, she taught religion classes at the primary level. I gather that she had a series of notebooks in which she used to write class material and hymns in an elegant cursive style. But marriage ended her career and converted her into a traditional, home-bound housewife. The ensuing life of domestic drudgery significantly weakened her intellectual skills. I recall that when they were older than fifty, both regularly read books of hymns, prayers and holy edicts. Father additionally read Gujarati novels and health books, and perused English newspapers. She did not. When I was in the USA in the 1980s, she wrote rambling letters that mixed Gujarati and English and had sentences lined up in an odd manner on the page. They took an effort to decipher. Father sent a letter only once or twice.

Hirji Sunderji, his father, died early, leaving a poor wife with many mouths to feed. Fatehali had to start work at an early age. His first job was to load and unload cargo from trucks. Then he learned to drive. At the time I was born, he had a small *duka* in Newala. As it did not thrive, two years on, with a new baby in our ranks, the family – Father, Mother and sons Mohamed, Karim and Nazir – moved to Lindi, a larger coastal town (Image 1 and Image 2: Appendix B).

As the British rule consolidated after World War I, the numbers of Asians in Lindi grew. The population of the town grew from 8,600 (African = 7,400; non-African = 1,200) in 1948 to 10,300 (African = 8,400; non-African = 1,900) in 1957. The non-Africans of 1957 comprised 100 Europeans and 1,800 mostly Asians (Census 1957).

The Ismaili presence in Lindi is traceable to the early 1900s. Around the year 1957, there were roughly 2,300 Ismailis in the whole of southern Tanzania. Of these, about 500 were in Lindi town (These figures show an order of magnitude as their accuracy is open to question). The other numerically comparable if not more numerous Asian communities were the Ithnasheris and Hindus. The Goan, Bohora, and Sikh populations were much smaller in number.

Lindi, the administrative and economic hub of southern Tanzania, was an amply spread place with large swaths of greenery. Its long streets broadly divided the central part into an elegant, beach front European section, a clean looking residential-commercial Asian section, a sports ground-school section and the market area African section. Some Europeans had houses in the hilly areas. The principal Asian area had one and two story Zanzibar style traditionally built structures standing some distance from each other. I recall produce and clothing stores, a fancy goods store frequented by the Europeans, houses of worship, a petrol station and a few two story commercial/residential buildings. Not far from the house we later moved to were the Novelty Cinema, a place I first entered when I was eight years old, and an elegant beach hotel whose interior I never had the opportunity to explore. Both were Ismaili owned. I also remember the Ismaili library and student hostel in Lindi.

The Asians of Lindi were primarily engaged in small scale trade. They also ran hotels, tea shops, photo studios, a pharmacy, carpentry shops, petrol stations, maintenance and repair garages for motor vehicles, and flour mills. Hindu artisans – barbers, shoe makers, washer men – plied their respective trades. Asians worked as clerks or middle level managers in banks and foreign import-export-shipping firms, as sales persons in major stores, as accountancy, insurance and law personnel, or served in the civil service. There was no Ismaili teacher or doctor in Lindi, but there was a Hindu doctor. The Hindu and Muslim teachers in our schools had been recruited directly from India.

The delicacies of the Ismaili run Sampully Bakery left a lasting imprint on your taste buds. It had a region wide reputation with its output prized by all, including the colonial wives. Every Asian of that era from Lindi I meet does not fail to mention it. But, except for freshly baked bread, my family had those delights only on very special occasions.

The well to do Asians ran wholesale enterprises and factories, owned multiple shops, and repair, trucking or petrol stations, and operated cinema houses and major hotels in the town and inland. They interacted closely with British company and colonial officials. Their houses were expansive and better built compared to ours. I was acquainted with these Ismailis in their capacities as the *Mukhi* and *Kamadia* (prayer house leaders), and as senior personalities in our community. As was generally the case throughout East Africa, the economic elites dominated the high positions – religious and secular – in the community institutions.

As far as I know, no Ismaili farmed in the Lindi area. Some inland families ran dairy farms. A few Asians owned large plantations. The 1950s witnessed the start of a push away from trading into agriculture. But it did not go far. Apart from the few large scale operators, it was a sector of the economy not welcoming or friendly to Asians in the same manner as Africans faced hurdles in obtaining licenses or loans to operate retail and wholesale shops.

Economic separation was an integral feature of colonial rule. Africans were restricted even from studying commerce related subjects. Such a set up made Africans stagnate and Asians rise up. But that unfairness was under attack. For example, in many areas, rural cooperative societies were denting the Asian monopoly in buying produce from farmers.

Early Days

My father first opened a small shop near the African area in Lindi in 1952. He sold salt, oil, sugar, biscuits, candies, matchboxes, flour, rice, soap, beans and kerosene. But his stock was tiny. My mind still holds the image of a ramshackle storefront with odd-shaped, mostly empty aluminium bins, and half-filled candy-toffee bottles on a brownish table with cracks running in all directions. A mostly bare wooden shelf stood at the back. His customers were largely African.

He had a difficult time making ends meet. I can still hear him complaining to mother,

> I just sold a few sweets today. The profit was ten cents. How can I feed all of you this way?

I wonder how I can recall this detail. I was but four years old. Is it a visualization of what I was told sometime later? Or perhaps it was because the conversation preceded a striking shift in our family life.

A faint image of the major rain storm that engulfed the south around that time lingers. Our roof was damaged; some of the corrugated iron sheets were blown away. I see myself shivering in the damp house. Roads were flooded and communications were severed for about two months.

A more solid image shows a filthy, pungent, unlit outhouse in the backyard. The floor was slimy, slippery. The rusted, sheet metal walls creaked with the wind. Long whiskered, giant cockroaches slithered in and out of the squat-hole. Too terrified to place myself over it, I mostly voided outside. For that, I was teased by my elders to no end.

Father closed his Lindi shop in 1954 (or perhaps 1955), and began work as a lorry driver. His truck plied between Lindi and inland towns, delivering imported goods to traders and returning with agricultural produce like cashew nuts, cassava, maize, beans and charcoal. The roads were treacherous during the typical three month rainy season. But he did not cease his runs, and was thereby respected by area merchants for his dependability.

After two years, he secured a loan of TSh 10,000 from the Ismaili run Diamond Jubilee Investment Trust. It enabled him to open a retail shop in Bunju. Mohamedali, his younger brother, was his partner and ran the shop. Father's transport work went on but on a more independent footing. Using a part of the loan and his savings, he got a truck of his own; a fellow Ismaili driver has told me that it was a BMC 7-ton truck.

Earnings from the Bunju shop did not pay the bills. So the two brothers moved to Ruponda, a lush forest-enclosed place that was more than a village but not quite a township. It was located about ten kilometres from Nachingwea, a key interior commercial hub. Father was already making regular deliveries to that area and had a good sense of the opportunities. His arrival enabled Ruponda to boast a grand total of two shops, his and a bigger one run by an Ithnasheri merchant. They sold general merchandise and bought cashew nuts, beans, honey and beeswax from local farmers, bagged it, and sent it to the merchants of the port towns, Lindi and Mtwara.

In consideration for our education, Mother and we three boys remained in Lindi, but now in a decently built, more spacious flat a walking distance from the sea shore. It comprised a long, narrow corridor with five rooms at one side, the kitchen being the last. The corridor opened into a small backyard with a Western type toilet, bathroom and storage room filled with charcoal sacks and wood for fuel. The front living room also served as a small shop in which Mother sold sundry items like sweets, matchboxes and salt. A sports goods store was next door to us.

The backyard had a tamarind tree that had been chopped off. Only the main stump with one side branch remained. Small shoots would emerge on a frequent basis, especially after the rains. The tender reddish-green leaves of the tamarind are edible and have a sweet-sour taste. Mohamed and I liked to chew them, so the poor tree never regrew well.

Our school vacations were spent in Ruponda. Nazir and I went up the mango and cashew trees. Scaling the coconut tree, even a short one, was forbidden. But that did not prevent us from trying. We made catapults with strong Y-shaped twigs and long but thin rubber bands obtained from vehicle and bicycle tires. They were for hunting birds, rats and large lizards. When we came upon a carefully camouflaged chameleon, we did not take aim but sat down and stared at it until it changed its colour. Hours upon hours went into shooting multi-coloured marbles.

Once we were given a shiny plastic ball obtained from the other shop. When we took it to the playground of the primary school, African local boys joined us in a game of soccer. It was an exciting event for them. Their ball was a bundle of wound up newspapers tied tightly with sisal strings. This was the real thing, a first time event for them.

I recall this as the only time that I, as a child, played with kids whose skin colour was black. They were playmates of convenience. As the owner of the prized ball, I bossed them around with an aura of superiority. All my friends in Lindi were brown-skinned; most were Ismaili. Strict racial boundaries were the norm in those times, and we observed them as a matter of course.

Social life in Lindi was restricted and religiously oriented. In commerce and civic matters, Asians from various communities competed and cooperated as the situation demanded. But each community celebrated its festive and holy days mostly on its own. Fairs, school issues and special ceremonies brought them together. Intermarriage was rare and frowned upon. Mother told us not to eat in the house of an Ithnasheri; a relic of the historic angst between the two groups. But in school, Asian children intermingled. In my standard 6 primary class, my closest buddies were a Hindu and an Ithnasheri. When I passed by the home of the former in the evening, he would call me. We then sat under a shady mango tree nearby and munched the generous bag of *ganthia* (fried chips made from garbanzo bean flour) and sharp slices of raw onion his mother had kept for us.

In my ten years in Lindi, I do not recall ever having a one-to-one engagement with a person of European origin, and I never witnessed my father doing so either. Actually, I did not want to. The thought aroused fear. While their residential area lay across from our prayer house, and no rule forbade it, we did not venture in that direction. Aware of the vicious dogs lurking in that area, the very idea of encountering one kept us at bay. One place where the white folk came into social contact with the brown skinned subjects was the Novelty Cinema. But they came on the day of the week reserved for English movies and would congregate in a corner of their own. Even though there was no law against it, other than the cleaners, hardly any African person entered the cinema theatre. It was understood that this was not a place for them.

Gastronomical Matters

The best friend of my brother Mohamed was from a rich Ismaili family. His father ran the best high-end textile goods shop in Lindi as well as an auctioneering joint. On weekends, the two friends took me along when they sauntered near a flour mill some distance from the town centre. I spent the time sailing paper boats in a small pond. It was wider in the rainy season, and would be awash with countless tadpoles and the clatter of hundreds of frogs jumping about and croaking. At times our trip was ruined by a colossal swarm of dragon flies. If you did not escape in time, they hurtled into your face, nose and ears ceaselessly, driving you crazy. Fried dragon flies were a delicacy for the local Makondes. Mother occasionally fried them with garlic and salt. It was a yummy treat.

When we went out, our mothers gave us boiled cassava, yams or *puri* (fried flat bread) for a snack. Mohamed and his buddy ate theirs with the chilies that grew wild around the mill. The tiny ones were exceptionally hot. I tried them but once. Instantly, my mouth caught fire. I must have cried for a long time. Traditional Asian food is spicy. But in our family, it was never too spiced. Father ate chilies on the side. That bite was my first encounter with *pili-pili hoho* (small red chilies). It was also the last. Unlike many of my Asian peers, I came not to fancy highly spicy food as an adult. I wonder if that ordeal influenced my aversion.

Our meals were Indian vegetarian dishes with lentils, flat wheat and millet bread, rice and an assortment of curried vegetables dominating the menu. Meat and chicken were rare. When meat was cooked, you got one or two small chunks. A glass of extra sour but diluted yogurt was a frequent presence. Breakfast was filling but nutritionally bereft most days – white bread, jam, margarine and tea. Sundays were different. Mother prepared *chapatis* (Indian flat bread) or pancakes, and served them with honey and a boiled egg. I loved the Sunday breakfast. Banana or papaya was consumed daily. We gorged ourselves on mangoes when they were in season, though the ensuing runs to the toilet were a bit of a nuisance. Once or twice a week, I got five cents to buy a packet of roasted ground nuts and popcorn during school break time.

We had a notion that some foods – *maharagwe* (large kidney beans), *ugali* (maize flour paste), *nguru* (dried king fish), *dagga* (dried sardines) and the like – were the sole preserve of the 'natives'. It was beneath our status to consume them on a regular basis. Some could be had on rare occasions provided they were cooked in a special style. Others, like red kidney beans, never. But there were a few notable exceptions.

Cassava was a staple crop in Ruponda. One farmer brought freshly dug roots with pure white innards. Boiled or cooked with *nazi* (coconut) milk, it was often eaten at lunch. Mother cooked fresh *kisamvu* (tender leaves from the cassava plant) with *nazi* milk and small red beans, and served it with rice. It was an exquisite dish. *Kisamvu* boasts a beyond-this-planet taste that clings to your tongue for hours. We also had curried *maboga* (pumpkins). These were among the exceptions to keeping a distance from the local tribal cuisine.

Jamaat Khana

Besides school and home, life revolved around the *Jamaat Khana* (prayer house, JK). The Lindi JK was a spacious two-story modern structure built around 1950. It was the largest JK in the south, housing the community library and a room for religion classes. We spent nearly an hour of each evening and the Saturday morning there. Father attended the daily dawn-time prayer session as well (Over his adult life, he rarely missed it). On festive and sacred occasions, we could be at the JK for three hours or more.

The rituals, beliefs and life style of the Ismailis differ in critical aspects from those of the followers of the general Islamic faith. We pray twice a day, do not face Mecca in prayer, do not have to fast during the month of *Ramadan* (though some do), and are not required to learn the *Koran*. Our mostly low caste Hindu ancestors in India were converted to Ismailism by Ismaili *Pirs* (distinguished missionaries). Our *ginans* (hymns) thus incorporate Hindu beliefs and mythology. Most are in Gujarati. Our pre-1954 prayer was in Gujarati as well.

The practices that set us apart from mainstream Islam had generated a cultural and political backlash in many countries. They also conflicted with the projection of Aga Khan III as a senior statesman of global Islam. He thus introduced an Arabic version of the main prayer in the mid-1950s. Most sections contained verses of the *Koran*. These changes were designed to more closely link us to the Islamic world. Another significant change was in the length: The almost twenty minute long, meandering prayer was replaced by a curt, five minute recitation – so it was a popular move.

It was 1957. I was barely eight. We were taught the new prayer during the Saturday religion class. We understood just a few of the strange words. A small booklet put out the Arabic words in Gujarati/English script, and contained a Gujarati translation. The meaning was beyond my grasp but since six months of rote chanting efficiently instilled the Arabic invocation in my head.

It was in this context that I 'spoke' — for the first time and in a formal manner — before a large audience. I recall the event with clarity. The JK was full. For the first time, a child was to recite the new prayer. And it was I. My oration was smooth. I did not misspeak a single word. Father fondly patted me, saying he was proud of me. Being at the nadir of the communal economic ladder, he had, apart from his generous spirit, little to display to the others. His child taking the centre stage raised his standing. The grand sum of five shillings (a tad less than one US dollar) was my reward. It was an ample one; over the following week, my best friend and I savoured a good many soda-and-peanut breaks. Six months later, I became the first child to recite the *Eid* festival prayer. I secured five shillings on that occasion too. But I was a bit disappointed as I had been expecting ten.

Friday is a special day for Muslims, Ismailis included. The JK is well attended; the offerings are classy. But for us, the kids, Thursday was the prime day. Once the JK ended, our small group of six to seven year olds ran towards the nearby shop of Parmar *mochi* (shoemaker). He was Hindu. After visiting the temple, he always returned with a sizable pile of small pieces of the white core of the coconut. It was a treat he reserved for us. On some Hindu holidays, a plate of sweets came along. The thought of those tasty snacks propelled us with speed. We had to make it before his shop closed around 7:30 pm. As far as I can remember, there was not a single Thursday on which he disappointed us. Daily, on the way back from school, we waved at him, and he waved back.

Primary School

The Indian Public School was my first school. Adjacent to a vast open field housing a soccer arena, the central rectangular one-story structure was encircled by a well kept garden. I see the hibiscus shrubs and the dispersed sunflower stalks swaying in the wind. Red, white and yellow roses bloomed aplenty. Sisal plants and cacti with menacing thorns defiantly occupied some patches. A number of fruit laden papayas stood aloof in the corners. There were I think four or five classrooms on each side.

The school received funds from the Asian communities, annual subventions from the colonial government and charged a modest fee. It enrolled pupils from grade 1 to grade 10, though later the higher grades were moved to a new secondary school. Though officially not segregated, in practice it was. Of the three to four hundred pupils in my days, just a handful were African. Sons of chiefs or officials, I now guess. Instruction until Standard 5 or 6 was in Gujarati. It then switched to English. Swahili, the language of the people, was not on our syllabus. Our teachers were directly recruited from India for the job.

My first teacher, Vatsalaben, was a young, plump Hindu lady with long, braided hair. A grim frown was affixed on her face with the same degree of permanence as the shiny red dot was affixed on her forehead. She is the only primary school teacher I can clearly bring to mind. I think it is because she was a notoriously mean lady.

Our morning began with monotonous recitations of the Gujarati alphabet and numbers. The class takes the cue from her pointer as it moves from one Gujarati character to another on a picture-laden wall chart. The chanting routine begins. If you foul up, she senses it at once. Then you stand on your desk till your feet ache, get a swift rap on the knuckles with the pointer, or worse, have your ear twisted until tears fill your eyes. Later, we recite these characters from memory, and learn how to write each one on a wood-framed slate. This is done by routing a slate pencil over and over and over the specimen thereon placed by our hefty teacher.

Multiplication tables resemble a series of songs chanted until they are firmly glued into our brains. Nowadays, I speak and think in English and Swahili. But I continue to do mental arithmetic in Gujarati. To recall the result of 12×9 in English, I pause briefly. But in Gujarati, the answer is instantaneous.

I despised Vatsalaben thoroughly. Occasionally, I threw a tantrum, and refused to go to school. On such days, Father tied my leg to a bed post, immobilizing me for the duration of the school hours. I sat on the floor, sullen and hurt. But when he went out, Mother would often untie me.

Unlike at the JK, I could be naughty at school. A friend and I once plucked a rose from the school garden. It was a dare: the plant was situated directly under the headmaster's office window. But luck was not on our side: he spotted us. The next day we were caned in front of the whole school. In my studies, and especially in mathematics, I was usually at the top of my class. In some subjects, Yasmin BK Velji would sometimes overtake me.

Family Matters

The adult person dearest to me by far was Uncle Dawood, Father's youngest brother. He stayed with us and was an easy going, at-all-times-cheerful and kind uncle.

I cannot think about him without recalling *Shree 420* (Mr. 420), the multi-award winning, internationally acclaimed Indian movie released in 1955. It is at once a comedy and a tragedy, a social satire, a romantic saga and a patriotic tale. Two of Indian cinema's top personalities at the time – Raj Kapoor and Nargis – have the lead roles. At the outset, the former is a tramp in the style of Charlie Chaplin. Later on, life events turn him into a smooth talking con-artist. The movie features several Hindi hit songs of that era. The most popular one, sung by Mukesh and mouthed by Raj Kapoor, begins:

Japanese Shoes

Mera jutta hei Japani	My shoes are Japanese
Ye patlun Inglistani	These trousers are English
Sir pe lal topi Russi	A red Russian hat on my head
Mera dil hei Hindustani	Yet my heart remains Indian
Mera jutta . . .	My shoes . . .

The scintillating songs of *Shree 420* have been hard wired into my brain from those days. Dawood *chacha* (uncle) looked like Raj Kapoor. And he dressed like the actor (not the tramp, but the immaculate conman) too. A creamy-white, stylish hat adorned his head in the slanted Raj Kapoor style. Perpetually singing or humming popular movie songs, *Mera juta hai japani* was a staple on his musical menu. I admired his colourful personality (Image 3: Appendix B).

The children adored him because he was so unlike an adult, letting us do what others would not. He did not scold us when we jumped over a fence, climbed mango trees, or took aim with a catapult at birds. He did not report us to our parents, but just smiled. Once he bought, to the annoyance of my mother, a couple of water pistols for Nazir and me. She was livid as we chased each other around the house, squirting and making the floor wet. But Father would never utter a word of reproach towards his often wayward young brother. He had a good reason, as I explain later. The fondest memory I have of him is of his actions during the annual Hindu Diwali festival.

I am anxious, impatient.

> *Dawood chacha, it is Diwali [Hindu festival] night.*
> *I know, Karim, I know.*

After dinner, Mohamed, Nazir, Nizam and I expectantly wait near his room. Sure enough, he comes out, a small box in his hands. A finger to his lips, he smiles broadly. We creep with him in silence to the dark vacant lot behind our house.

Stand here, do not come closer.

He takes out five small fire crackers, puts a match to one, and throws it in the air. Others follow: Bang, bang, swish, bang, bang. We jump with joy. He hands a fire stick to each of us and lights it. As it emits sparks and sizzles, we wave it like a magic wand. A big band of crackers joined at the wick comes next. It produces a fast succession of twenty bangs that illuminate the area. Again, we cheer and shout. Again, a few more crackers.

Finally, the big, red one, the-mother-of-all crackers, is taken out. *Chacha* takes an empty tin can, and makes us step back. Deftly placing the big one upright on the ground, lighting the long white fuse with a match, rapidly dropping the can upside down over it, he dashes away like a startled rabbit. A thunderous boom ensues, the can lifts off like a rocket into the night sky, and we scream with excitement.

Khel khattam (show is over).

We silently creep back to bed. I dream of flying off into space by holding on to a human size fire cracker.

This is my indelible image of beloved Dawood *chacha*. But he was unwell.

An African Wife: His upbeat personality, handsome demeanour and cinematic dress made him a popular person with unmarried Asian girls. Yet, none would consent to marry him. It was because he suffered from epilepsy. His illness was of sufficient severity as to prevent him holding a job or running a shop for any length of time. The medicine of the Lindi doctors did not work for him. My father had set up a shop for him in Mtama village, and found an African woman to stay with him. They were not formally married; she was his live-in wife. Neither the shop nor the informal union lasted.

I knew that my uncle had a shop in Mtama, but had no idea that I had an aunt there too. She never came home. Interracial marriages were a taboo. I came to learn about her from my father long after we had left Lindi for good. Informal, out-of-wedlock affairs between Asian men and African women, however, were not uncommon in those days, and too some extent, were openly tolerated.

According to the year 1957 official census, Lindi District had 175,591 African and 2,583 non-African residents. Included in the former were a grand total of five African wives of non-African men. Was my aunt counted as one of them? Reading this report, I was amazed at the level of race, tribe and religion related detail the British used to keep. In a way, it makes eminent sense since divide – along racial, tribal, regional and religious lines – and rule was a central pillar of colonial domination.

When Dawood uncle had a seizure, which was frequent, the sight was unbearable. When he got over it, Mother would pamper him and prepare special dishes for him. One evening, upon return from the JK, I found our home eerily silent. Dinner was not laid. Sitting with a group of women, mother was sobbing; Father whispered in a corner with other men. A white sheet on the floor covered a human form. What was afoot? There was no answer, but a neighbor escorted me and my brothers to our room, brought biscuits and warm milk, and put us to bed.

This was the first time I felt immeasurably sad. I was downcast for days; too much pain radiating from the inside. Mother said Dawood *chacha* had gone to heaven. But where was that place? Why did he have to go? Why now? Like a whipped dog, I sat in a corner, unable to play with my friends. I still recall the cruel taunts of the boy who called me a wimp.

I had attacks of malaria in Lindi. I was hot and listless. Mother fed me soup and a grossly bitter medicine. I felt weak for days afterwards. Father also suffered from malaria; it was frightening to watch him shiver and groan like a child. Once Mohamed and I had persistent cough that did not respond to the doctor's pills. One man advised my parents that donkey's milk was an effective remedy. Then, for nearly a month, we went daily to a farm near Lindi. The fresh, raw milk from donkey udders was warm, with a sharp, unique taste. When I think about it, it is on my tongue even today. The cough resolved eventually; whether it was due to the natural history of the condition, or the curative effect of donkey milk is unknown.

Zanzibar

A short while after *chacha* left us, Mother and three kids went to Zanzibar. It was my first sea voyage. A rusty ship took us from Lindi to Dar es Salaam. We sat on the open deck, the cold, uncomfortable journey lasting almost the whole day. Food was scarce. In anticipation, she had packed a good quantity of fried stuff. We munched it when hungry. We likely spent a night at her brother's place in Dar es Salaam. Roughly six hours on a smaller boat the next day put us on the island our parents had talked about extensively (Today a bus trip from Lindi to Dar es Salaam takes six hours, and a speed boat then takes an hour and a half to reach Zanzibar.).

It was a most memorable visit. I met my maternal grand uncle and aunt for the first time. Having raised my mother after her mother had passed away, they were, in essence, her dad and mom. Accordingly, we addressed them by *nanabapa* and *nanima*.

Nanima fed us huge servings of fabulous dishes like *pilau, muthia* and *khitchdo*. Fish was aplenty. She smiled constantly, urging us to eat. Cooking or at meals, from morning to sleep time, Mother and she kept on talking, without a break. Where did they find all those things to talk about?

Nanabapa, though getting on in age, was in robust health. Unusually tall, with a bulging chest and square face, he was an avid swimmer. Each morning, he aroused me and Mohamed from bed at 4 am. After praying at the JK, we went to the Forodhani Beach. The first day was not a pleasant one. Mohamed knew how to swim; I did not. He carried me to a depth of water that reached his chest, and without warning dumped me into the cold sea. For a while, as I struggled and yelled, he just watched. At last, he put his strong arms under my belly, held me on the surface, and patiently showed me the strokes. And it worked. In a few days, I was swiftly gliding on water. On the way home, he bought fresh fried *mandazi* (doughnut like pastry) or *vitumbua* (fried fermented rice balls) from the vendors. We avidly devoured these delights at breakfast.

It was in Zanzibar that I first tasted the bevy of succulent tropical fruits the island is famed for. Of unique aroma, shape, shade and consistency, they included *shoke shoke* (rambutan), *fanas* (jack fruit), *doriyani* (durian), *gulabi* (???), and *matufa* (water apple). It took guts to put the foul smelling *doriyani* into your mouth. These exquisite fruits could not be had in Lindi. Mangoes were plentiful back home, but the Zanzibar varieties evinced incomparable flavours, with the giant sized *embe boribo* (boribo mango) stealing the prize. The local market of the spice island lived up to its name. A variety of spices were sold at very low prices. Mother took a good supply of cloves, black pepper, cinnamon, nutmeg and cardamom back to Lindi.

Number Patterns ✥ ✥ ✥ ✥ ✥ ✥ ✥

My friendship with numbers began early. Mother set the ball rolling. I counted stones, marbles and seeds, and added and subtracted before joining school. My first formal class was the religion class at the JK. As I did well in reciting hymns and the prayer, Father wanted to send me to primary school a year earlier than usual. But I gather that my extreme unruliness discouraged him.

I was formally introduced to numbers by Vatsalaben. She taught me their names, in Gujarati and then in English. Our friendship blossomed as I migrated to larger numbers and grasped multiplication, division, fractions and powers. But it was not fun to play with my buddies in a setting of fear. The moment a human friend mishandled a number, he got a whacking. Though I despised her harsh approach and the boring drills, I learned arithmetic, and elements of algebra and geometry, and excelled in class.

Did my teacher know that numbers were attractive and funny? I do not think so. The world of maths contains beautiful figures, graphs and patterns – numeric and non-numeric – that entice and capture young minds.

Three Patterns

To illustrate this point, let us examine three multiplication patterns.

Pattern I results from multiplying two numbers containing only the digit 1 with the result containing all other digits apart from 0.

$$
\begin{array}{rcl}
1 \times 1 &=& 1 \\
11 \times 11 &=& 121 \\
111 \times 111 &=& 12321 \\
1111 \times 1111 &=& 1234321 \\
11111 \times 11111 &=& 123454321 \\
111111 \times 111111 &=& 12345654321 \\
1111111 \times 1111111 &=& 1234567654321 \\
11111111 \times 11111111 &=& 123456787654321 \\
111111111 \times 111111111 &=& 12345678987654321 \\
\end{array}
$$

Pattern I

Pattern II, in which multiplication is before addition, shows distinct digits on the left being transmuted into a number containing the digit 1 only.

$$0 \times 9 + 1 = 1$$
$$1 \times 9 + 2 = 11$$
$$12 \times 9 + 3 = 111$$
$$123 \times 9 + 4 = 1111$$
$$1234 \times 9 + 5 = 11111$$
$$12345 \times 9 + 6 = 111111$$
$$123456 \times 9 + 7 = 1111111$$
$$1234567 \times 9 + 8 = 11111111$$
$$12345678 \times 9 + 9 = 1111111111$$

Pattern II

Pattern III has a rectangular form on each side, and shares features of Pattern I and Pattern II.

$$123456789 \times 09 = 111111111$$
$$123456789 \times 18 = 222222222$$
$$123456789 \times 27 = 333333333$$
$$123456789 \times 36 = 444444444$$
$$123456789 \times 45 = 555555555$$
$$123456789 \times 54 = 666666666$$
$$123456789 \times 63 = 777777777$$
$$123456789 \times 72 = 888888888$$
$$123456789 \times 81 = 999999999$$

Pattern III

When the results of these exercises are laid out as attractive symmetries, they appear as wonders to behold, making us eye them as we eye a piece of fine art.

A vast supply of material of this type, suitable for up to high school, exists. Primary school pupils work with such patterns by proceeding from small to large numbers. They discover when the patterns change. Their findings turn into colourful diagrams placed on classroom walls. Dry arithmetical routines turn into fun-filled activities.

My primary schooling did not expose me to the enticing faces of my number friends. To the contrary, the climate of dread placed our budding alliance in jeopardy. I discovered the fine charms of numbers only after I entered the university. I realized their potential as tools for improving maths education much later. If my primary school teacher had ventured into that terrain, I think more of my human pals would have socialized closely, and on a long term basis, with this esoteric set of characters from number land.

— 2 —

Multiple Identities

*Our true reality is in our identity
and unity with all life.*
Joseph Campbell

❖ ❖ ❖ ❖ ❖ ❖ ❖

MY BIRTH CERTIFICATE has my full name, a number, and the hospital, town and date of my birth. Unless it is a matter of fraud, there is not and cannot be a second person with an identical certificate. Without genetic sequencing, that single document fixes my identity, once and for eternity.

Yet, it gets knotty as we meander through life. Our identity acquires many faces, individual and social, fixed and fluid, local and global. You are you, and you are also a man or woman; child or parent; student, worker, manager or employer; farmer or taxi driver; Muslim, Christian or what not; citizen of one nation and more. Your habits, actions, speech, personality and appearance define you. What people think of you is a basic aspect of who you are. A year on, you will not be what you are today. Our identity is forged in relation to people, places, events and time. Our lives make us who we are. At birth we are unique, but how, when and where we pass our years makes us even more so.

Origins
Before joining primary school, I was one of the Hirji family, plain and simple. People would point at me and say, "Fateh Bungu's son." At school, I had a circle of friends. As I came to see each friend as a distinct person, I felt like a special person too. Around my tenth birthday, it seemed as if I had crossed a threshold in life. I did well in school. My teachers praised me profusely; fellow pupils looked up to me. I was less at home. Activities centered around the JK took up a major chunk of my free time. I helped lay out the mats before the prayers began, and looked after the under five year old kids. I saw myself more as a young man than a child. In school, my eyes were set on Yasmin, the prettiest and smartest girl in our class. Boys competed for a chance to talk to her. When she said hello, which was never often enough, cold shivers ran down my spine.

I have a strange memory. I am reciting a prayer to the Lord, and urging him to never make me lose compassion towards young children. I do not know in what context or why I did it. Had I seen a child being treated badly? I do not remember. But the image of the prayer is a distinct one.

That my father now gave me greater freedom of movement was another reason why I saw myself in a different light. To the displeasure of my mother, I was permitted to go to cricket matches and, importantly, to the morning movie shows with my friends. Money for peanuts and soda made cinema day a day of thrills and fun. Our fare comprised romantic musicals from India, and Tarzan and cowboy extravaganzas from Hollywood.

But was I something more than an individual? Towards which group did my primary loyalty lie? Looking back, I see that three versions of the global sense of belongingness competed to capture me – the imperial version, the India-oriented version and the Ismaili community version.

Imperial Identity

I recall two Western films, *Shane* and *The Alamo*. The first, starring Alan Ladd, has a memorable scene in which a young boy sees that his hero is being stalked by an outlaw gunman. As he shouts: "Look out, Shane," Shane makes a smart dive to the ground, fast draws his gun and kills the evil fellow. We replayed the same split-second move with our toy guns. We imitated the cowboys and sheriffs, swung the lasso, and waved our shooters, and took delight in screaming wild words at the Red Indians and outlaws.

The Alamo stars John Wayne and Richard Windmark as two gunslingers among a group of vastly outnumbered defenders of a Texas fort under attack by Mexican forces. The Americans come across as pleasant personalities – brave, smart, colourful, kind and witty. Some had their shortcomings, but we sympathized with them. We laughed and cried with them; we shared their hopes and anxieties. The brown-skinned Mexican characters, cruel and blood thirsty that they were, thereby became our enemies too. Though I saw this movie a couple of years after I left Lindi, it represents what I used to see there.

One scene from *The Alamo* is etched in my mind. Whenever anyone nears the fort gate, the guard bellows: "Who goes there?" Failure to identify oneself carried lethal consequences. We made it into a play phrase. Such images from the screen stuck in our psyche. These movies gave us a lasting lesson on what and who was good, and what and who was evil.

Up Side Down History: Only later did I realize that these movies instilled an inverted version of history and reinforced the colonial projection of race in our minds. We came to believe that the whiter a person, the more respectable, decent, dependable he or she is; the darker the person, the more unreliable, untrustworthy he or she is. For my father and his generation, this was and remains the accepted way of classifying humans.

Beside movies and other official venues, the sense of being a part of a major global entity underlay what we were taught in English and history classes.

After a brief coverage of the Greeks and Romans, we learned about the splendours of the British civilization, parliament, democracy, the British empire upon which the sun never sets, and the benefits it has showered on humanity.

We came to know Her Majesty the Queen, and the princes and princesses, and the British governor. A man called Winston Churchill was celebrated, but I was not sure who he was. The Union Jack fluttered at key places. During official occasions, it was almost everywhere. At public events and the movies, we stood up as the musical rendition of the Imperial anthem played. Its first stanza runs:

God Save the Queen

God save our gracious Queen!
Long live our noble Queen!
God save the Queen!
Send her victorious,
Happy and glorious,
Long to reign over us:
God save the Queen!

In the colonial era, the Asians saw themselves as British subjects fully entitled to the rights conferred by that status. They struggled to be treated as equals of the white settlers and officials in the colonies. But the empire only granted them second class status. They had privileges the 'natives' did not have, but it was on a tacit understanding that they serve the empire as and when needed. The Asians were exhorted to be loyal, law-abiding subjects of the Empire and expected to show gratitude for the blessings it had showered on them.

Take a Lindi bank: A white man is the boss. His subordinates – clerks, tellers, accountants – are Asians. The cleaners and messengers are African. Because the Europeans lack partners, Asians can play tennis at the European Club, but are not permitted to enter the club premises for a drink. A timid move by two well-meaning Britons to change the discriminatory rule encounters such a ferocious response from the main funders that they instantly abandon their vaunted principles (Roden 2012).

I was too young to realize such socio-political intricacies. But their core message was instilled in my brain through the life I was leading and what I regularly heard around me. I came to accept that Africans were inferior to us and that Europeans were a special people, somewhat mysterious in their ways. We respected them, but did not interact with them in personal terms.

However, despite the imperial pomp and glory, and what I was taught or otherwise imbibed, I never developed even a tiny sense of loyalty to the crown. Other than football and cricket stars, there was not a single British personality, practice or thing I looked up to. The words and melody of *God Save the Queen* made no impression on my mind. One moment, they were there and, the next, they were gone. Observance of racial hierarchies is the main thing I learned from the colonialists.

An External Identity

Stories from our ancestral home land, on the other hand, created a firmer impression. The administrators and teachers at our school were recent arrivals from India. For the most part, they were Hindus. Hence we read Hindu tales and myths, mostly from the *Mahabharata* and *Bhagavad Gita*, at school. The extraordinary adventures of Ram, Sita and Hanuman, the monkey god, and the exalted stories of Lord Krishna excited us. Though more than half the school was Muslim, we recited Hindu hymns in the Gujarati lessons.

We learned about Mahatma Gandhi, and his fight for independence for India. The picture of the Indian national flag was commonplace. Indian movies projected patriotic themes and songs. *Mera Joota hai Japani*, the favourite of Dawood *chacha*, was a patriotic movie. We heard radio broadcasts from the Voice of India. Father listened to news programs and songs from the popular movies. The Indian national anthem, patriotic songs and Hindu hymns were heard. During school assembly, we sang popular Hindu devotional songs like *Ragu Pati Ragav Raja Ram* and *Jai Jagdish Hare*.

Jai Jagdish Hare

Om jai jagdish hare	Hail, Lord of the universe
Swami jai jagdish hare	Hail, Master of the universe,
Bhakta jano ke sankat	The sorrows of his devotees
Das jano ke sankat	The sorrows of his followers
Shah me door kare	Will the Lord instantly remove
Om jai jagdish hare	Hail, Lord of the universe

Vande Mataram (Mother, I Bow to Thee), a Bengali song with roots in the history of India, and which almost became the national anthem of India, was played, though not frequently. Apart from the title line, its meaning was lost on us. *Jagriti* (Awakening), a film with intense, India-oriented nationalist overtones has a song by Hemant Kumar called *Aao Bacho* (Come Children). It was a hit with us. The patriotic line, *vande mataram,* arises repeatedly in the song. We imitated scenes from the movie, sang the song and playfully marched to it in the school playground.

Our food, songs, music, movies and school material instilled a sense that we belonged to a distant, exalted place called India. In essence, we were Indians. Thereby, unless it was an issue directly affecting them, the Asians did not follow or take part in local political affairs. Their antennas were tuned to the goings on in the Indian subcontinent. The partition of India, the formation of Pakistan, and the slaughter that had ensued had, however, created a rift. Muslim Asians were not as attached to India and things with Hindu connections. Father, even as he regularly tuned into All India Radio, professed his loyalty to Pakistan. He often mocked things that were related to Gandhi, India and Hinduism.

But I did develop a nascent sense of loyalty to India, and did look up to Mahatma Gandhi. I think the Indian movies and school ceremonies had an effect. As I describe later, the basic moral values projected by the movies complemented the moral values we acquired from our religious teachings, especially the Ismaili hymns. The contents of these hymns also referred to ancient Hindu mythology. That synergy enhanced my emotional bonding to India.

The colonial authorities underscored those external loyalties by how they officially classified the Asians in Tanzania. The 1957 Population Census, for example, produced two separate reports; one of the African population and the other of the non-African population. The Asians were included in the latter, and further classified as Indian, Pakistani or Goan. It was one further illustration of the basic fact that the colonial ethic, rules and life were founded on a tripartite societal structure: African, Asian and European, standing hierarchically from low to high in that order.

Communal Identity

The Hindu-cum-India based orientation in the Indian schools in mainland Tanzania was not favoured by our *Imam*. He had promoted and supported an independent political movement for the Muslims of India. He urged the British authorities, with success, to set up a separate system of Aga Khan schools. One Aga Khan school was built in nearby Mtwara town but the numbers did not warrant building another one in Lindi.

The dominant sense of belonging for the Ismailis was not towards a geographically defined place or nation. It was to our community and spiritual leader. Once upon a time, we had ruled an empire in the Middle East. Though now scattered across the globe, our community remained a unitary entity. We recited the names of the 48 previous *Imams* in our prayers. It formed an unbroken lineage traced to Hazarat Ali, the son in law of the Prophet Muhammad. Prince Karim Aga Khan is the 49th *Imam*. We were a people without a land who strove to actualize a secular form of loyalty to the governments of the places where we resided. But our true, indivisible, uncontested loyalty was to the *Imam*.

The Ismaili flag is called *My Flag*. It has a green background and a red diagonal stripe. The communal anthem is *Noor-I-Rasoolillah* (The Light of Allah). The day our present *Imam* ascended his spiritual throne, July 11th, we joyfully sang it in a communal ceremony.

Ismaili Anthem

Noor-I-Rasoolillah se	O, the Light of Allah
Banai ho Aga Khan	Residing in the Aga Khan
Mowlana Shah Karim	Spiritual Lord Shah Karim
Tum ho Sahebe-zaman	You are the Master of all

Neatly attired, we were sent to the JK area. It was exciting to march with other children as our anthem was sung and My Flag fluttered in the background. Sometimes there was a small accompanying band. This day of festivities meant delicious food from morning to night. This was one of the principal highlights of my childhood. I knew the anthem from an early age, and understood its general meaning by the time I was ten years old.

I attest without hesitation that at that point in time, my primary identity was that of being an Ismaili. My community was my main object of loyalty. My religious teachers told me that it was a bond very different from any ephemeral worldly identity because it derived from an eternal spiritual connection. Foremost, I was an Ismaili, as my elders had taught me.

Correspondingly, I had no sense of loyalty to my land of birth. My elders declared it the land of black skinned people. We were apart from them; they were apart from us. It was just by a stroke of history that we happened to live in a place where there were many, perhaps too many, of them.

The general message conveyed to me and my peers during my final days in primary school, which were also my final days in Lindi, was on the positive, optimistic side. Our teachers, parents and the society at large impressed upon us that we lived in an era of social stability, harmony and progress. Life as we knew it would go on for decades. The current political clamour for change would die down and the 'natives' would soon come to their senses. Life was as good as it could be, for them, us and all. As the youth, our major task was to pursue our studies with dedication and diligence. If we did that, there was no reason why we could not attain our dreams. For the loyal subjects of the Crown in particular, a bright future lay ahead.

The Birth of a Nation

But that message proved to be a pipe dream. The days of colonial rule were numbered. The 1950s witnessed people rising up all over Africa. Earlier they had sought equality and social justice under the colonial umbrella. Now the primary demand was nothing short of self-rule. The struggle for freedom in mainland Tanzania gained momentum with the formation of the Tanganyika African National Union (TANU) in 1953. It was led by Julius K Nyerere (popularly known as Mwalimu Nyerere).

Mwalimu Nyerere sought to unite Christians, Muslims, the various ethnic and race groups, and workers, farmers and traders into a broad anti-colonial movement. Two salient facts of history facilitated his task: The socio-economic cleavages in our nation were not as acute as in some African nations. And, Swahili, spoken from one end of the land to the other, provided a strong basis for national unity. He confronted the colonial authorities with astute political skill. His firm stand on important issues and fair-minded persona boosted his following. He came across as an honest person whose words articulated the feelings of the common man. Unlike most politicians, he did not sway with the wind, but stood behind his principles in a consistent manner.

While other political parties emerged, TANU remained more popular by a wide margin. It undertook nationwide rallies, grassroots mobilization, boycotts and strikes, and worked on the legislative and international fronts. The efforts paid off as one concession after another was wrested from the British. By the time I left Lindi in December 1960, it was apparent (though not to my young, misled mind) that the momentous day of *Uhuru* was around the corner. And it was hardly disputed that Mwalimu Nyerere would be at the helm of the new nation.

The global Ismaili community underwent a decisive adjustment during this period. Aga Khan III passed away in 1954. His grandson, His Highness Prince Karim Shah, was the newly designated *Imam*. Then a student at Harvard University, he blended a spiritual persona with a liberal Westernized outlook, and assumed the title Aga Khan IV. He declared to his followers that that he would reinforce and extend the key changes on religious and social matters initiated by his grandfather. In international affairs, he began a gradual shift away from alliance with the UK to stronger ties with the Kennedy administration and harmonized his global actions with the US policy.

He paid a visit to the three nations of East Africa in 1957. In each capital city, the Ismailis held a grand coronation ceremony for him. Yet, it was more than a spiritually oriented visit. In public speeches and restricted pronouncements to the community, Karim Aga Khan dwelt on important social and political issues. He showed awareness that the strivings for national autonomy were fast gaining ground and would likely bear fruit in the near future. The ensuing transformation of governance and laws would have a life changing impact on his followers. He thereby earnestly urged them to fundamentally revamp their social outlook and behaviour. That was the only way, he said, that they could cope effectively with the loss of a way of life they had long taken for granted and adapt successfully to the era in the offing.

On the economic front, he urged Ismailis to broaden their horizons beyond commerce into farming, industry, services and the professions, placing special emphasis on education and health. On the social front, he stressed the need to transcend narrow racial boundaries and work towards the establishment of a peaceful, unified nation. His speech in Kampala, given after witnessing a boxing match between an Asian and an African student that ended in a draw, contained visionary advice (Aga Khan IV 1957):

> [T]he partnership between races . . . is the only condition of peace and prosperity. . . . I most strongly urge the Ismaili community to work hand in hand with all other citizens.
>
> Aga Khan IV

As noted earlier, colonial rule had fomented a deep animus between Asians and Africans. As the middlemen of the colonial economic domination, the former presented the concrete face of external tyranny. Frequent underhand practices by the Asian traders to shortchange Africans intensified the antagonism. They used false weights and tampered with the scales when buying produce. They sold imported goods at higher than warranted prices. The use of disrespectful language towards the black man was common. The African perception was succinctly captured by Mwalimu Nyerere when he said that '. . . *the Indian trader makes his living by downright dishonesty or at best by sheer cunning* . . .' (Nyerere 1966, page 23). The Asians were seen as beneficiaries of special privileges in education, housing, employment, business and public service. For such reasons and their cultural and social exclusivity, the tension between Asians and locals ran deep.

The Asians, on their part, did not have a free hand. They faced economic pressures and practical constraints from banks, British import-export houses and the authorities. As an employee of the state or European company, the brown man worked under a tight leash held by the white man. The role of Asians in produce marketing witnessed, first slowly and then rapidly, the growth of the cooperative movement that strove to protect the farmers and end the monopoly of the Asian traders.

Some moves by the European settlers or British authorities at times adversely affected both the Asians and the Africans. That led to the formation of a united front. But usually it was a temporary alliance.

Mwalimu Nyerere had steered TANU to adopt a racially inclusive policy right from the start. Though membership in TANU was then open only to Africans, the eventual goal was that all people, regardless of skin colour should, in theory and practice, have the same rights. No race or ethnic group should have special privileges. This fundamental tenet was expounded in his paper of 1952 quoted above. Notwithstanding his initial critical remarks, he ends his exposition with a conciliatory plea (Nyerere 1966, page 29):

> We appeal to all thinking Europeans and Indians to regard themselves as ordinary citizens of Tanganyika; to preach no Divine Right of Europeans, no Divine Right of Indians and no Divine Right of Africans either. We are all Tanganyikans and we are all East Africans. The race quarrel is a stupid quarrel; it can be a very tragic quarrel. If we all make up our minds to live like 'ordinary sort of fellow' and not to think we were specially designed by the creator to be masters and others specially designed to be hewers of wood and drawers of water, we will make East Africa a very happy country for everybody.
>
> Mwalimu Julius Nyerere

Signs reflecting this grand vision began to appear: A few African children were adopted by Ismaili families, the Aga Khan schools began to enrol African students. A few Ismailis like Amir Jamal assumed a prominent role in the struggle for Independence. In Lindi and other places, Ismaili businessmen assisted TANU by donating vehicles and resources for political mobilization campaigns. And the Ismailis continued their assistance to the Muslim welfare societies across Tanzania.

Such actions, though, were exceptions, not the rule. Some had a public relations motivation. Like other Asians, and despite a broad alliance between Muslims and Christians, the bulk of the Ismailis stood on the sidelines, eying TANU and the moves towards Independence with suspicion if not hostility. Asians also joined the colonial effort to undermine TANU. Thus, the principled stand and conciliatory gestures of Mwalimu Nyerere were not heeded. Even the sound advice of their *Imam* effectively fell on deaf ears.

Among my father's generation, race based ways of thinking and conducting oneself did not wane as the day of Independence drew nearer. They visualized the day as a moment of high trepidation, not of celebration. While the public pronouncements of the community stated to the contrary, their actual feelings remained as narrow and rigid as ever.

I was a ten year old child with little clue about politics. I did not know who Julius Nyerere and Rashidi Kawawa were. But I knew the names of the British governor and Lindi's white mayor; they were often mentioned by my teachers. The sentiment I gained from our elders at that time was unmistakable: Lock your doors. Pray that life will not turn nasty. We cannot know what these 'natives' will do. If they go berserk, as they did in the Congo, the British will not be around to rescue us.

Looking back, I see that it was a vision based on unjustified fear-mongering. In comparative terms, the political process unfolding in mainland Tanzania was a paradise compared to the situation in colonies elsewhere. No prospect of anything faintly like the blood bath which had accompanied the independence of India and Pakistan lay on our horizon. I gather we were actually better off than we would have been in our ancestral homeland. It is relevant to note that racial acrimony and violence were then more intense in the US than in our land. Accordingly, we owe a mountain of debt to Mwalimu Nyerere and the people of Tanzania for that atmosphere of tranquility. But blinded by racially tinted lenses, the Asians were unable or unwilling to learn the clear lessons offered by history. They could or would not see that the colonial past had been profoundly unjust, even by their own moral standards, and had to change. They only thought in terms of doom and gloom. Or as my *Vadima* (elder aunt) stated, in terms of *hai, woi*.

The wide prevalence of such attitudes at the morrow of *Uhuru* indicated that for the emergent nation and its children, major obstacles and troublesome days lay ahead.

Mathematical Identity ❖ ❖ ❖ ❖ ❖ ❖ ❖

I befriended two maths entities in primary school, One and Zero. I hit off instantly with 1, the unit guy. Of small magnitude, he shouldered the whole number system on his back. But 0 was a weird girl. This nothing person took a while to consort with. If you were alone with her – as when you had zero cents – you were in trouble. But if she was with one – like if you had 100 cents – you were in a splendid mood.

It was Vatsalaben who told us that the number after 9 was written as 10; the next after 99 was written as 100; and so on. First I could not understand it. It took time to grasp that the number 353 actually meant there were 3 of hundreds, 5 of tens, and 3 of units. This was the source of the dualistic personality of Zero. She was a number and a place holder symbol as well.

Additionally, One was an extrovert who had revealed himself to us eons ago. Zero had lain low for a long time. The ancient Egyptians, Greeks and Romans had not known her. My fair lady was first unmasked in India. The nations of Europe did not feel her charm until about eight centuries ago. Their number notation and computations were too cumbersome as a result. When she came to Europe via the talented mathematicians of the Middle East, the Church branded her a heathen. Only when the immense benefits she conferred on commercial transactions were realized did her popularity mount. And soon her utility was so high that life without her became inconceivable. Without my friend Zero, modern science and technology could not have emerged.

I was not aware of the history, charm and intrinsic utility of these residents of number land in our early days. I came to know that when I read the history of maths at the university. Else, I would have paid more attention to the pretty lady Zero from the start.

Their central status in the number system has earned my two friends royal sounding titles. I guess you know that

$$n + 0 = n$$

Adding zero to a number leaves it unchanged. If I have n shillings and my pal has no shillings, our total wealth remains n shillings. So Zero is the additive identity. Zero also gives rise to negative numbers. If I have n shillings and my pal has m shillings, but our total wealth is zero, then m is the negative of n. That is

$$n + m = 0 \quad \Rightarrow \quad m = -n$$

If I have n shillings and my pal has a debt of n shillings, our total wealth stands at zero. Zero is the boundary point dividing numbers into positive and negative numbers.

The use of shorthand notation is handy when dealing with residents of number land. Take repeated addition. If we have $(3 + 3 + 3 + 3 + 3)$, we write it 3×5, giving rise to the concept of multiplication. The unit number is special in that if you multiply anything by one, it does not change. That is, $15 \times 1 = 15$, and for any n,

$$n \times 1 = n$$

One has the noble title of multiplicative identity. Like his associate Zero, he gives rise to inverse entities. If the product of two numbers is 1, each is the inverse of the other.

$$n \times m = 1 \quad \Rightarrow \quad m = \frac{1}{n}$$

This leads us to the idea of division, and to fractions and fractional numbers.

$$\frac{a}{b} = a \times \frac{1}{b}$$

There is one exception to these operations. They do not apply when the bottom number is 0. You do not divide by Zero, unless you seek to land in a mysterious arena. This shows the volatile side of her personality.

> A student was asked why she had not submitted her
> maths homework.
> "Sir," she gloomily replied, "*I accidentally divided by zero,*
> *and my papers caught fire.*"

Now take a case of repeated multiplication: $3 \times 3 \times 3 \times 3 \times 3 \times 3 \times 3$, that is, three multiplied by itself seven times. The shorthand notation 3^7 is handy here. We say that 3 is raised to the power of 7. We discover two rules for powers.

$$3^6 \times 3^5 = 3 \times 3 \times 3 \times 3 \times 3 \times 3 \times 3 \times 3 \times 3 \times 3 \times 3 = 3^{11} = 3^{6+5}$$

and

$$\frac{3^8}{3^5} = \frac{3 \times 3 \times 3 \times 3 \times 3 \times 3 \times 3 \times 3}{3 \times 3 \times 3 \times 3 \times 3} = 3 \times 3 \times 3 = 3^3 = 3^{8-5}$$

When multiplying like entities, add the powers; when dividing them, subtract the powers. These ideas evolve to generate fractional powers like square roots and cube roots, and even negative powers.

My two innocent looking friends, Zero and One carry a huge weight on their shoulders. By interacting with each other and their progenies through two basic operations, they produce a complex edifice whose mysteries are still being probed. We discover negative, fractional, prime, perfect, friendly, irrational, imaginary, complex and transcendental numbers. We find that $\sqrt{2}$ is irrational and π is transcendental. But let me not get carried away. I meant no harm; I just wanted to shower praise on the creative powers of my friends.

Instead, let us look at an oddity we come across in school algebra. It is about powers. We know that $8^2 = 64$; $8^3 = 512$, but what is 8^0? To obtain the answer, look at a specific example and apply the second rule for powers.

$$1 = \frac{8^7}{8^7} = 8^{7-7} = 8^0$$

This implies that anything raised to nothing gives you the unit number. Even $100,000,000^0 = 1$. Like the alltime great boxer Muhammad Ali (see Chapter 7), Zero has the power to flatten a mighty number to the ground.

❖ ❖ ❖ ❖ ❖ ❖ ❖

In secondary school, one topic especially puzzled my classmate Abdul Karim and me. It was about arranging things. For example: In how many different ways can three chairs be placed in a line? The answer is derived as follows: The first chair can be selected in three ways. For each selection, the second chair can be selected in two ways, and after that, the final one can be selected in only one way. The total number of ways of placing three chairs then is: $3 \times 2 \times 1 = 6$. If we label the chairs as A, B, C, the six arrangements are $ABC, ACB, BAC, BCA, CAB, CBA$.

If there are four chairs, a similar logic shows that the number of arrangements is: $4 \times 3 \times 2 \times 1 = 24$. If there are n chairs, that number is: $n \times (n-1) \times (n-2) \times \cdots \times 2 \times 1$. A shorthand notation helps here as well. We write,

$$n! = n \times (n-1) \times (n-2) \times \ldots \times 2 \times 1$$

for integers larger than 1. We set $1! = 1$. Hence, $4! = 4 \times 3 \times 2 \times 1 = 24$. This is a neat way of writing a laborious expression. You may ask: Why not simply multiply and write the answer? That is easier said than done, for the result can be unwieldy. For example:

$$20! = 2,432,902,008,176,640,000$$

The formulas involving arrangement problems sometime yield the entity $0!$ What is this odd creature, we wondered? Then we found a proof showing us its true colours. For any positive integer n, it is known that

$$n! = n \times (n-1)!$$

Obviously, $6! = 6 \times 5!$. Now put $n = 1$ in this expression. This gives

$$1 = 1! = 1 \times (1-1)! = 1 \times 0! = 0!$$

Holy cow, we said. A zero (nothing) followed by an exclamation mark produces the unit guy, the basis for all numbers. Something arises out of nothing. Perhaps we should write $0! = 1!!!!$ The proof is a logical one but the idea does not sink in easily. I must say, I remain a bit perplexed to this day.

We also wondered what is 0^0, or $0/0$? I found out after many years that the answer depends on the context in which the entity arose. Many of the answers defy common sense but derive from sound logic. They open doors to greater wonders. The strange aspect of these esoteric ventures is that many have practical applications in science, engineering and even social sciences.

Let us explore further. The two numbers, 3^7 and 7^3, appear similar, but are far apart. The first equals 2187 and the second equals 343. A difference, but not a striking one. Next consider two expressions we do not expect to differ that much:

$$2^{2^2} \quad \text{and} \quad 3^{3^3}$$

Since $2^2 = 2 \times 2 = 4$ and $3^3 = 3 \times 3 \times 3 = 27$, the two numbers respectively equal

$$2^4 = 16 \quad \text{and} \quad 3^{27} = 7,625,597,484,987$$

Now that is a difference. If you go on to decode 4^{4^4}, you land in an arena where your fancy electronic calculator runs out of steam. But we shall boldly go even further. Observe that

$$10^{10^{10}} = 10^{10,000,000,000}$$

To write this number in full, we place 1 and follow it with ten billion zeroes. Let us print it out in a format with 100 zeroes per line and 50 lines per page. With 5,000 digits on one page, we need

$$\frac{10,000,000,000}{5,000} = 2,000,000 \text{ pages}$$

to print it. If one book has a thousand pages, we need 2,000 books for this task. If our printer churns out 1,000 pages per hour, it will take 2,000 hours or about 83 days to finish the job.

This numeric entity is larger than the number of atoms in the known universe. A simple notation and a few small numbers have landed us in a strange field. The power of powers has been unleashed. And that is just an initial taste of the avalanche of enticing mysteries you can plunge into headlong.

We were taught arithmetic and algebra in a mechanical style, and forced to memorize it. If we did not, we were caned. There were no illuminating illustrations, imaginative examples or anything that took your breath away. Maths was solving problems by applying a series of rules. Instead of being let loose, as good education ought to have done, our creative abilities were confined. Albert Einstein had once proclaimed: *Imagination is more important than reality.* Were our teachers aware of that? And what of today's teachers? Judging by their output, it seems that most are unable to do even what our teachers did. They need thorough retraining. Else, their maths classes will neither instill a sense of reality nor inculcate seeds of creativity.

— 3 —

Split Personality

Nobody can be exactly like me.
Sometimes even I have trouble
doing it.
                    Tallulah Bankhead

❖ ❖ ❖ ❖ ❖ ❖ ❖

OUR SENSE OF RIGHT and wrong comes from our parents, elders, peers, teachers, mass media, religious and civic institutions, and the society at large. As we grow up, assorted moral precepts impinge upon our psyche. Some take root; some do not. Some we accept in theory but flout in practice. We choose among competing values. Few people show ethical consistency over space and time. And our own judgment about the morality of our actions frequently differs from that rendered by others.

Arrival in Dar es Salaam in January 1961 began a critical phase in my youth life. I was pulled by two competing tendencies: One steered me to be a model student and religiously inclined, community serving lad. The other propelled me to assume the captaincy of a youth gang engaged in fun and petty theft. Each style of life had its charm. I acquired a dual persona: As the captain, I led an adventurous, risky, happy-go-lucky life. Yet, I was a docile, studious person at school and a religiously inclined boy in the JK setting. The latter roles were not pretensions; they too were emotionally fulfilling roles that emerged from within my inner being. It was as if matter and anti-matter coexisted in close proximity but without a strong reaction.

As in Lindi, my existential universe remained a racially and religiously isolated segment of the national universe. Consequently, as the nation moved towards ending colonial rule, my primary sense of being was essentially static. But social influences that had the potential to fracture my ingrained sense of identity were, unbeknown to me, also beginning to operate on me.

Dar es Salaam

Our new *Imam* emphasized education for Ismaili youth in the same way as his grandfather had done. Moreover, he directed a substantial amount of communal resources towards that purpose. To enable upcountry Ismaili children to access the expanded Aga Khan education institutions in Dar es Salaam, he issued an edict urging the Ismaili families in the city to house them as boarders. Like the other parents, my father aspired to send his children to these schools. His transport business was doing well. He had high hopes for me since I was one of the two top students in my grade. It was in this atmosphere that, in January 1961, I found myself dispatched to the capital city to join the famed Dar es Salaam Aga Khan Boys School (AKBS).

I had not been away from my family for an extended period before. But my uneasiness was compensated by the thrill of living in the metropolis. That I lived with close relatives – *Ada*, a soft-spoken uncle; *Vadima*, a plump, jolly aunt; and *Dadima*, my beloved paternal grandmother – made the abrupt transition bearable. Two Ismaili boarders, one of my age and the other, a year younger, also stayed at my *Ada's* flat.

Dar es Salaam had four types of residential zones: Oysterbay was for colonial officials and white people; Upanga and the central commercial area were occupied by Asians; Kariakoo and Changombe were mixed Asian, Arab and African areas; and the suburbs beyond were primarily African areas. The setup had evolved from the German times. Local residents had been evicted with minimal or no compensation from the prime areas near the sea shore, including Upanga. The British had continued the process; the infrastructure was developed for the needs of the Europeans and the business community (Asians) with Africans assigned the role of providing the necessary, but low-paid services within that set up (Brennan 2007; Brennan, Burton and Lawi 2007; Lusugga Kironde 2007).

My uncle lived in Upanga, an area of about four square kilometers. Only two African families resided in that area at that time. Our flat was in a two story, squarish, well-built structure on Upanga Road, less than a five-minute walk from the beach front, and about two hundred meters from the Upanga JK. Each floor had six flats. A corner ground floor flat, like the one we had, came with a large garden in the backyard. All residents of our flats were Ismaili. In fact, approximately a square kilometre surrounding the JK on its North, South and West faces, with some sixty large and small blocks of flats and a few mansions, was a virtually exclusive Ismaili residential enclave in those days.

Our household, with two cracked window panes, frayed sofa covers, old, dented utensils, mismatched crockery, and discoloured walls was the poorest one in the block. Next to us was Karim Master, a no-nonsense religious studies teacher who was more known for his peculiar gestures, speech and gait than for his erudition. He too did not seem too well off. The rest, families of merchants, transporters, and professionals, stood on a firmer economic pedestal.

My uncle was a beneficiary of the generous Home for All scheme set up under the guidance of our *Imam*. Flats built by the Ismaili Cooperative Society were available at a modest down payment and reasonable monthly instalments to community members. Even relatively poor Ismaili families owned a flat. That was the case with *Ada* too. Having made the down-payment with assistance from relatives, each month he paid TSh 150 (about US $25) towards the mortgage. When it could not be made, his brothers or sister helped him out. His main sources of income were a part-time low-pay overseer like job in a city centre shop, the few-item sales counter run by *Vadima* from the living room, and the fees from the boarders. My father was a major pillar of support for him.

It took a while to get over the novelties of Dar es Salaam. An eleven story tower not too far from our place was the tallest structure in the city and the nation. The two boarders, also recent arrivals from the hinterland, and I counted the stories one by one, and gasped: Boy, an eleven story building! How did those at the top feel? And you did not climb the stairs; a mechanized box took you to all the floors. It was like the contraption we saw in the movies.

The other thing that awed me was the majestic Upanga JK. A blend of traditional Islamic and modern architectural styles, it was a two story structure with halls larger than half a soccer field. An elegant, tall minaret with four giant clock faces at the top stood at one corner. On three sides it was surrounded with a picturesque garden with winding walkways and cool cement benches, enticing one to sit, admire the flora and regale in the aroma. A fountain with five powerful jets sprayed thin beams of water into the heavens. Focused light beams from the base converted the emergent droplets into glittering diamonds. On festive nights, the prayer hall was decorated from end to end like a grand party auditorium and was filled to capacity. The devotees dressed up. The children came elegantly attired as well. With my plain, loose Lindi clothes, I felt out of place in the early days.

On such nights, the *nandi* (food offering) tables in the centre were decked with mouthwatering dishes. To be auctioned after the prayers, their aroma was irresistible. I desired *kuku paka* (whole chicken cooked with coconut and spices) that almost always was the *Mukhi's* principal offering. But it was way beyond our means. My aunt usually purchased a couple of plain dishes like rice with beans, or *chapati* (flat bread) and vegetable curry from the side tables. Later, when my parents came to the city, Mother did cook *kuku paka* type of dishes at home. But the king-sized, elegantly laid out dish in the JK was of heavenly descent. In my more than seven years of attendance at the Upanga JK, I had the opportunity to taste that sumptuous *kuku paka* only once. That was when the *Mukhi*, as a token of his appreciation for our service, repurchased it especially for the JK volunteers.

Life at *Vadima's* place was enjoyable in ways more than one. A large open area behind the flats was our makeshift cricket field. My friends and I kept the grass short, and sanded and flattened the centre batting area. That there were well to do kids in our building and the adjacent block of flats ensured that we had the basic stuff like bats, balls, gloves, wickets and stumps. Two brothers – a fast bowler and a skilled batsman – played in the school team.

Two cricket luminaries, both of whom played for the Aga Khan Cricket Club, lived in a flat opposite ours. Badru Bhamji was the star batsman famous for his frequent hits over the boundary, and his brother, Firoze was, I think, a fast bowler. It was our unspoken wish that one or both of them would observe our play, and offer us a hint or two. But our dream did not materialize. An average spin bowler, I rarely batted more than ten runs.

Though I lived in a diverse metropolis, my cultural life was more restricted than it had been in Lindi. Not only did I not have a single African friend but my Asian friends were now all Ismaili. My social universe, from home to school to fun, games, social visits and the JK, was exclusively Ismaili. Not counting my teachers, I regularly interacted with only one Hindu person. He was Kanti Bhai, a youthful itinerant barber who, black bag in hand, went from flat to flat to trim the hair of boys and elderly men. He charged around one shilling per scalp. Once every six weeks, I was placed at his mercy.

Dadima

Despite its dismal state, our flat had a merry aura. My aunt was a popular personality with whom women neighbors gossiped and let off steam for hours. They played cards and exchanged wisecracks in the afternoon. *Ada* joined in, but *Dadima*, napping in a corner, sternly eyed the unruly lot with silent displeasure.

I walked to school with two friends, a five minute stroll through a thick growth abounding with mango, *zambarau* (jambolan, Java plum), *ambli* (spiral form of tamarind) and *khungu* (Indian almond fruit) trees and the coconut palm. We sometimes picked *zambarau*, *ambli* and *khungu* on the way back from school. The *mkakaya* (flamboyant tree, *gulmohar*) was a ubiquitous presence, providing shade and sustenance to birds and boys. In the flowering season, its resplendent pink-red panoply enlivened the mostly somber landscape.

Upon return home, first it was lunch, and then homework. At 4 pm, I had a hot cup of tea light on milk but doused with sugar, and two biscuits. *Dadima* sat on her bed, a rosary in hand. She would fondly address me as *bapa* (big father) as I snuggled next to her, the cup in hand. It was a daily ritual. In a soft, melodious tone, she would begin a family saga of the distant past. Even if it dealt with a sad event, her gentle tone reduced the bite. Her memory was phenomenal. The tales she retold did not vary. At other times, she would sing religious hymns, and I would sing along.

Dadima was born in Zanzibar in 1896. Her parents had set sail from the state of Gujarat in India, possibly in the 1880s. She married young and bore seven children, one died before he was five. My father, the fourth in line, was born in Zanzibar in 1921. Britain acquired the mandate to rule mainland Tanzania after World War I. Our *Imam* then advised the bulging numbers of Ismailis in Zanzibar to seek fortunes in Dar es Salaam and inland areas. I gather that my grandfather and family moved to the mainland around the year 1930. According to *Dadima*, his life was cut short by a chronic bronchial ailment. I think it was in 1936 or 1937. Hardly forty five years old, he left his widow to fend for three quite young kids. The two older sons helped out in making ends meet.

Throughout the year I stayed with her, *Dadima* narrated much about our ancestry and family events to me. I curse my feeble memory for having lost track of most of what she conveyed to me.

After tea, she took me to the backyard garden. Reveling in the scent of red and pink roses, the slender green-yellow *langi langi* (cananga, ylang-ylang) petals and tiny white *asumini* (jasmine) flowers, and ruffling the mystic *mehndi* (henna) leaves, she eyed the guava, mango, *sita fud* (apple custard) and sugar cane growth. Of the regularly available fruits, she preferred oranges, bananas and papaya. But, underneath, she craved the exotic fruits of her childhood days, those I had tasted in Zanzibar. Though sold near the main JK in Dar es Salaam, they were beyond our means. Once in a while, a relative or a neighbor gave us the chance to nibble on the desired *doriyani, shoke shoke, gulabi* and *fanas* (jack fruit).

Before getting ready for JK, I added up the sales figures from the small 'shop'. I always did it fast and accurately. *Vadima* assessed the profit, which was usually around five shillings, or what could buy six loaves of bread. Then it was time for JK. The days I walked with *Dadima*, we left earlier; but usually I left at 6:30 pm. She sat in the garden for a few minutes before entering the prayer hall. Home by 8 pm for a quick dinner, perhaps the unfinished homework, and, by 10 pm at the latest, it was bedtime. Except for the main religious occasions, that routine held fast.

It brings to my mind the sole unsettling aspect of life at my uncle's place. With three adults and three boys to feed, it was not uncommon at dinnertime that there was not enough food to go around. What *Vadima* placed on the children's plates did not quench our feeling of hunger. Now and then, I went to bed feeling queasy in the belly. Though we lived in poverty in our early days in Lindi, and rarely bought new clothes, Mother always ensured that there was more than sufficient food on the table. It was in Dar es Salaam that I came to know what it felt like going hungry to bed. *Dadima* sensed it at times, and would place a part of her share on my plate, saying she was not hungry. My fixation on the sumptuous *nandi* dishes auctioned at the JK dates from those needy days.

Two Friday evenings a month, I went to my maternal uncle's place. He lived in the mostly African/Arab Kariakoo area and had two sons (strangely, also named Mohamed and Karim) about my age, and a daughter, Yasmin. They too were in dire straits. Their house/shop was a ramshackle, tin roofed, thin-walled congested unit. He would give us, the three boys, one and a half shillings to spend at the JK. Instead of going to the nearby JK, we hiked to the main city JK, the prime reason being the selection of *nandi* on offer. On good days, we managed to get a plate of fried fish, egg-plant and *chapati*, and a decent plate of rice and *mung* beans curry at that price. Rarely, we landed the mouthwatering *chicken biriyani* (a spicy rice-chicken dish). The auctioneer, aware of our limited disposition, would steer an expensive dish to us at a low price. Sitting in comfort under the main stairs, we consumed the bounty with relish.

The next morning, the three of us woke up early, again to go to the JK. After prayers, it was time to head to the Kivukoni Beach front. A trove of *ambli* (tamarind), *khungu, zambarau* and semi-ripe mangoes awaited our plucking. My aunt would scold us. Yet, the family enjoyed the catch.

A Memorable Sting: My fruit lust gave me what I recall as my inaugural bee sting. On an early morning of 1963, engaged in a *khungu* hunt at the Kivukoni beach, I spotted a juicy bunch on a tree of medium height. Without hesitation, I climbed up. As I reached for the bunch, a bee stung my ear. A piercing wail, "mummy," ensued, the thin branch snapped, and I fell twelve feet to the ground. With an expansive internal bruise on one thigh, barely able to walk, and a throbbing earlobe, I do not know how I made it home.

As there was no bleeding, I was not sent to a clinic but was given a glass of hot milk and put to bed. Mother made and applied a paste of warm turmeric and flour over the bruised area. Within a couple of days, it cleared up, and I resumed loitering around with friends. (Scientific research, I can say now, provides some evidence that turmeric has detectable anti-inflammatory properties.)

Dadima spent hours taking care of her waist long hair. She regularly washed it with *aritha* (round, black seeds producing soppy suds) and dyed it with henna till it turned into a collage of glittering gold and brown streaks. On key religious days, she would have me pluck *asumini* flowers, and petals of the aromatic *langi langi* from the garden. With these precious jewels of nature secured in her small brown purse and draped in her reddish, laced shawl, she exuded the demeanour of royalty as she serenely glided towards the JK. The aroma and sparkle from her hair enhanced her elegance.

 Dadima knew traditional Indian medicine, and put it to use when one of the family or a neighbor was unwell. When I had fever, she applied a towel dipped in dill-water to my forehead. She remained in robust health and was physically active into a ripe old age. I do not recall her ever being ill. Rarely sitting still, she was perpetually in the middle of one chore or another. To the annoyance of my aunt, she redid what had been done a short while earlier – like rewashing a dish just washed. When visiting a relative or going on a shopping trip to the city centre, she preferred to walk rather than take up the offer of a ride from her sons or a neighbor.

 Of diminutive stature, the traditional shawl always on her head, a rosary in hand, and a spirit endowed with joy and gentleness, she was the beloved hub of our large extended family, holding together a conglomeration of otherwise bickering and discordant people. When she smiled, as she so often did, the world smiled with her (Image 4: Appendix B).

Ginans

The Ismaili hymns, or *ginans*, are recited in the JK each evening before the start of the first prayer, in-between the prayers and after the last prayer. They also feature in the dawn prayer sessions, at special *majlis* (prayer gatherings) and funerals. You get a pleasant tingling sensation in your ears and a warm feeling in your heart when a woman with a superb soprano leads the recitation.

 Our *Pirs* (saints) have composed more than a thousand *ginans*. Most are in Gujarati, and incorporate both Islamic and Hindu values and traditions. That culture has evolved over centuries. Some are general hymns; others suit particular occasions. Like my peers, I was immersed in *ginans* from childhood. And it was not just at the JK; they were an integral part of home life as well. Mother, in the kitchen or at rest, recited them in a soft voice, often without a break. *Dadima* was fond of them as well.

 By age ten, I knew several *ginans* by heart. Their enchanting melodies and poetic words sent you to a state of mental repose. As guides for spiritual and worldly conduct, their prime canons were devotion to the *Imam*, and abiding by the ethical tenets of our faith. *Monan na Man*, a popular *ginan* by Pir Hassan Shah, for example, eulogizes the devotional, simple life, and castigates selfishness, material greed, hypocrisy and deception. The first and third of its eleven stanzas are:

Spirit versus Matter

Eji moman na man em janjo ji	O being, your essence is spiritual
Tame kayano ma karso abhiman re	Discard physical vanity and pride
Moman	O being . . .
Dhonga to ene ene hare vasee	Hypocrisy will lead you astray
Teto lute sahebjino dhyan re	And estrange you from the Lord
Moman	O being . . .

In the *ginan, Eji Duniya Sirjine,* Pir Hassan Kabir Din wonders why you do not pay homage to the Creator of the world, food, air and water. Sinful ways will land you in unbearable suffering in Hell where heat of the intensity of a hundred suns prevails and morality breaks down to the extent that mothers disown their children. If you avoid sin, your heavenly rewards will include houses made with gold bricks, pillars bedecked with jewels, and walls plastered with pure silk. If you discard your sinful ways, and adopt a life of reverence, you avoid the former and attain the latter. Two stanzas of this *ginan* are:

Punishment for Sin

Eji duniyano lobh jivdo karvano laago ji, Duniyane lobhe jivdo bhulo ji,	Craving for worldly stuff captures his soul, And in that vile craving, he forgets his essence
. . . . . .	. . .
Eji bhulo te mathano bhejo kane nisershe ji, Til til na lekha saheb lese ji	That forgetful brain matter will ooze out your ears, A bit by bit account of your life will the Lord demand

These dreadful eventualities of a life of sin struck a distinct note of fear in my young mind. When a boy annoyed me in the extreme, I would angrily tell him that he would burn in Hell, and his brain would drip from his ears.

I understood the broad meaning of the *ginans,* but not their subtleties. The words were complex; metaphors, abstruse; and my Gujarati, patently deficient. The saving grace was that our missionaries explained their import and meaning in the course of their JK sermons. What I can say for sure is that the *ginans* played a primary role in the formulation of my internal moral code. If I missed a prayer session, I felt guilty beyond measure. What I came to regard as right or wrong largely stemmed from the values they projected. Selfishness, lying, greed, unruly conduct, harming others and disrespect towards elders – they were forbidden. On the other hand, kindness, generosity, integrity, simplicity, helping people in need, valuing the acquisition of knowledge, respectful behavior, regular prayer and meditation, and paying religious dues were the defining attributes of a genuine devotee of the *Imam*.

Incidental Rewards: Today I have a secular disposition towards the essence of human life. Yet, I still like reading and reciting *ginans*. I value their non-denominational ethical tenets. They invoke fond memories, and make me sentimental. Their poetic turns of phrase, and fine tone and melody continue to charm me.

They have three other benefits. One, I prefer the Gujarati script version and not the English alphabet transliteration. The latter sheds their authenticity. That preference has helped me retain a modicum of mastery of Gujarati. Two, when my respiratory passages get congested, as they so often do in this polluted city, a twenty minute recitation of the *ginans* (as indeed, of any poem or verse) in a loud voice facilitates mucus drainage and reduces the blockage. At least, it does that for me. Last but not least, the *ginans* are the only effective way through which I can get across to my ninety five year old, bedridden father. He is listless, and does not heed any call most of the time. But when I recite a *ginan* in his presence, he becomes attentive, takes up his rosary and starts reciting it as well. Ten minutes into the session, I can talk to him for a short while. But it does not last long. He soon relapses into his own mysterious universe.

Undali Street

Despite the pleasant days with my uncle's family, and no dearth of friends at school and in the vicinity, I sorely missed my mother. I desired her delicious dishes. I longed for the way she doted on her children. Only when my family permanently moved to Dar es Salaam at the end of 1961 did that gnawing sense of being alone fade away.

For the first two years, the seven of us first lived in a cramped, two room flat in Ismailia Flats, an eight flat building on dusty, crater-strewn Undali Street in Upanga. The residents in this block were all low economic status Ismailis. Next to us was a retired postmaster with nine children. Parvez, a boy a year younger than me, in the flat above ours, sold *jugu* (peanuts) roasted by his mother in the JK; he was nicknamed *juguro*.

My father got the job of a salesperson in a wholesale shop in Kariakoo owned by the eldest son of his sister. That family had wealth; her daughters were snobbish and uptight. When I went to their house, I felt uneasy and out of place. My hands trembled when I had a cup of tea on their elegantly set table. At the other relatives' places, it was just like being at home.

Father had a strict routine. Awake at 4:30 am for the JK prayers, back by 6 am, breakfast and a few chores later, he sped off on his bicycle to open the shop by 8 am. Located in the dense heartland of Kariakoo, right opposite the Msimbazi Police Station, it was a single windowless room about 20 meters long, and four meters at the doorway and seven meters at the rear. Near the door was a wooden stool, a giant weighing scale and a display counter made from glass and wood. Father mostly stood behind the counter, dealing with customers and directing three barely clad, barefoot African workers. When no customer was around, he sat on the stool. The floor area was cramped with sacks of salt, beans, flour, rice, cans of cooking oil, and boxes of soap and sundry items.

Father's lot improved in a year's time. A three ton delivery truck was garaged at our home. On weekends, it was used for family tasks. The owner wanted to focus on expanding his other businesses. Hence, Father was made a working partner in this shop. Two years later, he became the sole proprietor. Father later revealed to me that his nephew had overcharged him for the shop.

In the meantime, we had moved into a bigger house. Once in a while, I went to the shop. I saw that he hardly sat still. He told me to place myself near the door and keep an eye on what was coming in and going out. The profit margin was low, usually one to two percent. The loss of one cartoon of matches, or a sack of beans would make a sizable dent in the day's profits.

The Upanga JK was a five-minute walk from our place, with *Dadima's* flat being on the other side. I often visited her, and walked her to the JK. At times, we sat for a few minutes on a bench in the JK garden. She regaled me with her stories as usual. My father regularly brought supplies for their place from his shop and elsewhere.

Captain

I went on with my Standard 8 studies at the Aga Khan Boys School (Chapter 4). It was a ten minute walk from Undali Street. After school, Nazir and I played with a stable group of ten boys. Amilo Pipi, a boy with steel-like biceps, and his brothers Nazim and Shokat were the sons of the post master. The others were either from our building or the neighboring ones.

In time, we became a gang. It did not have a name, but I was the captain. Some twenty five meters across from the front of our flats lay a vacant grassy lot. We cleared the overgrowth, and built a three by three meters wide and two meters high structure using discarded wood, boxes, roofing material, nails and rope picked up from construction sites. It was the gang HQ. Weekday afternoons and weekends were spent in its vicinity. We played with marbles, climbed trees, practiced high jump, long jump and running, and kicked the soccer ball. Our meetings were noisy, but as the captain, I saw to it that no one mistreated another.

We were poor but ambitious. We fancied things other children had but we did not. It was time we too had them, we decided. For a start, we liked sugar cane and guavas. Around the evening prayer time, we sneaked into the large gardens of the well to do households. Many of them had a multiplicity of fruit trees. A small gap in the shrubbery permitted us to enter, and chop off a large branch of sugar cane. We sat near the JK, sliced off the tough skin with a knife (I always carried one) and enjoyed the bounty. On lucky days, we feasted on guava, mangoes, *sita fud, khungu* or *zambarau*. A juicy water melon was a prized item. We always returned home with the JK crowd, so our parents thought we had attended the prayer ceremony.

One flat not far from the JK had two sizable *daldam* (pomegranate) trees. The large yellow-red ripe fruits were impossible to resist. As people napped to secure relief from the tropical heat, the area was deserted on Saturday afternoons. Seizing the opportunity, we went over the iron gate and plucked two ripe fruits. Unluckily, a young girl at the window spotted us and raised the alarm. In panic, we took off, with five older boys in hot pursuit. Our initial move was to hide behind the Aga Khan Hospital that was near the sea shore. But the pursuers were too close. So we ran along the winding, sandy sea line going towards the Selendar Bridge. The tide was low, so we could run along the beach throughout. We evaded capture by hiding in a secluded, dark area under the bridge. The pomegranates were swell, but two of our buddies had been identified. The school headmaster was notified on Monday. Craftily and vigorously, they denied everything. It was not them, they innocently declared. Since there was no definitive proof, the case was dropped with a warning not to engage in such activities.

From fruits, our eyes moved on to chocolates. We would enter fancy shops like Patel Stores, split up into talkative groups, cause a distraction, look around several shelves, buy a candy or two, and walk out in jest. Back at the gang HQ, one or two among us would raise his shirt. Lo and behold, a nice chocolate bar was tucked underneath. Nazir was quite adept at delivering such fine blessings to us.

On a few occasions, one boy brought cigarettes and a box of matches to the hut. We puffed a few, passing each from person to person. But the practice did not catch on. My throat was irritated each time I smoked. I am happy to note that as adults, none us became regular smokers.

Cricket was the game of the era. So we cleared a wider area and made it into a cricket field. The pitch was measured and levelled, and boundary markers placed. Unlike soccer, cricket needs bats, balls, gloves, stumps, pads and the like. Their cheapest variants were too expensive for our parents. At *Dadima's* place, children from well to do families had provided the equipment. In Undali Street, we only had makeshift stuff – a tennis ball, an oddly carved bat and plain wood sticks for stumps. It did not befit a distinguished team like ours; we had to play real cricket.

No problem, it was concluded after a rancorous session. We then went to weekend cricket matches, innocently prowled about the changing and storage areas, and, when the chance arose, snatched an item or two. In a short while, a decent collection of cricket paraphernalia was stored in our hut, allowing us to play the game with gusto. Our bounty included a bat and a pair of gloves belonging to John Solanki, the reigning super star of Tanzanian cricket. His name was elegantly inscribed on them. Once we had the temerity to go to the Gymkhana Grounds late in the evening, roll up the practice half-carpet, and carry it to our field. But our luck did not last. The club *askari* (guard) scoured the Upanga area the very next day, and spotted his carpet on our field. When he angrily asked how we had got it, we said that we had bought it for five shillings from a fellow who had passed by. Needless to say, he did not accept our explanation, and made us carry the carpet back to the club.

Cricket, like soccer, was a British import. But unlike the latter, it was an elitist game. For the Asians in Tanzania, it was the premier sport, and most cricket teams were Asian community or school teams. Unlike Kenya or Uganda, whose national teams fielded two or more African players, I do not remember seeing an African player on a Tanzanian club or national team. And there were no African spectators at the games either.

Cricket had a different standing in the Caribbean and India. As a game of the people, it was embedded into the local culture and was a medium for nationalistic sentiments (James 1993). In Tanzania, to the contrary, it embodied a pro-colonial, parochial outlook.

The climax of our *taap-taap* (transference) endeavours affected a visiting Zambian dance troupe. It was holding its practice sessions at the Diamond Jubilee Hall. The instruments were left unguarded at lunch time. We waited till no one was around, entered the practice area and expropriated two small drums and one banjo. The next day, Nazir, Nazim and Shokat merrily banged away, inventing a unique musical style at the same time. But the theft had been reported. The cacophony aroused the suspicion of a policeman walking by. Caught red handed with the missing items, the trio were taken to the Central Police Station near the main railway terminal.

Our parents were summoned. Amilo Pipi and I accompanied my father. As we entered the station commander's office, we saw our buddies standing in a corner, eyes cast downwards. Given their youthful age, the commander did not want to take the matter far. But it was necessary to teach the naughty boys a lesson. So he made them hold the drums over their heads for about thirty minutes, and loudly repeat "We will not steal, we will not steal" over and over. A good dose of punishment awaited them at home too. The rest of us said we had no knowledge about the theft. This incident put a halt to consequential shady actions on our part. From then on, we were content to *taap-taap* a branch of sugar cane once in a while.

Yet, there was no shortage of fun-filled activities. We swam at the Upanga Beach, and afterwards, climbed the nearby mango, *ambli* (tamarind) and *khungu* trees. The wide crater like area facing our house filled up during the rainy season. At the centre it was almost four feet deep. We sailed that pond on wood boards, and waddled in the water that brimmed with tad poles and jumping frogs. We had set backs too. A one-story house was built near our hut in mid-1963. The occupants, a Sikh family, soon came to despise our noisy gatherings. One sad morning, the man of the house put a match to our gang HQ. When we returned from school, we were shocked to find it in ashes. The nasty but bulky fellow came out, and roared that he would thrash us with a stick if we rebuilt it. So that was the end of that.

In ways more than one, it was time to move on. Father, now a business co-owner, acquired a two-story flat on a hire purchase basis. It was located adjacent to the JK. We were slated to move in a month. By then, I had joined the Ismaili volunteer corps, which meant I had service duties during the JK prayer sessions. I thus interacted with more religiously inclined youth. Most of my daytime hours were spent at my new secondary school where my circle of friends was light years apart from any I had had earlier. In spirit and practice, the gang-banging mode of life had lost its charm.

Two days before we moved, I distributed the gang property – cricket balls, bats, gloves, etc. – among the members. I made sure that each person got his fair share. Amilo Pipi told me: "Karim, you are a good captain." To this day, at the age of sixty six, he calls me by that title. Once a captain, always a captain.

Uhuru Day

In the year I lived with *Dadima*, the foundation for a stupendous transformation in the manner by which our nation would be governed was being laid. A new set up for the Legislative Assembly in 1958 had accelerated the process. In the

1960 elections, TANU, the political party led by Mwalimu Julius Nyerere, won 70 out of the 71 Assembly seats. Self-governance was attained in May 1961. By the end of the year, full Independence would be attained.

Colonial rule had systematically fostered race based economic injustice, mistrust and strife within the nation. A *de-facto* Apartheid-like setup had prevailed for decades. On the eve of *Uhuru*, the black skinned people (the 99%) harboured a long list of mostly justified grievances against the hitherto more favoured brown skinned people (the 1%). Ethnic, religious and regional antagonisms were at play as well. Muslim and Christian leaders did not see eye to eye on some matters. The vision for the new nation was to form amicable, just and mutually respectful relationships among all its people, and establish a united, proud, peaceful and strong nation that could hold its own ground in the community of nations. It was a noble vision, but was it achievable under the conditions of the day?

Even if it was attainable, it was not going to be an easy task. Formidable obstacles stood in the way. Yet, four social factors in mainland Tanzania backed attainment of this vision. One: Even though our internal divisions had deep roots, they had not, unlike in some nations of Africa, reached an explosive stage. Two: A common local language, Swahili, constituted a major basis for sustainable unity. Three: One political party, TANU, had secured an almost unanimous mandate from the people. And four, but not least: It was led by a gentle, valiant man of sound, humane principles, a man who, moreover, was widely respected at home and abroad.

As we approached 9th December 1961, the day of *Uhuru*, rallies and festivities abounded. Hope and an unparalleled spirit of joy prevailed in an atmosphere of peace and stability. The flag of the new nation displaced the colonial flag. Dignitaries and the British royalty came, and parades were held. In an appropriately symbolic move, Lieutenant Alex Nyirenda placed the torch of freedom at the summit of Mount Kilimanjaro.

God Bless Africa

Mungu ibariki Africa	God bless Africa
Wabariki viongozi wake	Bless its leaders.
Hekima, umoja na amani	Wisdom, unity and peace
Hizi ni ngao zetu	These reflect our essence
Afrika na watu wake	Africa and its people
CHORUS:	CHORUS:
Ibariki Afrika	Bless Africa
Ibariki Afrika	Bless Africa
Tubariki watoto wa Afrika	Bless the children of Africa

The odd-sounding "God Save the Queen" was supplanted by what I later came to genuinely view as our own heartwarming and supremely melodious national anthem. The first stanza of this anthem is shown above.

A day before the *Uhuru* day, Mwalimu Nyerere called upon all our people to join hands, live in harmony and work to combat our three enemies: poverty, ignorance and disease. He expressed his full confidence in our abilities to do so. The motto of the new nation, he declared, would be: *Uhuru na Kazi* (Freedom and Work).

Mainland Tanzania faced a daunting uphill battle. For example, it had only 420 doctors in public health facilities that served over 10 million people, a ratio of less than one doctor for 20,000 persons. Most trained medical staff served the elites in the urban areas. The nation had no facilities for training doctors. It was but one aspect of the grim legacy of forty years of British rule. Yet, the mood at the grassroots was upbeat and hopeful. People were willing to play their part in building the nation. For example, workers from sisal plantations, whose pay hardly sufficed to feed their families well, contributed the equivalent of one day's wage to the national development fund.

The tranquil nature of the transition notwithstanding, news reports had Asians considering whether to emigrate to India or not. On the other side, there were calls from key political figures and the TANU newspaper to speed up Africanization of the civil service and other work positions, and provide better educational opportunities for African students. People did not want the inequities of the past to persist. The Asians could not take their privileged status for granted any longer.

The day of *Uhuru* was a couple of weeks before I moved to Undali Street to live with my family. The astonishing thing is that my recall of that particular day or the events leading to it is essentially zero. I do not retain a single image, even a diffuse one, of an event, person, place or idea related to *Uhuru*. Other than the visit of Aga Khan IV, I have no memory of the special events held at our school. Yet, I retain sharp mental pictures of friends, cricket, JK activities, school and home life from that time. What I have written in the preceding paragraphs about *Uhuru* comes from what I learned later on.

Apart from its title, the national anthem did not make an impression on my mind. I came to learn its words and understand its meaning three years later when I went to the Kinondoni National Service Camp.

Only one thing about *Uhuru* remains in my mind. This is the feeling of dread that pervaded the Asian communities. It was a fear of the unknown. We had seen Asian families escaping the turmoil in the Congo. Our elders thought, without any solid justifying evidence, that the same catastrophe was about to visit this land. Their fears percolated down to the children. Other than that, as our people struggled to realize their right to self-determination, the Asians, apart from a tiny nationalistic minority, stood on the side-lines. We went on with our secluded lives as if nothing was afoot (Jhaveri 2014). Even my respected teachers did not dwell on the significance of *Uhuru*. We were in a universe within a universe, impervious to the fundamental changes in the external dimension.

Both Prince Karim Aga Khan and Mwalimu Nyerere had promoted inter-racial harmony and cooperation, and urged us to adjust to the new life in a peaceful way. The quotes in Chapter 2 typify their vision. Yet their wisdom was not heeded as it should have been. At best, it garnered symbolic lip service. Instead of initiating a genuine process of developing mutual respect and solidarity, our community persisted with inward looking attitudes. The almost predictable consequences – at the economic and political levels – of that isolationist stand would unfold over time, and they would not be pleasant ones.

That psychological atmosphere meant that while I lived through a momentous year in the life of my nation, I have virtually no personal level descriptions or experiences related to it. A more telling sign of the degree of the racial isolationism I must have been immersed in would be hard to come by.

Poetry and Numbers ❖ ❖ ❖ ❖ ❖ ❖ ❖

Our sole female saint, Pir Imam Begun, composed theologically erudite *ginans*. My special attraction was to *Uth jag man mora* (Awaken, O devotee). It is both a literal call to rise up for the morning prayer and a metaphoric urging to eschew the life of spiritual slumber. The devotee is implored to avoid pride and pleasure, and seek salvation from the unpleasant cycle of reincarnation by fulfilling religious obligations and engaging in meditation. Often recited at funerals, its words and melody have been with me since the Lindi days. From the frequency with which she sang it, I infer it was a hit with *Dadima* too.

A second reason why it appealed to me was that it featured my friends from number land. Only a few hymns share this feature. One stanza of this *ginan* declares that the sinner returns to the material world in cyclic phases. First he/she does so thirty-five times, then twenty five times, then sixteen and finally eight times. The next line gives the total number of reincarnations, namely, eighty four. In my primary school days, I did the addition $(35 + 25 + 16 + 8)$ to check if the total was 84. A more learned interpretation multiplies this figure by 100,000, that being the counting unit for reincarnation.

Another stanza proclaims that we take twenty one thousand and six hundred breaths in a day. I thereby figured that:

- We take $21600/24 = 900$ breaths per hour.
- We take $900/60 = 15$ breaths per minute.

Using a wall clock, I timed my breaths. Mostly, I obtained fifteen breaths per minute. At times, it was higher by a breath or two. I now know that in normal health, the adult respiration rate at rest is between twelve and eighteen breaths per minute. The rate for a child is slightly higher. That Pir Begum, writing centuries ago, gave a rate that lies half-way in this interval testifies to the state of Islamic science of that age. With hindsight, I note that my counts of my own respiration rate were likely biased. As I had expected them to be fifteen, I may have subconsciously adjusted my breathing and/or counting to get the desired value. Observer bias is a common occurrence in social and natural science studies. Fortunately, many methods, simple and complex, to control such a bias have been devised.

Pir Imam Begum linked numbers with poetry. It was likely the first instance in which I saw numbers in a positive poetic context. Vatsalaben had made us recite multiplication tables as if they were songs. But the setting had been a distasteful one.

In Dar es Salaam, my friendship with numbers bloomed exponentially. As I narrate in the next chapter, two of my teachers at the Agakhan Boys School played an instrumental role in this process. One of them also connected mathematics with literary pursuits.

Poems are elegant constructs of words, with an emotive or paradoxical essence. In contrast, mathematics is an arena of arcane symbols and unfathomable formulas that follow strict rules of logic. Can they be enjoined? The usual view is that they cannot. But that view flows from a narrow vision of the subject. If you peruse beneath the surface, you discover that a steel-like cable with multiple strands links these two pursuits. Poems provide illuminative or humorous commentaries on mathematics or its subfields. Mathematical formulas and ideas have been expressed in poetic form. Poems whose essence embodies a mathematical idea exist. And we can analyse poetic structures with the tools of mathematics. A large body of work on each of these diverse strands exists.

Accomplished mathematicians have stood out in the world of literature and poetry. Take one case: Omar Khayyáam, the premier Persian algebraist and astronomer (1048 – 1131) also penned elegant verses. His major poetic work is the well known *The Rubaiyat of Omar Khayyáam*. Or, take a later case: Bertrand Russell, a leading mathematician of the last century, won the Nobel Prize for Literature for his popular writings and essays.

I illustrate the linkage between the two fields with the digits of π. While number lovers memorize hundreds of these digits, most of us at best recall the first three or four digits. However, there are many catchy poems and phrases we can employ to extend our reach. The verse below is often cited.

A Mnemonic for π

How I wish I could calculate pi
"Eureka," cried the great inventor
Christmas pudding; Christmas pie
is the problem's very center

The number of letters in the first word is the first digit of π, the number in the second word, the second digit, and so on. If you memorize the first line, you get $\pi = 3.141592$. Remembering the whole verse wins you the first twenty one digits of $\pi = 3.14159265358979323846$. If only the first line is used, it is modified as "How I wish I could calculate pie" so as to adjust for rounding.

Scores of creative mnemonics, prose or poetic, and in several languages, have been devised for this purpose. Designating remarkable literary creativity, entire short stories encapsulating the consecutive digits of π have been written. Below is perhaps a first Swahili mnemonic for the first ten digits of π. It is a translation of: 'I and my neighbour's child went out to buy six loaves of bread.'

A Swahili Mnemonic for π

Mimi na mtoto wa jirani
tulikwenda nje kununua mikate sita

Placing together the number of digits of consecutive words in the Swahili sentence [42526(10)3764], subtracting one from each digit and putting the decimal point, you get 3.141592653.

Over the course of centuries, prominent poets, mathematicians, scientists, and writers have categorically declared that the two endeavours share important features. I quote the views of five distinguished personages.

Inspiration is needed in geometry, just as much as in poetry.
Alexander Pushkin

A mathematician, like a painter or poet, is a maker of patterns.
Godfrey H Hardy

Pure mathematics is, in its way, the poetry of logical ideas.
Albert Einstein

A mathematician who is not also something of a poet will never be a complete mathematician.   Karl Weierstrass

The union of the mathematician with the poet, fervor with measure, passion with correctness, this surely is the ideal.   William James

These preeminent personalities are in essence telling us that literary and artistic pursuits, for one, and mathematics, for the other, are connected in a more than symbolic manner. The linkage between them is structural and integral. Many other heavyweights of history have expressed similar sentiments.

The number pattern given below, crafted by James Henle, is an example of mathematics in a poetic form (Henle 2011).

$$(1)^2 \ = \ 1^3$$

$$(1+2)^2 \ = \ 1^3 + 2^3$$

$$(1+2+3)^2 \ = \ 1^3 + 2^3 + 3^3$$

$$(1+2+3+4)^2 \ = \ 1^3 + 2^3 + 3^3 + 4^3$$

$$(1+2+3+4+5)^2 \ = \ 1^3 + 2^3 + 3^3 + 4^3 + 5^3$$

A Poetic Pattern

The number patterns in Chapter 1 are forms of poetic maths as well. The linkage between literary arts and mathematics is also illustrated in the other chapters. And there is so much more: An Internet search on the phrase "mathematics and poetry" opens numerous gateways to a treasure trove waiting for you to discover and enjoy.

— 4 —

Two Teachers

*Life stands before me like an eternal
spring with new and brilliant clothes.*
Carl Friedrich Gauss

TRANSFERRING FROM ONE school to another is normally an unremarkable event. We do it when we enter secondary school, or when our families change residence. At times, however, it turns into something more. Either in a deleterious or beneficial way, some persons or circumstance at the new school come to exercise a significant impact on the course of our lives. We may not realize it immediately. But years later, we discern that what then looked like a minor thing initiated a qualitative rupture in our mental repertoire, and affected our subsequent lives in a fundamental way.

That is what happened to me when I moved to the Aga Khan Boys School (AKBS) in Dar es Salaam. My two maths teachers at this school laid the foundation for my lifelong bonding with that subject. They had a crucial impact on what I subsequently accomplished. One of them also initiated my enduring addiction for reading fiction and non-fiction books. The realization of the major influence they had on my life, though, dawned upon me much later.

AKBS

One early morning of January 1961, my uncle walked me to the AKBS. My application to join the school had brought forth a summons to the school. Unsure what it was for, I waited in a classroom with about ten children who were in the same boat. A while later, a stern-voiced man entered and gave us a test paper containing questions on English and mathematics. We had an hour to complete it. I finished first, before the set time. Upon taking a brief look at my answer sheets, he smiled and told my uncle that I should report, attired in the school uniform, to a particular Standard 7 classroom the next day.

At home, everyone was happy. *Dadima* showered her blessings in the traditional way by gently clacking her knuckles on the sides of her skull and then repeating the action on my skull. She prayed to our *Imam* to safeguard my faith, bless me with a peaceful and prosperous life, protect me from illness, and help me reach my goals. The ritual ended with a kiss on my forehead. My uncle and I spent the afternoon buying two sets of the school uniform, two pairs of socks, a school bag, a few pencils and notebooks.

The next day I was up early. A cup of tea and two slices of bread layered with margarine sent me off to school with two boys in our flat. On the way, they tutored me on what to do and not to do. The main thing, they said, was to look out for the Deputy Head Master, the fiercest fellow in the place. If you want to avoid his cane, do not be even a minute late, I was gravely warned.

School began with an outdoor assembly. An Ismaili prayer preceded some announcements by the Head Master. Non-Ismaili teachers and students stood aside. On that day, I stood with them as I did not know the line for my class.

The main AKBS building was a rectangular two-story structure, far larger than my Lindi school. The geometrically austere set up containing some 25 classrooms, the office area, laboratories and the main hall symbolized an educational edict: You enter the premises to gain knowledge, only knowledge and nothing but knowledge. As if to strike a balance, the fragrant, lush gardens around the entrance and in the courtyard projected an aura of care-free relaxation. Daily watering and debris removal produced a fine pattern of flowery plants. Hibiscus was aplenty, and the white and red roses lent a royal touch. Bougainvillea made up a part of the front fence. The swarthy trees, with the flamboyant specie aplenty, held their own ground, flourishing as they pleased. Productive mango, tamarind and *khungu* trees shed their largess across the yard. My eyes strayed beyond the smaller front entrance where the humongous *mzambarau* boasted big bunches of the purple fruit. At one side of the main building, a mammoth sports field accommodated a full-size cricket pitch, an athletics arena, tennis courts and grassy open spaces.

The school had students in Standard 7 and 8 (middle/upper primary school), Form I – IV (secondary school) and Form V – VI (high school). The library shelved far more books than I had previously seen in any one place. Each student got a textbook for each subject, to be returned at the end of the academic year. The physics, chemistry and biology laboratories were state-of-the-art. A high-ceilinged large hall with a curtained stage was the venue for stage, music and dance performances, movies and meetings. Once a year, we watched a play staged by the senior students. I was told that the AKBS was ranked among the top five secondary-cum-high schools in the nation.

On the first day, a prefect directed me to my classroom. All eyes shone on me as I entered. Feeling intimidated, I sat in the last row. Soon our teacher came in. It was the same man who had administered the test the day before. Spotting me right away, he beckoned me to an unoccupied seat in the second row. That was how I came to know Mr Hirani.

In the initial days, I was not at ease: Too many new faces, hardly a friend, and none in my class. Some classmates bore the aura of nobility. They spoke stylish English and sat next to each other. I felt they had a special relationship with the teachers. With uniforms cut from prime cloth and not a hair out of place on finely combed, shiny scalps, they did not even glance at me. At break time I sought out my neighbourhood boys, but found them immersed in circles of their own.

Break time was the chance to spend the ten cents I was given daily; five cents for *jugu* and five for *bisi* (popcorn). It secured but a handful of nuts; but they felt good in the mouth. Friday was a special day. Then I had twenty more cents, and could buy a soda, the treat of the week. I had it in style. First I took a gulp of coke, burped, and then added salted *jugus* in the bottle, shook it gently to create foam, took a slow gulp, chewed a few moistened nuts, and continued the process until no nuts were left. A big burp climaxed the fiesta. This routine was usually followed with a group of boys. We felt as if we had had the grandest of drinks. Yet I envied the uppity ones who spent a shilling daily, had sodas frequently, and got prized items like *jugu mawe* (bambara nuts), *dariya* (roasted chick peas) and potato crisps.

The teachers were strict and demanding. Homework was aplenty. If you did not work hard, you were left behind. A competitive atmosphere prevailed. My aptitude for maths raised my standing among my classmates. Even in the A section, where the brightest students were placed, performance in maths was variable. I always had the correct answer; the teacher often called upon me. Soon, other students were asking me maths questions during break time or after school. I became a respected, but not a popular student.

On some Saturdays, I went to cheer the school cricket team. Otherwise I did not take part in school sport. In my second year, my spare time was devoted to the Undali Street gang. In that regard, I declare with certainty that as we scoured around for cricket equipment and other stuff, our *taap-taap* ventures did not ever target our school team. It was an inviolable boundary. But we did pilfer a few items from the Aga Khan Sports Club. Why the latter but not the former? I do not know.

We do not ask why we drink water. It is an act we take for granted. Similarly, there were two basic aspects of school life I did not think at all about at that time. My concern surfaced a decade later when it dawned upon me that generally there is more than one way of examining issues in life. One aspect was that the students were divided into streams – A, B, C, D, etc. – on the basis of ability. The A stream had the top-notch students; B, the next best students; and so on. The last stream was for kids considered dullards or misfits who were not expected to enter or complete secondary school. My entrance test results had put me in the A stream. I remained in that stream in the following year. I had no qualms about that system, and I did not hear any misgivings about it either. It was seen as an appropriate way to organize the education of a large group of students.

Tracking and Education: Ever since I started to teach in 1971, my classes have had students of varying ability or background. Effective teaching in that situation is a major challenge, especially if their range of abilities is wide. At first sight, stratifying students by perceived ability sounds sensible. However, forty years of experience and exploration in teaching tell me that it is an erroneous action. Tracking has major pitfalls. The tests used to assess ability are flawed. Students who do not perform well in one subject may excel in another. Tracking also brands children for life; does not consider that child development is an uneven process; makes teachers pay more attention to a select few;

deprives weaker students a chance to be inspired by and learn from their peers; often nurtures elitism; and perpetuates existent socio-economic inequalities. From pedagogic and societal angles, it is far from an optimal way of organizing education.

Dr Hassan Fazel was a lecturer in the Statistics Department of the UDSM in 1973. He had a PhD in Statistics from a Canadian University and was the first Tanzanian to attain that degree in that subject. He told tell me that he used to get failing grades in maths during his first two years of secondary school, and was considered a dullard.

Tracking was concordant with the hierarchical social-economic realities and visions of the colonial era. Thankfully, it was gradually set by the wayside when a national system of education came into being after Independence.

The second aspect of my school then deemed normal was the composition of the student body. Only one student in my class was African. As far as I can recall, all the rest were not just Asian but Ismaili. In Lindi, they had been a mixture of Ismailis, Ithnasheries and Hindus.

The majority of my teachers at the AKBS came directly from India. My two maths teachers were Ismailis – one born in Tanzania, the other, a recent arrival from India. Apart from religion studies, I had not been taught by an Ismaili teacher before. But they were also my last Ismaili teachers. It turned out that in all my subsequent studies up to the PhD level, I never again had an Ismaili teacher. At the AKBS, there were a few British teachers as well.

The teachers from India spoke English with a peculiar accent. Some pronounced 'm' as 'yum' and 'n' as 'yun'. We used to mimic them for a laugh. I cannot fault their deficient Swahili since most of the local Asians did not have a decent command of it either.

Fazli Datoo

Mr Fazli Datoo taught me maths in Standard 8. After securing his High School Certificate with flying colours a year earlier from the same school, he had plans, but not yet an offer, to join a university to major in maths. AKBS needed a middle school maths teacher. His excellent performance and upright character made him a suitable candidate.

Mr Datoo was the youngest teacher I have ever had. Though he was then not a qualified teacher, he has been one of the best and most influential teachers I have had in my life. Mesmerized by him from day one, I came to look upon him as a remarkable all-round person.

His friendliness was a world apart from the stern aloofness of my previous teachers. My Lindi maths teachers had been tyrants. By his youthful demeanour, he related to us more as a friend than as a person assigned to impose knowledge on us. He joked and laughed. That Lindi lady had borne a perpetual frown on her face; Mr Datoo was rarely without a smile on his face. And you could talk to him after class.

He dealt with you as a person, not as some nondescript boy in his class. Since I was adept at maths, he called upon me from time to time. He was not unduly swayed by the uppity students. During his session, you felt one among equals. He was instrumental in making me feel more at ease at the AKBS.

The young teacher was a master of his discipline. I admired how he deftly handled numbers, algebraic expressions, shapes and formulas, rarely referring to the text book. It was embedded in his brain. His facility to convert intricate topics and formulas into friendly entities ensured that his class was never boring.

And, he attended to the weak students. Always open to question, he went over a topic if he felt you had not grasped it. Among the many teachers I have known, I place him as one of the few who excelled at teaching simultaneously on two fronts: As he gently prodded those who lagged behind, he gave the rest harder problems. Some touched on advanced material. Such a teacher makes the stratification of students by ability superfluous.

Some rowdy students took advantage of his gentle nature. But the corridor-prowling Deputy Head Master – the terror of the school – would come to his rescue. With a keen sixth sense for detecting disturbance, the old man would step into our noisy room in a timely manner, order the rogues out and whack them with his thin sturdy cane.

Mr Datoo connected with students outside the classroom as well. As the Cub Master, he took students on bicycle rides and educational trips. I did not participate in such activities as they entailed extra expenditures my uncle could not afford. But those who did fondly recall the weekend adventures.

He was our most popular Standard 8 teacher. Though he did not deviate much from the curriculum, he taught in an engaging and effective style. You could see that he truly liked maths. Many a time, I went to bed with a hard exercise whirling in my mind. He (and Mr Hirani) laid the foundation upon which mathematics became a prime love of my life.

Apart from them, I barely remember my other AKBS teachers. He turned learning into an enjoyable experience. Over my life, I have had only a few teachers who have equalled that teaching style.

Mehrali Hirani

Mr Mehrali Hirani taught me maths in Standard 7 and a part of Standard 8. He was also our class master in the latter year. At first sight, he could not be more different than Mr Datoo. While Mr Datoo was gregarious and instantly friendly, he appeared aloof and stern. While Mr Datoo projected a casual persona, he always carried himself and spoke in the manner of a cultured English gentleman, and with only a tinge of the Indian accent. And he dressed in style. A wrinkle free, immaculate white or creamy white shirt, a finely creased brown pair of trousers, and shiny black shoes were his standard attire. At times, he donned a tie. His short, wavy, glistening hair effused the aroma of Brylcream. It was invariably combed to perfection, slanted like a 15 degree geometric wedge.

But appearances deceive. He was a demanding but not a mean instructor. He held us to a high standard but with a gentle, parental touch. He made us work hard but rarely delivered more than a stern rebuke to those who submitted assigned work late. When you made a mistake, he shook his head in a style of his own. But it was more effective than a cane; you felt ashamed and strove not to repeat it. If you were on the right path but stuck midway, he uttered 'think, think' to encourage you.

His systematic exposition introduced me to logical thinking. Each time he ended a proof, he looked at it as if it was a serene painting. He set problems more difficult than the ones in the textbook, and touched on topics covered in

Form I or later. These ventures made us feel as knowledgeable as pupils in the
higher grades.

It was from Mr Hirani that I first heard that maths was a science as well as
an art form, that it was as beautiful as a delicate sculpture. I did not grasp what
he meant since he did not provide enough examples to demonstrate his claim.

Once, he drew a five sided outwardly bulging figure on the board. Now I can
call it a convex pentagon. Dividing it into five parts, each a triangle, he derived
the sum of its inner angles in pictorial terms. We drew such figures on graph
paper, measured and added the angles. Whatever the shape, the answer was
close to what he had found with pure logic, namely 540 degrees. I remember
being struck by the idea that perhaps reality could emerge from thought! Could
I procure a hazel nut chocolate bar by intensely thinking about it? Then my
taap-taap ventures would not be needed!

When he taught us two-dimensional graphs and the (x, y) system of coordin-
ates, he said it was called the Cartesian system, in honour of René Descartes,
the French mathematician and philosopher who had invented it. And I think it
was Mr Hirani who first related to me the famous dictum of this philosopher: *'I
think, therefore I am.'*

Monte Cristo

Mr Hirani expanded our horizons towards reading. His approach was a hit, as
my classmate, Al-Noor Jiwan-Hirji, has reminded me. With a contribution of
one shilling from each student, a set of the comic version of the Greek classics
was placed in the class library. We borrowed a comic at a time for a week. It was
fun to learn the tales of the heroes and villains of the ancient Greek literature.

Comics heralded ventures into fine literature. In November 1962, having
done the primary school territorial examination, we anxiously awaited the
outcome that would determine our educational future. To our dismay, we had
to be at school for two more weeks. No Standard 8 student was in the mood for
formal lessons. The class masters left them to their own devices, provided they
did not generate a ruckus.

Not so for Mr Hirani. He brought a thick volume, the unabridged version
of *The Count of Monte Cristo* by Alexandre Dumas, to class. Saying it was
an adventure epic, he spent three hours daily reading it aloud. We were not
enthusiastic at first. But as the tale unfolded, the class turned attentive. His
oration was of an accomplished actor – amply audible, crystal clear, rhythmic
and entertaining. As abstruse words and complex paragraphs arose, he paused
to explain the literary intricacies, and summarize what had transpired in the
convoluted tale.

The cowardly betrayal of the young sailor Edmond Dantès, the miseries
inflicted on Mercédès, his bride-to-be, and on his father, and the treachery of
the perpetrators, kept us entranced. Every day we looked forward to the next
turn of events in the beguiling saga. Our emotions swung like a see-saw. But
the fun was short lived. Before we knew it, school was over, but the story was
not. Only the first volume had been covered. As he bade us a fond farewell, Mr
Hirani implored us to pursue education as far as we could, and put our best
into all endeavours in life. His last words, presented with a wink, were that the

eventual fates of Edmond and Mercédès could be readily discovered in a library.

I passed the territorial examination. With the interest in novels sparked, my vacation days were spent on popular adventure and mystery books. In the first week at my new school, I borrowed a library copy of *The Count of Monte Cristo*. After devouring the second volume, I reread the whole book. It was the first major work of literary fiction I read. It remains one of my all-time favourites. Time and again, I have returned to it. Each time, it ensnares me as tightly as it did when Mr Hirani narrated it. Each time I recall his vibrant rendition.

The Count and Beyond: My granddaughter Emma and I have spent three summers reading European classics, watching their best movie versions, and discussing the paper and screen versions. We began in 2011 with *Great Expectations* by Charles Dickens; in 2012, it was *The Count of Monte Cristo*; and in 2013, we tackled the majestic *War and Peace* by Leo Tolstoy. My wife Farida joined us for the movies. We laughed, felt sad and learned. I have acquired a copy of *The Black Count* by Tom Reiss, a biography of the all-round heroic but unknown Afro-French father of Alexandre Dumas (Reiss 2013). His adventure and novelty filled true life inspired Dumas to write the tale of *The Count of Monte Cristo*. It has been a pleasure strolling through this well-researched, mammoth biography.

Beautiful Addition   ✢ ✢ ✢ ✢ ✢ ✢ ✢

The year was 1778; the place, a rural locality in Germany with many destitute farmers. The man who taught arithmetic to their children looked down on his low class wards. Often, he assigned them laborious numeric exercises to keep them occupied. Once he made them add the numbers from 1 to 100. To his astonishment, Carl Friedrich Gauss produced the correct answer within a minute. When the teacher inquired, Carl said: He had taken the sum

$$S = 1 + 2 + 3 + \ldots + 98 + 99 + 100$$

and rearranged it in a decreasing order

$$S = 100 + 99 + 98 + \ldots + 3 + 2 + 1$$

Then he had added the two lines term by term to get

$$2S = 101 + 101 + 101 \ldots + 101 + 101 + 101 = 100 \times 101$$

Upon dividing by 2, he found that $S = (100 \times 101)/2 = 5050$.

This method is remarkable because it produces the general formula:

Sum of the numbers: 1, 2, 3, 4, $\ldots$, n: $S = [n(n-1)]/2$

Now suppose you had to add only the odd numbers from 1 to 99:

$$T = 1 + 3 + 5 + 7 + \ldots + 97 + 99$$

Consider the diagram below with alternate unmarked and marked sets of circles. The number of circles added equals the next odd integer.

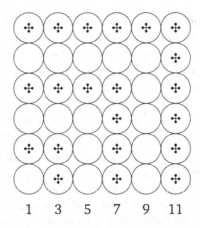

$$1 \quad 3 \quad 5 \quad 7 \quad 9 \quad 11$$

At the bottom left, there is a single unmarked circle.
Next: Three marked circles $\Rightarrow 1 + 3 = 2^2 = 4$ circles in all.
Next: Five unmarked circles $\Rightarrow 1 + 3 + 5 = 3^2 = 9$ circles in all.
Next: Seven marked circles $\Rightarrow 1 + 3 + 5 + 7 = 4^2 = 16$ circles in all.
Next: Nine unmarked circles $\Rightarrow 1 + 3 + 5 + 7 + 9 = 5^2 = 25$ circles in all.
Next: Eleven marked circles $\Rightarrow 1 + 3 + 5 + 7 + 9 + 11 = 6^2 = 36$ circles in all.
Since $11 = 2 \times 6 - 1$, we generalize from here to declare that:

$$1 + 3 + 5 + \ldots + (2n - 1) = n^2$$

With $n = 50$, and $2n - 1 = 99$. Therefore we find that

$$1 + 3 + \ldots + 99 = 50^2 = 2500$$

By astute reasoning, Carl F Gauss converted a time consuming task into an easy one. We turned a tedious addition into a straightforward one using a picture. Both methods show the creative beauty of mathematics.

With adroit strokes and apt colours, the painter projects her feelings, observations and imagination onto canvas in ways that astound us. With apt phrases, the writer renders real or contrived natural or social settings into essays, novels and informative works that hold you captive hours at a time. With her dense expressions and sublime diction, the poet evokes strong emotions in our psyche. None has a totally free hand. Each is in a way bound by the rules of the craft, the nature of the medium and the perceived audience.

It is not too different for a mathematician. Though her craft abides by stricter rules, there is abundant room for creativity. An authentic mathematician seeks elegant structures, simpler, unitary expressions, and even paradoxical findings. She juggles numbers, figures, shapes and abstract constructs to seek conceptual unity where none seems to exist. She desires to broaden her audience and impart to them the joy she feels from immersion in that imposing but picturesque edifice created by centuries of global intellectual effort. She creatively uses visual aids to enliven her world and welcome us into it.

I can only show but a tiny portion of the book loads of enlightening instances of the artistic face of mathematics. Navigating through them over decades, Mr Hirani's declaration that maths is beautiful has repeatedly appeared before me like a majestically radiant rainbow.

— 5 —

A New World

The sun is new each day.
Heraclitus

❖ ❖ ❖ ❖ ❖ ❖ ❖

THERE HAVE BEEN TIMES when I embarked on a path that took people around me by surprise. It was as if an uncontrollable bug impelled me to step out of the line. I made a sharp turn, or went into an uncharted terrain. These moves occurred on the personal, social and intellectual planes. Some emanated from forethought. A few were impulsive. And there were a couple whose rationale remains a mystery.

Yet, life is a school unto itself. The consequences of my decisions were usually not what I had anticipated. More often than not, I was propelled into a strange place resembling a parallel universe with its own laws of operation.

That is what transpired after my middle school ended. The school I selected for secondary education unexpectedly extracted me from the constricted mini-universe I was ensconced in since childhood into the external mega-universe I had barely taken note of. In consequence, my outlook on life and social relationships were reshaped, markedly and irrevocably.

Technical College

Up to the end of middle school, my main life choices had been made by my parents. I had moved from Lindi to Dar es Salaam not because I had wanted to, but because Father said so. I had joined the AKBS for the same reason. Not that I resented any of it; in fact, I took up the opportunities happily. The first time I alone made a major decision about my future was just prior to the Standard 8 final examination. We were given a form to indicate the secondary schools of our preference. We could put down three schools. For my friends, the first choice was our current school, the AKBS, which was also a secondary school. They would thus remain at the same physical location. It was the natural, expected and obvious course of action for an Ismaili pupil.

The secondary schools in our UK style education system offered virtually the same types of subjects. Some were stronger in science, and some, in the arts. The quality of instruction and the available resources, however, varied, at times to a pronounced degree. One school stood out in terms of curricular diversity. The Dar es Salaam Technical College (DTC), half a mile from my home, had a secondary-technical (sec-tec) stream. Besides the standard subjects like maths, physics, chemistry, English, history and Swahili, students in this stream had to learn wood work and technical drawing, and either metal work, electrical work or auto-mechanics. To balance the work load, subjects like biology, geography and literature were not available.

Such a practical education was the last option for a person in an upward bound social milieu. Asian youths rarely pursued it if they qualified to join a regular secondary school. My grades were at the high end. I could have gone to any school I wanted to. But I was bitten, for the first time, by that pesky bug of detachment. It solidly decreed that I was to be an engineer, and needed an early start. Thus, without consulting anyone, I put down DTC as my first and only choice. It was a magnetic attraction; my thoughts circulated around engines and power lines. Perhaps I was influenced by my gang peers. Their economic status propelled them towards a practical job. But being a grade below me, they did not face the need to choose at that point in time. To this day, I remain puzzled why I did what I did. Needless to say, my friends, teachers, parents and relatives were surprised. But I did not yield to their attempts to discourage me, and remained adamant. And DCT is where I squarely landed. (Six years later, one of my ex-gang buddies joined the DTC, but in the technical diploma program.)

All my previous schools had been – by custom, design or fact – effectively segregated by race. The AKBS was a multi-racial school in theory. But in the year 1961, only a few black faces were seen. In the two years I spent there, I had one African classmate. And we never became friends.

Though colonial rule was a thing of the past, its attitudes and arrangements continued to hold sway. For us, they were still the natural state of affairs. Parents in my community had lamented the opening up of the Aga Khan schools, nominal as it was, to African children. It was said that the quality of education would decline. We rationalized that the Africans were inherently inferior in mental ability. We had been raised by our parents and community to keep a distance from, to distrust and fear Africans. Almost never referring to them by their proper names, our talk was inundated with derogatory terms for black skinned people, like *golo, gaggo* or *kario*. Steeped in this mentality, the social implications of my choice to join the DTC were not apparent to me beforehand.

It was no wonder that my first day at DTC found me in a state of shock: I was the only Asian in my class. One boy was half-caste. Two had Arab blood. The rest, more than four fifths of the class, were black Africans. In the earlier two batches of the sec-tec program, now in Form II and Form III, there were a handful of Asian students. At break time, they banded together. So, in the first few weeks, I joined them with relief. Half a month into the school term, we had a spirited weekend picnic at a sisal ranch owned by the family of one student of Sikh background.

Yet, human commonality soon prevailed. In the struggle to tackle the demanding material the teachers poured onto us, I began to bond with those who shared my challenges. Within a month, my life was put on a new footing: For the first time, I had African friends. Like ice placed in bright sunlight, and without me realizing it, my race-based views began to melt. I encountered smart and dull students. I saw serious ones and happy-go-lucky types. I found well behaved students and naughty students. Among my classmates, a number were kind and friendly. With most I got along well, just as a few kept a cool distance. Surprise, surprise, it had been precisely that way in the schools I had previously attended.

Two arrangements at the DTC consolidated these bonds. First, lunch was provided free of charge even to those not residing in the campus hostel. Most Asian students opted to eat at home. I disliked the scorching sun. So, even though Mother disapproved, I did not. For five, and later six, days of the week, the Indian style lunch was not on my menu. Instead, in the flippant company of my new buddies, I devoured a substantial serving of rice, spinach and beans, or *ugali* (maize meal dish), cabbage and beans. Rice and beef stew, cooked in the mild Swahili style, was served once or twice a week. We looked forward to the day. Each meal included a fruit – orange, banana, mango or a slice of pineapple. In the first two years, we also had afternoon tea with biscuits in the cafeteria.

Another facilitator of the bonding was the time I spent at the school. Because the technical subjects included practical training, our school day ended later than at the regular schools. I was with my buddies from eight am to four or five pm, working on a multiplicity of tasks, and helping one another. Amer Mohamed El-Battashy became my best friend. Our close knit group included Isaac Marande, Abdul Karim Mohamed, Nassoro Mohamed Mitawa and Ram Jogi.

Amer and I regularly studied together, and the others joined in later. We cracked our heads to tackle a hard class assignment. Some assisted me in Swahili, the subject that made me stumble. I reciprocated by helping in maths. Technical Drawing required not just a fine artistic flair, but also a keen sense of three dimensional perception. A most demanding task was to visualize and precisely draw the interior facet of a complex mechanism. How, for example, the interior face of an angular slice of an engine block looked kept me awake at night. We often had intense arguments about how to tackle such exercises.

Isaac and Nassoro were on the DTC soccer team. It practiced at the Uhuru Primary School on Saturday mornings. The DTC athletics team was also present. I served as a linesman in matches, or performed a supportive task. After the sweaty, tiring practice, a hefty lunch was our reward. After leaving DTC, Isaac and Nassoro played in the first division of the football league. Isaac was a star player in the Tanzanian national team, shining especially in the East Africa wide Gossage Cup tournament.

Ram, a jolly fellow who laughed continually, made us laugh with him. His cackles poured out like the spurts and gurgles of a vehicle with a partially blocked muffler. With an Asian father and African mother, he lived on Msimbazi Street, a five-minute walk from the campus, and not too far from my father's shop. We visited him at home, and had tea and *mandazi*. The opportunity to engage in small talk with his lovely sister was an added attraction.

The ground floor of the main classroom building had a large locker room where we kept our overalls and tools for the practical work, books, and other stuff. Unknown to our teachers, we put Playboy pin ups behind the locker door. Amer had contacts with sailors working on international shipping lines. They were our source of the contraband photos. Being my first exposure to the naked female form, they caused my young blood to sizzle. Upon hearing that raw groundnuts increased one's virility, Amer and I began to consume them by the kilo.

DTC Teachers

Our teachers were a mixed bag. A wife and husband team from the UK taught History and English. I found their lessons insipid. English was rules of grammar and trite composition exercises, and history, mostly itemization of events and dates. Exciting ideas on social issues were absent. Neither encouraged broad reading or stimulated discussion. The Swahili teacher, a plump, aging Tanzanian, bored us to no end. He too was bored by his job. After setting a class exercise, he would doze off at his desk. On the other hand, the maths teacher (an American), the woodwork instructor (a Tanzanian), and the physics teacher (an Englishman), existed on an elevated plane. As transmitters of knowledge, they were in a class by themselves.

Mr Calvin Brooks, the maths teacher, was the first African American I ever met. His suave mannerism, fastidious appearance, drawling speech and warm personality captivated us from first contact, and held us in awe. What we had seen only on the movie screen came alive in flesh and blood.

Mr Brooks was a man of sports too. He coached the college basketball team and introduced a new game that was a mini version of tennis. Called platform tennis or paddle tennis, it had rules and field layout like tennis but with a smaller playing area. The bats resembled large table tennis bats. I have not heard of this game in Tanzania since those days; I may be wrong, but I suspect it came into and left the country with him.

Most of my classmates found maths a tough nut to crack. I had attended schools with good resources and proficient teachers. But my classmates had struggled through the colonial era Swahili schools with a dearth of books and qualified teachers. Their unease with numbers and formulas was understandable. The professional, yet gentle style adopted by Mr Brooks rapidly eased their unease. I was struck by the rapidity with which some who had wavered in the subject at the start began to show a worthy performance in his class.

Mr Brooks decorated his lessons with stories relevant to the topic at hand. That amused us and held our attention. One I recall was how the Greek mathematician Thales cleverly determined the height of the Great Pyramid of Giza without directly measuring it (I give the details later). He told us how measuring farm areas, assessing tax revenue, and planning construction tasks in ancient Egypt made use of basic ideas of arithmetic and geometry, including the Pythagoras theorem for right angled triangles.

The practical side of what he taught was soon evident. In metal work, carpentry, fine art and engineering drawing, we found that facts and ideas from geometry, trigonometry and algebra were indispensable.

Mr Brooks was an American Peace Corps volunteer, hailing from the state of Missouri. The colonial era had not exposed me or my classmates to a competent, confident, qualified and elegant professional whose skin colour was black. In my Asian circles, it was viewed as an improbability. For my African friends, it was a dream. But it was not. He demolished the colonial stereotype by personifying in flesh and blood the human capacity to excel irrespective of skin colour. I have no doubt that he made a big dent in my racist prejudices, and raised the self-esteem of my classmates notches higher. His term of service expired as we approached the end of sec-tec II. We were truly sorry to see him depart. A few DTC students, Amer among them, kept in touch with him by mail for a number of years.

A Ghost from the Past: I saw the movie *To Sir With Love* in the 1970s and subsequently read the book on which it is based (Braithwaite 1977). Sidney Poitier stars as an endearing, dedicated teacher of hard-nosed, working class kids. Always dressed elegantly, he projects a smart and confident persona. Yet, he is black, they are white. Racial prejudices of post war Britain hold sway. Despite their palpable unease, he relates to his students both as a friend and a consummate professional. His approach is firm but fair. The initial tussles and setbacks notwithstanding, his faith in their abilities and their developing confidence in and fondness for him eventually yield pedagogic and social dividends. As the drama unfolded, I felt as if I was again in the presence of Mr Brooks: About the same age, they uncannily looked alike. With their auras of cordiality and sublime self-confidence, both personified the ideal teacher in my mind.

Cold War Politics: While Mr Brooks was genuinely devoted to his students, the same type of motivation cannot be ascribed to the institution that had brought him to Tanzania. The principal rationale of USAID was (and still is) to promote US foreign policy goals. These goals then were, and still remain, detrimental to the real interests of the people of Africa. In relation to Tanzania, that situation came to a head in 1969. Because of major differences with our government on the liberation of Africa from colonial and racist rule, the war in Vietnam, and perceived interference in our internal affairs, the Peace Corps was expelled from Tanzania. And they stayed out for ten years. I am thereby saddened to observe that like many prominent African Americans of that period, our exemplary teacher possibly and unwittingly served US cold war interests (Thomas 2012; von Eschen 2004).

Mr Fred Isaya, our woodwork instructor, was a meticulous professional. Well versed in the theory and practice of his craft, he taught us to convert rough wood board and plain panel into utilitarian but elegant items. He had three requirements: (i) the product should have exact configurations, (ii) it should appeal to the eye, and (iii) it should be devoid of even a tiny blemish. A real craftsman, he told us, carves joints with such a perfect fit that no glue, screw or nail is required. Make a plan before you start; cut the wood as precisely as required; minimize wastage and cost – those were his primary tenets.

His words and deeds fitted each other like a perfect dove-tail joint. For demonstration, he made sturdy items with exact fittings and which radiated elegance. It was as if they were made by a high performance machine. It was not enough to make acceptably useful items; we should craft excellent items that could stand the test of time and rough handling – that was his expectation.

He too had a friendly personality, always joking with the class. We progressed from simple things to elaborate items. The most complex item I made was a drawing board and T-ruler usable for technical drawing. My output, like that of about half of the class, lacked the quality he expected, but he was patient, prodding us to improve on the next job.

In December 1963, two days before the academic year closed, Mr Isaya offered me the job of installing number plates on the office doors of the newly built Dar es Salaam Business School. The place was adjacent to the DTC. I agreed. A day and a half on the relatively easy task earned me 100 shillings, a handy sum when the monthly minimum wage was about 180 shillings. That was the first paid job I ever did.

Number Plates – Old and New: I revisited the Business College campus in November 2012. There were more buildings, more students, and a wider variety and levels of study programs. The simple, sturdy number plates I had installed had been replaced by fancy, rewritable plastic plates, but they had signs of wear and tear. Some were fractured. Most lacked the names of room occupants. No one seemed to mind. That is typical of neo-liberal modernization. If external funds for a task do not exist, even easily remediable eyesores linger on.

Mr Naylor, the physics teacher, was a demanding task master, but with a soft spot in his heart for struggling students. His clear explanations of phenomena like heat, light and air pressure opened my eyes to the mysteries of nature. His lessons on optics, dynamics and gravity, and the challenging problems he set remain in my memory. It was he who showed me that mathematics was inextricably woven into all the domains of physics. That was one more thing that drew me closer to maths.

Physics experiments produced the thrill of discovery; the finding verified the theory, at least within the margin of error. One thing Mr Naylor did not tolerate was fudging an experiment. He spotted it right away. If a graph was too perfect, he caught on. Then the student had to redo the work.

I single him out for opening the doorway to a new mode of thinking about life, nature and society, which was based on the scientific method. He taught me that acquiring reliable knowledge needs systematic, persistent effort, testing the ideas in practice and validation by others. Be it for electricity, magnetism or optics, he showed us that we too could reproduce the laws others had uncovered centuries ago. Imagination and creativity play a major role in science. But science is not a random collection of facts. It is a painstaking, on-going process based on critical thought and sound investigation. It was his class that began to embed the germs of those key ideas into my mind.

Scientific Method: I subsequently ventured, in theory and practice, into the terrain of science for five decades. The principal lesson I have learned is that the scientific method is the sole reliable method for gaining knowledge. Popular views regard science to be synonymous with the use of intricate instruments and complex formulas. That is not so. Science represents a method, not just techniques. This method has eight key pillars:

- Claims should emanate from reliable evidence.
- Evidence should derive from multiple sources.
- No scientific claim should be deemed perfect.
- Each claim comes with a margin of error.

- Employ methods to minimize random and systematic errors.
- Any scientific claim should be reproducible by others.
- Claims should be reviewed in the light of new evidence.
- Dogmatic adherence to a theory is harmful to science and society.

The relevance of these tenets goes beyond the natural sciences. They are essential in health and education, politics and economics, psychology and cooking, and sports and games. They are the master key for conducting national and international affairs in a just manner. If the people demanded adherence to them before permitting any major course of action, it would spare the world much of the strife and suffering it experiences today.

What prevails presently in social discourse is a pseudo-scientific approach – with much data collected and analysed – that has the appearance of science, but where these tenets are compromised, if not subverted outright. This is not a matter of a few quacks here and there. Many grandiose pronouncements in scientific journals and by hallowed institutions like the UN, World Bank and WHO are sorely deficient in terms of adherence to these fundamental scientific tenets.

Our Swahili class was the worst of all. The teacher lacked enthusiasm or persona. Normally, he started writing on the board the moment he entered the room. His focus was on rules of grammar and dictionary type explanation of words and phrases. The entire class was bored, and we often made fun of him behind his back.

A common occurrence: Amer and I sit in the rear left and right corners. As he writes on the black board, I utter an authentic sounding bird call of *njiwa pori* (wild pigeon): *ku-ku kukukku; ku-ku, kukukku.* A few seconds later, Amer repeats it. The irked teacher turns around sharply, and hurls a piece of chalk in the left direction. The room is deadly quiet. He sneers in disgust, and resumes his scribbles on the board.

That was the first and only time in my life that I have adopted a directly insulting posture towards a teacher. Over the course of my education, and especially at the university level, I frequently disagreed with my teachers. But it was not done in a personally insulting manner. Our differences, though sharp and contentious, concerned issues, and hovered around the validity and societal implications of ideas. The question of personality was secondary. That was also the case for a contentious incident at the Kibaha School I describe in Chapter 7.

The DTC Swahili teacher was mocked as a person by most of my classmates. His extremely rigid style evoked our hostile response. Had he told or read us stories from the existent literature, and taught in a livelier fashion, he could have turned us around with ease. Had he ventured into the rich realm of Swahili poetry or discussed linguistic ramifications of current issues, we would have been all ears. Our minds yearned for enticing tales and facts of life. Despite the unsettled atmosphere in the class, he did not modify his alienating style. Like a robot, he went on as if nothing was afoot.

There were two other factors at play as well. First, Swahili was not as yet a compulsory subject for the school certificate examination. We therefore did not take it as seriously as the other subjects.

Second, my classmates were being taught in English for the first time. Previously, they had been instructed in Swahili. English was the tongue of modernization. Commanding respect, it was a stepping stone for jobs and advancement.

On that front, Mr Brooks was the prime role model, though a questionable one in this instance. Everyone desired to be as smart and dress as stylishly as him. We attempted to converse in the eloquent and elegant way he did. Students mimicked his accent, phrases and mannerism. Hence, in a persistence of colonial era attitudes, Swahili was relegated to second class status.

For me, in particular, the long run consequence of this combination of events was positively detrimental. My prior exposure to Swahili had been minimal. I was then suddenly thrust into a secondary school level exposition of the subject. In the Swahili sessions, I became as lost as a fly in a bee hive. This teacher made matters worse. I think my frustrations explain in part my dastardly conduct. To add fuel to the fire, my classmates mostly talked in English in my presence. Hence, despite being surrounded by native Swahili speakers for three years at the DTC, my grasp of the language improved only in a marginal way. To this day, my mastery of Swahili is substandard. On that front, my mind still retains the shackles I have inherited from the colonial era.

English Worship: The five decades since *Uhuru* have witnessed major strides in the development of the Swahili language and its body of literature. Scientific, technical and legal vocabulary expanded vastly. Many Swahili books, plays and films were produced. Today many Swahili newspapers, websites, and radio and TV broadcasts exist. Its usage has expanded across Africa, and it is on the verge of being the regional language for East Africa.

Yet, the progress could have been greater. Thus, it is not as yet the medium of instruction even in Tanzanian secondary education. Government authorities have not provided clear guidance and funds for the job; and the academic community has not played its role to lead the process to the extent it should have. More troubling is the fact that the English-worship mentality of the colonial times has revived of recent. The elites send their children to private English medium schools. Politicians, up to the President, colour their speeches with English phrases to appear more erudite. Our newspaper, radio and television personalities not only mechanically trumpet the US line on global issues, but also strive to adopt an American sounding accent. The substance is propagandistic, and the imitation is pathetic. Yet the high minded imitator is blissfully oblivious of those comical but shameful realities.

DTC Life

I looked forward to the pleasant routine of school. Out of the house by 7:30 am, the half-paved, half-gravel path meandering through grown bush took fifteen minutes to traverse. The pleasant company of cashew, mango, tamarind, guava, *khungu*, coconut and *zambarau* trees enlivened the brisk walk. A majestic baobab hailed me mid-way. In their season from October to March, the abundant flamboyant trees glittered with red and pink flowers. Instead of using the main gate, I entered the campus via a scary, bushy burial ground. The early morning walk and late afternoon return thankfully spared me the harshest of the scorching rays of the tropical sun.

Be it physics or metal work, I was in tune and engaged. The company of supportive friends generated a feeling of being at home. I was the most diminutive person in my class. My 'big brother' Nassoro, however, would not allow anyone to tease or bully me. We were a raucous bunch, but took our studies seriously. It is no exaggeration on my part to say that we had a jolly good time inside and outside the classroom.

It was my first time to be immersed among buddies of varied background, creed and colour. In the process, and without me being aware of it, the racial prejudices I had imbibed from birth began to dissipate. I do not want to romanticize the situation, or play up the progress. It was a gradual process. Attitudes built up over generations do not evaporate as easily as water does in the sun. Racial distrust is furthermore a two-sided affair. Quite a few of my DTC friends despised the Asians, and did not hesitate to air their views. The colonial set-up and life experience had instilled bitter feelings in their psyche. But they made an exception for me. I felt I was not viewed as an Asian. They castigated the *wahindis* (Asians) in my presence as if I was not one. I now see it as a psychologically transformational period for both sides, a process of confronting one major form of societal antagonism carried over from the colonial days.

That process occurred within the context of formation of harmonious bonds at the national level. Inspired by the fair persona of Mwalimu Nyerere, Tanzanians from Lake Victoria to the Ruvuma River, from Lake Tanganyika to the Indian Ocean were acknowledging their shared humanity and joining hands on many fronts. There was a gradual but distinct change in the social attitudes of the people as a whole. Loyalties based purely on race, ethnicity, region or religion came under scrutiny. A new cohesive national identity and culture began to form. Swahili, now heard all over, and taught in the schools, provided a firm unifying glue.

There nonetheless was another side to my life that continued to cohere to the colonial era mode of conduct. My interactions in that segment of the universe distinctly contrasted with those I had at the DTC. Still, some of what happened even in that arena complemented the national trends. Here too, there were contradictory forces at work. Some hoisted me one way; others pushed me along an obtuse tangent. I describe the other side of the story in the next chapter.

But one thing I say with certitude: It was at the DTC that the slow process of seeing myself in a new light began. Previously, I had seen myself as Karim, a member of the Hirji and Kassam clans; Karim, an outstanding and helpful student; and Karim, an Ismaili enjoined with fellow Ismailis, devoted to communal faith, culture and institutions. That tripartite vision had thus far formed my primary sense of identity.

The new sense of self that was forming was that of being a member of an emergent nation unified and guided by a noble leader. He propounded humane ideas and policies based on equality – in dignity, rights and responsibility – for all the nationals. By law, I was already a citizen of Tanzania (see Chapter 6). Now I was propelled onto the path of being a Tanzanian in my heart and soul.

My attitude towards the key symbols of our nation began to change after joining the DTC. Instead of indifference, they evoked pride. Earlier, when the national anthem played at the movies, I had stood up because everyone did. Now I felt like doing it. Till then, I knew only its title. In those years, I learned and recited the entire anthem. When it was played at the movies, a few of my Ismaili friends continued to make weird faces as they stood up. I had previously gone along with such conduct. Now I resented it.

The anthem has two identically structured stanzas. The first eulogizes Africa and the second zeroes in on Tanzania. The melody and essence resemble the anthem of the African National Congress of South Africa (led by Nelson Mandela), and later that of the free Republic of South Africa. The first stanza of the anthem is given in Chapter 3. The second stanza is shown below.

God Bless Tanzania

Mungu ibariki Tanzania	God bless Tanzania
Dumisha uhuru na umoja	Affirm freedom and unity
Wake kwa waume na watoto	For women, men and kids
Mungu ibariki	God bless
Tanzania na watu wake	Tanzania and its people
CHORUS:	CHORUS:
Ibariki, Tanzania	God bless, Tanzania
Ibariki, Tanzania	God bless, Tanzania
Tubariki	And bless
Watoto wa Tanzania	The children of Tanzania

Serve the Nation

In this formative stage of my new sense of identity, one milestone stands out. This was an episode of one month duration at the end of my second year at the DTC. Before I go into it, I give the historic background.

The colonial set up had allowed Europe and America to extract immense wealth from Africa. In return, the people of Africa secured marginal benefits, and endured gross exploitation and horrific violations of the fundamental rights. The demise of direct colonial rule did not reduce the structural economic and geopolitical dependence of colonial times. Rather, it assumed newer, disguised forms. The classic book by Walter Rodney, *How Europe Underdeveloped Africa* and Vijay Prashad's recent work, *The Darker Nations: A People's History of the Third World*, explain this history in a clear manner (Prashad 2008; Rodney 1973). See also the revealing expose, Perkins (2005).

From Cape to Cairo, Africans struggled to vanquish the miseries imposed on them by history. They sought real independence, the right to determine their own destiny and to make decisive strides in fighting poverty, ignorance and disease. The advent of *Uhuru* was the first step in the process. Monumental tasks on diverse societal fronts had to be tackled. An arduous, long-term, uphill path lay ahead.

The pent-up cry for a better life was expressed in the proliferation of development projects, official and informal. Many projects bubbled up to the surface literally the day colonial rule ended. Construction of schools, health centres, affordable housing, water supply systems, farming schemes, dairy projects, factories and roads consequently assumed a rapid pace.

Jeshi la Kujenga Taifa (JKT) (The National Service) was born soon after *Uhuru*. Its main aim was to train youth to implement development projects. In the early 1960s, JKT camps were set up in several districts of mainland Tanzania with assistance from Israel. At the outset, participation was voluntary. The youths who joined the JKT fell in two distinct groups: Individuals (mostly male) whose schooling had not continued beyond the primary level enrolled for one year. Trained in varied practical skills, some found opportunity with the military, police or prison service upon completion of their term. The second group comprised students from secondary schools and colleges. They spent four weeks in a JKT camp during school vacation, and took part in farming, raising livestock and construction of houses and schools. They assisted with cooking, washing and cleaning tasks at the camp as well. Food, shelter, uniforms and basic supplies were provided free of charge to all camp residents.

My second year at DTC ended in early December 1964. Apart from the usual JK activities in the evening, there was no specific program to occupy me. The prospect of spending whole days at home until school resumed in January did not attract me. My mind was no longer receptive to the unceasing lectures by Mother on food, prayer, friends and leisure. Nothing I did escaped a corrective comment.

I was furthermore dismayed by the emergent strife between my parents. My elder brother Mohamed behaved in an odd way. He skipped school and spent hours sitting quietly. Father and Mother were convinced that someone had cast an evil spell upon him. They took him to Ismaili missionaries, Hindu gurus and local *malims* (holy men). But it was to no avail. They argued over and cajoled the poor boy to no end. Yet, the more he was pushed, the more he receded into his own cocoon. He ceased to talk and became aggressive. My father then took him to a psychiatrist at the Muhimbili Hospital. The electric shock therapy and pills calmed him down, but only for a while. A cycle of instability and hospitalization came to constitute his subsequent life. Little did we realize then that this was the onset of a gruesome descent into the devious recesses of schizophrenia from which he would never be able to escape.

Having entered an ethereal universe, he was with us but not with us. He talked to himself and laughed by himself. I did not understand what was going on. It was a sad sight. With him so withdrawn and unreachable, life at home turned distressingly uncomfortable.

A couple of weeks earlier, I had heard about the JKT on Radio Tanzania. I was stung by the bug of adventure once more. Impelled as well by nascent nationalist sentiments, I applied to spend the month in the Kinondoni JKT Camp. The place was barely two miles from home. Happily, Father gave his consent. And since I would be home one day of the week, Mother was not too unhappy. Amilo Pipi, my friend from the gangland days, signed up too. He had dropped out of school, and had yet to find a job. He too was looking for something to do.

The hundred or so volunteers in my batch were secondary school students. It was an all -male group in which roughly ten were of Asian origin. We slept in large military style tents, each with twenty beds. Our life adhered to a tight schedule. Awake daily by five thirty, we lined up, neat and clean, for inspection at six. A jog or parade was followed by marching to a construction site adjacent to the camp. The usual breakfast comprised a six inch thick slice of crusty bread decorated with a generous layer of margarine. A giant mug of steaming tea light in milk but doused with sugar helped wash it down. These delicacies were served slightly after 9 am.

Our principal task was to build affordable, two-room, single story family houses. The work involved clearing the bush, digging with spades, spreading sand and gravel, mixing cement, making and laying bricks, fitting windows and doors, putting plaster, nailing corrugated iron sheets on the roof and painting. All our work was directed and closely supervised by expert *fundis* (craftsmen) resident at the camp. We fumbled and made mistakes on the first few days. With time, the quality of our work improved markedly. My wood and metal work training at the DTC came in handy.

As we became drenched with sweat, we sang songs: Our spirits went up, the toil became lighter. A short patriotic ballad, *Tanzania nakupenda sana,* was most frequently on our lips.

Nakupenda Sana

Tanzania nakupenda sana	Tanzania, I love you a lot
Na jina lako ni tamu sana	And your name is so sweet
Nafurahisha moyoni	Happiness engulfs my heart
Nakuota	You fill my dreams

The camp *fundis* had not received formal training, but had learned on the job. Yet, most showed keen insight into the intricacies of the tasks. Despite the lack of quality tools, they were adept at what they did. With life experience as their guide, work plans were implemented efficiently. Their supervision reduced our blemishes. When it was called for, we redid the job.

The houses built by the JKT were placed under the control of the National Housing Corporation (NHC), which rented them to low income people at affordable rates. The main beneficiaries of the scheme were teachers, office clerks, public service workers, nurses, policemen and the like. In the colonial times, local personnel had congested dwellings with poor sanitation and deficient water supply. Now their families had a more decent life. Later on, electrical power lines reached these homes.

After four to five hours of grinding toil, we returned to base camp. Lunch was *ugali* or rice with a vegetable (mainly spinach, cabbage and carrots) or beans. Once or twice a week, we got meat. Food always tastes superb after intense physical work. The portion was humongous. We then had an hour to do personal chores – washing and ironing our clothes, polishing shoes, taking baths and resting. A lecture from a visiting personality or the commander, a film show, or a cultural event like *ngoma* (drumming and dancing) after dinner rounded out the day. It was lights out at 10 pm. Limbs aching, we fell onto our beds like a sawed-through coconut tree. Yet, no matter how gruelling had been the day, when we woke up early the next morning, we were refreshed and in bright spirits.

Amilo Pipi and I were in the same tent. The son of a wealthy Asian merchant stood out. A sour facial expression his trade mark, he hated the parades and constantly grumbled about food and work. He did not sing and laugh with us. We wondered why he had volunteered in the first place. We observed that he brought food from home and ate it surreptitiously at night. The smell of canned beef or sardines made our mouths water. After his hiding place came to our attention, once in a while we extracted a can from it when he was not around and shared it with another friend. In order to divert his attention, we pretended we were his friends and listened with feigned sympathy to his litany of complaints. We told him that we had seen people loitering about his bed, and that he should safeguard his stuff. I think he trusted and believed us.

In any case, he did not complain to the camp officers. But, they would not have viewed his practice of bringing food from outside with favour. And his complaint would not have been an unusual one. Some residents used to appropriate another person's item for temporary use. If you ran out of shoe polish, you 'borrowed' your neighbor's. It was not seen as stealing, as the stuff was mostly returned. In camp parlance, it was called *kusogeza* (to move a thing around). If you reported a loss, you were slyly advised to *sogeza* as well.

Tanzania gave refuge to and supported freedom fighters from Angola, Mozambique and South Africa. Consequently, we were under real threat from the Portuguese forces and from Apartheid South Africa. About three times a week, we had about an hour of military style training. In preparation for attacks from the enemies of Africa, we learned to handle a semi-automatic rifle, camouflage ourselves and crawl on our bellies. But it was a rudimentary style training that did not amount to much in professional terms. It was essentially a morale boosting, patriotism enhancing exercise. In particular, we did not handle live ammunition, or any dangerous device.

The month went by quickly: How emotional we became on the last day; no one wanted to go home! The four weeks of intensive, shared effort, the common meals and living side by side had fostered steel-like bonds. We were Tanzanians, united, without regard to our backgrounds, to build our nation. A few of the houses we had worked on stood ready for occupation. Sturdy and appealing to the eye, the sight filled us with pride.

A Milestone

It was 12 January 1965, our last day at the camp. We marched and saluted the flag. Then we held hands and sang *Tanzania Nakupenda Sana*. The camp commander took the stage to congratulate us for successfully completing our service. We listened attentively. At the end of the ceremony, we sang *Mungu Ibariki Afrika*. Tears formed in our eyes as we hugged each other and said goodbye.

By the time I went to Kinondoni JKT Camp, I had an official piece of paper declaring that I was a citizen of mainland Tanzania (see Chapter 6). My inner sense of being a Tanzanian had been maturing slowly since the day of *Uhuru*, gestating as if in a womb. If I have to place a date on when I firmly and irrevocably became a member of the Tanzanian family, I would say it was the day I completed my national service training at Kinondoni. That one month of camp life with fellow Tanzanians had permanently embedded the spirit of our national anthem in my cells, bones, blood and brain.

From that day on, I was a Tanzanian, heart and soul. This new-born baby did not need a paper document to know what it was. Breathing on its own, it began, slowly but surely, to utter patriotic sounds, be of service to fellow citizens, and explore the changing socio-political environment of the day.

This new identity did not conflict – emotionally, intellectually or materially – with what had been my primary identity till then, namely that of a faithful *Ismaili*. In fact, the similarity between the sentiments of the Aga Khan and Mwalimu Nyerere on the question of serving the nation made the two identities harmoniously complement each other. As I saw it, being a devoted Tanzanian was an integral aspect of the obligations of a devout Ismaili resident in Tanzania.

The middle of January 1965 found me back at the DTC. A week on we were assembled for the morning assembly. I wondered why one Kinondoni Camp officer stood with Mr Waldron, the principal. To my surprise, my name was called out. I went forward and was presented with my certificate of attendance in the National Service (Image 5: Appendix B). The *afande* gave us a short talk on the importance of the service. I was the first (and till then the only) student from the DTC to attend it. Mr Waldron later called me to his office to congratulate me, and I walked around the campus with chin held high. My buddies were envious. How come this *muhindi* went to the serve the nation and we did not? Happily, during the next vacation, Amer, Nassoro, Ram, Abdul Karim and Saleh Ramadhani spent a month at the Kinondoni Camp.

Separation

The bug of detachment struck me once more at the start of 1965. It foretold that my future did not lie in engineering. I did not have the necessary aptitude. Mr Brooks and Mr Naylor had swung the pendulum in my head towards maths and physics. I was driven to make a U-turn.

Patience has not been a hallmark of my life. So I marched to the office of Mr Waldron and requested to be allowed to skip Form III and join Form IV. He was taken aback but patiently heard me out. Some students had come to postpone their study program; none had asked him to accelerate it. He examined my file. My scores in maths and science were good enough for him to grant my request. Yet, he warned me that I was taking a risk. Sensing that I was determined, and as my good fortune had it, he allowed me to jump the grade.

As Amer, Isaac, Abdul Karim and Nassoro joined sec-tec III, I entered sec-tec IV. I was lucky in that my new classmates were a welcoming bunch too. Juma Balozi and Said Alawi became my good friends, though, at lunch time, I always sat with my sec-tec III peers.

The year was spent entirely in studies. Extracurricular activities were set aside as I had to cover an extensive ground in physics, chemistry and mathematics on my own. Every day, I slogged till late. To make matters harder, I signed up for the Additional Mathematics paper. I studied it independently and tutored two of my classmates who, under my influence, had taken up that challenge. Mr Pillai, the maths teacher who had replaced Mr Brooks, was not of much help. Even in the regular math class I had answers better than the ones he gave.

Excessive reading in poor light strained my eyes. Mother said my eyes were always red, and gave me more milk to boost my stamina. One JK missionary said walking barefoot on cool, mildewed grass and eating almonds refreshes the eyes and enhances memory. Strolls at the Gymkhana golf course at 6 am and almond powder in milk then became routine.

An optician said I needed eye glasses. They did make the world brighter; the fog dissipated. But there was a snag. The thin black frame had a top edge straight like a ruler. It conferred a geometric sort of personality on me. I became uneasy when a girl at the JK eyed me. But I realized it too late. I had selected the frame, so I had to live with it. Eventually, I got over the mental discomfort.

The certificate exams came and went. Amer and I went to the Royal Hotel for a sumptuous *biriyani* feast that he remembers to this day. We did not realize its significance at that time. A full forty six years were to transpire before we saw each other again. By then, both of us would be rusty, grumpy men no longer preoccupied by girls or an engineering drawing assignment. Instead, we would brag about our sweet grandchildren, whine about creaky joints, and curse lingering ailments.

The passage of time has not made me forget that it was at the DTC that I was thrust into a place novel in people, ideas and practice which eventually conferred on me a new identity. In the twenty years I spent abroad, the thought of renouncing my Tanzanian citizenship never occurred to me. Like the blood cells being daily formed in the bone marrow, the sense of being a Tanzanian continually regenerates itself in my psyche.

Similar Triangles ✛ ✛ ✛ ✛ ✛ ✛ ✛

Mr Brooks had a penchant for tales from history, making the austere mathematical entities friendlier. One tale was about the pyramid of Giza, the tallest structure from ancient Egypt that stands 140 meters from the base to the apex. Legend has it that in the sixth century BC, the King of Egypt asked Thales, the Greek mathematician, to determine its height. It looked like an insurmountable task. Could he find the answer without scaling the pyramid? Thales used his keen knowledge of geometry and physics to find a good answer using a method that needed four ground level measurements only.

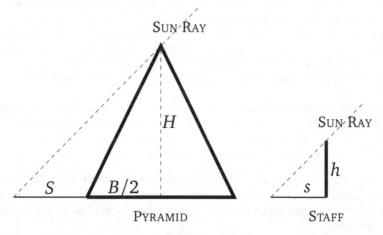

SUN RAY

H

SUN RAY

S $B/2$ h

s

PYRAMID   STAFF

He measured four lengths: of his staff (h), its shadow (s), the shadow of the pyramid (S), and the width of the side of the base that lay in the same direction as the shadow (B). Both shadows were measured at the same time of day. These distances, depicted in the diagram above, were found without much difficulty.

As the shadows arise from parallel rays of the sun, the triangle formed by the staff and that formed by the pyramid are similar. The ratios of the lengths of their corresponding sides have a fixed value, as we learned in geometry. Utilizing this property, Thales reasoned that:

$$\frac{H}{(S + B/2)} = \frac{h}{s} \quad \Rightarrow \quad H = \frac{h}{s}(S + B/2)$$

Assume a staff of height two meters casts a shadow of one meter. If the base of the pyramid is 66 meters, and its shadow extends 30.5 meters from the associated edge, then

$$H = \frac{2}{1}(35.5 + 66/2) \approx 137 \quad \text{meters}$$

Words of caution are in order. Measurements were not accurate in that era. The shadow of the pyramid is not a straight line but has a triangular shape. If the sun's rays run perpendicular to the face base, it will be symmetric from the opposite base; otherwise it will slope at an angle. Methods of calculation for this case were not known then. The evidence about the episode is tenuous. See Redlin, Viet and Watson (2000) for a good summary.

Whatever the case, it is an attractive tale with an elegant foundation. Spun in a flowery way and combined with a lively description of the Egyptian society, it converts a sleep-inducing lesson in geometry into a memorable one.

Learning From the Past: I told this tale to Emma in 2011. Later, we went around Upanga with a two meter long pole, a piece of string and a measuring tape. Applying the method of Thales, we estimated the heights of telephone poles and papaya trees. Passers by wondered what we were onto.

As we put theory into practice, concrete issues arose. Cloud cover makes the task difficult. The shadow can fall on a wall or uneven ground. Even on a flat surface, where it begins or ends is not easy to pin point. For a tree with a rough base or wiggly apex, it is a tricky issue. A slight tilt to the pole and varying the time affect the answer. Unless it is a long pole, the margin of error is high.

An accurate answer requires a series of measurements at different times and days. A plumb line to vertically align the pole is essential. About thirty measurements per structure limit the error. This approach links the maths of Mr Brooks to the scientific method of Mr Naylor. Applied well, it produces good estimates of the height and the margin of error.

Such stories depict the originality, logic, artistic side and practicality of maths, all in one stroke. They generate practical exercises. The material is at hand. Students estimate the heights of the poles and trees near the school, compile the data, and show the results in a graphical form. Geometry and statistics become fun.

With his knack for presenting the diverse facets of mathematics, Mr Brooks was Mr Datoo and Mr Hirani combined in one. His enticing tales and logical approach bonded me more firmly to the subject. Amer, Isaac and I fondly remember him.

— 6 —

Parallel Universes

*Common sense is the collection
of prejudices acquired by age
eighteen.*
Albert Einstein

OUR OUTLOOK ON LIFE derives from our social environment, of which the words
and deeds of our elders, peers and teachers constitute an important component.
By a certain age, we harbour social assumptions that we take for granted in
the same way as we do the sun in the sky. They underpin our world view, and
provide us meaning and comfort.

But the picture is complex: Our life axioms are generally anchored on a
shaky factual and ethical foundation. Our social environment may moreover be
fragmented and undergoing decisive change. These factors taint our already
dubious axioms about the world with sharp inconsistencies.

My years at the DTC found me entrapped in a strict race-based dualism. The
social setting in which I spent most of my weekday sunlight hours was a light
year apart from that which enveloped me at other times. My sense of normal
and abnormal was likewise affected, and my basic outlook on life experienced
fragmentation and inner discord. But I was not alone. It was a duality that
reflected the social disharmony in the nation at large.

But it was a dynamic picture since in the early post-*Uhuru* days, that duality
was in a state of flux. Vibrant trends foreshadowed a possible confluence, a
meeting of minds, between groups separated under colonial rule. I put on the
table one facet of this changing picture in the last chapter. Let me now turn to
the other facet, that is, my life when I was not at school.

A Devotee

A brisk trek home climaxed the long day at the DTC. A quick cup of tea prefaced
a routine ingrained from childhood: Attending the JK, the centre of the Ismaili
universe, a place that was both an indispensable venue for spiritual sustenance

and the hub of our social life.

The Upanga JK was next door to our block of flats. Since I had joined the Ismaili Volunteer Corps in the second half of 1963, I was usually there by 6:15 pm. Our responsibility was to ensure that the prayer session proceeded without a hitch. Among the multiple tasks we had were: to arrange prayer mats, chairs and the 12-inch high front desks, receive and set out the plates of food offerings, serve cold water to the attendees, give out *juro* (small pieces of sweet), man the shoe stall, direct traffic and people, auction food, babysit and control children, assist the elderly, count the donations, and at the end, clean up and switch off the lights.

Females and males sat on separate sides of the prayer hall. But there was no physical barrier, and it was not a sacrosanct divide either. For some tasks, a gents or ladies volunteer went over to the other side as a matter of routine.

My school friends were black Africans. My fellow volunteers – Navroz Lakhani, Nazir Nensi, Mohamed Budhani, Fidahussein Moledina, and Shiraz Esmail among them – were brown skinned Asians like me. At school, I conversed in English and Swahili. At home and in the JK, I switched to Kutchi and Gujarati. The outlooks of my evening and daytime compatriots differed in crucial aspects. And in a holdover from colonial days, the two groups lived in separate areas of the city.

Nevertheless, I was also close to my JK buddies, and in ways more than one. We were devout Ismailis. We lived in the same neighbourhood. We knew each other's families, and met daily. Apart from religion, Indian style food, cricket, music and movies formed common cultural pivots.

At least twice a year, in preparation for a major religious festival, we spent a series of nights decorating the spacious JK. We set up the celebration area, served food and organized the entertainment activities. After the festivities ended, we took down the decorations, disposed of the piled up litter and returned the place to its immaculate status. The Captain and his lieutenants directed our work. The smiling face of the diligent Lt Chaglani remains fresh in my mind.

The volunteers specialized to a degree. The cold water stall, for instance, was manned by the same two boys. I think they were twin brothers. I was often in the gents shoe stall, an unpopular assignment. This is where worshipers kept their shoes before entering the prayer hall. I assisted Mr Kassamali, a man employed on a permanent basis for the job. The walls of the stall were lined with wood shelves, with each containing numerous shoe box sized compartments. Our job was to place the shoes in the boxes and return them when needed.

He was a tall, elderly man in poor health. Yet, he lit up a cigarette, though discreetly, whenever he could. Perpetually chewing beetle nuts, he intermittently elicited a silent but deep cough. His trade mark was a red fez hat, an Ottoman era custom few adhered to. On Fridays and major holy or celebratory days, the place was full. He got tired quickly but I was on my feet all the time. The challenge was not to let a big crowd build up after the prayers ended. This required good memory. Upon observing a person headed to the shoe stall, you located his box and placed his shoes on the counter before he reached it. Fast delivery kept the faithful happy.

Mr Kassamali had high regard for me. Addressing me as his son, he used to repeat stories about how he had not been justly treated by the Ismaili Council. His clothes had a tear or two, and he was, like the *Jamaat Bhai* (Congregation Worker) and his assistant, the other Ismaili employees at the JK, at the bottom of the communal economic ladder. Their wages barely kept their families afloat. They were usually among the last persons to leave the JK. I stayed behind to help close the heavy main and side doors. My father (and others) gave him cash gifts for the *Eid* and *Khushali* festivities.

The motto of the Volunteer Corps was "Work, No Words." Many tasks consumed time, and on occasion, required exertion of muscle and limb. Yet, we did them in high spirits and, despite our motto, with large doses of chatter and banter. That made them pleasant. That it also afforded a chance to interact with female volunteers, many pretty girls our age, transformed a laborious task into a swell activity. And that is not to minimize our genuine desire to fulfil our sacred obligations.

Some Sundays, the volunteers picnicked at one of the fabulous beach fronts around Dar es Salaam. We swam, sang songs, recited jokes, played card games and volleyball, drank *madafu* (coconut water) by the gallon, and devoured spicy *channa bateta* (potato and garbanzo beans curry) and *bajia* (falafel). There were days on which we had a food guzzling competition. Skinny that I was, I once was able to munch and crunch to secure the second place, just one bite short of the winner. Predictably, a nasty stomachache gripped me that night, requiring Mother to administer mint water to sooth it.

Three of my JK friends were leading school cricketers. Some weekends, we went to cricket matches, especially if the AKBS or the Aga Khan Sports Club teams were playing or if there was a match between East African teams. The Upanga area had four large cricket grounds. One person hard to forget was Gulu White. Called so because of his ultra fair complexion, he was one of three cricket-playing brothers, and a well respected captain of the Aga Khan Cricket Club in the 1960s. From the late 1970s, he and Father became fast friends. When he was ailing in the late 2000s, Father assisted him on a regular basis until he passed away.

Friday or Saturday nights increasingly became movie nights. Besides Indian movies, we also saw English movies. Shiraz Velji was our connoisseur of English flicks. Among others, he guided me through *The Guns of Navarone, Vertigo, Rear Window* and the hilarious Pink Panther detective series.

On occasion, despite Mother's unease, we attended the late night show. One night, Navroz and I walked home after a horror movie, an Edgar Alan Poe tale I think. At the British veteran's cemetery on Upanga Road, we dared each other to lie down on a grave. You first, he said; you first, I said. In the end, none of us did. Another night, some hefty Africans gave us a chase. Black guys pursuing Asians meant only one thing: they were out to rob us. So we ran into a nearby flat. But, it was not so: They were the *mgambo* (neighbourhood watch patrol) following late night prowlers who may be up to no good.

Movies and Morality

Indian movies formed a crucial arena of our cultural universe, standing second to JK related activities. These extended sagas informed our conversation. We hummed their sentimental songs and admired the bevy of glamorous stars. Importantly, they moulded our perspectives on a central aspect of life, namely, that relating to girls, romance and marriage.

Hormonal activation was introducing us to the essential biology of life in strange ways. We were adrift in a stormy arena without adult guidance. The sole item of sexual wisdom our religious teachers and parents conveyed to us was that masturbation was a sinful act. Yet, it could not be escaped. It made one feel guilty, and pray for forgiveness.

The gap was filled by the Indian movies, most of which were dramas of love won and lost. The enticing story line, acting, songs and dances led us to at least one movie per month in one of the six theatres around. In our teenage minds, to see the latest major release was almost as obligatory as going to the *chand rat majlis* (new moon prayers). The actresses provided us images of an ideal partner. I was enchanted with the gorgeous Waheeda Rehman, who starred opposite the swashbuckling Dev Anand, or the handsome Raj Kapoor. A girl I saw daily at the JK had the build and face of Waheeda. Or so it seemed to me. In my recurrent day dreams, she and I frolicked for hours at the beach, just like Dev and Waheeda had done in *Fantoosh*.

Songs from the lips of Lata Mangeshkar, Mohamed Rafi, Mukesh and Hemant Kumar were as often, if not more often, on our teenage lips than the *ginans*. At the Volunteer Corps picnics, Shamshu Vellani sang his favourite songs. His downbeat mood, arising from a recent break up with a girl he had been crazy about, lent authenticity to his words. One boy would beat the drum as his sad voice entranced us. "Once more," a chorus would beseech him continually, until he was almost hoarse.

Odd as it may be, the Indian movies and the JK arenas complemented one another. The former provided the dreams and the latter, a chance to realize them. Boys and girls in our days did not intermingle as they do today. Communal activities were an opportunity to interact with females our age. I did not have a sister. The girls I usually met were close first cousins, whom I regarded as my sisters. So I grew up being shy when girls were present. But during the tasks in the JK setting, I was less tongue tied.

Eternal Love

Na ye chand hoga	This moon will vanish
Na taren rahenge	The stars will be no more
Magar dil hamesha	Yet my heart forever
Tumare rahenge	Will only be yours
Na ye chand ...	This moon ...

It was a traditional sexual morality. Attachment was a sacred, once in life act that came with total faithfulness and willingness to sacrifice one's life for the soul mate. Hemant Kumar's pleasant rendition of the romantic lyrics by SH Bihari in the 1954 movie *Shart* given above project that outlook on love and marriage.

Importantly, the values enshrined in these movies were not simply about the romantic aspects of life. They concerned life as a whole. These three-hour sagas of the struggle between good and evil upheld kindness, integrity, decency, honesty, self-sacrifice, simplicity, service to the weak and poor, devotion to family, community and nation, and bravery and courage. Handsome heroes and pretty heroines personified the noble traits, and scowling, flabby villains, the opposite set of traits.

The memorable lyrics of Shailendra Singh in the 1966 quirky movie *Teesri Kasam* brought to us via the hypnotic voice of Mukesh typify the values they espoused. Its first two stanzas are shown below.

Avoid Lies and Greed

Sajan re jooth mat bolo	My man, do not speak lies
Khuda ke paas jana hai	The Almighty awaits us all
Na hathi hai na ghoda hai	Not an elephant or a horse ride
Wahan pai dal hi jana hai	We just have to trudge along
Sajan ...	My man, ...
Tumhara mahal chaubare	Your palaces and wealth
Yahin reh jayange pyare	Will remain here, my dear
Akad kis bat ki pyare	Why do you fret, my dear
Ye sar phir bhi jhukana hai	Prostration is but inevitable
Sajan ...	My man, ...

The ethical precepts of the *ginans* complemented the notions of good and evil we gained from these movies. Our teachers at school conveyed a similar set of values. We saw role models who embodied them to one degree or another. I thereby looked up to Mr Datoo and Mr Hirani at the AKBS, and Mr Brooks and Mr Isaya at the DTC not just because they were outstanding teachers but also because I regarded them as kind, honest and noble people. That confluence of values from the three main dimensions of our lives – religion, entertainment and education – had a multiplicative effect. We cherished those values and strove to abide by them.

Let me not be misunderstood. It was not that adults around us were saints, and we became angels. Vice, deviousness and vile conduct were regular features of life. But unlike today, people of high moral stature and cases of admirable conduct were of sufficient scope as to make a difference. The values I stress embodied the spirit of those times in the same way as greed, hypocrisy, consumerism and selfishness embody the spirit of the current capitalist era.

That confluence of values began to develop a national dimension in the early post *Uhuru* days too. Before I venture into that broad arena, one concrete but rare instance of a linkage between my day and night time universes needs a hearing.

A Metallic Link

The gallery of lights atop the central JK and Upanga JK domes were switched on during the major religious and national holidays. They significantly enhanced the festive atmosphere. But not quite satisfied, the Upanga elders sought to bestow a mark of uniqueness onto our JK by converting the stationary light bands into rotating bands. With the funds secured, the layout was planned and an electrician was found. A group of volunteers including Shiraz Budhani, Fidu Moledina and I were assigned to assist him and implement the major parts of the job.

As the supplies were being collected, it came to notice that one essential item, a cam shaft with three aluminium connectors angled 120 degrees to each other, was not at hand. But it was the heart of the project. Joined to a motor, and wired correctly, the mechanism would create the illusion of rotating lights. I offered to make the unit at the DTC. My co-workers were not confident that I could produce a unit of the desired configuration and quality. They thought it should be made by a commercial workshop, but the supervising electrician took up my offer.

I made the contraption in the DTC workshop as a part of my metal work class exercise. The first step was to make three clay casts for the connectors. After pouring molten aluminium ore into the casts and cooling, the connectors underwent precision grinding and drilling. The main shaft, made from an existent cast iron rod, was sawed and accurately ground on a lathe machine. Precisely placed holes to join it to the electrical motor and connectors were drilled and threaded. Smooth electrical conduction necessitated an exact fit between the connectors and the shaft. A slightly loose fit would render the device unstable, and not of much use within a few weeks.

I completed the job in two days, brought the cam shaft to the JK, and held my breath as the electrician joined it to the motor and did the wiring. Good lord, it did work. Other volunteers had spent much effort doing the external and internal rewiring, ensuring insulation, securing the motor, and placing mercury contacts and switches. The eventual product was an elegant display of rotating green, red and yellow lights swathing the JK dome. It was switched on for the first time during a major Ismaili festival. Seen across the city, it became the hallmark of the place for a long time to come.

This was a major accomplishment by our group of volunteers. Together with those who had donated material and funds, the lead volunteers secured a public commendation in the JK. But my name was not in the list. Though my contribution had been critical, perhaps it was too small to deserve a citation. Or perhaps, our leaders did not even know about it.

Yet, I garnered benefits of my own. In a small but notable aspect, my actions in the DTC universe had produced a long term, eye pleasing outcome in the JK universe. Making the cam shaft was the first time I accomplished an intricate and practical engineering task. And it was done not only for a worthy, spiritual cause with fine heavenly rewards, but also, on this earth, I was blessed with a high grade for that practical class exercise.

Two other smaller items also passed through the worm hole linking my two universes. My father was a heavy smoker at that time. So, starting from semi-crude ore, I made a shiny aluminium ashtray for him. Later, I regretted that I had supported his harmful habit. Happily, he stopped smoking a few years henceforth, and did not resume. In the carpentry class, I made a round wooden board and matching rolling pin. It was for making *chapati*. But my mother never used it because it was not of the size and quality she preferred.

At least one book moved through that worm hole. I came upon the Harry Greenwall book, *His Highness The Aga Khan, Imam of the Ismailis*, by chance in the DTC library (Greenwall 1952). As it was a biography of our previous *Imam*, I excitedly loaned it out and poured over it. But a few pages on, I found the tone and material disturbing. I did not go too far before I showed it to my JK friends. It passed from hand to hand and after a while appeared to have been lost. We came to know that when the book had first come out in the early 1950s, our missionaries had warned Ismailis not to read it, or be swayed by it. They said the contents were largely untrue.

As it happened, until my last day at the DTC, the book did not come back to me, and I had to pay the fine levied by the library. About a year later, a JK friend handed it back to me. He said he had misplaced it. Since I had already paid for the book, and also because I did not like negative material about our spiritual leader to be in circulation, I did not return the book to the DTC library. It remains in my possession to this day.

Open Discourse: This has been the only act of narrow minded censorship which violated peoples' inalienable right to know that I have consciously done in my life. What I did was childish. If you possess genuine faith, you have no need to fear opposing ideas, or resort to trickery. Instead, you need to engage with those persons who espouse contrary ideas and respond, with reasons and knowledge, in a peaceful, graceful and transparent manner. If you desire long term respect and flowering for your faith, be you Hindu, Ismaili, Muslim or Christian; believer, agnostic, pagan or atheist, educate your faith holders to respect those who do not share your views.

Tolerance does not signify timidity. It reflects confidence. Yet, narrow-minded intolerance is a rising malady today. In my view, the only things we should not tolerate are concrete and actual injustice and suffering imposed on fellow human beings. Ideas, of whatever nature and inclination, have to flow freely in societal discourse.

Citizenship

The question of citizenship underlay the national dimension to the confluence of values I noted above. The attainment of *Uhuru* in 1961 posed a fundamental question to the residents of mainland Tanzania who were of Asian descent: To become citizens of the new nation or not? Some had Indian passports; a few had British passports. Many were British subjects in theory. But what that meant in practice was unclear. For the Asians, basic economic and cultural interests were at stake. They had been the vital commercial conduit linking the colonizer to the colonized. The colonialists had accorded them special favours that were denied to black Africans. They had established their own residential, educational and cultural enclaves. By now they had come to view their special status as their birth right. How much, if any, of that would be preserved under the new political environment?

Mwalimu Nyerere categorically declared that every citizen would have equal rights under the law. Culture and religion would be respected. But the special dispensations granted under colonial rule would not persist. Influential voices in the nationalist movement opposed the grant of citizenship to Asians, urged rapid Africanization of civil service positions, and called for moves to selectively favour Africans in the economic and educational spheres. The Asians were disturbed by those calls. But Mwalimu, the principal leader of the nation, opposed the race-based policies and voices. Nonetheless, the Asians did not trust him, and felt he had ulterior motives. Thereby at the outset, they hesitated to apply for citizenship.

The Ismailia community was the first to break the ranks. We sought guidance on this matter from our *Imam*. He issued a relevant spiritual edict not long after Independence. It implored us, in quite explicit terms, to regard and make Tanzania (then Tanganyika) our homeland. It was repeatedly read out in the JK. I was immensely moved by its wording, and know that it had a decisive impact on how I began to view myself.

Buoyed with divine guidance, the Ismailis applied for citizenship in droves. It was a short process. Many soon became bona-fide citizens of mainland Tanzania. Other Muslim Asian communities followed. But principally due to their stronger economic, cultural and family ties with India, a substantial portion of the Hindus held back.

The birth place of my parents was Zanzibar. My siblings and I were born on the mainland. The citizenship issue arose before these two nations united in 1964 to become Tanzania. Thus, at that time, my brothers and I did not qualify for citizenship of mainland Tanzania (Tanganyika) by birth. So my family applied for it. The valued certificates granting us that status were issued in 1963. After the formation of the United Republic of Tanzania, we became citizens of Tanzania by birth as well.

A National Confluence

The early post-*Uhuru* years exuded hope and unity. Our leaders regularly called upon the youth of the nation to serve the people. We were urged not be self-centred, but to work for the common good. We were encouraged to develop a genuine spirit of cooperation and understanding. The spirit of the youth shone with optimistic ideals. A good portion of the Ismaili youth was infected by it. The edict of Aga Khan IV and acquisition of citizenship had already stimulated a nascent sense of patriotism.

Thus, in addition to volunteer work at the JK, the Ismaili youth was steered towards general service to the nation. In town after town, they participated in the self-help, nation-building projects. Their schools became more multi-racial, and, like all schools, were placed under the central purview of the Ministry of Education. Many began to speak better Swahili, now a compulsory subject in school.

The Ismaili youth in Dar es Salaam organized day-long work projects in the Buguruni area. My JK buddies and I took part. We built a primary school and low cost houses, and cleaned public places. Area residents worked with us. We shared food and drink. If only for a few hours, it was the first time most of us had interacted on a person-to-person basis with black skinned people. Previously we had only known them as domestic servants, petty traders and hawkers, craftsmen or customers in our parents' shops. It was an unthinkable congregation just a couple of years back (Image 8: Appendix B).

Ismaili youth were inspired to enrol in the one month voluntary national service. Amilo Pipi and I were among the first, as depicted in the previous chapter. Navroz Lakhani went to the Kinondoni Camp a year later. I think one or two others from my JK group also enrolled. And there was a twist to Navroz's experience. His exquisite cursive writing style earned him summons from the Prime Minister's office to write the personal data on the certificates for the attendees. The other day he looked at my 1965 certificate. Unfortunately, it was not of his hand.

By participating in nation building activities, we not only fulfilled the wishes of our *Imam*, but also genuinely felt that we were playing our part to bring forth a nation in which all the races and creeds would live harmonious and mutually respectful lives.

The core values we imbibed from parents, teachers, elders, religion and Indian movies had hitherto been expressed in a restricted communal universe. Now their radius of application expanded to the national arena. Not just as Ismailis but also as Tanzanians, we should respect the truth, value simplicity, work hard, and assist the needy and the poor. That is what I meant by the confluence of values at the personal, communal, educational and national levels.

The presence of Ismailis in Mwalimu Nyerere's cabinet was an indicator of the national atmosphere. Amir Jamal, who had been active in the struggle for *Uhuru*, rose to be the Minister for Finance and a respected national figure. Al Noor Kassam first became a Permanent Secretary in the Ministry of Education and occupied other key posts in the public service (Kassum 2007). Over time, educated Asians in good numbers came to man high level positions in state institutions, public enterprises and the academy.

The integrative nature of that process was reflected in my personal sphere in terms of who my heroes of the day were. I venerated our *Imams* – Prince Karim Aga Khan IV, and Sir Sultan Mohamed Shah (Aga Khan III). In my mind, their inspirational words were the ultimate truth. Further, I admired the charismatic, sagacious leader of our nation, Mwalimu Julius K Nyerere. His simple words embodied a noble morality. His principled stand on racial equality, and his unflinching support for the liberation of Africa moved me. My vision of the local and global situations derived in large measure from his erudite statesmanship. Another key figure of influence was Mahatma Gandhi, the eminent humanist and leader of Indian nationalism.

I read the speeches of the Aga Khans and Mwalimu Nyerere. The first major non-fiction books I read were the autobiographies of two of my icons: *The Memoirs of Aga Khan* by Sir Sultan Mohamed Shah, and *My Experiment With the Truth* by Mohandas K Gandhi (Aga Khan III 1954; Gandhi 2008). It was probably in 1965. To be more honest, I should say I endeavoured to read them, as they were not easy to wade through. I read this page and that page, and took a while to reach the last page. The dazzling, eventful and colourful life of Aga

Khan III, his interactions on the international arena, the history of the Ismailis he outlined, the values he advocated, and his grandiose style, captivated me. The plain and decent life of Gandhi, the tenacity with which he adhered to his ideals, the principle of non-violence he espoused and faithfully practiced, and his firm dedication to the cause of self-rule for all colonized peoples uplifted my outlook on life and ethics.

In this era of hope and dreams, nothing seemed impossible. A rising segment of the youth and students of all races and creeds united under shared ideals. We began to feel and act, even though in embryonic ways, as members of an indivisible human family, drawn to treat each other as brothers and sisters.

The words of Mwalimu Nyerere on the occasion of the opening of campus of the University College of Dar es Salaam in August 1964 captured that spirit.

> *The people and the Government of the United Republic [of Tanzania] are aiming to build a just society of free and equal citizens, who live in healthy conditions, who control their own destiny, and who cooperate together and with other people in a spirit of human brotherhood for mutual benefit.*
>
> Julius K Nyerere

The Ismailis had firmer ties to Tanzania as compared to other Asians. Their presence was felt on many fronts in the national life – business, commercial services, education, health and general facilities. A number of Ismaili firms partnered with state institutions in sectors like manufacturing and tourism.

This was clearly articulated by Prince Karim Aga Khan in a November 1970 interview with an Ismaili–Tanzanian journalist. In a wide-ranging dialog, he lauded the multi-racial nature of Islam and commented on policies that favoured locals and side-lined the Asians for business licensing that was afoot in Kenya and Uganda. Many East African Asians emigrated abroad in consequence. The issue had been in the headlines for a while. He was asked why "*[v]ery few Ismailis were affected in the so-called Asian exodus from E.A. What reasons would you attribute to this situation?*" (Ladha 1970). His response was forthright:

> *Well, I think as a community, we probably have a very high percentage of people who took citizenship of the countries where they lived. This being the case, they are not affected by laws which differentiate between what a citizen can do and what a non-citizen can do. I think this is the first point. And the second point is an emotional one. The Jamaat [congregation] has been living in Eastern Africa for four, five or even six generations. And whether this is commonly understood outside or not, the Jamaats are deeply, emotionally and psychologically attached to East Africa. They may be of a different ethnic origin, but this does not mean that their psychological involvement is any less. If they leave, they depart from an area where they were born, educated and brought up with their families, where they have got a deep involvement which is profoundly personal. In view of this, I do not consider it surprising that only very few Ismailis indeed have left Tanzania.*
>
> Aga Khan IV

With my two principal icons expressing similar sentiments on fundamental issues, I began to develop a unified ethic on life. Not that I was aware of every speech or development. Far from that. What mattered was the atmosphere of the era, whose central ideas infected me and many of my friends.

The International Dimension

Events beyond the national boundaries also exercised political and ethical influences on Tanzanian youth. It was the sixties. Students across the globe were restless. From Algiers to Islamabad and Peking, from Tokyo to Mexico City and Jamaica, from London and Paris to San Francisco, they were taking to the streets in the thousands. They extolled the ideas of peace, social justice, economic equality, human solidarity and intellectual freedom. They scrutinized the dominant morality of the day and found it lacking in practice. They wondered how, on the one hand, the Western nations could claim to promote democracy and freedom and then wage brutal wars on civilians, arm dozens of thugs and dictators, and firmly give support to racist structures and regimes.

The last issue had a special resonance in Tanzania as it blended with matters prominent on the domestic front. Radio Tanzania broadcasts, the main local source of news and political views, regularly featured events connected to the Apartheid and settler states in Africa, the struggles against colonial rule in neighboring Mozambique and Angola as well as to the on-going civil rights struggles in the USA. They brought into the forefront leaders like Eduardo Mondlane, António Agostinho Neto, Nelson Mandela, Martin Luther King and Malcolm X. We of the new African generation empathized with the noble dreams of Dr King and Nelson Mandela.

A spirit of Africa wide unity, Pan-Africanism, entered the imagination of the youth in East Africa, including Tanzania. Leaders like Kwame Nkrumah of Ghana and Gamal Abdel Nasser of Egypt were admired, while turncoats like General Mobutu Sese Seko of Congo and Kamuzu Banda of Malawi were reviled. Mwalimu Nyerere's principled stand on matters in the international arena was admired widely. He stood up to the big powers with regards to racist and colonial rule and the right of self-determination. He championed Pan-Africanism and international non-alignment. That internationalist spirit formed the root of his moving call:

> We, the people of Tanzania, would like to light a candle and put it on top of Mount Kilimanjaro which would shine beyond our borders, giving hope where there was despair, love where there was hate and dignity where before there was only humiliation.
>
> Julius K Nyerere

As secondary school students, my friends at the DTC and the JK, and I did not follow such issues either diligently or in depth. Only a minority did. But these issues were a constant presence in our lives. And that rubbed off and affected our consciousness. At the Kinondoni National Service Camp, for example, we had several lectures on these topics. The songs we sang during drills and jogs roundly denounced colonial and racist leaders and views.

Globally, fundamental social assumptions were put under scrutiny. It was an era of critical inquiry. Venerated ideas, institutions and practices came under a microscope. It was a spirit that challenged social inequities and questioned blind allegiance to authority. In Africa, the partial demise of colonial rule and persistence of racist regimes added a new dimension to that global process. Stunted social interactions inherited from the colonial era faced a new climate of open mindedness. People's social vision expanded. Hitherto parallel universes began to converge.

A Disjointed Life

While the potential for the actualization of that vision existed, its practical realization was a different matter. The gulf between community and nation retained from the colonial era impeded the wider confluence from taking firm root. I continued to exist in two distinct universes, one centred at the DTC and the other, at the JK. I rocketed from one constellation to the other on a regular basis and at a dazzling speed. Those inversions split my persona. None of my DTC friends came home. My parents would not have approved. None of my JK friends did anything like eating lunch on a daily basis with African children. Most – and I talk of the period from 1962 to 1966 – did not have an African friend of their own age group. Some weekends I went to the Aga Khan School to watch or record scores in a cricket match. But it was an all Asian crowd. None of my JK buddies ever visited the DTC. Nor did they express an interest in the place.

I recall two major convulsions eliciting disparate emotions in my two universes. These were the army mutiny and the revolution in Zanzibar, both in the year 1964. The former saw the looting of several Asian shops in Dar es Salaam. The second saga witnessed scores of Asian Zanzibari families escaping to the mainland. Both incidents incited fear, anger and loathing among Asians, my parents and JK friends included.

When the news of the army mutiny and ensuing riots reached us, I ran home in panic. My parents locked the doors and listened to the radio. The next day, I went to Uhuru Street and gaped at the shattered shop windows. Both events had roots in the persistence of social divisions and economic inequities of the colonial era. The Asians, however, interpreted them purely in race terms, and blamed Africans as a whole. In a grand gesture, Mwalimu Nyerere toured the looted shops to reassure the traders that the state would protect them. Yet, that did not stop my father from uttering a barrage of unpleasant words – words too strong to repeat here – for him and Africans in general, even though his shop had not been touched.

Contrarily, my DTC friends viewed these events either with neutral curiosity or a favourable nod. Ram Jogi, for one, supported them without reservation. They deserved it, he said. During the day, I heard such voices. In the evenings, I listened to opposing views. Both emanated from close friends. I was thereby emotionally torn and confused.

Despite the contrasting tendencies, my universes were not static but in a state of flux. Fine voices propounding cooperative existence appeared in both camps. While in a minority at the outset, they were slowly gaining ground, especially among the youth.

Forces inclining our outlook in a retrogressive direction were at work too. The milieu that taught us sound ethical precepts through the *ginans* was also the one in which we acquired narrow minded racism, intolerance for other faiths, the tendency for material acquisitiveness, and hypocrisy in various guises. The wealthy Ismailis, who held leadership positions, did not practice what they preached. Their conduct, even within the communal context, was questionable. They viewed the nation building projects as exercises in public relations. Their aim was to further their business interests. That our residence and social life mostly remained segregated did not help either.

The generational gap was wide. While my father worshiped two of my heroes (Aga Khan III and Aga Khan IV), he derided the other two (Mwalimu Nyerere and Mahatma Gandhi). His views were based on purely racial and religious factors.

Such contradictions notwithstanding, a significant minority of the Ismaili youth was steered to surmount social barriers erected in the colonial era and embrace an inclusive, humanistic perspective. The process was a gradual one, but its direction was unmistakable. This was the context in which my patriotic sentiments matured. Slowly I came to disavow an outlook that reflexively judges humans on the basis of skin colour, ethnicity, nationality or culture. In comparison to most of my JK friends, I was propelled along that trajectory at a faster rate. But it was not due to anything special about me. Serendipity placed me in the DTC, a multi-racial, multi-religious universe which then produced positive bondings with my African classmates. Mwalimu Nyerere's words and deeds drew me further along.

Many on both sides were similarly affected. A gravitational force attracted my two universes towards each other. It was a tug-of-war as titanic forces from history sought to keep them apart. But the emergent force gained momentum. The balance began to tip in its favour. In an imperceptible but concrete manner, mainly the youth from the disparate universes began to eye each other with understanding, and took steps to connect with each other.

Yet, it was a temporary mirage. Life too often derails sublime trends. Promising prospects unexpectedly reverse. The inclusive trends of post-*Uhuru* Tanzania suffered a similar fate. Racial alliances ultimately triumphed over humanistic values. Eventually, the gap between my two universes not just ceased to narrow, but in fact began to widen untill it reached an unbridgeable extent. I then faced an irreversible separation from my Upanga JK compatriots in terms of proximity, national affiliation and outlook. This is a lengthy story that I set aside for now. I will return to it in the closing pages.

Number Patterns ❖ ❖ ❖ ❖ ❖ ❖ ❖

My DTC and JK universes were also linked by maths. Some JK friends excelled in science and maths. Senior to me, their talks covered topics like atoms and astronomy, or the link between science and spirituality. I grasped but a little of what they said, yet I liked to listen. These interactions introduced me to maths puzzles. Though not a systematic introduction, it was a captivating one.

Mohamed Abualy and Issa Shivji edited the *Volunteer*, the magazine of the Dar es Salaam Ismaili Volunteer Corps. Besides articles on science, the July 1967 issue had four mathematical enigmas. One depicts ten identical boxes with ten coins in each box. In nine boxes, each coin weighs 2 gm, and in one anomalous box, each coin weighs 2.5 gm. The task is to identify this particular box using only one weighing. One other enigma quotes a Roman who says all Romans are liars. The question is, are they?

Navroz was also enamoured by mathematics, and like me, studied Additional Mathematics. As with my DTC classmates, we jointly tackled tough additional maths exercises. He had, furthermore, developed a range of interests spanning philosophy, science and mysticism. It was fascinating to hear his ideas, and our discussions covered all manner of topics.

Mathematical puzzles held our attention. Though it is the sports and games facet of what is normally considered a uniformly austere discipline (see Chapter 11 and Appendix A), even the best of our teachers did not make more than a small foray into this exciting arena. So our introduction to it was superficial and unsystematic.

Let us savour a taste of this field with an examination of the whole numbers: $1, 2, 3, 4, \ldots$. We take them as simple, dry entities. Yet, like humans, many possess remarkable personalities.

Specific numbers carry special significance in different cultures. We find lucky and unlucky numbers, or healing and calming numbers. Seven is a holy number in Islam; a year 2013 survey found it the most popular number across the globe. In the West, people think the number 13 portends a bad omen. Some hotels in the USA do not have room no. 13; some airlines lack aisle no. 13. The fear of 13 is pervasive enough to deserve a name: Triskaidekaphobia. Yet, other cultures deem it a lucky number. For the Aztecs, for example, it was a sacred number and formed the basis of their calendar.

Examining the social basis of the cultural attributes of numbers has educational and recreational value. But my interest is in the objective features of numbers.

We know of even and odd numbers, and that a prime number does not have integer factors apart from itself and 1. Else, it is a composite number. $13 = 13 \times 1$ is prime; $12 = 3 \times 4$ is composite. And, this is just a start.

Take the number 40. Why is it special? It is the only number whose English name – forty – has letters appearing in an alphabetical order. Of the zillions of numbers out there, there is no other! However, this is a language based property, and not an intrinsic property.

What is special about 16? Consider numbers of the form x^y, where x and y are distinct integers. For $x = 3$ and $y = 5$, we have

$$x^y = 3^5 = 3 \times 3 \times 3 \times 3 \times 3 = 243$$

Is there an integer for which $x^y = y^x$? Yes, there is, since $16 = 2^4 = 4^2$. However, it is in a class by itself as it is the only number with this property.

And why bother with the number 2592? Because $2592 = 2^5 \times 9^2$. There is no other four digit number with this quaint property.

Some numbers have features which are, though not unique, distinctive enough to make them stand out. I present a few cases:

$$153 = 1^3 + 5^3 + 3^3$$
$$1233 = 12^2 + 33^2$$
$$3468 = 68^2 - 34^2$$
$$8833 = 88^2 + 33^2$$
$$93084 = 9^5 + 3^5 + 0^5 + 8^5 + 4^5$$
$$2646798 = 2^1 + 6^2 + 4^3 + 6^4 + 7^5 + 9^6 + 8^7$$
$$87654321 = 1^8 + 2^7 + 3^6 + 4^5 + 5^4 + 6^3 + 7^2 + 8^1$$

Based on their distinctive properties, groups of numbers have specific names. We have narcissistic numbers; triangular and pyramidal numbers; perfect and hyper-perfect numbers; amicable and vampire numbers; Cuban primes; and so on. A vast and curious arena awaits your inquiring mind.

Knowledge of the special features of numbers represents centuries of creative labour on the part of mathematicians and amateurs. You exclaim: But what is the purpose? That is a puzzling response. People allege mathematics is dry and boring. Some deem it too utilitarian. Yet, the instant it exhibits an artistic, entertaining side, they frown, and are at a loss.

Consider an analogy. A palindrome reads the same, forward or backward. It takes the form of words, phrases, sentences, names, art and design, chemical formulas and music. Cases of letter palindromes are:

1. Never odd or even   2. No lemon, no melon

Palindromes form a part of the global literary lore, a source of word-based fun and recreation. To generate a new palindrome in any language is a formidable task. Yet, it is one literary buffs like to undertake.

Numbers that read the same from left to right or right to left are palindromic numbers. But even a primary school child can find such a number. 7337 is one case. What is not easy is to find a palindromic number that also has another basic property, say like being the square of an integer. Thus, $676 = 26{\times}26$.

2
30203
133020331
1713302033171
12171330203317121
151217133020331712151
181512171330203317121512151
1815121713302033171215181
16181512171330203317121518161
3316181512171330203317121512151816133
33161815121713302033171215181613 3
9333161815121713302033171215181613339
119333161815121713302033171215181613339 11

Palindromic Primes

A palindromic number which is also a prime number is a palindromic prime. For example, 131 is a palindromic prime. With that in mind, look at the number pyramid above.

With 2 as the start number, this pyramid is built through three rules: (i) Each number is a palindrome; (ii) It is formed by adding the same two numerals (but in a reverse order) to the left and the right of the previous number; (iii) The result has to be a prime number. This pyramid satisfies these demanding properties!

Human cultures contain word games and number games. Both amuse and generate wonder. Both require skill and persistence. Sudoku, a game with numbers, has recently gained global popularity. Enticing mathematical games at varying challenge levels are easy to locate on the Internet.

If a cross-word puzzle captures our attention, we dive into it. We spend hours on a puzzle. Yet, we stick to it – for fun or to show off. The same spirit drives number games.

Products, puzzles and stories in recreational mathematics can leave you as much in awe as an exquisitely crafted poem or story. The palindromic pyramid, for example, is as magnificent as a *Makonde* carving or a delicate poem. Behind it, there likewise is a top-notch, diligent, creative artist with a flair for melodrama.

Navroz tells me that our teachers approached maths with passing the Form IV and Form VI exams as the sole goal. They did a fine job in that respect. But creativity and fun in maths was uncommon. We did well in the exams, but could not connect maths with other subjects except perhaps the natural sciences. You had students who hated maths but loved literature; students who loved maths but hated literature; and students who hated both. It was rare to find a student who loved both.

In this time and age, we must transcend such divisions. Numbers are not just a technical part of human knowledge. Both words and numbers are integral to our culture. Our children deserve to be amused, stimulated, enlightened and served by both.

— 7 —

From Carpentry to Calculus

Anyone who has never made a
mistake has never tried anything
new.
                    Albert Einstein

❖ ❖ ❖ ❖ ❖ ❖ ❖

A FEW LIVES FOLLOW steady paths. A great many drift on rugged terrains, face ups-and-downs and encounter stormy detours. We often have to start over. That is what I had to do in secondary school. I had joined the DTC to become an engineer only to discover that my abilities in that calling were wanting. As my fascination waned, my enchantment with maths grew exponentially. The bug of detachment, which had first whisked me from AKBS to the DTC, stung anew. I yearned for traditional schooling. Typical impatience led me to combine Form III and Form IV in a single year. That is how and why, in January 1966, I landed at the Kibaha Secondary School, a boarding school six and twenty miles from Dar es Salaam.

I do not look at the major reversals – there have been several – I have faced in life with regret. Each time I found that engaging in a new environment, even for a while, was worth it. It flavoured my life, gave me a chance to learn unusual things and meet wonderful people. Life setbacks should be taken in stride, and not allowed to rattle our self-confidence. If, after a downfall or rebuff, we adopt an optimistic attitude and persist in our endeavours, we can often land on an elevation loftier than where we were before.

While the DTC did not make me an engineer, it re-engineered my outlook on life. I bonded with splendid beings and marvellous teachers. It was a sojourn I would gladly relive. Down-to-earth issues had occupied a prominent place in my education at the DTC. From now on, the theoretical angle would dominate. Calculus and three dimensional vector geometry would supplant carpentry and metal work.

Medical Records

It was December 1965. The day to go to Kibaha was a month away. It was a time to relax, devour Agatha Christie, Erle Stanley Gardner and Alistair McLean – the books Mohamed had collected at home – and goof around with friends. But my nationalistic mood itched for an opportunity to serve the nation. Issa Shivji, who had completed Form V at the AKBS, shared my feelings. Our first step was to approach the Director of the Muhimbili Hospital, then and still, the largest hospital in the nation. As we offered our services, he was not receptive at first. Dr Sarungi said we were not qualified for a job at the hospital. He had misunderstood us. When we clarified that we sought to be unpaid volunteers, he was surprised but took us on board without further hesitation.

The Medical Records Section needed assistance, he told us. Armed with a letter from him, we were directed to report early next day at the section premises. The section head would assign our tasks. It being a ten-minute walk from my house, I reported by 8 am. But I was alone since Issa had changed his mind.

The section maintained and distributed inpatient and outpatient files. On the first day, I saw an impatient crowd of nurses and patients at the service window. Each clamoured for his or her file to ensure it was at hand when the doctor needed it. It was a noisy, chaotic scene. The section head welcomed me with obvious relief. To cope with the work load, he needed more than the two assistants he had.

The name of this genial man escapes me. Stricken with polio as a child, both his legs were shrivelled and deformed. At that time, he did not have a wheel chair. Hence, he moved about with a support rod, or by dragging himself on the ground. His agility was nothing short of amazing. Getting a file request, he would rapidly crawl to the shelf, reach up to collect the desired file using his rod, crawl back as fast, employ his strong hands to haul himself onto his chair, and deliver the file to the person at the window. Occurring in a matter of minutes, it was a stupendous spectacle to behold. I came to admire the manner by which he kept his cool with angry clients. After a few minutes of instruction from him, I joined the staff in the file location and distribution tasks.

In all, he had four assistants, two for each shift. Their main job was to store patient files in an organized way, and retrieve them in a timely manner when needed. But the place was in a state of disarray. Piles of files, with loose sheets, lay about on the tables and the ground. Misplacement was a common complaint. I soon came to realize why that was so. The times when the files were most in demand or returned in larger numbers closely coincided with the start and end of the shifts. A long line of patients and nurses formed at the window. The staff were busy. Files would be misplaced, or dumped on the floor. But when the work load was lighter, the time was not spent replacing the files in correct places. The otherwise harangued workers saw it as a time to rest. And it was claimed that when the out-patients returned the next day or week, it was easier to get files from the floor than from the muddle on the shelves. That strategy only compounded the disorder in the long run. The once in a while refiling that was done was done in haste and involved a large heap. Files were placed where they should not be, and things went from bad to worse.

The second law of thermodynamics says that in the universe as a whole the total entropy – a measure of disorder in phenomena – increases over time. This is what Mr Ibsted was to teach me in his physics class at Kibaha. The law of conservation of energy is easier to fathom than this law. I think we would have understood it better if the physics teacher had taken us on a visit to the Muhimbili Medical Records section.

After assisting at the service window for three days, I was given a new task. It was to arrange the files on the shelves in the right order. Any semblance of regularity on the grimy shelves had evaporated long ago. From eight in the morning to noon time, five days a week and for four weeks, I slogged. Except for the dust, I did not mind. A short break mid-way found me chatting with the section head and the staff, exploring the hospital, or resting on an outside bench, consuming soda and peanuts.

Progress was slow since I also reattached the loose sheets in the files. By the time I left, only a third of the shelves had been tackled. I am not sure if anyone took up the task after I left. In any case, I was glad to have spent my time in a way that had helped others. It was my own brand of national service, albeit beyond the setting of a camp. The friendliness of the staff had brightened the days, and my command of Swahili improved. I had a close glance into the disquieting, complex hospital environment. It took a few days to come to terms with adults in horrific plight, but a child writhing and wailing in excruciating pain was a sight too unpleasant to bear.

Kibaha

Until 1961, Kibaha had been an isolated, barren roadside township with a few shops and small eateries serving rudimentary meals and offering toilet facilities for bus passengers. Its face began to change after the foundation stone of the Kibaha educational complex was laid. The complex was funded by the four Scandinavian governments. Its opening in 1964 initiated a process that eventually turned the town into a regional capital with a booming population and diverse economic activities.

The almost six square kilometer complex had three main components: a secondary school, a health centre and a sprawling agricultural section. The health centre provided basic health services to area residents and housed a nurse training school. The agricultural section had a large farm growing fruits and vegetables, a dairy farm, a dairy products processing unit and a training unit for dairy and farm extension services personnel. The school was to enrol students in forms I to VI. At the outset, the senior personnel at the complex, such as teachers, doctors, veterinarians, agronomists and administrators, were mostly from Norway, Sweden, Denmark and Finland. They spoke fluent English, though some had an accent that took us a while to fathom.

Kibaha Secondary School began as one of the best equipped and largest secondary schools in the nation. A boys only school with students living on the campus, there were no tuition fees, and room and board were free too. Personal use items like soap were also provided.

There were four residential houses. In each house, the junior (Form I to Form IV) students resided in a two-story structure with large halls that contained at least ten beds. The Form V and Form VI students were in an adjacent rectangular single story structure with a grassy courtyard in the middle. The six rooms on each side of the courtyard had two students per room. Each house had its own spacious area for recreation. That is where we played table tennis, card games or chess, listened to music, read a book, or relaxed and yammered away.

With students drawn from across the nation, a cordial multi-racial, multi-religious, multi-ethnic atmosphere prevailed. I do not recall if there was any Asian student in forms I to IV. In the year I joined, there were six Asians in forms V to VI. Constituting about five percent of the students in the higher forms, all were Ismaili.

My group was the second uptake of students for this school. I was placed in Scandia House. Our house master, Mr Sedegreen, was a tall, upright fellow with short cropped hair. He bore the stern look and uptight mannerism of a disciplinarian military sergeant.

At the Form V-Form VI level, there were two science streams and the economics-geography stream. But there were no arts streams. I was in the physics, mathematics and chemistry stream. General Paper, covering general knowledge, civics and essay writing, was a required subject for all streams.

All my teachers were Scandinavian. Mr Knudsen was our class master and maths teacher. He was a gentle, popular person, but getting on in age. I found his teaching slow and dull, and his material, not challenging. Mr Falk, the chemistry teacher, was younger, shorter and chubbier. His effervescent persona made him as volatile as a cyclic organic molecule and as slippery as a drop of mercury. To demonstrate the malleability of some molecular structure, he would shiver and contort his body till we got the point. To illustrate how the electrons in an atom jumped from one orbital to the next, he would abruptly hop onto the front desk with a big thud. Yet, he was more than a man of action. Entertaining as they were, his lessons were highly enlightening too. He deftly guided us into the vast domain and subtle intricacies of organic chemistry. His laboratory exercises were planned in minute detail and demanded precise control. A tiny error here, and the game was fouled up; you had to restart.

The teacher who took us to the limit was Mr Ibsted, a man with whiskers as long as those of a bob cat. His physics lessons were systematic to perfection and, unlike those of Mr Falk, as solemn as church sermons. With a no-nonsense attitude, he plunged us into the inner recesses of each topic and set tough homework exercises. We were ever in fear of his habit of unpredictably posing a question and pointing to a student. That person had to respond right away, and it had better be with the correct answer.

Mr Ibsted once fingered Titus Kamulali. The poor guy knew the answer, but became tongue tied. The teacher was annoyed:

What is your name?

Titus was in a sweat. Mr Ibsted repeated his question. At last, Titus gathered up courage. Rocking himself forward and backward as if in a trance, he began to recite a cyclic melody:

My name is Titus Kamulali, Titus Kamulali, . . .

My name is . . . . . .

Thereafter, whenever we called upon Titus, we assumed a gentle head and torso rocking pose, and recited his full name, in a musical tone, three to four times.

A Disturbance

The names and faces of my Kibaha teachers remain embedded in my mind. That is, with one exception. Until a former schoolmate reminded me recently, I had forgotten the name of our General Paper teacher. My image of him is fuzzy too. I think there was a good reason behind this memory lapse; almost all of us loathed him.

General Paper was to cover topics like civics, history and science. Issues in science were to be addressed from a societal angle. Mr Meng presented us a range of material from current affairs, history, science and literature. We wrote an essay based on a covered topic almost every week. I liked it since it landed me in the library. While seeking relevant information, I got an opportunity to swim in an expansive ocean of knowledge.

Yet, several aspects of the class did not sit well with us. We were unhappy about his choice of topics. They did not seem relevant to our realities. We thought his approach looked down upon African culture and glorified European culture. His condescending attitude irked us. His views were rigid and he did not welcome dissent. But this was a subject where issues were to be approached from different angles. It was not like calculus where, say, the derivative of x^2 is $2x$, and nothing else. My essays laid out views that differed from his. I got a low grade not because they were poorly formulated, written or argued, but because they did not accord with what he espoused.

Shiraz Kassam and I used to compare our general paper essays. He had a superb command of the English language and his writing style was exquisite. He was also an avid reader of the American magazines *Newsweek* and *Time*. Though we were good friends, we perpetually argued about national and international matters. Most of the time, our views were poles apart. He drew on these magazines to back his standpoint. Once he said that Africa was less developed compared to Europe due to climatic factors; the tropical heat stifles economic progress. I responded by asking why Tibet, Kashmir and the Eskimo lands were not as advanced as Europe? I do not recall his answer.

His general paper essays regurgitated ideas from these magazines. Our teacher also held them in high regard. So Shiraz always secured a high score, often the top one. A series of low scores saw me redoubling my efforts. For each topic, I collected extensive supportive material. I brushed up my grammar and style, and wrote in a more systematic fashion. Yet, while my class rank in all other subjects was No. 1, in general paper, the best I attained one semester was No. 2 (Appendix B: Image 6). Even Shiraz was impressed by what I wrote and often remarked that I deserved a higher score.

Shiraz, to put it mildly, was ill at ease with maths. I could not decide whether to sympathize with or laugh at his agonizing struggle with the concept of the derivative in calculus. He simply could not fathom why, when the strange entity δx (pronounced delta x) tends to zero, the ratio

$$\frac{\delta y}{\delta x} \Rightarrow f'(x)$$

tends to a finite number. Raising his hands in despair, he declared that as delta goes to zero, Kassam goes to sleep.

Our general paper session came after the chemistry lab. The experiments ran over at times, and we would be slightly late to Mr Meng's class. It was not a deliberate deed on our part. Yet, he would admonish us as if we were kids who had done a terrible misdeed. His unkind words added to our resentment of a man whose smug, superiority-infused persona had already displeased us.

One day, the lab session ended on time. We knew he was waiting impatiently. Yet, we did not directly proceed to the classroom. Instead, we headed in a perpendicular direction, erratically went up and down the stairs, and managed to be five minutes late. All this time, he observed us from the doorway. Upon our entry, he did not say anything, and we too had no words. Red in the face, he then stormed out of the room.

He returned with the school principal at his side. The latter did not ask us any questions but said in an angry tone that by insulting our teacher, we had gravely violated the rules. He had no choice but to suspend us until our fate could be decided. During the next classless two days, we were restricted to our dorm area. Subsequently, we were asked to apologize as a group to the teacher. We had no regrets, but we complied to avoid worse punishment.

The General Paper class resumed, but Mr Meng mellowed. Matters did not go further. I remain amazed at how the incident occurred. There had been no forethought, no prior planning. It was a spontaneous event; a fellow at the front took the wrong turn; the rest had followed automatically and in unison. The consensus that we would not any more tolerate how he treated us expressed itself as if we were a unified colony of ants. This was the first group-based act of defiance to authority, on an issue of general interest, that I was involved in. I did not know that more were soon to come, especially after I entered the university. And, unlike the juvenile actions of mockery against the Swahili teacher at the DTC, matters of national policy would then be at stake (Hirji 2011).

Apart from this teacher, my classmates and I retain but pleasant memories of our Scandinavian teachers at Kibaha. They were seasoned instructors well versed in the subjects they taught. They set high standards, assigned a lot of homework, and pushed us to excel. But they were, as well, friendly, understanding and committed to our progress.

Student Life

Besides being academically demanding, life at Kibaha was regimented. We lined up outside the expansive cafeteria before breakfast, lunch and dinner. On entering the hall line by line, we sat in pre-assigned places. Each table had two large food containers, and two students served the food. That rotating duty came with an advantage: you could pass on the choicest portion – the largest sausage – to yourself or a friend.

A heavy load of class and lab work filled the day. After dinner, we returned to the classroom for an hour-and-a-half self-study session. Soon thereafter, the dorm lights went off. Though we had more time to ourselves on weekends, there were clothes to be washed, rooms to be cleaned and a load of homework. Once a month, we could spend a weekend in Dar es Salaam.

Our days were also peppered with fun and games. From 4 to 6 pm on weekdays and more hours on weekends, it was sports time. Our school had a modern track and field arena that surrounded a well-kept soccer pitch. With a good supply of equipment and expert coaching, our teams were often among the top three in the inter-school competitions. My gregarious Scandia house friend Anton Kaduri was a star basketball player. His skilful throws placed our team near the top of the league. I lost touch with him after Kibaha. Twenty two years later, when I joined the Faculty of Medicine at the UDSM, I happily found that the Professor of Anatomy was none other than this eye-twinkling, ever smiling man. His superb manual dexterity was now being applied to a rather different pursuit. Sadly, but as too commonly happens to the brightest minds in Africa, he passed away well before his time.

I played volleyball, and was on the house, but not the school, team. We won the inter-house competition for both my years at Kibaha. I was into boxing too, as I describe later. My circle of friends regularly attended soccer games and athletic competitions, rooting for our teams with noisy chants. There was no cricket at Kibaha, but I kept abreast of the national and international developments in the game.

Within a month of joining Kibaha, I learned chess. It soon became a prime reason why I eagerly awaited the weekend. It was a joy to spend the hours in the agreeable company of pawns, knights and rooks. Even the weekends I was barred from going to the city, not an uncommon occurrence, became enjoyable. I explained the rules of chess to Elias Kisamo and Salim Lalani, who then became my recurrent opponents. After I introduced it to Navroz, he and I dissipated long hours on the chessboard when I went on a weekend leave to Dar es Salaam.

A Swede who taught maths in lower grades was the patron of the chess club. A real master, he would tightly corner my king within a few moves. The ease with which he did that was astounding. Among the students, only Munisi made me sweat. The rest I trounced without trouble. I was the school chess champion in my first year. In the final year, I focused on the final examinations and set it aside. I wish I had not. Subsequently, I played chess only on a sporadic basis, yet kept up with the main events in the international chess arena.

Chess helped improve my memory and focus. My mind was closed to all else when I was in the midst of a game. At the end, I could recreate it from step one to checkmate and analyse my errors. Our chemistry textbook had numerous formulas of intricate organic molecules. I think chess improved my ability to concentrate, enhanced my memory, and enabled me to recall such material with ease.

I read mystery novels by the dozen, mainly on the weekends. Agatha Christie, Erle Stanley Gardner, Hammond Innes and Sherlock Holmes were my top authors. Mohamed had a big pile of books that he did not touch now. The mystery genre got so much into my head that on my school ID, which I still possess, I inscribed the initials *FBI*. A hitherto colonized mind was in danger of being unconsciously transformed into a neo-colonized bumpkin.

In a holdover from my gang days, I carried a small knife in my pocket. I also had a couple of throwing knives. Upon carving out a target area on the wide-trunked mango tree behind our dorm, I practiced knife throwing when I was free and bored. I would go on for hours at a time, the bark gradually chipping away. Some schoolmates still call me the knife-throwing guy.

On one casual stroll across the campus, Salim Lalani spotted a large crab some fifteen feet away and told me to liquidate it. To his astonishment, my knife flew swiftly and pinned the creature to the ground. It was a lucky shot; I was rarely that good. I now find it interesting that no house prefect or teacher ever raised an issue about my preoccupation with knives. It was probably viewed as a harmless, if strange, hobby. In the current hysterical educational arena, I do not think such an act would be tolerated even for a second. Not that I advocate knife throwing in schools; conditions of life today have changed. My point is that in general we need to be more tolerant of student behaviour that does not exactly subscribe to the official line.

A Knife Carrying Grandfather: Barry Lynch, a grandfather-of-five, was working on a cane farm in Australia when a crop sprayer suddenly collapsed and pinned him to the ground. He was alone in an isolated location. Not despairing, he started digging with his small pocket knife. After a six-hour strenuous and painful ordeal, he managed to free himself. Else he would have lost his leg (Saul 2013). Should I emulate him and resume my childhood tradition of carrying a knife? In this age, when even a pair of scissors arouses suspicion at the airport, I guess I better not.

Salim and I frequented the farm area on Saturdays. After purchasing fresh milk and fruits, we loitered around the vast complex. Once, we went overboard. Each gulped down a pint of warm-from-the-udder milk, and gorged on a medium sized pineapple. The instantaneous bellyful of delight became a day long bout of watery diarrhoea, and of teeth so sensitive that no food could be placed in the mouth. All output, no input – we were the joke of the week in Scandia House. Even the normally stoic Mrs Falk tittered when we went to her for relief. At another time, my friend bought and swallowed two raw eggs. Not to be outdone, I put down three, only to get a bothersome bellyache that night. This time around, I did not go to the clinic. It went away by itself the next day.

A Human Life = 30 Raw Eggs: Dhaou Fatnassi, a twenty year old Tunisian, accepted a bet to swallow 30 raw eggs in succession. He fell down after ingesting 28 and died on the way to the hospital (*Daily News* 2013). Occurring thirty eight years after our milder teenage day waywardness, this episode revealed a grim reality: he was a jobless man desperate for a few coins. The overthrow of a long reigning dictator did not change the fundamental nature of the neo-liberal economy. As democracy turned into an elitist sham, the value of human life was reduced to a pittance.

Mrs Falk, the school nurse, was the wife of our volatile chemistry teacher. Unlike her husband, she was as steady as a bulky baobab. Her kind treatment of ill students and follow ups in the dorm raised her popularity. If you contracted malaria or were injured, you were first treated in her clinic. If it was serious, you were sent to the Kibaha Health Centre. She had a curious way of responding to each sentence you uttered. It was like *yanh hanh, yanh hanh,* and was widely mimicked by the students. She as well patiently counselled us on the health risks of smoking, sexual activity and unhygienic habits. The image of a small poem on the clinic wall remains with me:

On Smoking

Ah, but to smoke
And calmly puff away
Calmly puff away
.... twenty years ahead
And think
.... of a quiet cancer bed.

The school rules on smoking were not aligned with what she espoused. Though the junior students were not allowed to smoke at any time or any where, we the Form V and Form VI students could do so in our dormitories.

Only a couple of students in my class smoked, and that only once in a while. Why the liberal policy on smoking? I had no answer at that time. Only after entering the public health arena in the 1980s did I realize that it reflected the conditions in the Scandinavian world. These nations have progressive health policies, but they have not been very successful in curbing smoking. The smoking rate for Norwegian teenagers, for example, has shown a smaller decline as compared to those for their British and US counterparts. Our teachers at Kibaha had afforded us the same liberty to puff away our lives as that given to the teenagers in their nations.

Though at the top of my class in academic matters, I was not a disciplined student. I broke the rules and was apprehended. One day I took a short cut to the Kibaha shops by climbing over a health centre wall. A teacher nabbed me in the act. It was a double offense since I was leaving the school compound without permission as well. At times, I skipped the after dinner study session and remained in my room to iron my clothes or rest. Mr Sedegreen made his usual rounds. The thump of his military boots gave him away from a distance. My room became dark, and I froze until he was gone. One cool evening, the ominous footsteps echoed. I became as still as a cement beam for fifteen minutes. Assuming all was clear, I then poked my head outside. To my shock and horror, the crafty house master was right there, waiting in silence. My punishment was the cancellation of a weekend leave.

On two free weekends, I walked the twenty six miles to Dar es Salaam. It was a matter of whim, and I walked on my own. Starting early on a Saturday morning, I made it to Ubungo by evening. A city bus then took me to Upanga. A couple of teachers had stopped to offer a lift, but I had declined. The return trip, however, was by bus.

Badru Moloo, my roommate, was in the botany/zoology stream. Hailing from Iringa where his father ran a dairy farm, he was the first Asian I knew who was emphatically attracted to a life surrounded by cows, goats and dogs. He had grown up doing chores around the farm, including milking cows by hand early in the morning. His arms were extraordinarily strong, yet he had a warm, soft and upright personality, and was seen as an exceptionally honest and organized person. Teachers and students alike treated him with respect. When he was appointed the senior house prefect, I told him he was the perfect person for the job.

Though I was a troublemaker and he, the nailer of troublemakers, we were on good terms. He frowned at my erratic tendencies but overlooked my minor deviations. That I excelled in my studies and helped other students sufficed to place me in his good books. His broad-minded nationalistic outlook was as well in harmony with my views.

My teachers were perplexed by my contradictory persona. I did the required classwork, did it well, and always on time. My subject grades almost always were 'A's. My class rank was number one. Yet my discipline grade was an invariable 'D' (Image 6: Appendix B) – another instance of dualism in my life.

Cultural Currents

As noted earlier, during my first year at Kibaha there were six Asians students who formed about ten percent of their peer group. All were Ismaili. The health centre had one Ismaili nurse. Two Ismaili trainees were enrolled at the agricultural centre. We met as a group on some Friday evenings for prayers. On key pious occasions, we gathered at the nurse's place near the health center. Her cooking was a welcome change from the cafeteria food. My lifelong daily routine of JK attendance was broken for the first time. But I recited my prayers every day before falling asleep. On the weekends spent in Dar es Salaam, the old routine went on.

Kibaha life placed me with the same set of people four plus twenty hours of the day. Apart from the absence of females, their diversity reflected that of the nation at large. Skin colour, ethnicity, religion or language no longer decided personal interactions. My friends, close and casual, were of varied backgrounds. We bonded as students facing the same academic hurdles, enduring the same living conditions, and having fun in a shared set of activities. My friendships derived from common interests, outlook, activities and a clicking of the spirit. It was a life light years apart from my socially restricted lives in Lindi and Upanga. The race-based dualism that had engulfed me during my three years at the DTC was at least partially cast aside.

My cultural horizons began to transcend the exclusive immersion in Indian movies and songs. Some of my JK friends were fans of the Beatles, Elvis Presley and Cliff Richard, etc. My DTC buddies were attached to Congolese music and Tanzanian bands playing Swahili songs. I was into neither of these genres. But Kibaha exposed me to both and more.

Each house had a radio, a cassette player and music cassettes maintained by the Prefect. Salim Msoma was the student assigned by the Principal to purchase the cassettes from the Dar es Salaam Music House. His choices were generally popular. The recreation area tingled with music after 5 pm during the weekday. The weekend was a melodic time all the time. In that pleasant atmosphere created by lively music and songs, I played chess or table tennis, or just sat around with friends.

The calypso beat of Harry Belafonte gripped me. *Jamaica Farewell, Island in the Sun* and *Day O* became my lifelong companions from those days.

Jamaica Farewell

Down the bay where the nights are gay
And the sun shines daily on the mountain top
I took a trip on a sailing ship
And when I reached Jamaica I made a stop

But I'm sad to say I'm on my way
Won't be back for many a day
My heart is down, my head is turning around
I had to leave a little girl in Kingston town

Congolese music and Swahili songs from local bands dominated Radio Tanzania and the cassettes. Popular bands of that era included Kilwa Jazz Band, Simba wa Mnyika of Tabora, Cuban Marimba Band, and the Police and National Service bands. But I paid scant heed to them. Mainly, it was because I did not go to the dances. I found their beat akin to Rock and Roll, a genre I was allergic to. I remained a captive of Indian movie songs and music. But there were exceptions. The first Swahili romantic song to reside firmly in my psyche was Miriam Makeba's ululating *Malaika*.

Malaika

Malaika, nakupenda malaika	Angel, I love you angel
Malaika, nakupenda malaika	Angel, I love you angel
Nigekuoa mali we	I yearn to marry you, O lovely
Nigekuoa dada	I yearn to marry you, sister
Nashindwa na mali sina we	Dejected and penniless
Ningekuoa malaika	Else I'd marry you, angel
Nashindwa na mali sina we	Dejected and penniless
Ningekuoa malaika	Else I'd marry you, angel

The popular song *Tenda Wema* from the Shinyanga Jazz Band, and composed by Zakaria Daniel, was a hit with me. He subsequently became so identified with his composition that he was thereafter called Zakaria Tendawema. The lyrics satirize modern human interactions:

Tenda Wema

Tenda wema	Do a kind deed
Nenda zako, O	And be on your way, Oh
Binadamu	For, human beings
Hawana wema, O	Have no gratitude, Oh

This song seems lost at present; but the versions it later spawned are heard. A Taraab version sung by Mwanatama Amir with lyrics by Khadija Kopa exists. The 2013 song of the same title and theme by Rose Mhando has popular currency at present.

We occasionally heard Taraab songs from Radio Tanzania and Radio Zanzibar. They attracted me because the beat was similar to Indian movie songs. Some were Swahili renditions of popular Hindi songs. The nasal voice of Juma Bhalo presented sonatas of up to ten minutes in length. Repeating a short phrase many times, they still grabbed your undivided attention in a way akin to a hypnotic effect. As I was completing this memoir, I was saddened to hear of the passing of Juma Bhalo in April 2014 (Kubegeya 2014).

Among the music stars I got acquainted with at Kibaha, my favorite by far was Jim Reeves. The instant I heard his soothing tunes, I was hooked. The soft, metallic voice and romantic lines of this country-gospel singer from the USA mesmerized me. I recall *Adios Amigos, This World is Not My Home, Am I Loosing You* and *Welcome to My World.* When I listen to them now, I fall in a Jim Reeves' induced trance as if it was yesterday. At the top of my chart was the scintillating *Rosa Rio*.

Rosa Rio

Aye, aye, aye, aye
My heart is in Rosa Rio, under the Argentine sky
There with a beautiful lady, with her dark and sparking eyes
My heart is in Rosa Rio, your sentimentae, aye, aye
There with a beautiful lady, that I'll love the day I die

For me, Jim Reeves was the English language equivalent of my two top male Hindi singers, Mukesh and Hemant Kumar.

Politics

In that broadened social and cultural atmosphere my interest in national and international issues expanded. I read the papers when they were available, listened regularly to radio news, read the speeches of Mwalimu Nyerere, and searched the library shelves for books on science and general knowledge. The crimes of Apartheid and minority and colonial rule in Southern Africa featured in the news. I followed the struggles of African Americans for civil rights, and became aware of the on-going war in Vietnam.

On the home front, there was a major student demonstration at the University College in Dar es Salaam in November 1966. They were opposing the new compulsory scheme that required all persons selected for higher studies to enter the national service for two years. Angered by their stand, Mwalimu Nyerere ordered instant expulsion of the protesters. For days, it was the main news item. We were shocked by that turn of events, but a sense of fear made us avoid discussing the matter openly in a larger group.

As we would be affected by the new law, the sympathy of most senior students lay with their fellow students at the university. I felt that expulsion was an excessively harsh penalty. Yet, having already been involved in it, I backed the idea of national service. The few who are lucky to receive free education have a moral obligation to serve the nation. If it involves some form of sacrifice, so be it. That was my forthright view. Though I was in a minority, I sensed that my colleagues were not as set against the national service scheme as those at the university. Many of us harboured strong patriotic feelings, and we had not as yet tasted the fruits of an elitist life.

Two new, path breaking national policies were enunciated in my final year at Kibaha. Both exercised a profound and lasting effect on me, and at that point in time, I endorsed both. The first policy was enshrined in *The Arusha Declaration* (TANU 1967) which made Socialism and Self-Reliance (*Ujamaa na Kujitegemea*) the national creed. It entailed state takeover of banks, major industries, large farms and commercial firms. A collective mode of farming was introduced and the accumulation of wealth by persons in leadership positions was restricted. The imperial powers, big business folk (including the Asians) and most bureaucrats were not enamoured by the Declaration. The ordinary people, however, were supportive. In many villages and streets, they marched and sang joyfully to affirm their backing for Mwalimu's policies.

On the educational front, the principles of *Ujamaa* were practically embodied in the policy paper *Education for Self-Reliance* (ESR) (Nyerere 1967). The prime tenets of ESR were: (i) The current system of education was set up to produce white collar workers; (ii) The graduates it generated had an elitist orientation; (iii) Africa needed youth who were versed in theory and skilled in the practical arts, and who were motivated to serve the nation; (iv) Primary and secondary education had to incorporate practical work like farming, livestock and dairy keeping, and carpentry; and (v) Student life should reflect basic values like cooperation, equality, discipline and service for the common good.

Most students at Kibaha were not too aware of or concerned with social and political matters. Besides studies, their preoccupation lay with games, girls and personal affairs. Only a few, including myself, paid attention to national issues in more than a cursory manner. And even among us, the level of understanding was somewhat shallow. As these events unfolded on the national front, the Scandinavian run campus went on with life, for the most part, as if nothing significant was afoot. But the spirit of the times could not be avoided, and quite a number of us were inspired by *The Arusha Declaration* and the policy of ESR.

I habitually raised and discussed socio-political issues with my friends and school mates. I remember long arguments with Elias Kisamo, Emmanuel Kigoni and Salim Lalani. I brought such issues up in my general paper essays but the conservative teacher was not pleased by what I wrote.

My vision was nationalistic and left-leaning. The main planks of my outlook were a belief in racial equality and acceptance of our obligation to the nation. Salim's views reflected the racially tainted retrogressive logic common to Asians in Tanzania. Our exchange generated much heat and persisted for hours. Being a close friend, he knew of my erratic proclivities first hand. So, after a while, he would angrily shake his head and exclaim with exasperation, "Karim, which is the real you?" What he meant was that how could a fellow who flouted disciplinary rules, was a knife-throwing buffoon and had weird tendencies claim to be a politically progressive person, and, moreover, a follower of Mwalimu, Gandhi and Dr King? He was perplexed to see such vastly disparate tendencies coexist in the same physical brain. Both could not be real; one must be fake, probably the latter one. Looking back, I too am perplexed. But, as my brief sojourn into boxing reveals, I was not alone. In fact, I was in good company.

On Boxing

My Undali street gang of 1962 did have minor skirmishes with other kids. But it was a rare event, and we never had a serious fight. We created mischief and pilfered stuff, but did not harm others. I carried a knife in my pocket, but it was for cutting sugar cane, peeling and slicing fruit and practicing knife throwing. At the sea front, we wrestled and sparred among ourselves, but in a friendly way. In our dreams, we saw ourselves as the muscular Hercules of the cinema screen and comic books. We imitated karate chops on wooden boards. But that was all.

I have admired the boxer Muhammad Ali from the day he hit the headlines. The speed with which he demolished his foes was astounding. A loud mouthed young man, a black man boldly standing up to the dominant white establishment nourished my rebellious tendencies.

Kibaha School had a boxing club. I joined it around the same time I took up chess, and was placed in the featherweight category. The practice sessions were held twice a week between 4 and 6 pm. Putting on the gloves the first time around gave me a sharp rush of adrenaline. I tried to bounce around as swiftly as Ali, and did well at the outset. In one cross-category competition, I trounced a heavier boxer only to get a bloody nose from a swifter, lighter boy. He feigned swaying to the left side, but landed painful blows from the right. Without the needed acumen, I did not last long. In three months, I was knocked out of the ring. As I told my friend Kassam, the incremental ratio between the blows received (δR) and those inflicted (δI) did not decline. Rather, it grew exponentially over time, leaving me little option but to throw in the towel. In differential calculus terms:

$$\text{As time went by} \quad \frac{\delta R}{\delta I} \Rightarrow \infty$$

Volleyball, knife throwing and chess were safer. Though I no longer exchanged blows in the ring, I remained an aficionado. One evening of June 1967, the Upanga JK library was the scene on an animated discussion on boxing. The participants were Abdulrab Ben Daar, the Tanzanian lightweight boxing champion, two university students (Hassan Virji and Shiraz Esmail) and three high school students (Mamti Bhatia, Fatima Somji and myself). I was in town for the weekend. Mohamed Abualy chaired the session. The transcript of our exchange appeared in the July 1967 issue of the *Volunteer* (Abualy 1967).

Is boxing a sport? Abualy posed the query to set off the discussion. He then adroitly steered us from one topic to the next. The panel was sharply divided. Ben Daar and I staunchly defended boxing but the others voiced serious reservations. They said it was an unrefined, brutal activity like war whose real aim was to inflict pain. It harmed health, shortened lives, was connected to lack of intelligence and was tainted by commercialization. We called it a noble art for entertainment, expression of a basic human characteristic, and promotion of mental acuity. We said that the criticisms levelled against boxing were exaggerated and, where true, applied equally to other high risk sports activities.

Rereading that transcript today, I feel that each side (i) had strong words but few facts, and (ii) lacked awareness of the global realities. While the linkage between war and boxing was a major point, we did not refer to the brutal assault against the people of Vietnam then going on. We ignored the fact that the nation where professional boxing was at its zenith was also the premier war mongering nation in the world. Our verbal duel was like a high school debating competition where points are made just to undermine one's opponent. Its lack of substance reflected the deficiencies in our education about local and global affairs.

My attraction to boxing dissipated after I joined the university in 1968. I learned that it was a vehicle for commercial exploitation of a basic human instinct, and that boxers faced major health risks. I read Jack London's *Iron Heel*, a futuristic tale about socialism that has a caustic remark on how in the past (that is, in our days) people fought for money (Hood 2012; London 1908). This was the last straw. I no longer deemed boxing as a worthy sport, and favoured a worldwide ban on commercial boxing.

Muhammad Ali: My U-turn on boxing did not affect my admiration of Muhammad Ali. Actually, it increased by leaps and bounds. He is the greatest heavy weight boxer, if not the greatest all round boxer, of all time. But few people know that he was also an activist for civil rights in the USA, and worked with Malcolm X and Dr Martin Luther King. On converting to Islam, he espoused peace and non-violence. For him, it was not a matter of words only, as indicated by his courageous refusal to fight in Vietnam and kill innocent people. As he so aptly declared:

> *Why should they ask me to put on a uniform and go ten thousand miles from home and drop bombs and bullets on brown people in Vietnam while so-called Negro people in Louisville are treated like dogs and denied simple human rights?*
>
> Muhammad Ali

His principled stand cost him his boxing license and title (Wikipedia 2013a). Eventually, he prevailed in the court of law and made a spectacular comeback. In the 1980s, he began to show signs of Parkinson's disease – likely caused by the numerous head blows sustained over a long time. His deterioration has been a sad spectacle to behold.

I bring up his profile not just because I have been his fan, but also because he represents a noble face of humanity. He shows us that life can be full of strange dualities: That one can simultaneously be a rambling comic, a rough-tough boxer and a gentle, non-violent humanist. Maybe a quirky knife-thrower can be a decent human being too.

And, there are people who combine the skills of a master thinker with that of a champion fighter.

Chess Boxing is a sport in which the two competitors alternately play a game of chess followed by a round in the boxing ring. The winner has to excel in both. As a test of the combination of mental and physical agility and prowess, it is a unique game. A serious competitor needs a high standing in both the fields. The 2013 world championship tournaments in the middleweight, light heavyweight and heavyweight divisions for Chess-Boxing were held in Russia. It was put on the international arena in 2003 by Iepe Rubingh of the Netherlands (Wikipedia 2014d).

Though I never chess-boxed with a single opponent, I may have the dubious honour of being the only Tanzanian, at least in those days, who took part in both games concurrently. This is of particular interest at this juncture because my five months after finishing Kibaha School were spent in an environment in which physical prowess, stamina and acuity were the desired qualities and where, moreover, thinking and intellectual pursuits were not only discouraged but actually forbidden.

Encounters with Infinity ❖ ❖ ❖ ❖ ❖ ❖ ❖

Elias Kisamo, the tallest person in our class, resided in Scandia House two doors from me. As he shared my passion for maths and chess, we many a time sat together in the recreation area. Though a soft spoken person, once a conversation with him took off, it was hard to see when and where it would end. I prodded him on current affairs, and he, unlike my other classmates, was predisposed to raising abstract, puzzling questions. For example, when comparing carbon-based and non-carbon-based molecules, he was not content to list the differences. He asked why they were different. His stock query, always posed with a smile, was, "Karim, why is that so?" Hearing my reply, he would inquire what lay behind it. The unending cross-examination got on my nerves at times. But I enjoyed putting my wits against his cleverly constructed probes.

Elias was my Kibaha counterpart to my friend Navroz in Upanga. The latter too played chess with me, was wedded to mathematics, and liked to discuss philosophic and mystical issues. The whole slew of hours I spent with them are among my most pleasant teenage memories.

The idea of infinity reared its head in our maths class in varied guises. Some quantities, as the elusive δ that put Kassam to sleep, became infinitely small; some, such as the slope of the exponential curve, turned infinitely large; and there were some for which it was exacting to figure out where they were headed. Elias, Navroz and I grappled with infinity in our chatter. I think we generally ended up as perplexed as we had begun.

The symbol ∞ stands for infinity. My first notion was that it was a specific number far larger than the number of atoms in the universe, beyond any number any one could think of. But that was a simplistic view.

Is ∞ a Number?

---

1. *Assume that there is a largest number. Call it ∞.*
2. *But $\infty + 1$ is larger than ∞.*
3. *This result contradicts our assumption.*
4. *Hence the assumption cannot be correct.*

This mode of reasoning is called proof by contradiction. Pythagoras used it to prove that there is no largest prime number. Since then it has been applied to resolve a host of intricate problems in diverse branches of mathematics.

Infinity is perhaps the most beguiling idea in maths. It defies common sense and generates paradoxical results. One way to understand it is in terms of the relationship between wholes and parts. One point of view, called reductionism, proclaims that a whole is best understood by studying its parts, that it equals the sum of its parts. A train is made up of the engine, and passenger and goods wagons. The contrasting view, the holistic or wholistic view, focuses on the relationships between the parts. The units comprising a train must be in a specific order, else it is not a train. The whole is more than the sum of its parts. Complex systems demonstrate properties that are strikingly different from those of any of their parts.

The notion of infinity defies both these views. An infinite entity is by definition equivalent to at least one of its parts. Let us look at the set of whole numbers:

$$\mathcal{N} = \{\, 1, 2, 3, 4, 5, 6, 7, \ldots \,\}$$

Since there is no largest number, this set goes on forever; it has no end; it is an infinite set. Now consider another infinite set, the set of even numbers:

$$\mathcal{E} = \{\, 2, 4, 6, 8, 10, \ldots \,\}$$

$\mathcal{E}$ is also an infinite set. Moreover, it is a proper part of the set $\mathcal{N}$ in that every element of $\mathcal{E}$ (like 12) is also an element of $\mathcal{N}$, and there are elements of $\mathcal{N}$ (like 17) that are not in $\mathcal{E}$. Common sense tells us that the set $\mathcal{E}$ has fewer elements than the set $\mathcal{N}$. But here common sense misleads us. Careful reasoning finds that both sets have the same 'number' of elements.

To prove this claim, first suppose we have two bags. One has black beans and the other, red beans. Suppose we can form pairs of beans, one red and black, in such a way that each red bean has its own black bean partner, each black bean has its own red bean partner, and no bean is left over. Then, even without counting, we can declare that the two bags have an equal number of beans. Now apply this logic to the sets $\mathcal{N}$ and $\mathcal{E}$ by using the following system of pairing.

$\mathcal{N} ::$	1,	2,	3,	4,	5,	6,	7,	,...
	↓	↓	↓	↓	↓	↓	↓	↓
$\mathcal{E} ::$	2,	4,	6,	8,	10,	12,	14,	,...

Infinite Sets

An element n in $\mathcal{N}$ is paired with the element $2n$ in $\mathcal{E}$. Each element from $\mathcal{N}$ has its own partner from $\mathcal{E}$, and vice versa. And nothing is left over. The two sets thus have the 'same number' of elements. They are of the same size. Can you believe that?

Now visualize a conference held at the centre of the Andromeda galaxy in the year 2300. Authors and academics from star systems and cultures across the universe are gathered to ponder translations of the exemplary works of multi-galactic literature into a universal language that can be accessed by all.

The venue, Hotel Infinity, has an infinite number of rooms. Ms Granulatum, a writer from an exceptionally remote corner of the universe, is a day late. All rooms are occupied. Not wanting to miss this once-in-a-millennium event, she pleads her case to the manager. As she has endured a hazardous trip, he sympathizes with her plight, and comes up with a neat plan:

> *Madam, we can make a special arrangement for you. But as it will mean some effort and expense on our part, we have to triple the daily room charge for you.*

She agrees. The receptionist then moves the occupant of Room 1 to Room 11, of Room 2 to Room 12, and so on. A person in Room n goes to Room $n + 10$. These moves give each current occupant a unique new room. There is no double placement. At the same time, ten rooms are emptied. Ms Granulatum takes up Room No. 7 that also gives her a splendid view of an exploding super nova.

Elias, Navroz and I came to learn about such features of infinite entities when we pursued university level mathematics. We found that there are levels of infinity. Some infinities are 'larger' than others. To our surprise, it was proved to us that the interval between 0 and 1 has more elements (decimal numbers) than does the set of whole numbers $\mathcal{N}$. And that was the beginning of a magnificent intellectual journey that continues to this day.

Yet, I have come to see that for human societies, the interaction between wholes and parts, between small and big, is more beguiling than in maths. The linkage between individuals and society, or between race, religion and nation, can be complimentary or contradictory, depending on the circumstance and issues. Confronting the moral dimension of such connections between wholes and parts requires wisdom and courage. Failure to do that underlies many dualisms around us. These dualisms, formed in ways too intricate to be adequately captured by mathematical models, paint our lives with novelty or rigidity, fun or boredom, dignity or shame, cruelty or kindness, peace or violence, and intellectual feats or idiocy.

Navigating between wholes and parts in an ethical and just manner is the most profound challenge societies and individuals confront. Usually no one way is the right way. Often there are obviously wrong ways and some promising ways. It is only when we cooperate with fellow humans that we avoid the former and move towards the latter. Recent and ancient histories unfortunately indicate that, instead of doing that, we more often connect with our immediate circles in order to seriously harm perceived outsiders. The day a majority of us will think and act like members of a single, harmonious family is not as yet on the horizon. But it had better come before catastrophic global climate change and unchecked capitalism decimate the biosphere as a whole. In that event, all the wholes together with their parts – you and your family, your family and your community, your community and your nation, your nation and the human family, humanity and all living beings, will descend into the infinite oblivion. The natural ∞, like the mathematical one, will be submerged into an unfathomable, power driven entity, $\aleph$.

— 8 —

National Service

*The real danger is not that computers
will begin to think like men, but that
men will begin to think like computers.*

Sydney J Harris

❖ ❖ ❖ ❖ ❖ ❖ ❖

KIBAHA SCHOOL WEDDED ME to mathematics for life. At the start of 1968, I eagerly awaited university studies in order to dive into its complexities. But it was still six months away. In the interim, as required for all high school leavers, I was to enrol in the National Service and live in a military-style camp.

I had no qualms about the prospect, thinking it would pass painlessly and rapidly. Little did I know that the five month sojourn would be a time of confronting dualisms, milestones and U-turns of titanic forms, a time of scaling extremes on the moral, physical and intellectual dimensions. And not all of these ventures would be of the desirable kind.

A Mild Start

The final days of 1967 returned me to Upanga, once more active in the JK Volunteer Corps (Image 7: Appendix B). But I was emotionally unsettled. Cute girls made me dreamy. Yet, I was too shy to approach any. My JK friends joked with them as a matter of course. I could only envy them. I played volleyball, chess (once in a while), and attended cricket matches and movies. The song and romance infused Indian flicks resumed their central position in my cultural life. I recall two: *Mera Saya* and *Gunga Jumna*. Accompanying my female cousins to these three hour long dramas added the needed spice to my life.

Life at home followed the clock. At times, I assisted my father in his shop. He taught me to drive. I read *The Standard* and took a keen interest in national and global events. Discussing social, spiritual and political issues with Navroz and Issa became a norm. The latter, a law student at UDSM, made me aware of facts and ideas I had little clue about.

I viewed myself as a devout Ismaili and committed patriot. In my mind, both visions were in harmony with each other; my politics and spirituality were in unison. Loving my country, supporting the policy of *Ujamaa* and the liberation of Africa was an affirmation of the ideals of compassion, generosity and equality in the eyes of *Allah* that I had imbibed from Ismaili teachings and hymns. Most of my Ismaili friends did not subscribe to that perspective, at least not to the extent I did. We had sharp arguments about racism and injustice. I was anguished when my parents mistreated African workers at home and in the shop, and did not pay them well.

Tanzania faced problems putting the Arusha Declaration into practice. Its pillars – equality, communal solidarity, self-reliance and rural development – were laudable, but required a thorough plan and broad mobilization. Mwalimu inspired the nation, but whether the ruling party would deliver was an open question. Across Africa, the fight to end Apartheid and Portuguese colonialism gathered steam even as internal conflict plagued the new nations. A tragedy loomed in Nigeria. The civil rights struggle in the US was vibrantly alive. America's genocidal war in Vietnam and Israel's oppression of the people of Palestine drew global condemnation. Students everywhere rose up to denounce racism, injustice, inequality and militarism.

I was broadly aware of such happenings, but my comprehension was of a superficial variety. I did not know the essential facts, and did not fathom the details, scope, history, logic or their interconnectedness. My outlook derived from the philosophy of a specific religion and plain nationalism. It was an eclectic and diffuse outlook. As for my career pursuit, I had a restricted goal: To immerse myself in pure mathematics, only pure mathematics, and nothing but pure mathematics. Accordingly, I did the Further Mathematics exam paper, and assisted Navroz in his preparations for the Form VI maths exam.

National Service

Soon, it was time for national service. My posting was the Ruvu National Service Camp located some fifty miles west of Dar es Salaam. Standing atop a small hill, it had densely forested areas on two of its sides, and a farm and grazing field on the other two. It housed approximately a thousand residents.

One early afternoon in late January of 1968, a group of forty boys and girls alighted from a bus and set foot on its hot, dusty yard. Our baggage was light since we had been told that almost everything we would need at the camp would be provided.

An *afande* (officer) – the assistant camp commander, no less – welcomed us. We stood in a line, posture upright. He had a sour mood. His first sentence, loudly uttered, concerned the main rule at the camp. It was '*Obey Your Officer.*' No questions were allowed. And there were no exceptions. If commanded to jump in a well, you jumped – that was it. Any disobedience or even hesitation would lead to severe censure.

The second rule was to respect the officers: Stand up and remain still when you talk to or are addressed by an officer; seek permission before doing anything; and salute when you encounter an officer. An impromptu lesson on saluting was given. To our embarrassment, our awkward gestures drew derisive howls from the camp residents standing nearby.

Then an essential dictum of life at the camp was forthrightly decreed: Place your own ideas, diplomas, education, erudition and imagination under lock and key in your bag. That kind of stuff is plainly worthless here, we were told.

> Out there, you may be a learned fellow. But in the camp, you are a blank slate. What, how and when you think, or if at all you need to think, will be determined by us. The earlier you accept that, the easier your life will be. Do not make it hard on yourself by resisting. One way or another, sooner or later, you will come around.
>
> Ruvu Camp Officer

This grim message from the stern-faced *afande* was regularly repeated in the next two weeks. From childhood, I had been taught that one did not query or doubt ideas of a spiritual nature. These were matters of faith beyond human comprehension. As a devotee, you wholeheartedly, and without question or doubt, adhered to the main tenets of Ismailism and the guidance of the *Imam*. That was the end of the story.

The camp *afandes* conveyed to us that an injunction of the same spirit applied to worldly affairs. It was the first time I heard it stated explicitly: Thinking was not a desirable activity. Indeed, it was a forbidden pursuit at the camp. What was the point of letting your mind loose when everything was to be decided by the *afande*? Our one and only responsibility was to follow orders – exactly, promptly and to the letter. And, we had better do as told. The dire consequence of this disobedience would not wait till afterlife but would be felt here and now as back-breaking punishment or behind-the-bars confinement.

We stood in the hot sun for over an hour listening to a most unexpected and disheartening welcoming tirade. But we were too tired to be shocked. Other than his metallic tone, not much registered in my mind. Finally, we were led to our tents, and ordered to wash up. Our basic supplies – uniforms, shoes, shoe polish, brush, soap, mugs, etc. – were distributed half an hour later. My supply form, which I retain to this day, states that I was given twenty seven items including a bed, mosquito net, bed sheets, boots, berets, belt, vests and so on. And we had earned the derisive designation of a *cruto* – camp slang for a know nothing recruit. I was a *cruto* with force number A0810.

Twin Primes: If both of the two successive odd integers prime, they are called twin primes. For example, (11,13) and (41,43) are two sets of twin primes. Since (809,811) are twin primes, my force number was a pivot for twin primes. One unresolved problem in number theory is whether there are an infinite number of such pairs or not.

Our first day ended with a steamy, humongous meal of rice, spinach and red beans. Soon thereafter, it was bed time. The instant the lights turned off, our exhausted bodies switched off our benumbed, conscious brains. The process of identity erasure had commenced.

Camp Life

Camp life was arduous and strictly regimented. From jumping out of bed at exactly 5 am to retiring at exactly 10 pm, we were on the move. One physically onerous action followed another. When it ceased, there were cultural shows, singing sessions with patriotic songs, lectures and radio sessions. We had no personal time to speak of. Yet, the next day we were to present ourselves for an early inspection in a well-groomed manner, with shiny shoes and starched uniforms. It became clear from the start that my one-month stint at the Kinondoni Camp would be like a joy ride compared to what lay in store at this place.

Before breakfast, we practiced drill, marched, ran for miles, or worked in the farm. At 9 am, a copious, steamy, super-sweet mug of milked tea and half a loaf of bread with an invitingly thick layer of margarine were served. Once or twice a week, a boiled egg was on our plate. Then came up to five hours of arduous work in the hot sun. Depending on the assignment, it varied from clearing the bush, cutting down trees, digging the ground and planting seeds, working on the rice farm, harvesting papayas or pineapples, grazing cattle, tending to poultry, mixing cement and making bricks at a construction site, cleaning toilets to kitchen duty. The last one was a coveted assignment as it was comparatively light, done generally in the shade, and, to cap it all, promised the tastier morsels from the dish of the day.

In the course of our stay, we did things that previously we could not have imagined that we would ever do, or were capable of doing. A commonly uttered phrase in these months was: There is always a first time. It came up when we talked about the novel things done that day, and it was the standard response from the *afande* when a recruit was bold enough to say that some task was beyond his or her capability.

The first and only time in my life I was party to slaughtering a cow is a case in point. The job began with pinning the creature to the ground. It took six of us to hold down the loudly braying, writhing animal. Then the butcher applied a long, sharp knife, almost effortlessly, to the jugular vein. Warm red blood drained into a bowl. It groaned in agony, jerked spasmodically. But we held it down. Precious life ebbed away in minutes. Then came the formidable job entailing first skinning the carcass from head to toe; separating meat, bones, leather, hooves, entrails, head and tail; cleaning the entrails and the leather; and so on. We had no gloves or masks. The first timers like me soon found ourselves soiled all over with pungent, foul stuff.

Our regular diet at the camp was large servings of kidney beans with maize flour *ugali*, or cabbage/spinach curry with bread. Items like meat and chicken were rare. On that day, beef stew with bread graced the dinner menu. Yet I did not touch the savoury stew, had a slice of plain bread and went to bed quite hungry. For a week, I was not disposed towards food. Not having had Biology in secondary school, I had not dissected even a frog. Chicken slaughter I had seen. But the killing of the cow shook me to the core. But my aversion did not last. The rough demands of camp life soon encased the painful visions of the beast and the associated pungent aroma in a remote mental drawer.

Six weeks on, the military component of our training expanded. Each recruit had his/her semi-automatic rifle. We learned how to disassemble, clean and reassemble it. We had to take utmost care of this lethal weapon now at our side in parades and route marches. We learned to load bullets and fire the rifle and the semi-automatic machine gun. Towards the end of our stay, there were three days of range practice with live ammunition. It was not my best time: my performance was lousy. On the last day, only 3 of my 35 bullets barely landed on the target. The girls in my group did better and giggled at my pathetic showing. Being an adept knife thrower does not imply that you will be a good sharp shooter too.

In the course of the training, we cleared the bush, pitched tents in the forest, dug trenches, practiced camouflage techniques, crawled on our bellies for long distances, tackled obstacle courses, and learned the field craft. We were systematically conditioned towards more strenuous and hazardous work. We first did *mchaka mchaka* (jogging) with our gear for a mile. Then it was for two miles and then, three miles. Rhythmic, loud chanting sustained our stamina and spirit. The initial five mile march with a light load on the back evolved into a twenty mile march with a heavy load, and eventually into the forty five mile route-march in which the night was spent in trenches we had freshly dug.

The aim was to strengthen our physical and mental stamina. Almost every day, we did a new thing or performed an older action but at a level not done before. The setting of the sun found us in utter exhaustion. Yet, we invariably rose early the next day. And that could be at 2 am to start a march. No matter the exertions of the previous day, the new dawn saw us refreshed, re-energized and animated. Many *crutos*, especially Asian girls from affluent families, complained loudly at the outset: They had never done such a task, and would never be able to do it. It was astonishing and amusing to observe the most vociferous complainer successfully completing the toughest exercise and then, in as loud a tone, happily boasting about it.

It was a lesson, in concrete and unmistakable terms, that peer influence, group solidarity and personal resolve can interact in ways that enable us to scale supreme heights. How high we reach is not simply a matter of innate ability or genes. Our social environment plays a major role in how, where and when we do or do not excel in our lives.

Cultural Activities

Cultural activities were integral to camp life. We had sports, primarily soccer and athletics, and song and dance performances. Radio Tanzania was the primary provider of music and songs. Live traditional *ngoma* (drum) groups and music bands entertained us on occasional evenings.

Lectures on social and political topics by speakers from the TANU Youth League, the TANU Political Education Unit and officials and dignitaries were given. Once there was a talk from a representative of FRELIMO, the Mozambican liberation movement. It was in Portuguese; the Swahili translator spoke haltingly and mumbled; so it was not that informative. Michael Manley, the Prime Minister of Jamaica, paid a visit, accompanied by his host, Mwalimu Nyerere. Mwalimu did not speak, but it was the first time I stood near him. I do not recall being impressed by the visiting leader.

Central to the camp culture were the songs we sang and the chants we uttered, loudly and in unison, in the course of jogging, drills, marches and other activities. Many were patriotic in nature, and were led by an *afande* or a *cruto*. One praised our national leaders:

Tuna Imani

Tuna imani na Nyerere	We have faith in Nyerere
Hoya, hoya, hoya ×2	Aye, aye, aye ×2
Nyerere kweli, kweli ×2	Nyerere truly, truly ×2
Kweli, kweli, kweli	Truly, truly, truly
Nyerereeee	Nyerereeee

Then came identical stanzas naming Vice President Kawawa, Zanzibar President Karume and so on. The national and local commanders of the JKT were included. Apart from Mwalimu, we doubted their dedication and honesty. Blind adulation bred cynicism, not loyalty.

Another chant targeted our enemies. The Apartheid regime in South Africa, the state of Portugal viciously ruling African colonies, and the white minority regime in Rhodesia led by Ian Smith were the main foes. Tanzania supported the liberation movements and faced real dangers from the brutal colonial armies. Two frequent chants during sweat drenching jogs ran:

Matata Huyo

Kaburu matata huyo	That devious Boer guy
Huyo, huyo, huyo	Him, him, him
Mreno matata huyo	That devious Portuguese guy
Huyo, huyo, huyo	Him, him, him
Smithi matata huyo	That devious Smith guy
Huyo, huyo, huyo	Him, him, him

Ko Ko Liko

Ko ko li koooo
Ko ko li ko kajogo kambeba ko ko
Haya haya ko ko, haya haya ko ko we ×2
Ko ko li koooo ......

From strongly worded chants to the tribal songs, there was a message. Like the one given above, some had a diffuse implication but sounded pleasant. To the bemusement of Farida, this quirky chant is heard at home to this day. Loud chanting raised our spirits and bonded us to one another. It diverted attention from the burden weighing down on us, the hazards we faced or the tough road ahead. The harder the task, the louder our chants. Before we knew it, the job was done and gone. Only then did we collapse in a state of extreme exhaustion.

The post-Arusha Declaration period witnessed an outpouring of patriotic and socialistic songs. They were a staple on Radio Tanzania. The emotive *Tanzania,*

Tanzania was a lead one (Chapter 17). One other on my list of the Top Ten was *Tazama Ramani*:

Tazama Ramani

Tazama ramani utaona, nchi nzuri
Yenye mito na mabonde mengi ya nafaka
Nasema kwa kinywa halafu kwa kufikiri
Nchi hiyo mashuhuri huitwa Tanzaniaaaaaa...
Majira yetu haya, yangekuwaje sasa
Utumwa wa nchi, Nyerere
ameukomesha, ameukomesha

Look at the Map

Look at the map; you will see, a beautiful country
With rivers, and valleys abundant in grain
I say this aloud, yet upon deep meditation
This famous land is Tanzaniaaaaaa...
Our fine disposition, what would it have been
Enslavement of our nation, Nyerere
Terminated for good, terminated for good

Hearing *Tazama Ramani* on the radio, which is rare now, makes my eyes watery. My musical abilities are worse than deficient. My singing is barely bearable. In particular, I just cannot capture the intricate melody of this song. Were I to sing it aloud, I think even a grumpy old goat would beat its tail.

Not that my primary enchantment with songs from the Indian cinema waned. A segment of the cultural locus that had entered my bone marrow from an early age, they will remain there until I am six feet below the ground.

A sizable portion of the Indian movie songs espouse moralistic and patriotic values. But the patriotism they proffer is, of course, to India. While I retain a cultural alliance to India, I have not visited that country. Neither did my mother. My father, in his 95 long years, has been there but once. I reconcile my attraction to the beautifully rendered Hindi patriotic songs with my loyalty to Tanzania by locational substitution. The movie *Upkaar* starring Manoj Kumar has a charged nationalistic song entitled *Mere desh ki dharti* or (The soil of my nation). When it strikes my ears, it is the intense majesty of my homeland, Tanzania, that resonates in my mind.

Jis Desh Me Ganga Baheti Hai (The Land Where the River Ganges Flows) was a popular 1950s Hindi movie starring the master actor, Raj Kapoor. Its songs exude romantic, moralistic and nationalistic values. I have watched it several times, including once around the time I was at the Ruvu Camp. Its signature song promotes national pride, honesty, simplicity and treating guests like family.

These are values Tanzanians ascribe to as well. When I sing it (in the privacy of my home, of course), I replace the river Ruvu for the river Ganges. (The Ruvu Camp is named after the nearby Ruvu River.) My slightly modified version of the first stanza is:

Hothon pe Sachai

Hotho pe sachai raheti hai	Truth blooms on those lips
jahan dil me safai raheti hai ×2	where purity lives in the heart ×2
Ham us desh ke wasi hai ×2	I reside in that land ×2
Jis desh me Ruvu baheti hai	The land where Ruvu flows

Salutary Effects

Camp life lasted a tad more than five months, yet it modified our outlook on life in critical and long term ways. On the balance, I found it a gratifying and memorable time. The hardships we endured notwithstanding, it overflowed with joy and laughter, with thrills and adventure. Close and lasting friendships were formed. As I wrote in my diary after two weeks at camp:

> *Life here is so different from and in contradiction to what I have been leading so far, and shall lead in the future, that I must enjoy it to the fullest extent possible.*

Yes, there were some activities I disliked and some, like the monotonous marching drills, that I even despised. Let me first describe those aspects of the service that, in my view, were beneficial and wholesome. In the next two sections, I discuss those aspects I regarded to be personally harmful and ethically wanting.

Improvement of physical health was a major beneficial outcome. I have never felt more energetic or healthier than I did during those demanding months. It is not just a question of age. I saw in practice that the limits of my physical endurance and ability far exceeded what I had presumed them to be. I was able to undertake hitherto unthinkable tasks and endure extreme hardship as a matter of course. Enhanced physical prowess and stamina buttressed my self-confidence. I felt emotionally fortified, and prepared to confront dire eventualities and challenges of life.

Ordinarily, we underestimate the connection between physical wellbeing and our sense of self-worth. Yet, our health status forms the bed rock of our social persona and emotional bearing. Only when afflicted with a chronic or serious malady do we realize its overarching role. In the past fifteen years, I have had to deal with major health problems. It is only since then that I have realized how health critically moulds our sense of who we are, our moods and style of interaction with others.

Blood Donation: As a sign of my robust health, like many other *crutos*, I donated a pint of blood to the Red Cross near the end of my stay at Ruvu. It was interesting to know that I was an O+ person, but it was my first and last time to donate blood. My health status after leaving the national service has been on the shaky side, and donating blood has been out of the question. Neglect of physical exercise and poor dietary habits were the main factors leading to that state of affairs. I realized this a bit late, and changed my habits even later. By then, the damage had been done.

On the moral front, national service reinforced five fundamental values that had earlier been given to us by family, school, community and society. These were (i) simplicity — that one can live a decent and contented life with few material belongings; (ii) respect for physical work — that farming, making useful objects, protecting one's environment, cooking, and even washing dishes are fulfilling and enjoyable activities; (iii) diligence — that hard work builds character and self-esteem; (iv) solidarity — that cooperation and mutual support can convert mountains into molehills; and (v) progressive patriotism — that in a poor nation like ours, everyone has to play their part in building the nation and improving the lives of our people. These were the attributes Mwalimu Nyerere continually emphasized, and our teachers and religion also promoted. The national service placed them more firmly in our hearts and minds, rounding out the confluence of values I have been talking about. It was also in conformity with the policy of Education for Self-Reliance.

In these early post-Independence days, as I noted before, the patriotic spirit and a sense of optimism flourished. Mwalimu inspired us through eloquence and example. We championed the total liberation of Africa, aspired to contribute to national development, and sought to go beyond the restrictions of race, tribe, religion and social class. We did not feel that the pot-bellied politicians and service higher-ups who lectured us on such points meant what they said. We abhorred their hypocrisy. Yet, by and large, the lectures, films, plays and cultural activities together with the nature of life at the camp instilled hopeful, forward-looking ideas and ideals in our psyches.

Asian and African *crutos* intermingled more closely in the camp setting than they had done before. I detected a gradual dilution of racist and exclusive modes of thought on both sides. My Asian friends and I saw our command of the national language improve. The persona of Sadru Champsi encapsulated such tendencies. In the same tent as I, he was the only Asian *cruto* who spoke Swahili as if it was his mother tongue. His tone, rhythm and phraseology were authentic. His fine vocabulary put native speakers to shame. Having attended a multi-racial boarding school, he had a slew of African friends. Unlike me, he had integrated with ordinary Tanzanians in a robust manner. I did not find even a tinge of racism in his interactions with African people. Sadru was not one of those who displayed one face here and another one there. The firm nationalistic sentiments he harboured and his support for Mwalimu and his policies, was a primary basis upon which our friendship was founded.

The convergence of my two universes, the union of my black and brown friends, climaxed in the national service. Thereafter, the bonds began to fray, and a few years hence, I am sad to say, it was to be a very different story (Chapter 10).

Another salutary consequence of service life was to bring home the idea of social equality in concrete terms. At its root, the camp had a hierarchical structure. The *afandes* ruled the recruits; there was no question of equality between these two groups. But among the recruits, equality was an ideal upheld in theory and deeds. No matter your background, you did what everyone did, and in the same measure. It did not matter whether you were rich or poor; a *Muhaya, Mzaramo* or *Muhindi*; a Muslim, Christian or Pagan; son of a farmer, businessman or state official. You cleaned the toilets, washed your clothes, jogged for a mile on an empty stomach, or stood at attention when talking to an *afande* just like everyone else did.

In particular, gender equality was not a distant goal but a way of life. Men and women had similar responsibilities and did the same things. I was astonished at the robust females who showed stellar accomplishments in a diversity of activities. Their performance brought well-built, boisterous macho guys to shame. At range practice sessions and during activities like crawling under barbed wire with a rifle in hand, I was regularly outdone by frail looking girls.

A Robotic Life

These fine features of national service, however, came with two impediments that, in my view, damaged the very foundation of what makes us human. One blockage occurred on the intellectual front, the other, on the moral front.

The edict conveyed to us at arrival and oft repeated by camp officers was: Stop thinking. Your commander will think on your behalf. You just have to follow orders. Your knowledge and opinions, even if relevant and appropriate, are irrelevant and unwanted unless you are specifically ordered to present them.

The capabilities and functions of the human brain distinguish us from other animals. They make modern life and social conditions possible, and enable the emergence of individual personality. More than any organ, our brains embody what we are in this biosphere. This edict was thus tantamount to stripping us of our essential humanness.

Inducing physical exhaustion and making the quality of our existence depend on the *afandes* were the main components of this process. By sunset each day, you were drained of energy. Your body demanded sleep. You had no time to reflect or dream. And when the *afande* offered a slight respite from the drudgery, you felt he was according you a major favour. The slightest easing of the load weighing down on you earned your gratitude; you forgot that it was he who, in the first place, imposed the burden on you.

Gradually but surely, we began to think and live as automatons. At the emotional level, we came to terms with obeying orders without a second thought. It was as the Borg of the Star Trek TV series declares: 'You will be assimilated, resistance is futile.'

Obedience was instilled, not earned. Most *afandes* were feared; genuine respect was rare. To appear tough, they became too harsh. Insulting language was used. A sense of disquiet was gradually building up among the recruits, and was felt by the senior officers. Captain Mushi, the camp commander who took over during the middle of our stay, told us that he would take our concerns into account. But it turned out to be empty talk.

Being treated as persons with neither the right nor the ability to determine any aspect of our lives was a denial of the core of our individuality. You were not a person, but a cog in a large machine. The human sense of self is deeply ingrained. It may be suppressed temporarily with relative ease. But it cannot be erased, even under the most egregious of conditions. René Descartes proclaimed: *I think, therefore I am*. But its obverse, *I am, therefore I think*, is as well an inseparable facet of human life.

The attempt to curtail thought by persons who in our eyes lacked moral standing, wisdom or charisma backfired. It made us cynical, and diluted the positive effects of camp life. These worthy traits did not sink as deeply into our psyche as would otherwise have been the case.

There was a historic foundation to the contradiction between the recruits and the officers. We were a group chosen for university level studies, a rarity in Tanzania in that era. As I noted in the previous chapter, the government and the university students had come into conflict over the national service scheme in 1966. To an extent the students were driven by a streak of elitism. Yet, they also doubted the motives of the politicians who thundered about serving the nation, but were bent on lining their own pockets (Ivaska 2011). I say with confidence that our misgivings at the camp were not against national service as such, but on the manner in which it was run. We saw instances of dubious conduct among the officers. We felt things could be done better, with less waste and better outcomes. But our views were deemed superfluous, unneeded. We thus ended up grumbling among ourselves, a state of affairs that promoted attitudes of negativity towards camp life and its rationale.

A few recruits raised probing queries during political education lectures. But more engaged in small acts of disobedience. That was the case with me. It was that bug taking its bite once more, another manifestation of dualism in my life. At times, I did not wash or iron my uniform well; in parades, I marched out of step. These transgressions earned me sharp insults from the *afande*, and unceremonious ejection from the parade. I became adept at 'taking cover,' that is, surreptitiously vanishing from the scene. Tired or not in the mood, I at times evaded the radio or *ngoma* programs.

I was caught twice: the penalties I got were uprooting two tree stumps, and an extra drill. The last punishment entailed forty five minutes of non-stop marching, crawling and running, as commanded by the *afande*, and with a heavy load on the back.

To leave the camp without authorization was a graver offense. Some late evenings a friend and I went by the back door to the nearby township to get roasted corn or fried fish. Three times, I took a bus to Dar es Salaam to watch a movie. Between the camp and main road lay a water-logged terrain. I had to return before dawn. The delightful Hindi movies I saw — *Upkar, Ram aur Shyam* and *Guide* — were worth the risk. The first time, I was not noticed. The next time, I was spotted but managed to slip away. Then my luck ran out: I was nabbed on my last trip by an *afande* who had lain in wait. The following day I was charged before the camp commander, found guilty, and locked up in the guard house for three days. Apart from the cold, hard, filthy floor on which I sat and slept, plain boredom, and swarms of buzzing, stinging mosquitoes, it was bearable. The meals were a bellyfull, there were no clothes to starch and iron, and luckily, there was no parade march to slog through. So I was not too unhappy.

But let me clarify, as recorded by both my memory and diary, I was not a lazy recruit. I did not have a rejectionist attitude towards national service. A fair segment of the recruits abhorred it outright. Others had a neutral disposition.

But as my previous voluntary deeds attest, I favoured and basked in it. I put in more than my best in productive activities like *shamba* (farm) work, kitchen duties, construction and cattle grazing. Though others did, I never took cover or feigned illness for such meaningful work.

When I goofed off or broke the rules, I was indirectly resisting the prevailing authoritarian atmosphere and the requirement to obey orders blindly. My mind rebelled, and defiance to authority was an expression of my individuality and a protest against the irrational aspects of camp life.

Degraded Morality

The animal species, even the ferocious ones, share a fundamental trait. Each specie has a deep-seated disinclination to kill one of its own. It is a hard wired device to protect itself as a specie, and its individual members. Exceptions do occur. We find within-specie infanticide, cannibalism and fights for food or mate ending in death. But such happenings are not the rule. When they occur in a systematic way, they express an underlying survival aspect.

Humans share that fundamental characteristic. On top of that, our history has generated elaborate moral and legal codes to reinforce it. Such codes have evolved in all corners of the planet. When a human, as an individual, kills a fellow human, he or she faces the risk of severe sanction. But at the group level, it can be another story. Then humans can perpetrate mass killings, with genocide and war being the most horrific manifestations, and often with impunity. These actions bear a stamp of approval from the state and society. Those who kill efficiently are celebrated. In that shameful practice, we outperform all other animals on this planet.

Lethal violence among humans, individual and collective, is not primarily due to intrinsic or genetic characteristics. It emanates in large measure from the social structure, economic disparities and access to material resources. Historical factors like culture, nationality and religion also come into play, and have a cumulative and cyclically reinforcing effect. Violence on a mass level requires extensive social conditioning. Overcoming the biologic inhibition to kill needs conscious and extensive effort on the part of those in society who wish to unleash such violence (Grossman 2009).

Trained to Kill: Each nation spends a sizable portion of its resources on weapons and armed forces. Social, political and economic factors affect recruitment into these forces. The dominant ideology and culture lend them prestige. Still, the individual soldier has to be trained and converted into a willing killer. A prime aim of military training is thereby to disrupt the sense of unity we feel with fellow humans. It seeks to instil in our psyche that it is acceptable, indeed moral and patriotic, to take the life of a human being if commanded by an officer. That order, like any other, must be executed instantly and automatically. Hence, the military training is accordingly designed not just to instill the skill to kill, but also to create the frame of mind facilitating the performance of the act. Killing has to be psychologically efficient (Grossman 2009).

The ideal soldier suppresses critical thought unless needed to implement the order given. In Cartesian terms, he ceases to exist as an independent moral being. He is a man authorized by law and the state to take the lives of designated human beings. And when he does so, he is called a hero, cheered and decorated.

Our training lacked the thoroughness of professional military training. Yet, the key elements were present. We were taught to effectively bayonet human-like dummies placed in upright and supine positions. The supervising officer emphasized that our attitude towards the act was as important as keeping the appropriate angle and force of the thrust.

> *When using a bayonet, you cease to be a human being and become like an animal.*
>
> Ruvu Camp Officer

I found this denigration of the universal moral edict — Thou Shall Not Kill — a profoundly disturbing facet of camp life. Though an endorser of the pronouncements of Mahatma Gandhi and Martin Luther King, I was not a strict pacifist. I agreed that the people of Angola and Mozambique were justified in resorting to the armed form of struggle to gain freedom from the barbaric Portuguese colonial rule. To me these actions constituted reactive acts of self-defence.

Militarism of a blind variety did not appeal to me. Killing done by an authoritarian structure in which the main actors are deprived of the basic right to use their own judgment produces unnecessary killings. This feature of camp life troubled me to no end; the implied denial of the common humanity of all on this planet was a dagger thrust in the core of my outlook.

Socialism and Militarism: The armed forces set up in a socialist society, which Tanzania was striving to build, should reflect the tenets of equality, grass-roots participation in decision making, and respect for human life. Camp life should reflect the principle of ground level democracy. All residents as well as nearby villagers should be represented in the main decision making bodies. Discipline should be instilled by example, respect, patriotism and the force of morality. Rather than deny them their right to think, the officers should welcome suggestions and ideas from the soldiers. Financial matters and use of camp resources must occur in a transparent manner with the records accessible to the public. Hierarchical structures must be kept to a minimum. Persons given the responsibility of issuing lethal orders must be under the strict and continual control of society, and be openly accountable.

What I underwent at the Ruvu Camp was not that different from the training given to police and soldiers in colonial times. The political context and rationale were not the same. But the armed personnel were being trained to serve an authoritarian state structure, and not the common person in the street or the village. The training was designed to teach skills for subduing the people in the case they exercised their right to self-determination. In essence, it did not conform to the numerous laudable nation-building activities we were engaged in. It was an instance – and a morally sordid instance at that – of the dualism of post-colonial society.

Fortunately for me, the mode of existence that bluntly restricted my thought processes and demeaned the worth of human life did not last long. By the middle of June 1968, I returned to a non-regimented life. The five vital values instilled by camp life – simplicity, respect for physical labour, diligence, cooperation and patriotism – had left a mark. And I had concretely seen the benefits of social and racial equality.

The attempt to shut down the mind had a rebound effect, at least in my case. The coming three years saw me asserting intellectual independence to a degree I had not done before. My life was imbued with a spirit of inquiry that did not leave any stone unturned. Instead of the camp instituted motto of accepting edicts from above and social conventions without question, my new motto aligned itself with the signal cry of the 1960s: 'Doubt Everything.' Blind obedience to authority was replaced by 'Question Authority.' In the place of an outlook and identity based on simple nationalism, I began to internalize – gradually but surely – an identity based on the vision of humanity as an indivisible, loving, caring family of equals.

A detailed narration of that story may appear in a future work. If you desire an immediate though limited glance, consult: *Cheche: Reminiscences of a Radical Magazine* (Hirji 2011).

Infinite Steps   ✛   ✛   ✛   ✛   ✛   ✛   ✛

My Kibaha buddy, Elias Kisamo, was also my companion at Ruvu. Being a person of upright character who performed his duties diligently, he frowned upon my erratic tendencies. While consoling me when I endured the backbreaking extra drill, he would pose his usual query:

> *Karim, why? Why did you do that?*

My response,

> *Why are the afandes so nasty?*

was wisely countered with

> *You cannot control what they do, my friend, but you can control what you do.*

His school day habit of inquiring into nature, life and philosophy persisted. He astutely summed up a unique lesson of camp life:

> *The possible and the impossible are closer than we think they are.*

He had in mind the litany of arduous tasks we had managed to accomplish. After we had successfully laboured through it, the gruelling forty five mile route-march dominated his talk for days:

> *Karim, I thought I was like Zeno's arrow.*
> *How is that?*
> *You know, to reach its destination, the arrow first has to go half the way. When it is there, it has to go half of the remaining distance, then the next half, then the next half, and so on.*
> *Meaning what?*
> *The arrow can never reach its destination. It has to take an infinite number of steps. We reached the half-way point, I was very tired but there was the next half. When we reached the next half-way point, another half remained, and on and on. A half-way always remains. I felt like that during the march. My exhaustion mounted exponentially. During the later halves, I thought I would collapse at the next step and never make it.*
> *But you did, Elias!*
> *That is true, but I am still trying to understand why and how!*

What my friend was alluding to is shown in the diagram below. The stages in the path of an arrow fired from the point Start to the point Finish are: the first half, then a half of that, and then a half of that, and so on.

Zeno's Arrow in Flight

Start   *Consecutive Half-Way Points*   Finish

This is one of the paradoxes posed by the philosopher Zeno in ancient Greece. Say an arrow has to fly the distance $2a$. It must first reach the point a, then the point $a + a/2 = 3a/2$, then $3a/2 + a/4 = 7a/4$, then $7a/4 + a/8 = 15a/8$, then $15a/8 + a/16 = 31a/16$, and so on. There is always a small distance left. Since the number of halves it has to traverse is infinite, the arrow can never reach the finish point. At least, that is what plain logic tells us.

Yet, in reality we see that while the arrow takes an infinite number of steps, it reaches its destination in a finite period of time. It took centuries to resolve the paradox. Today we tackle it by looking at the sum of the half-steps taken. This sum is:

$$d = a + \frac{a}{2} + \frac{a}{4} + \frac{a}{8} + \frac{a}{16} + \ldots$$

This is known as the geometric series

$$d = a + ar + ar^2 + ar^3 + ar^4 + \ldots$$

with ratio $r = 1/2$. We learn in high school that the sum of these infinite series is given by

$$d = \frac{a}{1 - r} = \frac{a}{1 - 1/2} = 2a$$

Even though the number of steps is infinite, each successive step becomes so small that the sum of the steps has a finite value. A finite distance can be traversed in a finite amount of time. Such calculations were not known in that era. Modern mathematics demonstrates that it is not a paradox.

This has been rendered in a poetic form by Alice Major (Major 2013). The opening lines of her poem are:

Zeno's Paradox

We've solved the paradox.
Motion is possible. The arrow's flight ends
even if its fractions interlock
to infinity – half a distance, yet again
half, and half . . . . We know this series sums
to a finite thunk and shudder.

Apparent paradoxes like this form the initial point of a strange tour into the world of infinite entities. Some paradoxes remain unresolved. Along that journey, we encounter numbers so gigantic as to defy ordinary imagination. As seen in the case of Hotel Infinity (Chapter 7), some violate the ordinary rules of arithmetic.

Our appreciation of the largeness of really large numbers is deficient. Yet, such numbers are nowhere near infinity. Once we move towards infinity, we find ourselves in a mind boggling arena (see also Chapter 11). Let us continue our exploration of this arena.

A sly mathematician advertised an apparently enticing lottery scheme. Each lottery ticket was priced at $1. A million serially numbered tickets would be sold. The winner would be picked by selecting a number between 1 and 1,000,000 at random and would win exactly $1,000,000.

The generous scheme produced a rush, and the tickets were soon sold out. The winning number, 008128, was held by a high school boy. When he went to collect the prize, he was told the pay-out scheme:

Starting from that moment, a partial payment would be deposited into his bank account every second. At the first second, the deposited amount would be $1; at the next second, $1/2; at the next, $1/3; at the next, $1/4; at the next, $1/5; and onwards in the same fashion. Payment would stop once the total amount paid reached $1,000,000.

The pace of payment, every second, is a fast one. But the amount deposited at each step gets smaller and smaller, and tends towards zero. Will the boy ever get the prize money, or was he being taken for a ride? To answer the question, we look at the infinite series called harmonic series shown below.

$$S = 1 + \frac{1}{2} + \frac{1}{3} + \frac{1}{4} + \frac{1}{5} + \frac{1}{6} + \ldots$$

As in the geometric series with $r < 1$, the terms become progressively smaller, and approach zero. In the geometric series, the sum is a finite, small number. It is logical to expect that here as well the sum will be a finite number, and most likely, it will be a number much smaller than 1,000,000.

Yet, this is a false conclusion. Careful calculations show that the value of S is not finite. If you select a sufficiently large number of terms, it can be made as large as you would like it to be. In the long run, the sum will exceed $1,000,000. The only problem is that you have to go very, very, very far out in time for that to happen.

There are $60 \times 60 \times 24 \times 365.25 = 31,557,600$ seconds in a year. With additional calculations, the boy finds that while a total of about $10 will be deposited in the first 10 hours, it will take roughly 10 years for the total to reach $20, and roughly 10 million years for it to reach $35.

By the time the deposit reaches $1 million, a truly unimaginable period of time will have elapsed. Zillions upon zillions of universes will have imploded, exploded, or been created. But one thing is absolutely certain: One day the promised amount will be paid.

Technically, the lottery organizer is not a cheat. For all practical purposes, however, he is. More than 99% of what he collects from the lottery will remain under the control of his family for generations to come. Deposited at the compound rate of interest of 1%, it will more than double every 100 years.

Now consider another scheme in which the payout was $1 at the first second, $1/(2x2), at the second second, $1/(3x3), the third second, $1/(4x4), the fourth second, $1/(5x5), the fifth second, and so on. This gives us a modified harmonic series,

$$T = 1 + \frac{1}{2^2} + \frac{1}{3^2} + \frac{1}{4^2} + \frac{1}{5^2} + \dots$$

If he uses this scheme, the lottery owner could be charged for cheating. Here the value of T is finite, and can be shown (using the methods of calculus) to equal $\pi^2/6$, or roughly, 1.6. If the payments per second under this scheme continue for zillions upon zillions of years, the total can never be larger than $2.

Some infinite series whose terms tend to zero have finite sums and some do not. This is an intricate arena of inquiry. Mathematicians from different continents have contributed to it. But none mastered this field with greater acumen than Srinivasa Ramanujan, a self-taught Indian mathematical prodigy who died at an early age. From his modest room, he came up with amazing formulas that still puzzle the experts. The collection of his elegant formulas constitute the Mona Lisa of mathematics.

The science of mathematics abounds with perplexing yet elegant ideas. The idea of infinity represents their zenith. Some ideas are relevant to high school. If a teacher introduces them in a maths class together with relevant historic anecdotes, it can spice up the subject to a delicious degree.

Part II

Musings

Now I move from mainly describing life events to mostly giving views and opinions, from narration to reflection. My theme is education, on the personal and social fronts. These next three chapters discuss key educational issues arising from my schooling up to the high school level. I discuss my informal education within the family, the role of teachers, matters of race and education, national education policy and the teaching of mathematics in schools. Relevant episodes from my life are interspersed within the text.

— 9 —

Education and Family

The difference between school and life? In school, you are taught a lesson and then given a test. In life, you are given a test that teaches you a lesson.

Tom Bodett

❖ ❖ ❖ ❖ ❖ ❖ ❖

OUR PARENTS BEQUEATH us our life molecule, determine what we do in our early days and substantively affect our future. The family is our first school. Beside food choices, life style, language, practical skills and ways of thinking, we ingest values that mould our outlook on things around us. These values, though, do not breed in isolation, but derive from religion, community, media and other sources.

In this chapter, I reflect on how my parents, within the context of a community, affected my outlook on life, in both positive and negative ways. I do so with the understanding that we rarely possess a balanced view of family derived influences. Our memories of our dealings with our parents are laden with emotion. As such, they often are selective and biased. Nonetheless, as they generally are an integral component of our coming to age, as was the case with me, I am driven to bring them forth here.

Family Life

I often wished I had a sister. Though they never said the word, my parents treated their five sons with much love. Of family life in Lindi and early days in Dar es Salaam, my recall finds no incident of an antagonistic interaction with them. That is, apart from when my conduct was beyond the pale. Their prime concern was that we were well fed, in good health, went to school and the JK on time, and did not stay out late at night. Otherwise, we were left to our own devices. Mohamed, when not engrossed in crime and romance novels, was mostly not at home, presumably with friends. Nazir and I went about with the Undali Street gang. The two youngest, we generally ignored. Our cousins visited us periodically, and were welcomed and fed. It was much the same when we went to their homes.

My parents were not communicative persons. I rarely had an extended talk with them. You asked about something and got an answer. Otherwise, they talked and you listened. Mother sang the same song every day: do this, eat this, recite your prayers on time, don't climb the trees, don't play in the rain, etc. When a friend came home, her song was louder, making us unable to converse among ourselves. Father was open minded, and gave me more freedom to do what I wanted to do. Around that time, he taught me to drive, but I did not get a driving license until after I joined the university.

When I returned from Kibaha School in the last month of 1967, home life went on following the clock. My parents worked hard. After tending to his shop from early morning into the afternoon, father tinkered with his pickup truck, got supplies for the home, and helped out *Dadima* and others. Mother was perpetually holed up in the kitchen, squatting for hours on a small stool. Two stoves – charcoal and kerosene – alight nearby, the pan or pot sizzled or simmered with edible delights like *rotli, rotlo, puri, chilla, bajia, samosa, lapsi, mithi sev,* fried or spiced bananas, vegetable, beans or meat curry, plain or beans rice, *khitchdi* (rice and split mung bean paste), and other dishes. The days she fried egg plant, okra, potatoes and fish and served them with *khitchdi* or *chapati,* I was in heaven. With five hungry sons and a hardworking husband to feed, she cooked by the ton. Without fail, one plate was an offering for the JK. Later, in her late fifties, she developed a chronic cough. It was, I think, due to the volumes of noxious fumes she had inhaled in dedicated service to those she cared for.

One thing I now find odd is that we never sat down as a family for a meal. The children ate on their own – before school, after school, and after JK. Father had his meals by himself, and mother ate after everyone had eaten. If she made chicken curry, she gave the choicest pieces to her children and husband, and left the bony ones for herself. In June 1968, a month before I joined the university, I often visited Issa at his home. It was then that I met Farida, my future wife. I was pleasantly surprised to find that at lunch and dinner, the whole family sat at the table, and talked about personal and general issues. It was a gathering unknown in our abode.

Father brought home delicacies like Kraft Cheese, corned beef and sardines. We loved them but some were wont to take more than their fair share, a habit that did not sit well with me. Rafik had a marked tendency to grab a bigger chunk. He still remembers the angry glares he got from me. As in our Undali Street gang, I was a stickler for equality.

Every day, the family was at the JK by 6:30 pm and back home, except for me, or on sacred days, by 7:30. A quick supper, and it was time for bed. I returned just before my father set the radio dial to Radio Tanzania. There being no TV in Tanzania at that time, it was a ritual for the nation to listen to the 8 pm Swahili news bulletin and commentary. He sat on the floor slurping his dessert of papaya, banana and a pinch of milk. After everyone had retired upstairs, I would creep down to the living room, and read till mid-night or beyond. Mother would come down sometimes, and send me to bed with words to the effect that excessive reading puts sinful thoughts in the mind. She was quite prescient, though it was not at all in terms of the sins she had in mind.

But one thing was sadly amiss. Mohamed's schizophrenia progressed from bad to worse and took its toll. He did not complete secondary school. His mood swings turned extreme, making life at home erratic. When he was in a functional state, my father got him involved in different lines of work. A motor vehicle shop hired him as an apprentice mechanic. Later, he got his own furniture shop in Kariakoo. I sat with him at his shop. The effect each time was transient. At the outset he was attentive, and fared well. But his resolve slackened in a while, and he progressively receded into that unfathomable, distant galaxy of his own.

When his agitations intensified and turned violent, he was admitted to the psychiatric ward of the Muhimbili Hospital. This would begin a routine of daily visits, over a week or month, to give him food and change of clothing. In addition to potent drugs, he received electro-shock therapy. He was released when he was subdued. The cycle unfolded about every six to nine months. Seeing my gentle brother endure that horrible process over so many years has been one of the saddest things in my life.

Positive Lessons

What I learned from my parents came not so much from their words as from what they did. The way they lived their lives instilled five major values in my psyche: diligence, devotion to family, simplicity, frugality and generosity. For five decades, I saw them toil from dawn to dusk. But they hardly complained. What had to be done had to be done. They did not seek luxuries, but were content with basic necessities, and a little bit more. My father drank beer before lunch, but it was always one bottle. Even when out with his friends, it was the same story, one bottle and only one. I never saw him drunk. My mother loved chocolate flavored toffies and fruits like *bor* (jujubes). Her face lighted up whenever you gave her what she liked. But that seemed to be the limit of her desires.

Their philosophy towards money was: Every cent counts. Spend it with care, or save it. Not that they were stingy or miserly. The boys had adequate clothing and pocket money. Though we had limits, I never felt deprived. There was good food, in sufficient quantity, at the table every day. But none was wasted. Every morsel counted. Edible stuff was never thrown away. The leftovers were consumed by Mother, the house worker, beggars, cat, dog or chickens in the yard. Father kept everything – newspapers, paper and plastic bags, cans, bottles, torn clothing, etc. – for reuse or sale. An African vendor took the old cans to solder into kerosene lamps. Newspapers were wrapping material for street sellers. His single pair of shoes lasted for years; when a shoe was worn out or torn, it was re-stitched or repaired. The sturdy pair I brought for him from the US in 1988 was worn for nearly twelve years.

Father was not rich. But he generously assisted, in material and monetary terms, relatives and Ismailis facing hard times. He always paid his religious dues on time, and made regular monthly contributions to the Ismaili Welfare Society.

No words I have can capture the immensity of the energy my parents spent to further the welfare of the family. It was my father who primarily took care of his youngest sibling, my uncle Dawood, who suffered from epilepsy. As soon as he had sufficient funds, he set up a small shop for Dawood in a township near Lindi. Then he got him married – on an informal basis – to an African woman. The severity of *chacha's* illness, however, meant that neither the shop nor the cohabitation lasted beyond six months (Chapter 1).

My parents cared for Mohamed with utmost patience for thirty years. Whether he was very aggressive, made a stinky mess, or refused to do as told, in their eyes he remained an ill child who deserved kind attention. I was upset when Mohamed soiled the living room but not they. When he was admitted at an upcountry hospital, Father, then more than sixty five years old, would brave the hazardous bus trip to visit him, and send him supplies and food. At times the bus was filled over capacity, and he would stand during the six-hour rough ride.

Not infrequently, Mohamed went out and did not return for days. Father and I, if I was in town, scoured area police stations, hospitals and public places. It entailed a whole day's effort. Often, we returned empty-handed to face the sad eyes of Mother. The exercise was repeated the next day, and the next, until he was found. Half the time he came back on his own, ragged, hungry and exhausted. We rarely knew where he had been. As years went by, the effort they devoted to search for him did not diminish. When he returned, their joy was boundless. He was fed and feted like a prince. One fateful day in 1993, Mohamed departed from home, never to be seen again. An intense search, mounted with the help of relatives and friends, and extended with newspaper and radio announcements, failed to find him. He is unlikely to be alive; yet, for some three years, Mother kept on staring intently at the main door, hoping against all hope that her son would come knocking.

When her health began to fail after the year 2000, and she was bedridden, Father was at her side throughout the day, serving her with unparalleled devotion. In positive spirits, he cooked, fed her, kept her company and prayed with her. She was hospitalized with acute pneumonia in December 2003. Father was 84 years old, but still went to the hospital twice daily to feed her. One evening, as he was tired, he was advised to stay home. But he was not one to break the routine. A minibus rear ended his car just before he reached the place, landing him in the same hospital with severe bodily injuries and brain trauma. Mother passed away while he was unconscious in the emergency ward. It took him two years to make a modest recovery from his injuries. Now his memories are highly diminished, and he does not even remember Mother.

The laudable traits my parents displayed were those of their generation. But they adhered to them well. Values like kindness and simplicity are enshrined in the hymns composed by Ismaili saints, that are an integral part of daily JK prayers. The material things of life, they tell us, are a transitory fad. True joy and advancement comes not from the jewelry you own or the luxuriousness of your home, but from following the path of enlightenment. What is solid and eternal is the spiritual component of life, including devotion to the Imam. This is what my parents believed, and made a genuine effort to uphold in their daily lives.

A wall poster I once obtained in Los Angeles read

> *Live Simply That Others May Simply Live*

It remained on my wall for a long time. But my parents and their peers did not need a poster to put that precept into practice. It was an integral part of their life style. I think they can teach modern environmentalists many a sound practical lessons on how to take care of Mother Earth.

Like Father, Like Son: Among us brothers, the one who resembles Father the closest, in fact displays a spitting image, is the Munir, the youngest. Settled in Canada for nearly thirty years, he is a mechanic and has two sons, Alim (24) and Nadim (20). Like Father, he is devout, never missing the daily prayer sessions, be it snow or rain; works hard at his job and at home; prefers simple vegetarian meals; is frugal to the limit; dresses and lives in a plain style; and has a humble, considerate and friendly personality. Unfortunately, both his sons have been afflicted with severe autism since birth, and require continuous, close care and attention. In the same spirit as my parents displayed towards Mohamed, Munir has devoted his life to them and, at the same time, has remained a calm, cheerful and optimistic person. He did not fare well in formal education; but in terms of essential wisdom and fortitude, he outshines us all.

Negative Lessons

Yet it was not a tale sparkling only with roses. My father's generation at the same time exhibited traits that, from a moral and rationalist perspective, we would not like our children to possess. My parents also embodied these negative traits. The two I single out were vehement racism and parochialism, and dependence on rigid, traditionalist ways of thinking.

My parents grew up in an era when total separation between the races was a pervasive fact of life. The Aga Khans had urged the Ismailis in East Africa to adopt African children. But it was a token gesture with not more than 50 children adopted. These African Ismailis were integrated into community life, but they were the exceptions to the rule. In the colonial and early *Uhuru* days, the secular communal institutions like the Ismaili health and education facilities, and economic support organizations did not involve people outside of the community.

Ramzan Meghji was one of six brothers born into a mixed race family, his father being Asian Ismaili and mother, an African. Having grown up speaking Swahili, his command of Kutchi and Gujarati was distinctly poor. He told me how Ismaili children made fun of the way he and his brothers spoke Gujarati, and socially isolated them. It disturbed him a great deal and was the principal reason why he stopped going to the JK.

Fifty years after *Uhuru*, as their outward behaviour modified, the inner perspective of my parents and most Asians on race hardly budged. After I had made African friends at the DTC, I became sensitive to the way our African house and shop workers were treated. Not paid the minimum wage, itself not a living wage, they were given food about to go bad and spoken to in a harsh way at the smallest mistake or presumed mistake. Humans were denied decent food while delicious dishes daily went to the JK. I was of the view that our *Imam* would prefer that we better fed those who toiled hard for us. But if I gave a worker extra money or food, and my parents came to know, they made a face. You are making them too big headed, I was sternly told. They can get special stuff only on an occasion like *Eid*.

A common occurrence in the 1990s: Nizar Visram – an Asian friend – comes home. As is customary, I offer him a cup of tea and snacks. After he leaves, my mother complains:

> *Why did you not offer him more?, There is so much food in the kitchen.*

A week later, Joachim Mwami – an African friend – comes home. I offer him tea and snacks. After he departs, my mother complains:

> *Why did you give him so much? We need to keep some for your brother.*

For both I had put the same stuff on the table.

Aga Khan III and his successor strove to modernize out culture and life style. He promoted education and work opportunities for women, establishment of community health centres, Western mode of dress, and cooperative housing and economic ventures. While these ideas were accepted by my parents in theory, in practice, especially on health issues, contradictory traditional ideas often held sway.

While my parents had healthy dietary and lifestyle habits, their minds were closed to other views, unless presented by a missionary in the JK. Whether he felt unwell or not, Father had to visit a doctor every three months for an injection of penicillin. He had to have it, else he would get sick, he said. If the doctor did not give him what he wanted, he went to another one. Sometimes the doctor gave him a placebo injection. In his younger days, penicillin was the miracle cure for all ailments. That belief was irrevocably implanted in his mind.

My mother developed osteoarthritis of the knees in the 1980s. Dr Hassan Amir, a colleague of mine, and senior surgeon at the Muhimbili Hospital, came home, and carefully evaluated her. His advice was:

> *Ma, you should not take too many pain pills and lie in bed all the time. Try to stand up and walk around.*

Pointing to the indoor flight of stairs, he said:

> *Try to climb one step first. Do that for five days. Then try two steps. Do that for more days. When you can, climb three steps. You should tell yourself that after one year, I will go half the way.*

Dr Amir explained to me that her restricted mobility made the joints stiffen at a faster pace. Taking pain pills too often masked the deterioration. Over time she would require higher doses, and be susceptible to serious adverse effects.

Mother said she would follow his advice. After he left, my parents started to laugh:

> *What kind of doctor is this? Instead of medicine, injection or an operation, all he does is to tell us to climb stairs!*

The joke was repeated for months.

Subsequently, Mother's eye-sight began to fail. This time I took her to an eye specialist from the same hospital. After evaluating her eyes thoroughly, he told me,

> *Karim, I will be frank. She has advanced cataracts in both eyes. I can correct that easily. But she has macular degeneration in both eyes as well. It has progressed too far. I do not think anything can be done about it. Even if I replace her cloudy lens, her vision will not improve.*

When I conveyed the message to my parents, they dismissed it instantly. They wanted an eye operation, and did not get it. Since the specialist was an African, the racial mode of thinking surfaced.

> *What do these black doctors know? They are corrupt.*

But if the doctor was corrupt, he would have performed the eye surgery and pocketed the fees. Father did not see the stark contradiction in his statement.

Three years later, they secured their Canadian Immigrant Visa. To Father, Canada was Heaven and Tanzania was Hell.

> *Just wait and see,*

he told me,

> *In Canada, your mother will get brand new knees and her eyesight will be restored. She will walk and see again.*

With hopes raised high, they left for Vancouver in early 1995. Sadly, it was not to be. The orthopaedist who evaluated my mother said that her knee joints were too deformed, and her age and health condition contraindicated surgery. Perhaps climbing the stairs could have arrested the pace of the deterioration. Her Canadian eye doctor, however, was not an ethical person. He performed the cataract surgery, but did not mention the macular problem. Why miss the opportunity to make a fast buck on the back of this immigrant? Her eye sight not only did not improve, but she lost all vision in the eye that had some. Bitter and feeling let down, she became depressed. After two unhappy years, they returned to Dar es Salaam. Predictably, their experiences did not alter, even in a small way, their rigid views on life, race, health, Tanzania or Canada. It was the will of *Allah*, they declared, and went on with their daily routine of regular prayers and showering curses on the black people.

Mother Tongue

What is your mother tongue? When asked this question, I am at a loss. My first words were in Kutchi. I spoke in Kutchi with Mother but conversed in Gujarati with Father. He replied in Kutchi. Mother spoke in Gujarati with him but in Kutchi with us. My brothers and I talked in Kutchi in the early days, but switched to a mixture of English and Kutchi later on.

Kutchi is a dialect spoken in Kutch, a province of India from which many of the Ismailis had originated. It is the most common language in our homes. But our Kutchi is not the Kutchi of our ancestors. We employ it with Swahili, Arabic and English words. Our vocabulary is restricted, and we pronounce words and construct phrases in ways that may not sit well with a bona-fide resident of Kutch.

Other Ismailis came from Gujarat. They primarily speak Gujarati, a mature language with its own alphabet, numerical characters, an extensive body of literature and a strong tradition. But how they use it differs markedly from the original. In East Africa, it is combined with Kutchi, Swahili, Arabic and English terms. Our religious hymns – *Ginans* – are in Gujarati. But that is an erudite, poetic version of Gujarati not encountered in our daily lives.

My education until the fifth grade was in Gujarati. But all the rest of the way to my doctoral degree, I was taught in English. After primary school, I did not get or seek a chance to learn Gujarati further. I did not take to reading and writing in Gujarati. During the two decades I was in the US, my ability to read and write Gujarati deteriorated immensely and is abysmal at present. But I converse reasonably well in Gujarati. Of recent, I have begun to remedy the deficit and started reading material in that language.

Our prayers are in Arabic; but apart from having some familiarity with the English/Gujarati translations of the various sections of the prayers, the local Ismailis do not know much else about Arabic. Unlike other Muslims, they do not normally read or recite the Koran.

Movies from India have been a central part of the Asian culture in East Africa. The medium of the cinema screen thus exposed me to Hindi from a young age. But I have a mediocre grasp of this poetic, mature language with a long history. Like most local Ismailis, I neither read, write nor speak it with any degree of fluency, and understand it only to the extent that enables me to follow the action on the screen, and gauge the basic meaning and emotions in the songs.

The colonial era upbringing kept me away from Swahili until late in life. When I studied it at the DTC, the prevailing attitudes impeded my progress (Chapter 5). At the university, I took evening classes in the language for six months. It helped. Nowadays, I regularly listen to Swahili radio programs and read Swahili newspapers. I converse in it on a daily basis. Yet, my command of the principal language of my nation remains substandard.

My secondary and post-secondary education was in English. In secondary school I did not study English Literature. But I have been an avid reader of books in that language since middle school. Living in the USA for nearly two decades improved my English language skills markedly. Nevertheless, there remains an air of artificiality in my English expressions and speech. My vocabulary is not as vast or versatile as that of a native speaker. When I refer to artificiality, I do not refer to accuracy, but to ways of expressing things. My English has a professional flavour, not a home baked flavour. My US students tittered at how I pronounced some words. In Tanzania, my students strained to pick up my Americanized accent. In comparison, when I talk in Swahili, Kutchi or Gujarati, though my vocabulary is restricted and grammar questionable, I do not get that feeling of unnaturalness. What I say in those tongues comes more from the heart than just from the brain.

With this admixture of languages learned or imbibed in a partial or hodge-podge way, I am at a stage worse than a jack-of-all-trades and master of none. It is more like a pretentious jack-of-many-trades desperately attempting to master at least one trade, but just making wrong turns in the process. On top of this murky state of affairs, complications of a socio-cultural variety add to what language I use or do not use.

In the early 1970s, I developed a specific aversion to speaking in Kutchi with fellow Ismailis. I became sensitive to racist expressions. Terms learned from childhood like *golio* (dark man), *kario* (black person) and *salo janwar* (that animal) infuse our talk. So unless absolutely necessary, I did not use Kutchi. If my Ismaili friends spoke in Kutchi, I responded in English. I expressly told my wife that at home I would talk only in English or Swahili, but not in Kutchi. She does not like it, but has grudgingly though not wholly adapted to it.

Racism is not associated with one language only. English and French have been vehicles for propagating racial bigotry. In Apartheid South Africa, Afrikaans was a language of racist oppression. But we deal with what we face. I have found that if I talk with Ismaili or Asian friends in English or Swahili, the terminology is less racist and, ethically, is more palatable.

With Ismaili or Asian elders and those with a limited grasp of English, I use Kutchi or Gujarati. Until July 2009, this included my father. Now I mostly talk to him in Swahili. The change came about upon a series of sad but unacceptable incidents involving our house workers who care for him. He was quite angry and said,

Why do you talk the language of those people?

I replied that it was the language of our nation, a language that projects respect and dignity onto everyone. His reaction was to ignore my words. But it was the least I could do. We must honour our parents, appreciate the plight they face in old age and deal with them with due patience. But at the same time, we cannot sit back when we witness excessive humiliation imposed on fellow human beings on a regular basis. We have to draw a firm line somewhere.

Logical Thought ✤ ✤ ✤ ✤ ✤ ✤ ✤

Humans raise questions and seek explanations. They formulate ideas to guide action. From the stone age to the computer age, the growth of scientific and general knowledge shows us the successes so achieved. Nevertheless, even in this era of wide cell phone use, people continue to hold ideas and theories that are riddled with serious flaws. In particular, we generally draw erroneous conclusions when we are confronted with coincidences or unusual occurrences.

Take an event of early 1976. Farida, two year old Rosa and I were on a bus from Moshi to Dar es Salaam. When purchasing our tickets, I had selected seats in the middle, a location that promises the least bumpy ride. Strangely, another family had the same seat numbers, thus relegating us to the very last seat on the bus. And what a bouncy ride it was.

It had rained hard. The road was slippery, but the driver sped along. A third of the way, our bus skidded and was rammed in the middle by a truck laden with wood poles. People in the front and rear escaped serious injury, but of those in the middle, eight died on the spot, and a number sustained major injury. A couple had their limbs chopped off. More passed away either on the way to or in the hospital.

Awakened by the crash, Farida and I found ourselves jammed next to each other. The bus lay sideways; Rosa was not to be seen. In panic, we clambered out through the flung-open emergency door. A cry was heard; our baby was on a wet grassy patch about ten meters away with not a single scratch mark on her. Farida too was unhurt, but I had a long gash on the forehead and was bleeding profusely. It was later stitched up in the Korogwe Hospital. To this day, I am haunted by the piercing cries of the traumatized, dying patients on the ward beds next to mine.

Three months after this accident, one early morning Farida went to the kitchen to warm up milk for Rosa. Usually the hungry, impatient kid would follow her mother. But that day she remained in bed. Due to a leak in the stove, gas had accumulated in the enclosed area. The instant Farida struck the match, an explosion ensued. The next moment, I was rushing her to the hospital. With second and third degree burns on her legs, it took her months of fever and extreme pain to recover. Her left leg remained scarred.

Is Rosa an exceptionally lucky child? Was it an amazing blessing of luck that sent her and us to the back of the bus, ejected her safely during the accident and made her remain in bed the day the kitchen turned into an inferno? As parents, we are thankful to the force that may have overseen her safety. But what of the family that took our seat in the bus? Why had luck, chance or divine providence favoured us and not them?

Years later, on the day of her wedding, Rosa had a dental appointment. And it was precisely on that day that the dentist, an experienced professor of dentistry at a leading American university, made a major blunder, and caused her serious injury. Poor Rosa attended her wedding ceremony with a swollen mouth and in extreme pain. Should we say that her good luck had been exhausted? Or was it divine providence?

Is luck – bad or good – a term for chance or randomness? What is a random event? Is it an event that is inherently unpredictable? Or is it an event that we cannot predict on the basis of available information? Can the exact circumstances of an event like our accident and the gas fire be envisioned ahead of time? Is it possible to jointly predict the exact paths of a bus and a lorry traveling from distant places together with the duplication of seat numbers? That cannot be done even by the most powerful computers we can construct. Just too many factors affect the process. A small change in one, say the speed of the bus, can produce a decisive change in the outcome.

Randomness is an inextricable part of our natural, social and personal environments. It is not inherently good or bad; it is simply there. Not recognizing that fundamental property commonly leads to flawed inferences. We draw incorrect conclusions regarding cause and effect upon witnessing a series of coincidences. More often than we think, an amazing series of events can occur due to purely random fluctuations in the social or material environments.

Another error we make is to equate randomness with total disorder. That is also not so. For example, while the exact ways in which people express their views on a topic may differ, the gist of what they say has a common basis, and may derive from regular media sources. Random actions at the unit level often produce identifiable patterns at the aggregate level. While we cannot predict the outcome of a given journey, we can reasonably estimate the chance of an accident on a particular route. With sufficient, relevant data, we can estimate the increase or decrease in the accident risk during the rainy season or night trips.

Chance factors generally operate with systematic factors – a fundamental principle we fail to grasp. We are especially prone to make the error in relation to the outcome or diagnosis of a disease. If you mention a smoker who has lung cancer, the cynic retorts that his uncle smoked for a life time, yet died uneventfully in old age, or notes a man who succumbed to lung cancer but had never smoked. We confound plausibility with inevitability, and perceive complex events in simple, rigid binary terms.

The risk of lung cancer is affected by many factors. Say, the baseline annual risk of dying from lung cancer in a population is 1 out of 1,000. In a population of 1,000,000, a thousand people (give and take a few) are expected to die from it even if no one smokes. Say, chain smoking raises the risk of dying from lung cancer a hundred fold, that is, to 1 out of 10. If all smokers are chain smokers, and there are fifty thousand of them, the total number of deaths from lung cancer is expected to be

$$\frac{100}{1000} \times 50000 = 5000 \quad \text{among chain smokers}$$

and

$$\frac{1}{1000} \times 950000 = 950 \quad \text{among non-smokers}$$

The additional number of deaths per year then will be

$$5000 + 950 - 1000 = 4950$$

Nevertheless, there will be chain smokers who will not die from lung cancer and people who never smoked who will die from it. Smoking does not make it inevitable that your death will be caused by lung cancer; it increases the chance of that eventuality by a large margin.

In viewing our life occurrences, we play down random effects and consider other factors in a selective and biased manner. Say you get high marks in a maths examination for which you were quite unprepared. Still, you attribute the result to your ability. You do not say the questions by luck were on the topics you knew well. But if you fail the exam, you claim you had not slept well, or that the others had cheated. In a good outcome, we praise ourselves; in a bad one, we blame external factors. It enables us to retain our self-esteem. If you blame yourself too often, or if you totally side-line external factors, you build mental barriers that impede your progress in life. Psychologically edifying explanations maintain our peace of mind.

In general, we view evidence in ways that support our beliefs and question what we doubt. If it favours what we deem valid, we accept it at face value and if it does not, we set it aside. Whether or not we rush to judgment depends on the outcome, not on the reliability of the evidence, or of the process which produced it.

In the colonial era, the government officials, Christian missionaries and Asians believed that African children were naturally inferior. To invest more funds in 'native' education was thus felt to be a waste of time and resources. But such racist beliefs emanated from superficial observations and illogical thinking, and served to rationalize the unequal educational and social system of the day.

Let us consider one scenario that can give rise to such a view. Take a hypothetical case. A total of 11,000 students sit for the Form IV maths examination in 1961. Say, 3,940 or 36% pass, and the pass rates differ by race. There are 1,000 Asian and 10,000 African candidates. The pass rate for Asians is 74% but for Africans, it is 32%. The details appear below.

Performance by Race			
Race	Pass	Fail	Total
Asian	740 (74%)	260 (26%)	1000
African	3200 (32%)	6800 (68%)	10000
Overall	3940 (36%)	7060 (64%)	11000

My uncle looks at these results and loudly declares,

Africans are not capable of understanding mathematics.

For him, it is a clear proof of what he firmly believes. Nothing more needs to be said, it is the end of the story.

A survey by an education scholar finds that there are two types of schools: Well Endowed Schools and Poorly Endowed Schools. The former has the needed, qualified maths teachers, adequate supply of books, and a good system of administration. In the latter, maths teachers are in short supply and are not well qualified, and a shortage of text books prevails. Plus, they are poorly managed. He compares the performance of Asian and African students by school type and finds the results shown in the table on the next page.

From this table, we see that in the Well Endowed Schools, the pass rate is 80%, overall and for each race. In the Poorly Endowed Schools, it is only 20%, but again, does not vary by race. Looking at the evidence closely, the conclusion is unmistakable: what affects outcome of the exam in a decisive way is not the race of the candidate, but the type of school he/she attends.

African candidates, who are ten times as many as the Asian candidates, mostly (or 81%) attend Poorly Endowed Schools. But only a small proportion (9%) of Asians attend such schools. If we overlook this basic fact, we arrive at a biased, flawed conclusion.

Not everyone in the good schools passes and not everyone in the deficient schools fails. Some good school candidates fail and poorly endowed school candidates pass. This gives us an additional message: Besides the quality of the teachers and schools, other factors, like personal motivation and parental status, as well as random effects can and do influence the examination outcome.

Performance by Race and School Type

Well Endowed Schools

Race	Pass	Fail	Total
Asian	720 (80%)	180 (20%)	900
African	1600 (80%)	400 (20%)	2000
Overall	2320 (80%)	580 (20%)	2900

Poorly Endowed Schools

Race	Pass	Fail	Total
Asian	20 (20%)	80 (80%)	100
African	1600 (20%)	6400 (80%)	8000
Overall	1620 (20%)	6480 (80%)	8100

In general, when we gather information to assess if the outcome A is or is not caused by a factor B, we must pose several key questions:

➢ Is the information relevant and comprehensive?
➢ Is it reliable or laden with major errors?
➢ Does it emanate from a representative sample?
➢ Was the sample of subjects sufficiently large?
➢ Have natural time trends been considered?
➢ What other factors are of relevance here?
➢ Have their effects been allowed for?
➢ Has random variation been taken into account?

Even if we find good justification to infer A is related to B, it may not be a cause and effect type of link, or there may be hidden causes behind the surface level cause. Students who turn in their homework regularly do well in the examination. But the students who do not do so live a long distance away, or lack electricity at home. So it is not just that the student who seems to work hard gets a high exam grade. Another student who is equally inclined to work hard is exhausted by the long trip to the school and back, faces dim or no lights upon arrival at home, and thus is unable to submit his homework in a timely fashion. His exam performance is thereby affected.

For my parents' generation, life and life events were explained by resorting to ideas like will of God, luck, predestination, racial superiority and so on. If we remain glued to that form of thinking, it will spell a disaster for our nation. My generation attempted to go beyond it, but not with much success. We only took half-hearted measures. The education system in the early post-*Uhuru* days made progress in instilling scientific ways of thought. But then it got stuck, and reversed course. Now that system not only teaches practical matters in a deficient way, but also it does not promote a rational, scientific way of analysing issues.

Our children need bolder steps to transcend simplistic explanations in personal, general and national affairs. They need to learn well the natural and social sciences. In health matters, for example, they need to appreciate that diseases have varied causes that require specific actions for prevention and treatment. The scientific way of thinking has to guide lives and the development of the nation. Poverty, ill health, inequality and injustice can be tackled only through the adoption of an evidence-based, logical approach toward every issue of public interest. That approach will also assist us to recognize and avoid flawed policies and to combat prejudice, societal bias, discrimination and similar ills.

An integral aspect of promoting rational, scientific perspectives in social affairs and personal lives is to devise a sound strategy to teach maths in schools and higher education. We need to bear in mind that high levels of numerical literacy, general literacy and civic literacy are the three complementary educational pillars of a just, democratic and economically progressive social system.

— 10 —

Education and Community

*The whole purpose of education is to
turn mirrors into windows.*
Sidney J Harris

THOUGH THE PAST CANNOT be relived, it may be revived in our memories. That revival may, however, accurately portray or woefully distort our life story. How we bend our recall is not just a function of our mental powers, or the quality of the records we have. Our social environment is, as noted earlier, a cardinal factor.

That is what I found when I talked to people about the history of education and its relation to race and religion during the colonial and early *Uhuru* days. Most viewed the matter from a personal or communal angle. They drew major conclusions from selective events which, moreover, were recalled inaccurately. Such tendencies prevail not only among Asians, but also among Africans, and even among seasoned academics. Education has become a fertile ground for simple and convenient narratives of dubious validity.

In this chapter, I present an alternative that queries these parochial views. My approach is based on the facts of history. However, given the nature of this book, it lacks the rigor of a scientific analysis. For a glimpse into a scientific approach to analyse social issues, see the last part of Chapter 9 dealing with logical thought.

Education after Independence

My primary schooling occurred in the homogenized company of brown faced students and teachers. I had one African classmate in middle school, but we did not become friends. At that time, I could not visualize an African teacher. My bias reflected the realities. On the morrow of *Uhuru*, a mere twenty African graduate level teachers taught in the secondary schools across the nation, constituting less than 2% of the national pool of well qualified teachers. Just at the Aga Khan schools in Dar es Salaam, there were more than twenty well qualified Asian and European teachers.

Uhuru saw the inception of a single nationwide secular system of schools. Race, ethnic and religion based control over education diminished. All subjects acquired common syllabuses. History, geography and literature featured relevant content. Swahili was taught in all the schools. New schools were built. The existing ones were expanded. More boarding schools were established. School funds were allocated on fairer terms. The entry system became merit oriented. Teacher training was stepped up, and a uniform scheme of service for teachers was established.

The student bodies increasingly reflected the ethnic, religious and racial diversity of the nation. That a good number of the youth interacted in a multicultural environment promoted tolerance and harmony, and cemented bonds of national unity. This was seen, for example, when I was at Kibaha School. While regional, racial and religious imbalances did not vanish as such, the nation was making strides in the right direction.

Implementation of the new educational policy was not without glitches. The dearth of local experts and the enormity of the task made serious problems unavoidable. The short term achievements nonetheless were nothing to scoff at. In 1959, a mere 89 persons got primary school teacher training at the Grade A level; by 1966, it had risen to 720. Secondary school enrolment in 1962 was about 12,000; by 1967, there were twice as many, 25,000. Different types of institutions of higher education were also established across the nation.

In sum, the 1960s witnessed substantial educational progress. Opportunities for all societal groups expanded. The system began to embody greater social fairness and to cater for the needs of a developing nation. It was a remarkable contrast with the minimal and biased pace of educational change in the 1950s (Cameron and Dodd 1970; Resnick 1968).

These changes affected my life trajectory in a decisive manner. I say without hesitation that to me personally the effects were wholly beneficial. These policies ensured that I obtained high quality, free education of the type I wanted, and in places of my choosing. I have the solid impression that my fellow Asian peers who put in due effort in their studies also garnered similar rewards.

Before I elaborate on this point, let me place the matter in a broader context. The process of converting an educational system that has been organized along race or ethnic based lines into a fair and just system has never been a smooth one. The beneficiaries invariably oppose any step to rectify the situation. That challenge has been faced in many nations. For example, when the process of desegregating the entrenched racist system of education in the USA began in the 1950s, a violent backlash from the white community ensued. As black school girls and boys were harassed and murdered, the scale and brutality of the reaction took the world at large by surprise.

The Tanzanian Asians were predictably angered by the state takeover of their schools. The prevailing sentiment was:

We built them. They should build new schools, not target ours. This move will only lower the high educational standards we have attained with major effort and expenditure.

Pointing to such policies, they exclaimed,

> Look, Nyerere is anti-Asian. He utters grand words but in reality, he
> is a racist.

Such views dominated Asian thinking then, and unfortunately, they persist to this day. The fact of the matter is among the schools taken over by the state, a half or more were mission schools. Did that imply that Nyerere was anti-Christian? Some Christians said he was! To interpret education policy in purely racial or religious terms is to distort history. The aim of the new policy was to set up a common system of education for all the children of Tanzania. In light of the long colonial history of discrimination, and objectively, it was a morally necessary and practically desirable move that deserved the support of all parents in the nation.

The issue of education was connected with two key issues that came to the forefront after *Uhuru*: Citizenship and the rights of citizens. As I noted in Chapter 6, the Asians of mainland Tanzania had the option to apply for citizenship within two years. The social context, however, complicated this process. The role played by Asians in facilitating colonial domination and their exclusivity made most people view them with hostility. Antagonism of this form has been seen in colonies across the world. Often, the brown man or middleman was hated more than the white man.

The decision to offer citizenship to Asians was not a popular one. Influential actors in TANU and outside opposed it. They wanted rapid Africanization of the civil service and the major institutions of the economy and society. They argued that those who had unjustly benefited from colonial rule and had stood on the side-lines in the fight for freedom should not reap the rewards that came with it. These exclusionary voices resonated far and wide. Only a handful of prominent personalities, led by Mwalimu Nyerere, opposed them. His view was that a policy based on explicit racial categorization went against the main principles that had driven the struggle for Independence. From the outset, he opposed racial favouritism in any sector of society and government, and consistently maintained that stand.

Africanization was an official policy only for the first two years after *Uhuru*. As soon as the transition period came to an end, Mwalimu issued a directive that stated that it was dead. This move was in contrast to the other East African nations, Uganda and Kenya, where Africanization was implemented rigorously, and which saw a greater exodus of their Asian communities.

To the fervent Africanizer, Mwalimu was a pro-Asian politician. If what they advocated had come to pass, the Asians of Tanzania would have landed in a steamy political soup. It thus speaks volumes to the sagacity of the people of Tanzania that, despite their deep misgivings regarding Asians, they backed Mwalimu, and not the populist politicians who opposed his liberal stands on citizenship, race, education and employment.

Ismailis and Education
The British aimed to construct a three-tier race-based system in Tanzania, with separate schools for white, brown and black people. For the Asians specifically, local colonial officials strove to establish a unified Indian education system for

all their communities. But this plan was not accepted by Aga Khan III and the Ismaili leaders. They sought separate schools for the Ismailis that would be controlled and funded by themselves. Because of the influence Aga Khan III exercised at the UK Foreign Office, which saw him as a major ally in its geopolitical strategy, the local officials were obliged to permit the Aga Khan system of schools and even provide it financial subventions. In some towns in Tanzania, this move led to discord between Ismailis and other Asian communities (Paroo 2012).

An Aga Khan school was built in most major towns. Until 1935, these schools did not enrol children from other Asian communities. African children were not enrolled until the 1950s. But until 1961, the multiracial, non-denominational setup of these schools was never more than a minor affair. Apart from the towns where no other school for Asians existed, up until 1961, some 90% of their students were Ismailis. They also took up unqualified Ismaili students. These students with very poor grades were put in the D or E stream. African students were always a token presence, only one or two faces now and then. The morning prayers were based on Ismaili beliefs, similar to the practice in the Christian mission schools.

This system, however, yielded substantial dividends for the Ismailis. Thus at the dawn of *Uhuru*, it stood head and shoulders above other Asian communities in terms of education. Further, Aga Khan III had placed special emphasis on education for girls. That my mother reached secondary grade II in the 1940s is illustrative; until the late 1950s, non-Ismaili Asians girls rarely went beyond primary school. On the promotion of gender parity in education, Aga Khan III was undoubtedly more broad-minded and far-sighted than the colonial authorities were.

Aga Khan IV, who inherited the *Imamat* in 1957, continued the emphasis on education but with a difference. His pronouncements stressed racial inclusiveness as well. Thus, on the issue of education, the Ismailis witnessed a convergence of the communal and national policies. This earlier mentioned point deserves to be stated again. From that time, the pronouncements of the national leadership mirrored the spiritual guidance from Prince Karim Aga Khan. The latter urged them to acquire citizenship and express genuine loyalty towards their homeland. He was a distinguished guest at the *Uhuru* ceremonies, where he was seen to be on good terms with Mwalimu Nyerere. His sermon to his followers in Dar es Salaam on that day expounded that theme in unmistakable terms.

> *For years now, my grandfather and I have advised you that sustaining the dignity of your nation, working diligently for its progress, and taking pride in national matters are essential things. While you have well adhered to our words, it is my desire that you adhere to them more faithfully. You should all the time keep in mind the need to fulfil your duties towards your country, to work hard for it, and to live for the sake of it. I shower you with my blessings.*
>
> Prince Karim Aga Khan

Though barely twelve years old, I recall those words vividly. They planted the seeds of a nationalistic spirit in my young mind, and encouraged Ismailis to apply for citizenship. And, in a short while, most of them became citizens.

Citizenship was not just a formality. It promised and gave concrete rights and real benefits, irrespective of race, religion or ethnicity. This was acknowledged by Aga Khan IV in the interview I quoted in Chapter 6 (Ladha 1970). He stated that because his followers had acquired citizenship in higher numbers, they, unlike other Asian groups, had not been that adversely affected by the rules and laws that favoured citizens over non-citizens.

The synergy between the edict of Aga Khan IV and national policy was particularly marked in the arena of education. The issue of teacher training illustrates the point. From the time of the *Uhuru* ceremony, he began to steer young Ismailis towards teaching. His speech to the students of the AKBS, at which I was likely present, but of which I lack recall, identified teaching as a noble calling. The message to the Ismaili youth could not have been firmer. He went on reiterating the same point over the next few years.

I quote his words from 3 December 1964. Announcing a major expansion to the system of Aga Khan schools in Pakistan, he said:

> *It is my special wish that my spiritual children become teachers. For some years now, my spiritual children in East Africa have been doing precisely that. ...... [M]y spiritual children who teach religious and secular subjects are the valiant pioneers of our community. ...... It will make me immensely happy to find my spiritual boys and girls resolving to enter this noble and wonderful line of work.*

> Prince Karim Aga Khan

For the Ismaili youth, it was not pure worldly advice. It was a holy edict, a sacred duty which inspired and influenced many Ismailis of my generation.

Around the same time, the Tanzanian Ministry of Education unfolded a multi-year education plan, in which expansion of teacher training was a central component. New training colleges were opened up and recruitment at the existing ones was boosted.

Not all of the Ismaili students completing Form IV had grades high enough to enrol in Form V. Previously, they would join their family business or seek employment. Now, as citizens, they were eligible for the teacher training programs. Many applied; many were accepted. Of the entering batches at some of the main teacher training colleges – Changombe, Morogoro and Mpwapwa – in the early 1960s, up to a fifth were Ismailis. Girls almost equalled boys. No other Asian community was that well represented in these colleges.

And it went beyond teacher training. Asian, and particularly Ismaili, students joined nurse and health related training schools, business colleges, technical institutions and agricultural training centres. Most of the Ismaili students who finished Form VI joined the University of East Africa. Those who studied at the Dar es Salaam campus later became secondary school teachers in science and arts subjects, economists, lawyers, librarians, finance officers, social and political scientists; those who studied at the Nairobi campus became civil, mechanical, electrical and electronic engineers; and those who went to the Makerere campus became doctors, dentists, pharmacists, and health related professionals. Some were sent for higher degree studies and became university lecturers.

These Asian students, like African students, received good quality education that was paid for by the government of Tanzania. In many higher education institutions, their presence was at a level higher than their relative presence in the population. For instance, the Tanzanian Asian students at the University College of Dar es Salaam in my day were up to one eighth of all the Tanzanian students. The corresponding ratios for Tanzanian students at the Nairobi and Makerere campuses were higher. And the majority of them were Ismailis. Even for the very bright Ismaili students but from poor families, scaling such heights was a dream in the colonial era; *Uhuru* made it a reality.

Upon successful graduation they, like African graduates, were hired by the government into the civil service, teaching, medical service or professional work in the expanding para-statal sector. Given the state of our nation, the salary was modest, but work benefits like low rent housing, free health care, annual paid leave, generous maternity leave for females, free transport to place of work, etc. were nothing to scoff at. Asian professionals accompanied the para-statal director or senior ministry official on overseas business trips, and qualified Asians were sent for higher study abroad under state organized schemes.

Again consider the broader context. Nations with a history of social imbalances have often adopted measures to rectify them. Affirmative action was deployed to deal with gender bias and racial discrimination in the USA; in India, it was used to improve the economic status of the so-called untouchables; and in South Africa, to correct the inequities of Apartheid rule. Those who had received unfair levels of benefit in the past opposed the step, branding it reverse discrimination. In reality, remedial measures of some form are not only ethically unavoidable, but are also essential for long term social harmony.

Africanization was a form of affirmative action. In Tanzania, it was in place only in the first two years of Independence. I do not say that we had a perfect system. Many instances of favouritism based on race, tribal origin, religion, social class and political connections did occur. But there was no policy to that effect. No data showing systematic bias against the Asians in education and employment exist. Those who proclaim that it existed can only note a few anecdotes, or quote the words of political figures. They do not differentiate between measures that favour citizens against non-citizens and those that favour a particular race as such; measures that target an economic stratum and those that target a racial or ethnic group. They forget that Africans had been the victims of serious, legalized discrimination just a few years back, and that the Asians had benefited substantially from it. Further they ignore the fact that even after *Uhuru*, many Asian employers continued to have double standards for Africans in terms of salaries and appointment to senior level positions.

Any objective evaluation worth its salt would demonstrate that the Asian youth who were citizens derived substantial benefits from the post-*Uhuru* policies, and they did so to a degree that exceeded their numeric level in the population. If there was affirmative action, it had a marginal impact indeed.

The thesis of anti-Asian bias in education and the occupational disposition of the graduates is a flawed thesis. In the first decade of *Uhuru*, a merit based system prevailed. You were judged on the basis of your grades and performance. Black and brown Tanzanians secured similar treatment. If there were practical problems, of which there were plenty, all suffered similarly. If there were delays in payment of teacher salaries, Asian and African teachers bore the consequences together.

Things began to change from the 1970s. From around the middle of that decade, education in Tanzania experienced major setbacks. Quality and standards declined. It is in fashion to ascribe that outcome to the state takeover of schools. But that is an erroneous view. If you pursue the matter in scientific terms, you find major structural causes behind the reversal. The negative trend in education was seen across the Third World. Identifying the principal causes needs careful study and analysis. I partly look at this issue in the next chapter. But for now I say this. That poverty among African Americans in the US intensified after the abolition of slavery or that South Africa is still afflicted with stupendous problems does not mean that either slavery or Apartheid was an acceptable societal arrangement in any shape or form. Similarly, there was no moral basis to the race and religion based elitist education system instituted by the British in the colonial era. It was a profoundly immoral set up and had to go.

I firmly hold that Tanzanians of all backgrounds must extend heartfelt gratitude to Mwalimu Nyerere for overseeing that process and implementing the construction of a national system of education in a wise and egalitarian manner. And personally, I owe an immense debt to him and the people of Tanzania for providing me, free of charge, the wonderful educational opportunities that have made me who I am today.

Convergence

As the Asian youth of Tanzania benefited in substantive and disproportionate ways under the new educational policy, opportunities hard to come by during the colonial rule opened up. Higher benefits accrued especially to the Ismaili youth. The number of Ismaili teachers, doctors, dentists, engineers, economists, civil servants and professionals in the decade prior to Independence could be counted by the fingers of one hand. But the decade thereafter churned them out by the score. Educated freely by the public, they were engaged, like other Tanzanians of similar educational background, to serve the nation. It was not a state of high affluence, but neither was it a state of systematic discrimination or exclusion.

Interacting with African Tanzanians in schools, colleges and at places of work on an equal footing brought forth a change, gradual but on-going, in their attitudes. The Asians of my father's generation remained stuck in racist modes of thinking. But my peers were opening their hearts and minds and adopting an inclusive outlook. Life was not a paradise; it was challenging, frustrating too. Yet, compared to the convulsions in other African nations, the harrowing racial antagonisms in the USA, violent religious strife in India, the mass murders of the Chinese in Indonesia, or the expulsions in Uganda, it was a harmonious and tranquil state of being.

Despite the strong antipathy between the adults of the Asian community and the political establishment, among the youth from all races, religions and communities, the colonial era exclusionary attitudes were on the wane. I give an outstanding example of this tendency in the section after next.

Divergence

Life too often severs close knit-bonds and derails sublime trends. Promising prospects can unexpectedly reverse. That occurred in Tanzania too. The picture of convergence described above did not persist and actually began to unravel from the early 1970s. The gap between my two universes began to widen in terms of physical proximity, world outlook and national affiliation. And it became an unbridgeable gap after the life changing decision taken by the majority of the Ismailis in Tanzania to leave the country for good.

The hopeful vision expressed by Aga Khan IV in his 1970 interview transmogrified into its opposite in just two years. Intense gravitational surges from previously undetected masses of dark matter decoupled the anticipated stability. In the ensuing disequilibrium, most of my JK based friends were catapulted to locations light years away. By the early 1980s, most of them were not only not in Tanzania, but also not in Africa. No more citizens of this fine land, they and their families were scattered, essentially upon their own volition, across Canada, the UK and the USA. The rest were settled in other equally distant lands.

Numbers reveal the scale of the transformation. In the mid-1960s, roughly 35,000 Ismailis resided in Tanzania. By the year 2014, they had dwindled to no more than 4,000. And some of the latter are citizens of Canada, here temporarily on a business venture. There remains but one Ismaili family in Lindi, a far cry from the past. The JK where I prayed as a child was given to a charitable group. And so a galaxy of my childhood universe vanished into the thin air.

The Arusha Declaration of 1967 was the key trigger in the eventual turn of events. It made Socialism and Self-Reliance the creed of the nation. Major firms, industries, farms and banks were taken over by the state. Commercial and rental buildings, and large property owners were similarly affected in 1971. This policy also put strong emphasis on cooperative farming and control over the wealth acquired by political leaders.

In theory, it was a positive move, an essential step for overcoming neo-colonial dependency, promoting genuine development and improving the lives of the people. At the outset, it was a popular policy. It must be stressed that the policy was not aimed against any race, religion or ethnic group, but derived from the principles of social justice and economic equality.

Apart from supportive public relations pronouncements, the Asians did not react towards it with favour. Neither did the leaders of the main Christian denominations. They castigated it as a step towards communism. Predictably the major capitalist powers like the UK and USA disliked it as well.

While major multinational firms had sizable investments in Tanzania, among the locals, the business, property, farm and factory owners were mainly of Asian origin. And these wealthy Asians were the leaders and influential lights in their communities. Their decisive weight made political moves affecting their interests to be seen as moves affecting the community or Asians in general. Such skewed thinking led most Asians to regard nationalization as a move against Asians as such. The mood was more sombre among the Ismailis. They had acquired citizenship at a higher rate, and had established a deeper socio-economic foothold in the nation. Seen objectively, the move was an expression of the conflict between a rising local middle class and the colonial era middlemen. It was basically an economic conflict. Leading lights, however, portrayed it as a racial conflict, and the Asian youth were taken in by that way of framing the issue.

Another thing that is often ignored in the prevailing narratives extolling Asian investments in post-*Uhuru* Tanzania is that most Asian businessmen of any standing engaged in illegal transfer of funds abroad. Some communities did that on a greater scale than other communities; but it was a part of the game for all, thus depriving a young nation of needed capital. For example, I know that my father sent some US $5000 to a relative in London in 1970. Also, like all enterprises, Asian firms also benefited from a very low paid labour force.

The racially based perception about *Ujamaa* did not accord with the facts on the ground. During the forced villagizations, ordinary African villagers suffered much more than any Asian ever did. Further, I would say that 90% of the Asians were not affected by the nationalization of industries and houses. Most of them were owner occupiers or renters. As such, they were not the targets here. Those whose flats were nationalized in error eventually got them back.

For example, my family lived in an owner occupied two story flat. My father ran a wholesale produce shop with three employees. The nationalizations did not affect him. The flat that I occupy now was nationalized by mistake. But it was returned, and I have the title deed to it. My brothers and I, like all citizens, remained eligible for free education up to the university level, and had good job prospects in the expanding state entities. We continued to get free health care at governmental facilities as well. And that was the story for the majority of the Asian youth who were citizens.

Nothing is perfect. Individuals faced obstacles which were, rightly or wrongly, ascribed to racial, religious or tribal factors. But it was a multi-sided affair, with the Asians continuing to discriminate against Africans in business and job allocation. I surmise that official actions in education and employment until around 1973 were by and large merit based. Overt racial bias was a small and unofficial part of the story. Race based considerations came into play after hundreds of Asian employees in the state sector, including teachers, began to abandon their posts, tore up their contracts, and disappeared abroad without warning.

The nationalization of commercial buildings in 1971 was the last straw that set in motion the mass exodus of Asians, particularly Ismailis, from Tanzania. Just ten years earlier, in the wake of the spiritual edict to make Tanzania their homeland, they had taken the lead in the acquisition of citizenship. Now they paradoxically led the emigration from Tanzania. It was a sorry time for me: I witnessed one friend after another, one relative after another, packing his or her bags, and departing forever from their decades old abodes.

Consequently, we have the situation in 2014: About 90 percent of my relatives and Ismaili friends reside in Canada. A smaller number are in the US and the UK. Two of my brothers are settled in Canada and Rafik lives in the USA, though Rafik remains a Tanzanian citizen and regularly comes here to work on water development projects. My parents were twice admitted into Canada as landed immigrants. Unable to adapt to the Western way of life, each time they returned within a couple of years. Mother passed away in 2003. My ninety-five year old father stays with us in Dar es Salaam. He is in a frail state of health.

For my part, from 1980 onwards, I studied and worked in the USA for about 18 years, and returned in 2004. My daughter, her husband and two lovely grandchildren are US citizens, and reside in Los Angeles. The only thing Farida and I regret is that our grandchildren are so far away.

Despite the difficulties of starting afresh in a strange land, many of the Asians from Tanzania who migrated abroad in the 1970s did well in life. Hard work and persistence helped them obtain good jobs or set up successful business ventures. The solid educational foundation acquired from Tanzania served them well. Their children obtained high academic qualifications in science and the arts from prominent universities; a number distinguished themselves in their fields. For Ismailis in particular, overall it is a story of a community that has prospered, and at the same time, has managed to retain its cultural heritage.

But there is a curious aspect to this: While they had praised the communal based, private education system of the past in Tanzania, in Canada, the UK and the US, their children benefit from state run and funded education systems that are multiracial and multi-cultural. Calls for separate Aga Khan schools were not heard in those places. If they had been made, their legality and moral standing would have been called into question.

Not that the land in which they landed is a racial nirvana. These countries, including the UK, Canada and the USA, continue to function under the rubric of institutionalized racism and religious bigotry. They are divided societies in the arena of education, work, residence and political positions. Having taught at US universities for nearly two decades, I have experienced it first-hand. In the media and among politicians, anti-immigrant, racist type of rhetoric rears its ugly head periodically. Asians in the UK, for example, face violent attacks from white skinheads. The scale and rootedness of racism in all sections of the US justice and education system is enormous. Look up the appropriate news sources and you will be astonished. If the Asians of Tanzania thought they were escaping racism, they went to the wrong places.

The migration of locally trained professionals from Tanzania in the 70s was mainly an Asian affair. But it is not so any longer. Tanzanian professionals of all races now seek opportunities for relocating outside on a permanent basis. It was a common goal for my post-graduate students at the Muhimbili University. In a nation beset with an acute shortage of trained medical staff, about 8% of the local doctors, of all races, tend to move on to greener pastures. Of those who remain, about 40% cease to practice clinical medicine after a short while (Kisanga 2013; Msonsa 2013; Songa wa Songa 2013). Needless to say, the best and most qualified brains show a greater tendency to depart.

What in my days was a predominantly *Muhindi* affair, is currently a colour-blind matter. Children of the well to do – African or Asian – seek a way out. I meet many African friends whose children have settled in the UK, USA and other places. I am not saying that it is a bad or a good thing. My point is that economic motives rather than racial factors play a greater role in social affairs.

To reiterate, the fundamental issue is not (and was not then either) a matter of skin colour; it is (and was then as well) a matter of economics. It was largely a question of putting self-interest above national interest. A black person can be a patriot, and a brown person can be a patriot; a black person may not care about his/her nation, and a brown person may not care about his/her nation. It makes no moral or practical sense to judge people according to their race, religion or similar feature. We should judge people individually, by their deeds, over the short and long terms. The sooner we learn to view social issues in broader, factual lines, the better we will be able to deal with the underlying problems.

A Model Teacher

Social contradictions generate forces that propel individuals in directions beyond their control. The sweep is broad and strong. Oftentimes, a large group finds itself relocated far from its place of origin. At times they are forced to move; at times they chose to move; but usually it is a combination of both.

In societal acts, the matter of personal responsibility, especially for acts that harm other human beings, cannot be overlooked. Yet, in general, the blame game does not lead us far. History takes its own course. Individuals face daunting choices that pit personal, family, communal, professional, or national interests and duties against one another. Persons of noble bent are swept away by a surging tide. Under those conditions, who am I to say to anyone that you should or should not have done this or that?

Yet, I raise an analogy. When a serious problem afflicts your home, it behoves you to work with your family to resolve it. You do not run away; you do not abandon your folks to their own fate. The precept enunciated by Aga Khan III – *Struggle is the Meaning of Life* – implies that in times of trouble, you struggle with your fellow humans for the sake of the common good. It has resided in my brain since I was a young boy, and in my view, it applies in the context of our national family as well.

A few brave souls defy misguided hysteria even in times of major societal stress. They swim against the tide and remain faithful to their ideals. In order to work towards a more hopeful future, and in its own right, we have to acknowledged such people, and hold up their fine example.

I have in mind my UDSM roommate, Nazir Virji who completed his BA degree in literature and education in 1971. Like any other Tanzanian graduate, he had signed a five-year work contract with the government. This included a two-year national service engagement. Nazir was assigned to teach English Literature at the Dodoma Secondary School, a few miles from his home town. He was lucky and glad because Dodoma is where he had grown up and that school was exactly where he had wanted to plant his feet.

When Farida and I visited him in September 1973, we found him in merry spirits. He had a spacious two-bedroom house adjacent to the school that had a large backyard. Rent, water and electricity came to ten percent of his salary of about TSh 1,200 per month. Though the pay was the equivalent of about US $120, it sufficed for a decent life. He told me that he managed to save nearly a fourth of his earnings.

His living room was scattered with books by Dickens, Brecht, Hardy, Ayi Kwei Amrah, Ngũgĩ wa Thiong'o, Ousmane Sembène and others. This fellow truly enjoyed reading and teaching that kind of stuff. Apart from harsh complaints about the ministerial bureaucracy in delivery of school supplies, he was the same jolly guy I had known earlier. With his broad-minded patriotic outlook and cooperative spirit, he got along well with his fellow teachers. His kind and gentle demeanour, and hardworking ethos made him a popular and respected teacher.

But Farida and I were worried. He had been afflicted with insulin dependent diabetes since childhood. We felt he was not careful about his own health and personal affairs and needed a person to reside with him to oversee his nutritional and health needs, and keep his place in order. We found the kitchen in disarray, bedrooms dusty, and piles of stuff strewn around, and spent our first two days returning a semblance of order to his house. His relatives in Dodoma town had urged him to keep a house worker, and had a found a suitable person for the job. But Nazir was a stubborn fellow. He relished his independence from restrictive cultural norms and family practices. Further, he insisted on doing everything at his home by himself. Our imploring was to no avail. *You worry needlessly*, he told us.

But we should have been more worried. Just six months after we saw him, Nazir was found frozen stiff one grim morning by a fellow teacher who had come to find out why he had not shown up for class. At night, he had sunk into a diabetic coma. All he needed was a sugary drink, but was not able to access it on time. Had another person been around, the episode would have been a minor footnote in his life. Instead, it marked his ultimate day on planet earth.

Nazir had options, other choices. His sister who was settled in England wanted to facilitate his entry into that country. Like many of his Ismaili peers, he could have gone to Canada. But he would not contemplate such choices. As a young man he had taken to heart the edict of Prince Karim Aga Khan to become a teacher; he was inspired by his Imam to live for his country; he broadly supported Mwalimu Nyerere's socialist policies and was a patriot to the core. Moreover he loved his students. Having discovered his calling, there was nothing more he enjoyed than to ramble on about the style, prose and essence of an Ngũgĩ or Achebe masterpiece with his students.

In the wake of the post-1971 social hysteria among Ismailis, he did not suddenly shred his contract and leave his students in a lurch. Despite daunting personal problems, he remained a loyal teacher and citizen, and above all, a decent, noble human being. He lived and died for his nation. It is ironic that Nazir, who was then not that devout a person, was effectively more faithful to the edict of Aga Khan IV to make Tanzania his home than my spiritually inclined Ismaili friends. It was from examples like his, the few that they were, that I drew hope that a new dawn was afoot. Yet, in the long run, it was a not to be (Chapter 11).

Mathematics and Literature ❖ ❖ ❖ ❖ ❖ ❖ ❖

In our room at the university, Nazir's side was always neat and clean; his big pile of literary texts arranged in an orderly fashion. My side was in a perpetual state of disorder; and my bed was rarely made. When he saw me struggling through arcane formulas, he asked how I could enjoy that stuff. He had never liked maths, and had barely managed to pass it in school. When I said that mathematical entities were as beautiful as well written poems and prose, he laughed as if I had made a dirty joke. While he respected my views on general issues, when it came to this question, his forthright response was:

Do not talk nonsense, Karim.

Once I gave him my copy of a book called *Flatland* to read (see below). It took him a while to tackle it. I also told him the story of rice grains on the chess board (Chapter 14). In our subsequent interactions, I saw that he was developing a more accommodating attitude towards my favourite subject.

It was in Standard 7 that Mr Hirani had said to us that maths is beautiful. I came to realize later on that the assertion can be interpreted in four ways: (i) Maths possesses an inner structure and outer facet that are aesthetically equivalent to fine drawings, delicate paintings, well-crafted poems, evocative prose or pristine natural scenery; (ii) The intricate patterns in visually or acoustically appealing products of nature like sunflowers and sea shells, or those made by humans like architectural designs, wood sculpture, handicrafts and music can be explained with the help of mathematical formulas; (iii) Artistic entities like literature, poems, plays, sculpture and the crafts can incorporate or be enjoined with different aspects of maths to make an appealing product; and (iv) The endeavours of mathematicians and the makers of artistic, musical and literary products require parallel forms of creativity, effort and imagination to scale conventional mental barriers.

I learned in secondary school that a few seemingly self-evident premises can be combined with careful reasoning to generate the stunning edifice of Euclidean geometry. At advanced levels, I learned that relaxing one key assumption generates non-Euclidean geometries that are equally rational. They have a sound logical footing, but produce counter intuitive results that rankle the mind. Such mental constructs do not just have a purely theoretical value. For instance, hyperbolic geometry is as integral to Albert Einstein's relativistic model of the universe as Euclidean geometry is to Newtonian physics.

Einstein described mathematics as *the poetry of logical ideas*. I guess Mr Hirani was driving home the same point. The mathematical illustrations in the previous chapters are in line with that idea too. Let us look at four more examples linking mathematics to literature.

1. *Flatland: A Romance of Many Dimensions* by Edwin A Abbott tells a short story that unfolds in a two dimensional universe (Abbot 1992). Its residents are geometrical figures who move sideways, and front and back, but not up or down. Their society is stratified by geometric shape. Labourers are elongated isosceles triangles; traders are squares; women are pin-like needles; high priests are circles, etc. The residents have evolved ingenuous ways to enable them to undertake daily activities and communicate in this restricted setting.

This enduring classic was not written by a mathematician but by a teacher of English. The narrator, a square, is visited by a being from our three dimensional universe. It takes an effort to convince him that he is not under an illusion. When the square relates his experience to fellow Flatlanders, they think he has lost his mind, and he is locked away.

A pleasant but provocative tale first published in 1884 and continuously in print to this day, it appeals to the young and old. It can enrich school geometry lessons and show how strict social hierarchies stifle thought and progress. Further books expanding on that theme were published later, and it has spawned at least three science fiction movies.

2. *Alice in Wonderland* and *Through the Looking Glass* by Lewis Carroll are witty fantasies about a girl lost in a landscape where animals talk, things unexpectedly change shape and residents behave in an odd manner (Carroll 1981a; 1981b). Each is sprinkled with puzzles and allusions based in numbers and logic. First published in 1865 and 1871, they have generated several variations, fictional and semi-fictional, on paper and screen. In the hands of a broad-minded, articulate teacher, these stories can amply enrich maths classes from elementary to high school.

3. *The Man Who Counted* by Malba Tahan is a work by a Brazilian author but from an Islamic cultural perspective that was first published in 1938 (Tahan 1993). Set in the vicinity of Baghdad of the early Islamic era, it has an attractive series of short stories that revolve around mathematical themes. They record the amazing adventures of Beremiz Shamir, a man of prodigious mathematical talent. Blending culture, science, religion and commerce, the author gently exposes us to the complex entanglements our hero has to navigate. His keen reasoning rarely fails to come up with solutions that satisfy all the parties in contention.

Consider one case. Beremiz and his friend are on a road trip. Encountering an injured man, they kindly take him along, and share their bread with him. Beremiz has five loaves of bread and his friend, three. At the end of the trip, the rescued man shows his gratitude by giving five gold dinars to Beremiz and three to his friend. Beremiz objects to this simple division. He says that at each meal, a loaf was cut into three pieces, one for each person. The five loaves of Beremiz yielded fifteen pieces. Of these, he ate eight pieces and gave seven to the stranded man. His friend's three loaves produced nine pieces, eight for himself and one for that man. This exact division implies that Beremiz should get seven dinars of gold and his friend, only one.

That logic is faultless. So the gold dinars are divided accordingly. Beremiz remains unhappy. It is not fair in the eyes of Allah, he says. Both he and his friend assisted the stranded man with all they had, and ought to be rewarded equally. In that spirit, he keeps four gold dinars and his friend gets the other four. That, declares the wise Beremiz, is perfect division.

Wading through such tantalizing tales we learn aspects of mathematics rarely touched on in the school curricula. Their pace is slow, the style, popular, and exposition, elementary. The ensuing exhilaration makes you return to the first episode the moment you finish at the last one.

4. *Conned Again, Watson* by Colin Bruce is an illuminating work in the same spirit (Bruce 2001). Containing a series of short detective stories featuring Conan Doyle's famous Sherlock Holmes and his assistant Dr Watson, it is written in the quirky style of the original. Set in Victorian London, each story concerns a crime investigated by the duo that moreover has an underlying mathematical

or statistical theme. The reader is simultaneously entertained and educated as Holmes solves each case, and explains the maths with clarity and elementary examples to Dr Watson. It is suitable for high school students in the science streams and beyond.

Let me give two more instances intertwining maths with literature. The book *War and Peace* by Leo Tolstoy is one of the highest rated works of global literature. But it is not known that Tolstoy befriended mathematicians, and admired the discipline. Several of his books contain mathematical metaphors, a thing not appreciated by his contemporaries. Yet, now those metaphors are seen as sublime expressions encapsulating deep insight into the human condition and relationships (Ahearn 2005; Tammet 2012).

Lord Bertrand Russell ranks among the top ten mathematicians and philosophers of the 20th century. He made pioneering discoveries in mathematical logic and produced authoritative books on the subject. But he also wrote numerous books on popular science, ethics, social issues and literature, and was a globally renowned activist and pacifist who opposed war and the nuclear bomb. Interestingly, the literary quality of his general writings secured him the Nobel Prize for Literature in 1950.

Examples of the intersection of maths and art can be multiplied many times over. Numerous books reflecting that spirit and which are suitable for elementary to high school, have come out. Material is freely available on the Internet. Websites devoted to mathematical fiction exist. But which teacher of maths, especially among those in Tanzania, describes, explains or even mentions such material to his or her students?

I return to Nazir Virji. While Mr Hirani had introduced me to serious literature, it was Nazir who was my mature guide into that field. He would describe the books he was reading, and expound on their social and literary qualities. It was under his influence that I came to read books like *Great Expectations*, *A Grain of Wheat* and *The Hunchback of Notre Dame*.

At the UDSM, both of us read socially critical novels like Ousmane Sembène's *God's Bits of Wood*, Émile Zola's *Germinal*, Upton Sinclair's *The Jungle* and Robert Tressell's *The Ragged Trousered Philanthropists*. But while my choice was a confined one, he had a broad-minded stand. In particular, he had a high regard for Thomas Hardy. He would tell me in a lecturing tone that it was an error to see Hardy purely as a writer of romantic tales. In his view, Hardy's finely crafted sagas are also insightful commentaries on the workings of the English society. At that time, I did not pay attention to those words. Only years later, after going though Hardy's *Far From the Madding Crowd* (1874) and especially the not so well known *Two on a Tower* (1892) that I began to appreciate the literary wisdom of my friend.

Nazir showered particularly lavish praise on Hardy's *Jude, the Obscure* (1895). Aware of my socialistic political leanings, he told me:

> Read this truly progressive novel, Karim. It will tell you more about the
> effects of social stratification on human relations and life opportunities

than those political and sociological tomes I see you reading.

Though I had promised, I did not read it at that time. Only after I took up writing these memoirs did I remember the novel. But I did not have it, and it was not in the bookshops of Dar es Salaam. There was a free e-book version at Project Gutenberg, but I am not a fan of the e-book format. I prefer the paper version. Luckily, in June 2013, I got a well-kept copy from a street vendor for a mere US $2.00.

I take this opportunity to inform my friend in the Heavens that finally, not only I but also Farida has read it. Both of us had a jolly good time. And I fully agree with his take. This elegant, convoluted romantic tangle insightfully depicts the multiplicity of barriers faced by intellectually capable and diligent persons who come from poor families. The setting is Victorian England, but the lessons are universal. Many exceptionally gifted but lower class youth in the modern era find it extremely difficult to pursue their education dreams. The book also presents a keen insight into the position of women in education and society, and casts a critical look at the conservative norms of the place and time. The writing style and descriptions are of a master of words, alternating between dramatic, poignant, intensely emotive and deviously comical, as the situation demands.

By appreciating the integration of good literature, basic geometry and social commentary in *Flatland,* Nazir had begun to respect my assertion that mathematics is beautiful. Having kept my promise, I stand in awe at his acute literary acumen. I hope my long lost friend will look down from his lofty dwelling and project his radiant smile in my direction.

— 11 —

Education and Nation

I am not afraid of storms, for I am
learning to sail my own ship.
Aeschylus

❖ ❖ ❖ ❖ ❖ ❖ ❖

THE EDUCATION SYSTEM critically affects the fate of a nation. A progressive system enables people and institutions to acquire, store, enhance and transmit the knowledge, skills and tools that facilitate broad-based development and economic independence. It promotes unity and harmony. It encourages intellectual creativity and cultural practices that endow a distinctive identity to the nation. It fosters national pride, self-confidence, loyalty and intellectual autonomy.

That is the ideal. In reality, the education system often has retrogressive features. Despite being an efficient vehicle for imparting academic and practical skills, it can foster parochial attitudes and interests. It can fail to serve the goal of social and economic development for the majority. It can engender unemployment and frustration among the youth. It can impart dogmas and falsehoods that justify an unjust and irrational social structure. Education can promote or hinder unity, cultural renaissance and economic advancement.

How has the education system in Tanzania fared on that scale? The answer is complex. I give a perspective based on my experience.

Education for Self-Reliance

A brief picture of the growth of the education system in the early post-*Uhuru* period was painted in Chapter 10. Because it had taken off from a shallow base in 1961, the results were impressive. We had more schools, more teachers, and new higher education institutions. However, for the purpose of long term, sustained development, proceeding in that conventional direction was a recipe for major problems down the line. Extensive, consequential changes were required.

The policy of Education for Self-Reliance (ESR) unveiled in 1967 noted two crucial limitations of the existing system.

One: It prepared students for white collar jobs. Yet, most of its recipients were in rural areas where such jobs did not, and for a long time, would not exist. Office and service type of work opportunities were limited even in the urban areas. The system did not impart to the bulk of the students the skills and knowledge needed to make a decent living and be economically self-supportive in a developing society like Tanzania.

Two: The set-up, content and operational style of this system inculcated a self-centered, individualistic ethic. This did not conform to the national goal of building a society based on cooperation and dedication to the common good.

The system was thus flawed both in terms of promoting practical autonomy and inculcating the desired form of socialization.

ESR proposed to remedy these shortcomings by introduction of training in relevant practical skills at all stages of the educational ladder, and orienting the system along lines that would inculcate the spirit of solidarity and social responsibility. In principle, it was a bold policy that had the potential to fundamentally alter the content, structure and outcome of education. Implemented appropriately, it could produce a stable, effective, high quality, universal system of education that would enable the nation to accelerate genuine economic development, improve the lives and health of the masses, and foster social harmony. Progressive social scientists and broad minded educational experts the world over lauded ESR. Myopic conservatives called it an intrusion of politics into education. But they forgot that the existent system of education was also political in that it was concordant with the setting and ethic of a neo-colonial, dependent society.

When this policy was announced, I was in Form VI at Kibaha School. It was a relevant issue for the General Paper class. But, our narrow-minded teacher did not bring it up. We learned about it from the radio and newspapers. As the implementation directive for schools came later, the new policy did not affect our school life during the remaining months. Yet, I was a supporter of ESR from the day it was announced.

Interestingly, my secondary schooling had actually incorporated aspects of the policy. At the DTC, I had studied, in addition to the usual subjects, metal work, welding and wood work. Our final examinations included both types of subjects. Theory was integrated with practice. Further, the Kibaha School was situated in a complex that contained agricultural and health activities and training. In my time, the interactions between these parts were rudimentary. The complex, however, was an ideal setting in which the links could be made systematic and provide an education in which theory reflected practice. If they were reorganized along participatory lines, the two schools were well placed to be exemplary pioneers of how ESR should be implemented.

From 1968 on, ESR introduced practical activities in primary and secondary schools. These included planting fruits, grains and vegetables, running a poultry farm, carpentry and cleaning the premises. A number of schools rapidly established well run, productive projects. ESR was bearing fruit.

But the ESR work was not formally integrated into the curriculum. Unlike my practical DTC courses, ESR activities were not examinable subjects or listed on the school certificate. This was the basic source of tension in the scheme. On top of that, the ESR projects were often initiated without a good plan, and lacked area wide guidance and coordination. Because of the lack of a formal incentive, they were not performed with due diligence. The quality and output varied yearly. With the traditional curriculum prevailing, ESR work became an added burden on top of a loaded program, and that in a resource constrained setting. In a few places, ESR *shambas* (farms) improved nutrition and generated funds for school supplies. But that was rare. Cases of administrators misusing income from ESR projects for personal benefit came to light. To make matters worse, cleaning and *shamba* work were often assigned as punishments for misdeeds.

Instead of being adopted widely, the DTC sec-tec model was ended soon after ESR came along. At Kibaha, the usual curriculum prevailed. Students worked on the project farm, but a formal integration of farm work into education did not transpire. Grades on subjects like agronomy, dairy farming, health and hygiene did not feature on the student report card or the school certificate. Countrywide, there were five secondary technical schools, but under ESR, this model should have been the norm rather than the exception.

The fate of ESR was typical of the initiatives started under the policy of *Ujamaa*. Potentially worthwhile projects were poorly implemented. The state bureaucracy had little inclination and creative zeal to transcend conventional boundaries, be it in agriculture, dairy farming, water projects, health, agriculture, transportation, industry or education. Basic components of the old system that had earlier been faulted were kept in place, the old ways of operation were not re-evaluated, and a hodgepodge of new modalities was imposed on top. No fundamental change occurred. Apart from dogmatic political education, personnel were not retrained. The mode of functioning of all enterprises remained basically the same; even though now they were called socialist enterprises.

As the political rhetoric did not reflect reality, it engendered cynicism. The enthusiasm that had greeted the policy of *Ujamaa* waned rapidly. Moronic propaganda that just repeated what the Arusha Declaration said or what Mwalimu had uttered did not inspire any more. Instead of marching in a novel direction, like the socialist government of Cuba had done, what we got in Tanzania was essentially the worst of both worlds. Half here and half there, we landed nowhere. In particular, the standards of traditional education fell precipitously and a viable socialist alternative was not put in place. We continue to pay the price for this muddle to this day.

There was also an historic issue, namely, that of perception. In the colonial times, Africans faced major impediments in obtaining education leading to better paying white collar jobs. Missionary schools offered practical training to Africans under the rationale that it was what they were suited for. Asians and Europeans attended schools that qualified them for office and civil service jobs. It was not surprising that from the early Independence days, there was a huge demand from African parents for good quality, traditional style education for their offspring.

But just seven years after *Uhuru*, their own leaders were declaring that such an education was not what the nation needed. The justifications appeared sound. Yet, social conditions remained unfavourable. The expansion of the civil service and economic sectors notwithstanding, office jobs needing Form IV or lower level of schooling remained limited. Jobs that required practical training did not expand rapidly either. Opportunities for and the incomes from self-employment showed marginal improvement. People wondered: How will their children advance in life? Was the new policy an indirect way of keeping them in place while the children of the elite secured better education? Since the state organs continued to interact with people along authoritarian lines; since the administrators and politicians did not set examples of self-sacrifice which would inspire trust from ordinary people; and since the policy was practiced in a haphazard manner, public support evaporated. Among most of the teachers, parents and students, negative attitudes about ESR hardened in a short time.

From 1971 to 1973, while supervising the teaching practice of mathematics teacher trainees at the UDSM, I visited about twelve secondary schools across the nation. In the same period, I gave talks on current affairs and maths at schools in Morogoro, Moshi, Iringa and Dodoma, and my alma mater, Kibaha School. Everywhere I found serious complaints about ESR. Teachers blamed it for lowering the standard of education in general and of maths teaching in particular. They decried the sloppy manner of implementation. While politicians extolled it to the sky, I did not find a single school where ESR was embraced with even a minimal level of enthusiasm.

From what I gathered through visits to these schools, I wrote a long critique of the policy of ESR for a magazine published at the UDSM (Hirji 1973). My main theme was that, although the policy was laudable, it was not integrated with sectors of the economy and society, and its actualization left a lot to be desired. But my words fell on deaf ears. They also produced a backlash: In April 1974, I was ejected from the university, and summarily dispatched to the chilly remoteness of Sumbawanga, the place where political exiles were banished during the colonial era. Instead of lecturing on linear algebra and statistics, I became an assistant regional planning officer in a stagnant bureaucracy with not much to do other than report to work on time and read two-week old newspapers.

Over time, what I had envisaged occurred: ESR died a natural death. The manner in which it was implemented could not promote self-reliance and cooperative ethics at the individual, school or national level. In contrast to the stated aims, it perpetuated mental and economic dependency, and provided sub-standard traditional education.

Lest I be misunderstood, let me stress once more that I accept the essence of the policy of ESR. In my view, it is what Africa needed then and does so even now. My point is that what we saw in Tanzania in the 1960s and 1970s was not ESR of any reasonable form. Rather, it was a haphazardly undertaken and thoroughly mismanaged scheme that critically damaged the foundation that had been laid earlier and placed nothing viable in its place. In the end, it gave us the worst of capitalist-oriented and socialist-oriented education systems.

To sum up: In the first one and a half decades after *Uhuru*, the education system in Tanzania made major strides. Progress was made at all levels of education. However, the change was not sustained, and the attempt to place the system on a more relevant footing backfired due to poor actualization and lack of coordination with other sectors of the economy and society. Rule by a top-down political party the vast majority of whose leaders paid lip service to socialism in public, but undermined it behind the scenes, was another key factor that turned ESR into a confused, damaging parody.

A Dysfunctional System

The current education system of Tanzania has four tracks: primary, secondary, vocational and higher education. All the tracks have private and state run institutions. At first sight, it seems that the system has improved in significant ways in the past ten years. Enrolment has skyrocketed; many new schools have been built; each administrative ward has or is on the verge of having a secondary school of its own. Further, the number of higher education institutions including universities has grown astronomically.

The apparent progress belies the fact that the system is critically dependent on resources from abroad. The quality of education at the universities and colleges is awful, and that is no exaggeration. Expatriates teach science subjects and maths in schools. A great number of schools are schools in name only as classrooms lack desks, blackboards or windows. The ratio of one teacher per 200 or more students prevails in many secondary schools in rural areas. Toilet facilities are poor. Teacher housing is a pressing problem. Many teachers spend nights in classrooms they teach in during the day, and visit the bush to relieve themselves. Books, stationary and essential materials do not meet the high demand. Consider two not that atypical cases.

A Modern School? In February 2013, the Kibiriani Primary School in Dodoma Region had 388 pupils in grades 1 to 7. Yet, there was only one teacher, who was also the headmaster. There was not a single well-built toilet in the vicinity. The closest health facility lay 21 kilometres away on a rough road. Usually, no vehicle was available for sending a sick child to the facility (*Mwananchi* 2013).

A Place of Learning? Kongowe Primary School in Kibaha District had 1,502 pupils in 2013. Though the number of students was twice that allowed, the school had only seven usable classrooms. With class sizes exceeding 200, pupils sat on the floor or stood. Special facilities for the forty two disabled pupils were not at hand. One wonders how learning can take place under such circumstances (Mwinyi 2013).

A Herculean Task: In the year 2014, two primary schools in Iringa district, one with more than 600 pupils and another with 102 pupils, had only one teacher each. The two teachers were exhausted from the Herculean effort expected of them (Ally 2014).

At the other end of the spectrum are private schools that charge high fees and have up-to-date facilities, an adequate number of qualified teachers, books and computers, and are run well. However, most students attend schools having a serious shortfall of some kind. These dire conditions are mirrored in the national examinations. It reached a crisis point in the year 2012: some 70% of the candidates for the national Form IV exams failed to achieve the basic pass level (Division III or above), and 40% attained Division 0, a level that does not entitle them to a school certificate. That is, their four years of post-primary schooling was – for themselves, their parents and the nation – essentially a waste of time and resources. In the ensuing uproar, the results were standardized, and the pass rate was jacked up. But that is a tactic to mask, not solve, the underlying problems.

In response to public and media outcry, the authorities often resort to disciplinary measures with a publicity value, but which do not tackle the roots of the problems. In 2010, a district commissioner in northern Tanzania visited each school in his district that had shown poor performance in the national exams. At each school, he had the teachers paraded in public and caned by a group of militia men. In another case:

A Political Reaction? The District Education Officer in Kilindi District identified fifty primary schools with poor outcomes in the year 2012 national exams. His remedy was to demote, at one go, all fifty headmasters of these schools. It was his way of completely overhauling the schools (Semdoe 2013).

Underneath such extreme examples lies a sea of ineffective, short term actions to improve education. A sound, comprehensive remedial policy and developing an appropriate implementation mechanism are as rare as a unicorn.

The relationship between the teachers and parents is strained to a breaking point in many districts. Unceasing demands for financial contributions angers parents. They wonder why, despite the numerous payments they make, the exam performance of their children remains unsatisfactory. Parents and teachers blame each other, and the conflict occasionally takes a violent turn.

Parents Against Teachers: In a February 2013 incident, the headmaster of the Misingeni Primary School in Kigoma District found a group of students guilty of gross misconduct. As a result, all were caned. One student ran home to complain. Thereupon, twenty angry parents marched to the school, and severely beat up the three teachers who were on the premises (Abdallah 2013).

Long standing distrust between parents and villagers on one hand, and teachers and school officials on the other, can lead to actions that only endanger the students.

A Destructive Episode: The friction between school employees and area parents boiled over at the Kinjumbi Secondary School in Kilwa District. Distinctly annoyed by the conduct of the former, parents visited the school at night and plastered the classroom walls with faeces and drilled holes in the walls of the school dormitories. The message was clear: the parents had lost trust in the school. To resolve the dispute, the District Commissioner held a public gathering in March 2013. His main plea was that the ongoing damage to the school property had to end (Maumba 2013).

Students against Teachers: Elsewhere, two students who were thoroughly dissatisfied with their education went to the headmaster's office to demand a refund for the school fees they had paid. When he refused, they inflicted extensive injuries on him using a machete (Maregesi 2014).

This is but the tip of a nation-wide iceberg. The education system is replete with numerous fundamental organizational, economic and political problems. The trust between educators and the society at large has been shattered. Teachers no longer get the respect they once upon a time commanded. Harrowing signs of indiscipline occur on a wide basis. A state of acrimony prevails between students, parents, educators, administrators and politicians. It is the norm for each group to blame the others. Misuse, abuse and pilferage of the resources meant for education are entrenched, and take a heavy toll on educational quality and student morale. Violent strife is too common.

Corporal Punishment

The heavy handed spirit particularly affects the students. Media and members of the public complain that they lack discipline, and do not take learning seriously. The usual incentives are deemed ineffectual. It is said that a hefty dose of physical punishment of the colonial era variety has to be resurrected as it is the sole effective way to rectify the behaviour of the students and raise pass levels. Politicians and bureaucrats clamour for enhanced application of caning in schools. A few commentators, teachers and experts disagree with that stand, but most favour the stinging remedy (Kaigarula 2013; Macha 2013; Mwita 2014; Qorro 2013).

In the 1950s, corporal punishment was widely applied. In fact, this was the one aspect of schooling whereby African, Asian and European students were treated similarly (Edwards 2011). After *Uhuru*, it continued but in a restricted form. Current law permits caning only for major breach of discipline. It can be administered only by the headmaster, and not more than 4 lashes may be given at a time. The law is commonly flouted, sometimes with severe consequences. The following incident occurred in a school in my town of birth.

Students under Assault: In October 2013, two books went missing in a Form II class. The culprits not known, the teacher punished the whole class. Each student was required to bring in TSh 300 (about US $0.25) to make up for the loss. On the collection day, Salim Shamte did not have the money. When asked the reason, he said that he was not present on the day the loss occurred. He was told that all students, including him, had to pay. Salim replied: "OK, teacher, I will do it." This reply was interpreted by the teacher as very disrespectful because Salim ought to have said: "Yes, teacher, I will do it."

Thoroughly angered, he started hitting Salim with his fists. Taking Salim to the back of the class, the teacher shoved him twice against the wall, forced him onto his knees and beat him. Hours later, Salim developed severe headache and began to wail loudly. His parents took him to the district hospital. A few days later, he was sent to the Muhimbili National Hospital. Salim had sustained memory loss and was not able to speak clearly, both signs of brain injury. The prognosis was bleak (Bakari 2013).

In Zanzibar, the authorities acknowledged that caning was being excessively and inappropriately applied by teachers, and this was leading to rising discord in schools. A few schools have been placed on an alternative track to test substitutes to caning. The results of this experiment have yet to be known (Sadallah 2013).

Having experienced it first-hand, I concur that most present day students have an attitude towards education that is poles apart from that prevalent in my school days. The current batch is more undisciplined, and less inclined to study with focus and diligence. The student rebellions of the sixties had both a material basis and a progressive, societal orientation. The uprisings and fracases of today are more akin to an injured person lashing out without a sense of direction or broad purpose.

Mass failures and student unrest make most people support harsh measures like dismissing or demoting teachers, and caning the students. Such a quick fix approach, however, cannot work as the roots of the problems are systemic. It is not just the student who has changed, the conditions in schools and society today are vastly different too. We live in a world of gross inequality in all the facets of life, including education. The sons and daughters of the rich and well-connected attend costly private schools with books, teachers and supplies. The rest endure conditions of the type depicted above. Pass rates for rural schools are very low. University education no longer guarantees a job, let alone a decent job. Modern teachers remain a frustrated lot, no longer getting the respect or remuneration they deserve. In that situation, they too have largely abdicated their responsibilities.

Adult attitudes to children are not consistent and go from one extreme to another. We either treat children with excessive harshness or are oblivious to their egregious deeds, losing sight of the rational centre. We strive to respect the needs and rights of children. Yet, we treat small violations severely. Under the dogma of zero tolerance, dominant in the US educational system, and now spreading globally, a slight instance of perceived misbehaviour earns a legally mandated sanction like suspension from school. The calls for greater application of corporal punishment accord with that philosophy.

If a zero tolerance policy had prevailed in my childhood, where would my gang buddies and I be now? Pravez Vira not only became a praised fast bowler with the Aga Khan Cricket Club but also did well in business, while Amilo Pipi and Shokat worked hard in varied practical occupations. Bhanji joined the DTC and became a competent boiler plant engineer. As an adult, he has developed such a gentle, honest persona that no one would believe it that once upon a time, he shoplifted candies and ransacked people's gardens. For my part, I think I have not done badly in life. My brother Nazir was a hardworking engineer and responsible parent at first. Later, he became an astute con-artist. But I have relatives who were well behaved as children, but then ended up as con-artists.

As Sosthenes Mwita observes, there is a sociological basis to children's misbehaviour that we have to identify and tackle. Among these factors are coming hungry to school, a home life of discord and penury, and uninspiring, uncommitted teachers (Mwita 2014). If we do not tackle these basic problems, measures like caning will only backfire. In any case, caning and the like have no place in education, whatever the circumstances. The claim that they are beneficial does not arise from relevant and accurate data.

Traditionally, not only in Tanzania but broadly, maths teaching was associated with drastic teaching methods (Raizada 2011). To say that they were effective methods is to confuse learning basic arithmetic skills and memorizing multiplication tables with understanding the basic concepts and promoting a long term attraction to the subject. Caning at best favoured the former, but decisively inhibited the latter.

Determination of the causes of poor examination performance requires a series of short and long term retrospective and prospective studies. That includes examination of the records of the national examination body; interviews with students, parents, teachers, administrators and members of the public; on the spot audits of the examination process; and randomized field experiments. The evidence from these studies has to be synthesized using appropriate methods. Only such an investigation can enable us to unearth the personal, local, systemic and external factors that affect the outcome of school examinations.

Yet, the official commission charged to investigate the issue thinks along other lines. In the year 2013, it conducted an investigation without a scientific plan. On top of that, its report has been kept secret; the people are not to know what ails their education system. It has worked on the premise that a short term cursory survey of the different components of the system suffices to uncover the main problems and potential solutions. This is a misguided approach. A transparent process deriving from scientific studies that are comprehensive in nature and a public debate about the findings of report are essential for improving the education system in a substantial and sustainable way.

How this commission has done its job is a manifestation of the tendency of our leaders to avoid the root causes of the problems we face. When problems generate social strife, they apply strong measures. The advocates of stringent application of corporal punishment in schools betray the same mentality. It is not a remedy or a part of the remedy for the major problems of the school system. Student performance can improve only with a sufficient number of competent, motivated teachers. Adequate supply of necessary items like books is essential. The well trained teachers have to be given a living wage, low cost housing, and free health services for their families. Importantly, the education system has to be linked to the social and economic policies. Privatization benefits only a few. What the nation needs is a well-run, compulsory, free, effective public education system for all students.

We need to address fundamental matters like the dearth of teachers and support staff, frequent and unexplained changes in syllabus, inappropriate utilization of technology, adoption of multiple choice exams; classrooms lacking desks, blackboards or windows; hungry, barefoot students; few books; poor quality and sub-standard textbooks; and lack of basic amenities like water and toilets. You find a whole school with just one textbook on the premises. Yet, district authorities regularly focus on using aid-funds for physical structures and do not accord due attention to critical shortfalls. Thereby, numeracy and literacy skills remain quite low. A one time availability of funds for books, as happened in relation to an international corruption scandal, cannot be a long term solution (Kahangwa 2014; Kimboy 2014; Liganga 2013; Mgamba 2014; Sylvester 2014; *The Citizen* 2014).

I regard the politicians and administrators together with the Western funders who pull the strings behind the scene as the main culprits in this drama. Drowning in dollars, they do not devise and implement policies that can liberate us from the morass. Their abysmal record in delivering election day promises makes people view all they say with derision or cynicism. Consequently, everyone just complains and complains. Advocates of thoughtfully developed, evidenced-based yet bold measures are few and ignored. Battered by powerful socio-economic-political storms that have descended upon it, the edifice of education is presently adrift in high seas. It and the nation have lost their compasses, and we know not where we are headed.

Self-Determination

Human beings prefer to determine their own destiny. We take pride in what we can do for ourselves, and feel a sense of shame when we fail to meet the needs of our loved ones. No one accepts external assistance with the fullness of his or her heart. The cleavage between the giver and the recipient, even when good intentions prevail, is unbridgeable. We hold on to our dignity when we receive aid by reasoning that there is no other option, and hope that one day we will get a chance to return the favour. This logic applies at work or in school, in home or social life, in community or national affairs.

Yet, the word that has characterized and dominated the African development agenda over the past fifty years, and which shows no sign of losing steam, is 'aid'. Our economic and social plans and programs were based on major, if not decisive, funding and support from external, especially Western, nations. We were told that Africa cannot prosper without it. It was the primary message of the departing colonial rulers. And it is the same message we get today from the international agencies and foundations. When you ask why, despite fifty years of 'aid', the vast majority of people of Africa remain stuck in poverty, ill health and dreadful conditions of life, they say it is because our leaders misused the assistance given with good intentions. Instead of using it to benefit the people, the leaders lined their own pockets. But that is only half the story. The 'donors' too profited immensely (Danaher 1994; Torrie 1986; Toussaint 2007).

Almost all of our leaders, academics, experts and media overlook this basic reality and have internalized the aid-oriented outlook. Even though they occasionally stress that we need investment and trade rather than aid, mostly it is superficial talk. Their actions belie their words. Also such words ignore the fact that trade and investments directed at Africa are essentially exploitative in nature. In the long run, external economic intervention, of whatever form, mainly generates riches for a few, poverty for the masses, dependency for the national economy, and exacerbates internal social tensions (Bello, Cunningham and Rau 1999; Irwin, Kim, Gershman and Millen 2002; Torrie 1986; Toussaint 2007).

My issue is not with intentions. I saw that a number of externally funded projects in the early days of independent Tanzania came with good intentions and promising possibilities. I rate the Kibaha complex among them. Our Scandinavian teachers were well qualified and dedicated to giving us high quality education. Most were friendly persons. Overall, we had nothing but good feelings towards them.

But there was a social gap not easy to cross. Their houses were near our dorms, but I never visited a teacher at home. The question could not arise. They were the noble benefactors and we, the poor grateful receivers. That was the unspoken feeling in the air. And there was a fundamental contextual issue: that Europe benefited vastly more from its ties with Africa than Africa did with its ties to Europe. I learned the details and mechanism of this economic structure when I joined the university (Hayter 1971; Jalee 1968; Leys 1975; Magdoff 2003; Nkrumah 1966; Perkins 2005; Prashad 2008). But at Kibaha School, we felt it in our bones. Yet, it was taboo to say it. Patrice Lumumba was murdered precisely for saying it loudly and clearly. Mainstream figures on both sides thereon mostly maintained a discreet silence on the matter.

The giver/recipient relationship at Kibaha was expressed in subtle ways. One arena was the food served in the cafeteria. We complained constantly – the taste was too bland. Often, it was awful. The two standard responses were: the food budget per student in our school was higher than that in other secondary schools; and, more money could be allocated but the proposal was vetoed by the Ministry of Education. The clear message was that we are doing more for you than your own government can do for students like you, and that your own government is blocking us from doing more. You have no cause to complain. Just sit back and enjoy what we are serving you!

We found such responses condescending and insulting. Even our right to speak was being denied. Like starving refugees in a camp, we should accept the assistance given and shut up. And yet, the issue was not about money. We felt that if the same food was cooked in a different way with a few spices added, it would be palatable. The meat and sausage dishes served several times a week, supposedly special items, had a chalky taste. That was one reason why Salim and I used to gorge ourselves at the dairy farm. This point could not be conveyed to the administration, and the problem persisted. It is not the bland food, but the superiority infused responses that we got that has left a lasting sour taste in my mouth.

Our rebellion against the general paper teacher was founded on similar sentiments. On the cultural front, the administration did not restrict the type of music cassettes purchased for us from the city. But it was an attitude that reflected lack of interest in African culture. The word was that many Scandinavian teachers labelled local music as akin to 'organized noise.'

A few years after Independence, we became aware of the serious limitations of foreign aid. The Western nations used it as a device to institute projects that would keep us dependent. Often, it was a means for political manipulation. The terms of trade remained unfavourable to Africa, and the limited foreign investment that occurred did not promote self-sustaining development (Coulson 2013; Rweyemamu 1973).

Hence, during the initial days of *Ujamaa* and the policy of ESR, the issue of self-reliance garnered centre stage in the national political and social arena. Mwalimu told us in categorical terms that if we as a people, village, community or nation wanted development, then it could only come through our own effort and by standing on our own feet. There was no alternative to self-reliance; it was indispensable. This did not mean isolating ourselves from the world. Rather, it meant deciding our own destiny and seeking assistance only when it was essential, and that also on terms that were of benefit to us (TANU 1967).

Sadly, Mwalimu Nyerere and TANU reneged on that lofty goal within a few years. The issue of self-reliance became secondary as Tanzania sought and obtained foreign aid for projects in all sectors of the economy, including health and education. By the mid-1970s, Tanzania was one of the highest per capita recipients of foreign grant and loan funds in Africa. Even projects that we could do with local resources like health education and literacy campaigns were funded by Scandinavian countries. The decision as to the technology employed, say for water supply projects, was taken by the funder and not by us. Eventually, all the regions were parcelled out among the 'aid-givers' as exclusive operating territories (Cliffe and Saul 1973; Coulson 2013; Mapolu 1979; Rweyemamu 1973; von Freyhold 1979). This laid the foundation for the woes we face today. Below, I give two instances of my contact with the faces of dependency.

Medical Records II

My youthful sojourn among medical patient files in 1965 (Chapter 7) had an analogous sequel. Twenty five years later, in 1988, I joined the Faculty of Medicine of the UDSM. The teaching hospital for the Faculty was the adjacent Muhimbili Hospital. Because of my expertise in medical statistics, I was appointed to the Medical Records Committee of the hospital! The Records Section was still at the same location. Though extended, it was even more congested with shelves and files. The staff of 1965 were long gone. My visits to the section and attendance at the committee meetings indicated that many of the problems I had encountered earlier persisted. The problem of non-locatable files at times of need was particularly acute.

In 1989, I initiated a research project with my students that had a two-fold aim. One was to address a key question about outpatients who had been given appointments with specialists at the hospital: Were their files available when needed? Two, it was a practical exercise for my students to implement the research and data analysis methods they had learned in class. We jointly designed the research along scientific lines. An almost random sample of about 200 patients was interviewed. The response rate was close to one hundred percent. Upon compiling the data, the main complaints we found were: patient files were frequently misplaced and there were long delays in procuring urgently needed files. Some patients alleged that one had to bribe the staff in order to get one's file in a timely manner.

I presented the report in a meeting of the Medical Records Committee. After detailing the findings, I proposed that supplementing the incentives for the section staff was a central part of the solution. Their salary, equivalent to US $30 a month, could not cover the high and rising cost of the basic necessities of life. As a result, they sought extra income through dubious means; hence the allegations of bribery. I also suggested hiring two persons with the sole responsibility of replacing returned files. If a file was misplaced, the responsible party would be known.

At that time, the Swedish government had expressed willingness to fund computerization of the medical records at the hospital. The committee saw it as the magic solution. As I gave my report, I recall the sceptical expression on the face of the Swedish expert present. Our report was the product of a zero-cost study. Though done by students, it was scientifically sound. Data collection had been monitored for quality, a thing rarely done in internationally financed projects. Moreover, our report put forward low cost, home-grown, sustainable recommendations to deal with the problem.

The Swedish expert laid out a lavishly funded project that promised financial fall out to the committee members. Everyone listened with rapt attention. What he proposed was followed up. But it was a different story for our report. They appeared to take what I said seriously, but promptly forgot about it in the subsequent sessions.

Today, the hospital has both paper and computerized record systems. Some problems have been reduced but others remain. Computerization spawns problems of its own. In a setting where advanced technology does not have internal roots, they can be very serious. Accuracy and completeness of records are put on the back burner. Regular backup is not scrupulously observed, and unstable power supply affects access. Since the entry of patient data is in a standard format, and doctors are overworked, unique case details are not recorded. Looking at the dire situation of the patients in that hospital today, the claim that computerization has served its desired purpose is hard to sustain. When the basic work ethic and organizational acumen are wanting, technology cannot be a substitute.

Modern Maths

One case of externally driven action was the introduction of 'modern maths' in secondary schools. With inspiration, ideas and funding from the USA, local educators and external experts drew up a plan and devised textbooks for introducing maths of the type used in US schools into the Tanzanian curriculum. It started with concepts and aimed to reduce drill. Topics like sets, functions, relations and transformation entered the syllabus. The approach inherited from the British had stressed memorization and mechanical use of formulas. The new one was supposed to enhance understanding of basic ideas and facilitate long term retention.

For example, students first learned the distributive property: $a(b + c) = ab + ac$. Then they applied it to a few examples. In the past, we had learned the topic through hundreds of examples like $15(20 + 10) = 15 \times 20 + 15 \times 10$. Without knowing its name, the distributive property became embedded in our brains by the brute force of repetition.

The 'modern maths' approach did not thrive. Teachers were not retrained, and most were not enthusiastic about it. The high level of abstraction impeded learning. The fact that drills form the foundation for conceptualization was ignored. The exercises were not challenging. As the misguided nature of the policy became apparent, a retreat occurred and we were left with a strange admixture of the old and new. This fiasco took place at the same time as the policy of ESR was being introduced, exemplifying the disconnect between grand statements at the national level and the concrete trends in education.

The teaching of maths in schools never fully recovered from that US funded fiasco. Output of well trained teachers from the UDSM cushioned the fall and improved the teaching of maths across the nation for a while. But ultimately, the whole edifice tumbled down and today the Form IV pass rate in maths is the lowest of all the subjects.

Omba Omba Nation

By the end of the 1980s, half-hearted, aid-dependent policies and wasteful, uncoordinated implementation in education and all sectors of the economy landed the nation in a state of crisis. The neo-liberal era of the 1990s threw the final monkey-wrench into the system. In an amazing move, experienced school teachers were laid off, and school funding fell. User fees were introduced. But it only made parents remove their children from school. The error of this World Bank driven calamity was realized ten years on (Rowden 2013). External funds once again poured into education. They set the priorities and goals; and our government carried out the task, but in inefficient and dubious ways. School enrolment expanded rapidly, but without a corresponding increase in teaching staff, improvement in teacher training, or desired levels of essential supplies or facilities. The outcome was the state of chaos into which I gave a glimpse above. Maths and English are the subjects most severely affected. The standards and performance in these two subjects remain abysmally low at all levels of the system.

Fifty years on, after receiving billions of dollars in external assistance, Tanzania has attained the status of a favoured beggar in the international arena. Virtually all important projects are undertaken with foreign funds and external direction. Our priorities are set beyond our borders. Experts and academics bow down on a daily basis to 'donors' and investors. Self-reliance is not on the national agenda. Western ambassadors lecture us daily on governance and tour villages to dish out trifles. Simple public health messages air daily on public and private radio stations with 'the generosity of the people of America.' The prevalence of blatant mental subservience in such an open manner bespeaks volumes as to the loss of shame, sense of dignity and patriotism prevailing among our fashionably attired, smart phone-armed political and intellectual classes.

Take a central issue: Zanzibar operated a comprehensive school meals programme in the 1960s and 1970s. The economic crisis of the 1980s weakened it; the neo-liberal era of the 1990s put the final nails on the coffin. There was a precipitous fall in consistent attendance at school and exam performance thereafter. The revival of the feeding programme in June 2014 was gratifying news. But there is a snag: It is a limited, experimental scheme under an external NGO and is being coordinated by a UK university (Yussuf 2014). The case of Uganda is relevant: It launched a wide ranging meal provision programme for schools four years ago. While politicians boasted about fulfilling election pledges, it was dependent on external support for subsidized supplies. That support had a major setback of recent. Hence the year 2014 Uganda education budget avoids the issue of school meals. The focus now is on construction and supplies. Especially in the north, a big decline in attendance will likely ensue.

Our bureaucrats have no desire to learn from experience. They place an essential activity under experimentation by patronizing Western academics. What can and must be done by our own resources and our own plans is dependent on external charity. When and how we feed our children is decided by outsiders. Our bureaucrats and scholars get trips abroad and generous allowances from the project. And, one year our children are at school with full tummies but no books, the next year, they have books but are hungry.

While similar conditions exist in most African nations, my impression is that the attitudes of *omba, omba* (beg, beg) and donor-worship are more entrenched in Tanzania. Once in a while an editorial, commentator or academic rails against it. But the 'donors' effectively rule the nation. When Barrack Obama visited Tanzania in July 2013, the capital city came to a halt. The print and broadcast media, politicians and state officials, NGOs and experts, loudly, in unison and without exception, acted as if the Master of the Universe had graciously landed to bestow his majestic blessings on us. This humiliating puppet show of epic proportions beyond doubt demonstrated the depth of mental and economic slavery into which we have descended. From being the stalwart foe of foreign intervention in Africa, Tanzania is now perceived as one of the principal lackeys of US imperialism in the region. And 99% of our journalists, intellectuals and politicians are comfortably aligned with that state of affairs.

And this is the bottom line. So long as we do not uphold our national dignity, so long as we do not display confidence in our ability to solve our problems with our own resources and brains, so long as we let others do the thinking for us, so long as we do not encourage and train our children to develop inquiring minds that probe issues without fear or favour, and to the extent that we forget crucial lessons from the history of Africa, our ship will be stuck in shallow waters, and our destination will remain beyond the visible horizon.

Mwalimu Nyerere encouraged us to value self-determination and self-reliance in the spirit of cooperation and equality. It is the key to solving our problems. None are easy problems. Each arena – health, education, agriculture, sports, transportation, housing etc. – requires extensive effort, singular dedication and creativity. We will make mistakes, at times, serious mistakes. That is a part of any process of sound development. Yet, with zeal and persistence, one day in the not too distant a future, we will land where we want to be.

For a start, as we reorganize our house, let us ask the foreign 'donors', NGOs and investors to take a five-year unpaid leave of absence. When we have put our house in a better state, we can invite back the few whose presence will truly benefit the common person, and who are willing to work with us on the basis of equality.

The essential, uncompromisable principle is that we dream and plan for ourselves, use our own resources and uphold national pride and dignity. Barring that, we will lament fifty years on as we do today. Our great grandchildren will get substandard education and face the prospects of joblessness and poverty while, by that time, our mineral wealth will have been siphoned off to America, Canada, Europe and China, and we will be staring at empty holes in the ground.

Recreational Maths in Schools ✣ ✣ ✣ ✣ ✣ ✣ ✣

The teaching and learning of mathematics in the primary and secondary schools of Tanzania is beset with major problems. The roots lie in the dire condition of the education system as a whole. On top of that, there are problems specific to the subject itself. They include the basic approach used; syllabus, books and teaching materials; the type of examinations set; and the training of mathematics teachers.

Historic Legacy: We inherited the colonial era style and content for maths in schools. The UK derived scheme started with drill based counting, numbers and arithmetical operations. Then came memorization of multiplication tables, followed by basic arithmetic, algebra and geometry in which numerous, repetitious exercises were given. In secondary school, a formal approach in Euclidean geometry and algebra set up a unitary edifice. Drills remained central, but a fair amount of theory was included too. Additional maths was available for the better performing students. The topics in basic maths were not easy; the Form IV examination paper had difficult questions. Without a capable teacher and extensive effort, a high grade was difficult to attain. By conventional standards, it was a stable, well-functioning system. In part, that functionality stemmed from the fact that the number of students was, compared to what we have today, quite low.

There were two problems connected with this approach. One, by secondary school, most students were alienated from maths. The new material did not rekindle their interest. Two, the sole aim of secondary and high school maths teachers was to prepare students for the certificate exams. A seasoned teacher knew the type of questions on these exams, and had a tested strategy for propelling the best of his students towards a high grade. Much effort was devoted to varied practice problems in the expectation that some of them, with minor deviations, would appear in the exam paper.

This basic mold persists today, with the difference that standards are lower, the process of examination is not a consistent or well implemented one, and the quality of teaching has diminished substantially. In addition, the current syllabus contains remnants of the modern maths fiasco.

Take one illustration of the current scenario: In February of every year, the National Examination Council (NECTA) releases the results of the Form IV examinations. The next day, they inform the headline of each and every daily newspaper, be it English or Swahili. I have been closely looking at these reports since the year 2008. Each year, the media reports are full of astonishing arithmetical and interpretive errors; some of them emanate from the NECTA press release itself, but many are added by the journalists and editors. You find simple additions and percentages calculated wrongly and interpreted in a way that conveys an impression opposite to that of the reality. Numerical errors in educational reporting are one instance of a generalized phenomenon affecting reporting of data from health, agriculture, transport, finance and other sectors.

Alarmed at this display of below primary school level mathematical compet- ence among the journalistic community of Tanzania, and under the sponsorship of the Media Council of Tanzania, I wrote a detailed, accessible book, *Statistics in the Media: Learning from Practice.* It is not a formula driven, traditional statistics book. Rather, it is full of actual cases of media reporting of numbers in Tanzania and other nations. Clear explanations of how to and how not to report and interpret numbers and social statistics are given (Hirji 2012). The book was well publicized when it was launched and was then freely distributed to all print media outlets in the nation.

As I write these words in 2014, NECTA has released Form IV exam results once more, there have been the usual headlines and commentaries, and I have looked at all the reports once again. And I find the same errors, misinterpretations and inconsistencies. It is as if my book was never published. Our journalists and editors seem proud of showing off their ineptness at handling simple numbers to the world. Simple additions seems too difficult for them. As they complain that too many students are getting Division Zero, they show a performance that deserves placement in Division -1. I see this as a good indicator of the depths to which mathematics education in Tanzania has sunk.

In the meantime, mathematical education has expanded by leaps and bounds across the globe. A monumental outpouring of literature, events, international competitions, teaching methods, computer resources and software, paper and electronic books, and physical teaching tools related to school maths has occurred. But we are stuck in a toned-down version of an ancient scenario where even the regular tasks of the past are done in a flawed way by all the parties to the equation: students, teachers, parents, examination bodies, local experts and the national administrators.

To improve this situation in a substantive and sustained way, we need to adhere to five key principles: (i) enhance intrinsic appeal of maths, (ii) balance drill and concepts; (iii) enjoin theory with practical applications; (iv) introduce field work and projects; and (v) make use of computer resources in a selective manner. But this is not the place to go into the details. Here I have a limited aim, namely, to point out the key role recreational maths can play in this endeavour. I do so because this vital area is left out altogether from the local discourse.

I first clarify what recreational maths is, and then discuss a series of points relevant to the improvement of maths education in schools.

Recreational Mathematics (RM) is a broad field covering all branches of mathematics. Embodying the entertainment, fun and sports facet of maths, a good portion is within the reach of people who are not maths wizards. A large segment is suitable for school children. One example is the popular numbers game, Sudoku.

Many of the mathematical illustrations in this book are related to RM. In a maths class, such stuff provides relief from the drills, illuminates intricate ideas, and broadens the student's horizon. The main segments of RM are listed in Appendix A. Here, I give two mathematical jokes.

> Teacher: "*How many seconds are there in a year?*"
> Student: "*Twelve. January second, February second, March second, April second, . . .*"

> The teacher was explaining a basic rule of algebra: only subtract like terms. Thus $7x^2 - 4x^2 = 3x^2$. But $7x^2 - 4x$ cannot be reduced further. To drive the point home, she stated a daily life example, "*You can take four mangoes from seven mangoes, but you cannot take four papayas from seven mangoes.*"
> One smart girl raised her hand and asked, "*Teacher, can we not take four mangoes from seven trees?*" Another chimed in, "*And, can we not take seven mangoes from four trees?*"

Enhancing Appeal: Right from first grade, we need to teach maths in a way that sparks and retains interest. It has to become a fun-filled activity that generates wonder from the day they begin to count, add and multiply.

When I looked through the pre-primary, primary and secondary schools maths books in five bookstores in Dar es-Salaam, I found the supply, from several publishers, plentiful. The books up to Standard 1 had pictures, rhymes, and stories. But after that level, all the books followed a uniform, bland scheme – a statement of a key principle followed by page after page of routine exercises. This is when the typical young mind begins to detach itself from the subject. Drudgery and plain manipulation of symbols is boring. That is not so, for example, with general science. Science books at all levels contain attractive and colourful material – plants, flowers, animals, birds, oceans, stars etc.

Yet, there is no reason why maths textbooks cannot be enticing. Inclusion of mathematically linked pictures, designs, patterns, short stories, poems, historic anecdotes, songs, jokes, puzzles and revealing facts from nature and society serves that purpose. Eye catching stuff is spread throughout in a relevant manner. Songs and poems are recited by the students. Stories are told by the teacher in a dynamic style. Patterns are drawn by the students, and their origin and meaning explained by the teacher. Jokes, catchy definitions and word play are invoked as appropriate.

Class projects, involving physical and mental activities, are a crucial part of this effort (see Appendix A).

An approach to teaching school maths in a form that integrates the usual lessons with RM and practical projects has the advantage of broadening appeal while also enhancing rigor and retaining high standards. In the hands of an able teacher, it can improve performance to a significant degree as well as facilitate long term conceptual grasp of the subject matter.

Several school books in US schools partly reflect this approach. But they compromise rigor in order to make the subject appealing. The material is too simple, and exercises are of the easy, repetitious type. Challenging topics and inclusion of content from all continents are needed. Linking theory with practice, incorporation of field work and moderate computer use are to be stressed. Overuse of computers does more harm than good to the developing brain.

The challenge is to develop a school high standard, varied curriculum with material relevant to our socio-economic reality. It should have intrinsic appeal to the majority of students as well. Recreational material of appropriate level is thereby essential.

These artistic and recreational diversions do not replace systematic development or real life applications. They hold student attention as more rigorous material is developed. They do not dilute the standards, but enhance them. Creative teaching of maths will imprint into the young mind that it is a fun-filled endeavour, with a solidly logical basis and many real life uses. In the process, the bond between the teacher and the students – a bond that is too frayed at present – will be strengthened.

The maths teachers have to take the first plunge with a revamp of how they are trained. It has to include recreational maths, history of maths, and connecting literature to maths. And it has to give them a deeper and wider immersion into maths, challenging exercises and practical projects.

Relevant Books and Websites: For a sample of books and websites related to recreational mathematics, see Appendix A.

While maths teaching is in disarray, simplistic calls for a return to the past – like caning and drill – will not take us far. We need to identify, construct and embark on creative paths. The comprehensive, entertaining but also rigorous and practical approach I have outlined will expose our students to maths in a friendly style. It will instill better understanding, facilitate creative effort and encourage critical thinking.

Part III

Spirals

A foray into the past stimulates you to seek the presence of the past in the present. My venture into my childhood made me ask: Where are my school friends and teachers? How have they fared in life? How have my old places of residence changed? In what ways do the values and behaviour of modern youth differ from those of my days? Does the current socio-political atmosphere have much, if anything, in common with that of the 1960s?

Reuniting with people and places from my boyhood days was the best part of the exercise of writing these memoirs. The underlying human interest drives me to share aspects of my encounters with my readers. They give my tale a sense of closure.

Additionally, for many encounters, I felt as if I had moved full circle. This is my second reason for presenting them: They well illustrate the adage that the trajectory of human life is like a multi-stranded, intertwined helix. Some strands spiral up; some strands spiral down; and the resulting admixture imbues spice and splendour as well as pain and misery to our existence. The next eight chapters present key spirals from that scenario.

— 12 —

Spirals of Nature

Growth is a spiral process,
doubling back on itself,
reassessing and regrouping.
                Julia M Cameron

❖ ❖ ❖ ❖ ❖ ❖ ❖

HISTORY REPEATS ITSELF – a familiar statement, yet correct only in part. Society is perpetually in flux. When an aspect of the past reappears, the conditions are altered, and the causes and effects are probably not the same. Neither linear nor cyclical, our life journeys resemble a brocade of upward and downward spirals. Life changes even when we feel it is mired in a morass.

With most of the 1980s and 1990s spent abroad, Farida and I resettled in Upanga in 2004. We found our long time family home run down; kitchen furniture was cracked; the stove was rusty; water pipes were clogged; electrical wiring, dangerously frayed; water storage capacity, grossly inadequate; doors and door frames, hollow and emitting wood dust – a few among many problems. My elderly father had not had the energy to maintain it. Plenty of work lay ahead, but the exhilaration we felt at lounging in the homely setting neutralized any concerns. When you sleep in the same bed you had slept in thirty five years earlier, the depth and tranquillity of your sleep has no parallel.

About half the immediate neighbours were the same. Amilo Pipi's family was still where it was fifty years ago, and Farida's brother and his family, but a five minute walk away. Yet, nine out of the ten faces I saw around were new.

Spaces, structures and nature looked alien. With four times the number of residents, it had become a congested area. Most open spaces had closed up. The play ground, water pond and abundant vegetation on Undali Street (near our 1962 gang HQ) have vanished. Old residential flats, new fifteen to twenty story tower blocks, shops, electricity fenced plush bungalows, old and new schools and preschools, communal complexes, military headquarters, office buildings and an assortment of eateries joined with vehicles parked haphazardly envelope a once forested low density neighborhood. As we resettled in our old neighbourhood, indications from all directions emerged that we were in a place distant from the Upanga or Dar es Salaam of the 1960s. With every passing month, the gap between the old and the new widens, and things proceed in directions that generally are not pleasant to behold.

Housing

The current population of Dar es Salaam is more than eight times what it was in 1960. A shortage of housing is an acute city-wide malady. Once more, there is a building boom. And once again, the NHC is a key player. Yet, how things are different. My mind flies back to the Kinondoni National Service Camp and the modest, but sturdy houses we built for the NHC in 1964. In a sharp contrast, the modern boom envelopes the city with scores of high rise structures underwritten by local and foreign tycoons, finance groups and pension funds. In a nation mired in poverty, sturdy buildings with a long life ahead of them are demolished to make room for elegant looking tall towers. To add insult to injury, the construction quality of many of these towers is so pitiful as to make any decent civil engineer worth his salt have sweat drenched nightmares.

The process displaces low income tenants and favours the elite. Only wealthy businessmen, senior staff of local and foreign companies, diplomats, expatriates and high government officials can afford the rent or purchase price. Individual units in the city centre range from US $200,000 to $400,000. It is akin to purchasing a condo in Los Angeles. The new twin towers next to the former DTC have units with rents around US $1,200 a month. A typical city dweller, who barely earns US $100 a month, can only gape at them. Once for service to the ordinary citizen, the modern NHC is a captive of the logic of wild capitalism. The law governing its operation and the national land law have been altered to comply with the capitalist agenda of the West. The state institutions now uphold the economic interests of the common person to an even lesser degree than they previously did.

There is much talk about low-income housing. But it is political and public-relations talk. For instance, in November 2012, a scheme to construct 578 units in fifteen interior areas of the nation was announced by the NHC. The total cost was put at TSh 24 billion, or roughly US $25,000 per unit (Faustine 2012). A lucky secondary school teacher earns TSh 500,000 ($\approx$ US $320) per month. The high and ever rising prices of essential goods and services do not enable a decent life for a family of three on that salary. If he is able to set aside US $50 per month, and not considering the down payment, surety and the high rates of interest, it will take him more than forty years to pay off the loan. If you factor in these other costs and the maintenance fees, and tax, it will not only take him forever to pay up, but once he moves in, he may not be able to stay in.

In any event, even if you take into account the few public housing schemes, the so-called affordable houses are too few to meet the demand. Most remain within the reach of only the top level employees of the state and private sectors. With camouflaged dealings the norm today, I wonder who their real owners will be. I suspect that teachers, nurses, clerks, journalists, low rank police personnel and small business people will only dream about owning them or living in them.

Consider the past. In 1963, my father was paying installments of about US $15 per month for hire-purchase of a spacious two-story flat in Upanga. Teachers across the nation were guaranteed housing during the 1970s with rent set at 10% of their salary. At the UDSM in 1973, I had a large, furnished one-bedroom flat. My rent of about US $12 per month included water and electricity services. The houses built under the national service scheme came at a very low cost since we built them through our own efforts. They were the genuinely affordable houses, the likes of which are unknown today.

A diluted form of compulsory national service for Form VI leavers was revived in 2012. But, due to absence of coordination with the Ministry of Education, the school year overlapped with national service dates. Existing camps lack adequate facilities and health services. For these reasons, and the lack of clear rationale and motivation, enrollment has remained low. Of the 15,000 enrollees expected in October 2013, only 1,000 showed up. A re-emergence of an effective, large-scale low-cost housing construction scheme of the 1960s type in these circumstances, and especially in the prevailing profit oriented climate, is improbable (Mjema 2014).

The NHC and two other public bodies have proposed an ambitious plan to train 6,400 young people, recruited from all districts, to make compressed soil building blocks. They will be provided with block making machines and a modest initial capital (Mwakyusa 2014). It is touted as the seed to spark nationwide expansion of construction of low cost dwellings. It sounds promising. However, the scheme is not a part of a national plan that integrates housing with other sectors of the economy. State and corporate leaders of today treat such projects as publicity generating, by the way type of schemes, and not as the essence of their duties. Most fall by the wayside once the start-up funds are exhausted.

The high rise boom in Dar es Salaam has a distressing facet: The liquid waste matter and water drainage system has not been upgraded. Blockage is thus a common occurrence, especially in the rainy season. It typifies the paradox of modernity: Skyscrapers dwarfing the eleven story building that once upon a time held me in awe now stand along streets awash in raw human waste. The affluent residents holding their noses as they emerge from these fancy abodes attired in the latest fashion and designer shoes are a sight to behold. The other day, I passed by the Kisutu Market, now surrounded by many newer buildings. It had rained the previous day. Vendors displayed fresh, mouthwatering fruits and vegetables. But about three meters away, vomit inducing raw sewage gurgled out – the extremes of a duality in stable coexistence. And that is in the city business district; the situation in the outlying markets is worse.

The Upanga area is also gripped by demented capitalism. Local and external tycoons have majestic, gated, electrified residences. Officials from multinational firms, embassies and NGOs have special places. Elites prevail in the new high rises. Communalism and racial exclusiveness of the colonial era are ascendant. Low and middle class folk, of whatever creed and colour, are on their way out. Luckily, I purchased my house in the 1970s (My father was the main funder). A similar unit opposite rents out at US $1,800 per month. Even with a decent pension, a retired professor like me cannot afford it. And, we live in a state of insecurity, as the new land laws can turn the tide against us overnight.

Upon our return we found a tonnage of garbage rotting on the streets of Upanga. The municipal authorities progressively raised the collection fees. Now they are five times the original amount. A company whose trucks have modern waste-compressing equipment got the contract. Streets became cleaner as garbage was collected twice a week. But after a year and a half, it slowly turned into an up and down situation; collection followed the schedule for a while, then became erratic. Unpredictability is the norm now. Likely, the fancy trucks are in disrepair. Perhaps spare parts are not available or are too expensive. Or they cannot reach the rain clogged dump site: Another tale of the folly of using technology that is not suitable to our concrete conditions. Thereby, in the global ranking of dirty cities, Dar es Salaam is near the top. Only seven global cities rank dirtier than our Haven of Peace (Editorial 2014c).

The only solace, if you can call it that, is that Tanzania is not an exception. Mal-development in housing and infrastructure is observed across the Third World. Under the rapacious rule of international capitalism, dominated nations from Bangladesh to Malawi to El Salvador exist under a model of superficial, uneven economic growth. The few rich reside in palaces, a small middle class has a modicum of decent housing, but the masses dwell in congested slums where dirty water, disease and filth are the order of the day.

Fruits

On the way to the city centre or Kariakoo, I tread the road I walked daily some fifty years ago. The two majestic baobabs no longer hail me. Umpteen fruit bearing trees have departed from the scene. And those that remain serve more to provide shade rather than fruit.

Khungu, the fruit of the Indian Almond tree, was once commonplace. A ripe fruit has a multi-coloured, half a centimetre top layer that is soft and edible. The taste goes from tangy to mildly sweet, and the hard seed encloses an almond-like but thinner and sweeter kernel. Some afternoons our gang collected *khungus* scattered under the trees. Back at the HQ, we split the shells with stones and iron bars to extract the almonds; it was a laborious job but worth the effort. After dividing up the pile of a hundred or so almonds, we enjoyed the bounty and chatted away. The modern child, brown or black, does not even glance at such nutritional pearls.

Khungu sellers were then spread out across the city. Today, only two city centre street corners have one. And their overpriced *khungus* are not the thick-skinned variety of yesteryear. Once in a blue moon, a hawker near the main JK has small packets with ten to fifteen *khungu* seeds. They are exorbitantly priced: TSh 5,000 per packet (To put it into perspective, a casual labourer in the mid-1960s earning four to five shillings a day could get eight to ten such packets. Now with the official wage of TSh 3,000 per day, he cannot get even one). I guess the nostalgic ex-Tanzanian Asians, hundreds of whom have taken to visiting their erstwhile homeland of recent, and who routinely put up in TSh 150,000 per night hotels, fork out the sum without a second thought.

And what I am going to say now is not a fantasy. In the years 2012 and 2013, each morning we found two to five *khungu* shells, bereft of flesh, in our backyard. We thought that the crows who daily create a cacophony on our roof were dumping what was left after nibbling the fruit. In December 2013, Farida discovered that it was a small monkey who was showering the fine blessings on us. Collecting these remnants untill she had a good number, she split them open. The ten or so edible seeds brought culinary joy to her and Hadija. I cannot touch them due to a digestive ailment. However, in March 2014, the blessed creature decamped as mysteriously as it had arrived.

The guava and *Sita fud* (apple custard) were once ubiquitous inhabitants of the Upanga gardens; now I see them only in a couple of places. Happily, both of them and the sister fruit *Ram fud* are seasonally still aplenty in the city centre and Kariakoo markets. In 2010, we planted *Sita fud* in our backyard. Now two tall trees have sprung up. They seasonally bear sweet but small sized fruits. Each year, we harvest them by the dozen.

The once familiar *bor* (jujube fruit) and cashew trees have taken permanent leave from our area. The former looks like a three quarters of an inch diameter marble and has two varieties. The light green variety, which I like, is bland or acidic. The yellow-red skin variety is as sweet as an over ripe mango. Their flesh has a roughish texture that rankles your tongue. Mother did not have a preference for fruits, but with one exception: She loved *bors*. They were sold near the entrance of my school in 1961. But I have not seen them anywhere in Dar es Salaam in the past fifteen years.

Zambarau is an oval shaped fruit resembling a damson. From the Java Plum tree family, its purple skin and mushy layer are edible, but the seed is not. In my youth, it was abundant in the Upanga area, and was highly popular with us. Voluminously productive in season, a long, hook-ended stick would yield a hefty bunch of *zambaraus*. The ground below was littered with a purple mush of over-ripe fruit. That sight is a distant memory. The few trees that remain display an occasional ripe bunch lurching in the wind, and that too high above. Fortunately, and especially from December to March, it is sold in local markets. An itinerant bicycle vendor brings it to our home. In a rare case of carryover from the past, he sells the fruit in the traditional, home spun straw packets that preserve freshness and do not damage the soft skin. Plastic has yet to conquer his domain.

Mouthwatering small and large mangoes that once swung hither and thither from high and low branches by the ton are barely visible, even during peak season. I cannot get used to the absence of the plump *embe dodos* in our area. On the positive side: In the past five years, the supply of mangoes, papaya, plums, oranges, pineapples, peaches and apples from upcountry has increased appreciably. In season, they are aplenty across the city. I have the impression that these days mangoes are available in more months of the year than was the case in the 1960s and 70s. But they are pricey. The other day, I got superb *embe dodos* at TSh 1,000 a piece; an appropriately paid day labourer can get but three of them with his whole day's earnings.

Thorny trees of the spiral shaped tamarind remain plentiful. But the branches hold less fruit and the edible layer is not as thick, soft and sweet as it once was. The papaya and banana plants are far fewer in Upanga, but happily no shortage of their fruits prevails in the city markets.

On my walks around Upanga, I halt alongside my old friends to count the fruits on display. It does not satisfy me. Too few, I mutter to myself. When I see the *khungus* just with thin, crusty skins, I wonder why. As I stand gazing at the branches, passersby wonder. The old man has taken leave of his senses – that is likely what they feel. Who knows, perhaps I have.

And I find trees unseen by me as a child. There are numerous synthetic looking palm trees, and more so, rows upon rows of tall, standardized, droopy eucalypti. Growing adjacent to bungalows, the army HQ and elsewhere, they are supposed to symbolize urban renewal and protection of the environment. It is doubtful that they do either. An outcome of externally inspired, NGO driven schemes, they diminish the natural diversity of the area, and damage the ecosystem. I find them a depressing sight.

The remaining large trees at least provide shade to young men who do not have much to do. Others shelter banana sellers and fellows who roast cassava, maize or sweet potato. Accompanying them are peddlers of cigarettes, ground nuts, artificial juice and sweets. Trees are our free enterprise zones. But these torn-shirted entrepreneurs barely make ends meet. And instead of rotting fruit, plastic bags, bottles, paper and packaging foil dominate the ground.

That once lonely, picturesque path I used to traverse from my home to the DTC has acquired murky colours. Now it is a poorly paved road. I seek the fresh air and botanical aroma of my youth, but only ingest noxious lung scarring exhaust fumes from vehicles zooming by. The drivers, particularly the motor cyclists, display scant respect for traffic rules. A two-wheeled speeder can emerge out of nowhere to hurtle directly towards you. The road designer did not give due thought to pedestrians. Your choice is to stand your ground or dive into the ditch. Walking along or crossing this once tranquil road entails an enhanced risk to limb and life. The other day, a young lady trying to cross it waited for a good while, but the traffic did not let up. In frustration, she made her move, only to earn nasty insults from speeding drivers. No one had the decency to slow down. It was a display of our neo-liberal brand of modernity: as assertive vehicles and vendors conquer even the footpaths, the millions of pedestrians essentially have no rights on the auto-dominated, chaotic streets.

Flowers

Our gang had also collected flowers. Not that we were a bunch of sissies. We had reasons. First, we were always hungry. That is why the *mkakaya* (flamboyant) tree was coveted. In flowering season, its branches sparkle with medium sized, five petaled flowers. Four petals are pinkish red but one is deep red on one side and bright white on the other. The white side is doused with small pink dots. It is edible, having a mild lemon like taste. We plucked and chewed two to three flowers at a time. The nascent bud has swell-tasting innards as well. You bite off the leathery bottom, squeeze out the contents directly into your mouth and chew away in delight.

It was the same with the nascent buds of *rosella* (hibiscus). Their milder taste, though, attracted fewer fans. Another prized entity was a shiny yellow, three inch long, bell shaped flower with nectar sweeter than honey. The trick is to gently pluck it in a sideways position, quickly put it in the mouth, and suck the nectar before it drains out. But there was a danger; bees and wasps were fond of them too. We did not approach the plant if we saw these buzzards buzzing about. I think it is called yellow bells or yellow trumpet flower. Like the flamboyant and rosella flowers, the trees are still around, but in significantly lower numbers.

The second reason for collecting flowers was to be in the good books of our mothers. If we came home late, but had a bunch of flowers, we would be spared sharp words or worse, complaints to our fathers. My mother was fond of the intensely fragrant *langi langi* (ylang-ylang, cananga), the white, unopened *asmini* (jasmine) and the white-yellow, overlapping petaled *plumera* flowers.

The latter two carry a religious significance. She folded the five petals of a plumera into the stem, and linked five to ten folded flowers by a sewing thread, making a garland. The *asminis*, if she had them, would be threaded therein as well. The garland was hung across the photo of Prince Karim Aga Khan on the living room cabinet. A handful of *asminis* were taken to the JK, and sprinkled near the foot of his large photo on the centre stage.

With such goodies in our hands, Mother tolerated our late arrivals. But we had to exercise care. If the amount was excessive, sharp questions arose. And, it had to be an occasional occurrence. Hence, we brought flowers along only on the few days we were late. At times, I had a small raw papaya plucked from someone's garden. Not aware of its origin, she would cut it into thin slices, and fry them with turmeric and salt. It was Father's preferred side-dish.

You still find jasmine plants in some gardens, and plumeras near foot paths. Our neighbor has an expansive, productive *asmini* plant. Hindus revere it and place the flowers at the foot of a picture or statue of their deity. When I pass by the Hindu temple during my evening walks, I sometimes buy a plumera/jasmine garland for Farida. Distinctly pleased, she places it in a bowl of water on the dining table. However, she notes that unlike in the past, these *asminis* are not mature, and lack the distinctive aroma. These vendors, like most people in this noble land, have taken to compromising quality and taking short cuts as a standard practice in life.

Birds and Bees

Bees, wasps and butterflies are now a rarity. Natural beehives hanging from or attached to the branches of trees, an unremarkable sight then, have melted away. Is that why the *mzambarau*, mango tree and the *mkhungu* bear too few fruits? On the other hand, the ugly fly has run amok; the instant the main door opens, they penetrate the kitchen area. The mosquito population fluctuates; at times, none is seen; soon after the rains, you feel their bite. Malaria was an integral part of life in the 1960s. But then it was an eminently treatable condition with the cheap, though bitter tasting chloroquine. Now they are changing biting patterns and do not emit the usual zzz-ing sound. Presently, a mosquito bite exposes you not just to the possibility of a severe episode of malaria, but increasingly to dengue fever and filariasis. The hospitals in the city are overcrowded and chaotic. Their fees are nothing to smile about, and despite the high cost, you face the potential of flawed laboratory tests, mis-diagnosis, sub-standard or fake drugs, incomplete follow up and poorly trained and not-that-professionally behaved medical staff.

Mornings and evenings, noisy crows circle the sky. If a morsel of food is on the ground, a couple land swiftly in our back yard, making our four tiny kittens scatter in fright. The fine bird songs of the past are seldom heard today. In particular, in these seven years I have not once been rejoiced by the guttural calls of the wild pigeon (*njiwa pori*) that Amer and I competed to imitate. That cool *kuku, ku ku, kuku; kuku, ku ku, kuku* tune we had convincingly irritated our DTC Swahili teacher with has died out, at least from this part of town. Perhaps a zoologist can explain these changes in the insect and bird life of Dar es Salaam.

Sea Shells

The Upanga Beach was a favourite haunt for my 1962 gang. If the tide was high, we swam; if not we ran, jumped, raced or played with balls, pebbles and marbles. My hobby of collecting sea shells dates back from that time. I was intrigued by their exquisite designs. Varied sized cowrie shells, with light grey, yellow to dark purple skins, and striped and spotted cones, were prized. I had a small box in which I kept my best shells; and did not allow anyone to touch them.

The habit minus the possessiveness persists. During the weekends, Farida and I walk along the sea front. The fresh breeze takes you away from the fumes, dust, heat and grind of the congested and unruly city. Regularly, I pick up sea shells. At low tide, the catch can be a fine one. Split clams and cockles, and brownish flask bubbles are plentiful. Small and medium multi-coloured cowries, resplendent olives, and distinctly patterned cones are also found. On a good day, small button tops, augurs, rosy harps, the odd South African turban, and rarer items are spotted.

The children see me stooping and sifting the sand. They gather nearby and inquire, "*Babu*, what are you doing?" I explain and they join in. In a sweet gesture of kindness, they search and hand me what they find. Of recent, enterprising youth who make shell necklaces and bracelets for tourists have been gathering up all the bounty from the sea. Not much remains. But then, my beach walks have also lessened in number.

The bulk of my seaside gatherings, including the exquisite shells I buy from the Kigamboni market, has been passed on to Emma. She lives far away, in Los Angeles. I think she now has a larger and more beautiful treasure trove of sea shells than any other child in her area. Until 2011, when I used to visit her once a year, one of our joint activities was to catalogue the items in her burgeoning shell museum. Going through a sea shells book, we identified the pieces, and labelled and organized them. Cataloguing is not a straightforward job. The sub-varieties resemble each other in a confusing way. A magnifying glass and ruler are needed to pin point the exact identity. Emma remembers the names and patterns better than I do. Many a time, she has corrected my error while pointing to a pattern better matching the shell in hand.

A Distinctive Calendar: Imagine my delight early in 2008 when I received a sea shell calendar booklet designed and constructed just for me. Emma (with the help of two friends) had made it using a 10 by 12 inch plastic folder with twelve transparent plastic inlets. With two sides for each month, the right hand side has a photo of shells from her collection that are organized in a creative pattern. A hand written phrase appears next to it. Below it is a computer generated monthly calendar page in the usual format, but with key historic events and family birthdays noted. The left side features a Ten Things to Do blank lined page. The cover is decorated likewise. Of the creatively constructed pages, I best liked the month of October. It had honey, snake head and blue top cowrie shells in the form of the international peace symbol with the label 'I love peace.'

Aging has its blessings – I was plainly enthralled by the gift. My heart swelled with the feeling that I possessed an item unique in the whole universe. I showed it to others with pride. Month after month, I noted down the tasks to be done in those pages. A few were completed; some were not even begun; some were re-listed; some, abandoned. But at the end, a few major tasks saw a successful outcome. I thank Emma for her love, and instilling greater discipline into my then hectic life.

My attraction to shells inflicted on me an experience I would rather not have had. On a sunny February day of 2009, I spotted a sparkling brown tun. A shallow stream stood between us. So I jumped across, only to lose my footing and fall face down. I lost my pair of glasses, got my clothes sandy and wet. Worse, as the stream was adjacent to a sewer pipe, I ingested a hefty dose of noxious bacteria. Given my already shaky health status, a long course of antibiotics was needed to clear up the nasty belly ache that ensued. It took nearly two months for me to re-gather the confidence to resume my walks. Now I tread the ground with care, and remember that the agility of youth is not everlasting.

That sort of infection would have been unlikely in the 1960s. Then the sewer pipes went under two long cement jetties that dumped the city effluence into the sea. At high tide, we swam from one jetty to the next. Both the jetties are rubble now. Malodorous, slimy sewage emerges at the shore line. The water is a toxic brew. Yet scores of young and older kids, some supervised by parents, swim and play in these waters as if all is hunky-dory.

The kids who played at Upanga Beach in the 1960s were exclusively brown skinned. Now 90% are black skinned. But that welcome change masks an unchanging aspect. While the earlier era children were from the lower or middle strata of the Asian community, today the children of the middle level African elite in shiny four wheel drive vehicles spend weekend hours swimming and playing in Upanga Beach.

In those days, the high class Asian kids went to Oysterbay Beach, which had posh hotels. Today, Dar es Salaam boasts many more high priced, astoundingly luxurious beach front hotels. Most are in distant places. I do not enter them. From what I hear of their amenities, I wonder where we as a society are headed. The real high class elite children – black, brown and white – frolic in the large pools and relish Los Angeles style ice cream. The run down, smelly Upanga sea front is not their piece of cake.

It goes without saying that the kids of the ordinary African folk from Manzese, Buguruni and Tabata remain where they have always been. If they come to the beach, it is to sell roasted ground nuts, sweets and biscuit packets.

That is the essence of the change from the colonial times: Race based economic elitism has been replaced by a multiracial form of economic elitism. The degree of elitism, the gap between the rich and poor, is far beyond anything we could then have imagined. To cap it all, racial attitudes and separation persist, in camouflaged but solid forms (see the following chapters). Yes, there is change, but without substantive change.

Food

I am drawn to ponder on three goodies from the past: *kisamvu* (tender cassava leaves); *maboga* (pumpkins) and rosella (hibiscus) flower.

Kisamvu: Way back in the 1950s, Mother cooked coconut laced *kisamvu* curry and served it with rice. Its exquisite flavour has been permanently imprinted on our taste buds. As Rafik craves it to this day, Farida prepares it in the classic style when he visits us. He takes it with *ugali* and *maharagwe*. Father and I relish the soup she crafts from dried *kisamvu*, tomatoes, green onions, turmeric and garlic.

The current availability of *kisamvu* in Dar es Salaam is sporadic. The leaves are too aged, even at the Kariakoo market. Once I found succulent bunches at the Keko market. But it is too distant for regular procurement. In early 2009, I saw, for the first time, three types of local leafy vegetables including *kisamvu* in a dried, packaged form. The leaves are soaked overnight and cooked in the usual way. The taste is similar to the fresh variety. Originally for the expatriate, tourist and export sectors, and niche supermarkets, I was lucky to find it in a Kariakoo market stall. Unfortunately but predictably, the packages were too expensive for a typical local family. So, like most indigenous goods, they became sporadic. By the middle of 2013, they were gone. I inquired why but could not get a straight answer. But suddenly, in early 2014, they reappeared though in fewer places. As people become attached to chips, roasted meat and the like, the local demand for home grown nutritionally blessed foods is not high enough to sustain regular production. We throw away our gold for the sake of shiny brass.

Maboga: Another hangover for me from the 1950s Ruponda days is *maboga* (pumpkins). A staple in parts of rural Tanzania; in most urban centres, it forms a dish for *Ramadan,* the Muslim month of fasting. Large and small pumpkins of varied shapes and colours abound in the markets during that month. But if you search well, you can find it year around. We buy it regularly. With steam, it cooks fast. Unlike the bland stuff in the USA, many Tanzanian varieties are naturally sweet. If I am up to it, I scoop out the soft pulp, add baker's chocolate, cinnamon and a pinch of salt and heat the mixture for five minutes. With a pinch of honey, my father slurps this delicious chocolate *maboga* with delight. Mother used to prepare it in a curried form, and served it with rice or *chapati.*

Unethical Consumerism: Two things that perpetually bugged me during my years in the USA were endless shopping and extensive waste. The case of the pumpkins is illustrative. The USA produces nearly 800 million kg of these nutritious entities every year. About a quarter is used for decorative purposes during Halloween. Pumpkin pies are cooked or purchased in excessive quantities during this time and also at Thanksgiving. A historic tradition is now an imitate-thy-neighbor consumer fad. A large amount is dumped; tens of thousands of kilos of candies also find their way into the dust bin after Halloween. In a world and nation where millions go hungry, such incredible waste is profoundly unethical. It greatly harms the environment. That my grandchildren happily partake in such wasteful rituals without a second thought pains me to no end.

The fate of the pumpkin in our backwaters of capitalism is different in a way, but similar in essence. It grows in vast quantities in southern areas of Tanzania like Ruvuma Region. But inadequate attention to improving transport facilities, absence of canning plants, and skewed agricultural policies that do not prioritize development of local foods and creation of an internal market, mean that a large proportion of the harvest does not reach potential consumers in the cities or other regions. The price paid to the small scale farmer is a tiny proportion of the final selling price. Apart from during the Muslim holy month, a significant portion rots at the origin.

The leaves and seeds of the pumpkin plant are edible too. While the former is used in Dar es Salaam as a substitute for spinach, the seeds are often discarded. Unlike their elders in their home villages, our house workers threw away pumpkin seeds. When I said that they were prized items in America, they felt I was joking. You find roasted pumpkin seeds mostly in city supermarkets, but at a price few can afford. Once I took a small packet home. At the sight of the TSh 2,000 price label, they were aghast. Since then, we keep the seeds and dry them in the sun. When a decent amount has accumulated, it is roasted and enjoyed by everyone.

Pumpkin is a nutrition power house. A source of calories mostly as complex carbohydrates, it has good levels of dietary fiber; potent amounts of a Vitamin A precursor; Vitamin C and Vitamin E; modest levels of the B group of vitamins; adequate quantities of minerals like magnesium, zinc, potassium and iron; and a smattering of calcium too (Wikipedia 2013b). This home-grown, traditional vegetable can significantly enhance the nutritional status of the children of Tanzania. For that to happen, the Ministry of Agriculture has to plan and oversee expanded cultivation on a yearlong basis. Transport and storage facilities and canning factories are needed. Subsidized pumpkins and pumpkin products, in sufficient quantity, must be available to public schools.

The raised demand would sustain the chain of activities from farming, distribution, canning and sales. The taste buds of children would be attuned to pumpkins from an early age, thus creating future consumers. Pumpkins pies, cakes, biscuits and desserts should grace shops and restaurants across the nations. It should be a national staple. This is but another one of the many dreams I perhaps foolishly harbour.

Rosella: This flower represents a positive development. In 1962, our gang used to pluck it from the wild and munch it. Now dried rosella flowers are available in markets and supermarkets, and at a modest price. There are rosella tea bags too; but they are on the expensive side. You can buy bottled rosella juice at the Muhimbili Institute of Traditional Medicine. But it is cheap and easy to make at home. Boil a handful of the dried flower with two liters of water for five minutes, cool and sieve. Drink it as it is, add ice, or sweeten to taste.

According to recent scientific research, it has good mineral and vitamin content, and may assist the control of high blood pressure. But the latter claim has to be subjected to large scale, longer term human studies.

Globalization

Globalization has significantly altered our environment, flora, fauna, and taste buds. It has converted traditional nutritious dishes into tourist delicacies. And we ingest starchy, oily, sugary or salt laced junk foods.

A man who sells us vegetables was having his lunch. In his hand was half a loaf of white bread and an ice-cold soda. I asked him why he sold us gold only to buy rusted iron. What about a banana or an orange with cold water? He looked at me and shrugged his shoulders. Once I brought home buns made from whole sorghum. Farida ate and liked them, but our house worker did not; she prefers the sweet *mandazi* made from refined wheat flour. Was not what I had brought consumed by her parents in the village? Yes, it was. But she had moved forward in life!

Our taste buds have been neo-colonized. Nutritious vegetables, beans and whole grains that generations have consumed have been replaced by attractively packaged but sugary biscuits and Coke, Fanta or synthetic juice from China and South Africa. It is all around. Arguments over whether Fanta or Mirinda is more satisfying are loudly heard on the streets. The ads for these drinks permeate the airwaves. And obesity is equated with status and progress.

Apples and grapes from South Africa are easier to procure than pumpkins from Ruvuma. In advanced capitalist societies, overconsumption and waste prevail. Decorative use trumps nutrition, generating large corporate profits. In the dominated capitalist nations of Africa, under consumption prevails as a result of myopic donor-driven governmental policies and lack of investment for the creation of an internal market. Instead of enhancing the health status of our kids, tons of vegetables rot at the source. Poverty and malnutrition hold sway quite needlessly.

I could go on with examples, but the basic point has been made. It is but one of the many critical, internationally influenced forms of dualism that keep Africa mired in poverty and ill health.

I see NGO based attempts to rescue the situation. Well-funded reports on the promotion of traditional foods are written; a small booklet is printed. But it is sold in one or two city centre bookstores, and at a sum no ordinary person would part with. I suspect many if not all of them are bought by visitors and tourists. Instead of such feeble, transient attempts, a solid national nutritional strategy is required. How can that happen when our ministers and high officials are busy traveling abroad, and pocketing huge allowances. Can they envision and oversee such an effort? They cannot and will not until we learn the key lesson: Take our destiny into our own hands, and tell the 'donors' and foreign investors to go home and cool off for a while.

Last year, Farida and I went around Upanga with Emma to show her the flowers, fruits and trees we as children were familiar with. Some were there but many were not. Of the missing were the gigantic baobabs that once looked after their smaller brethren, and the cashew, jujube and pomegranate trees. Healthy sugar cane foliage was less visible. No *zambaraus* bunches were seen. Emma has the keen instinct of a naturalist, and her ears are well attuned to the distinct sounds of birds and bats. She gave us a splendid lesson on flowers and birds.

I came back with the impression that nature has been denatured; its aroma, its soothing melodies reduced. Have the creatures which pollinate plants and increase their bounty been driven away by exhaust fumes and the onset of climate change? By restricting the quality and quantity of its bounty, is nature sending us a warning?

My feeling is that most strands in the spiralling process engulfing the environment around us are on a downward trajectory. Only a few depict an upward spiral of hope. Generally, it looks as if we are spiralling towards a state that portends gloom. But perhaps it is all in my mind. Perhaps, my senses are too biased by nostalgia. I hope I am wrong, but deep down, I feel I am not.

The Golden Spiral ❖ ❖ ❖ ❖ ❖ ❖ ❖

Browsing the maths section of the UDSM library in 1971, I saw a book with stunning photos of sea shells, flowers, pine cones and classic architectural designs. Each had a spiral based pattern in its structure.

The outer casing of sea shells like the nautilus, helmet, cone and tun shells has a spiralling pattern. The arrangement of the seed bed of the sunflower shares that feature. Two spiral forms we can generate by simple maths formulas and which resemble these natural entities are the logarithmic and golden spirals.

The golden spiral is named after a number known as the golden ratio. Denoted by the Greek letter ϕ, it appears in structures of natural and man-made things, though not always in a precise way. By definition, ϕ is a positive number such that the difference between it and its reciprocal is one.

$$\phi - \frac{1}{\phi} = 1 \quad \text{or} \quad \phi^2 - \phi - 1 = 0$$

Using the quadratic equation formula, we get that

$$\phi = \frac{\sqrt{5}+1}{2} \approx 1.6218; \quad \frac{1}{\phi} = \frac{\sqrt{5}-1}{2} \approx 0.6218 \text{ and } \phi^2 \approx 2.6218$$

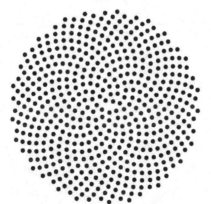

Sunflower Floret Pattern

A number of formulas using the golden ratio provide a fair representation of the arrangements of the florets in a sunflower. Let r be the distance of a floret from the centre, θ, the angle the ray from the centre to the floret makes with a fixed line through the centre, and n, the index number. One set of relevant formulas is:

$$r = c\sqrt{n} \quad \text{and} \quad \theta = \frac{360 \times n}{\phi}$$

Here c is a scaling factor. To obtain the spiral, we set a value for c, and calculate the pairs (r, θ) for say, $n = 1, 2, 3, 4, \ldots, 500$. Placing these on a graph paper, we get the pattern shown above. Note: It is easy to do this on a computer.

That library book also introduced me to Fibonacci numbers. These numbers are obtained by setting the first two Fibonacci numbers to be 1 and 1, and computing the rest of the Fibonacci numbers with the following rule:

Current Number = Sum of Previous Two Numbers

Using this rule we get the series of numbers:

{ 1, 1, 2, 3, 5, 8, 13, 21, 34, 55, 89, 144, 233, 377, 610, ... }

Fibonacci numbers often appear in the same context as the golden ratio because they are related in a basic way. First, as you proceed along, the ratio of successive Fibonacci numbers approaches the golden ratio, ϕ. For example, the ratio of the 15th and 14th Fibonacci numbers, 610/377, equals 1.6180. Second, we can express the nth Fibonacci number (f_n) in terms of the golden ratio.

$$f_n = \frac{1}{2}(\phi^n + \phi^{-n}) = \frac{1}{2}\left(\left[\frac{\sqrt{5}+1}{2}\right]^n + \left[\frac{\sqrt{5}-1}{2}\right]^n\right)$$

These properties allow us to construct the golden spiral either by using a formula based on ϕ, or approximately with the use of Fibonacci numbers.

The golden spiral is alternatively formed by placing squares whose sides are proportional to Fibonacci numbers next to each other in the cascading pattern shown in the diagram below.

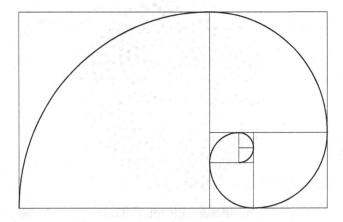

The Golden Spiral

Attractive spirals, the golden ratio and the Fibonacci numbers link my hobby of collecting sea-shells with my passion for maths. Both interests arose in my teenage days, yet I did not link them until I had graduated from the university. Suppose our maths teacher had taken us to the beach, made us collect shells, talked about their intricate patterns, properties and history. Would the proposition that maths is beautiful have encountered the indifference it did?

As I bend down to collect a sea shell these days, I give a nod to the view that:

To find a seashell is to discover a world of imagination.

Michelle Held

And I dream of Tanzanian children scouring the beach with excitement, hunting for shells, rocks and crabs. I dream that they seek the myriad of beautiful spiral patterns in books or the Internet, and compare them with their own collection. I dream their curiosity about nature and the mysteries of the realm of numbers is sparked. When will it no longer be a dream?

And I have fears. Sea shells have evolved for more than 500 million years. The one you found strewn along the sea shore may be tens of thousands years old. The unfolding global climate change patterns, however, do not bode well for these beauties of nature. Irrational modes of economic development unleashed by neo-liberal capitalism, which depend on ever increasing the use of oil, coal and gas as main sources of energy, are spewing billions of tons of carbon dioxide into the atmosphere, changing our climate and leading to further acidification of the oceans. Sea shells are highly sensitive to change in the acidity of their environment; a slight change and these apparently sturdy structures begin to dissolve with rapidity (Germanos 2014). Will the children of my grandchildren inhabit a world where a walk along the beach will no longer be an opportunity to admire and touch these marvelous products of nature?

— 13 —

Spirals of Solidarity

For humans, no circle is ever closed.
We walk ever in spirals.
R Scott Bakker

❖ ❖ ❖ ❖ ❖ ❖ ❖

A SERENDIPITOUS ENCOUNTER with a childhood friend: I am ecstatic. We hug and talk as we did eons ago. We recall and exchange news of mutual friends. But the euphoria does not last. Our current lives are a world apart; our priorities are so unlike. Only in a few cases does the contact continue. In most, the chance meeting is actually a formal good bye. We recede into our own worlds, worries and memories.

As I foresaw retirement from full time work, I made concerted efforts to locate people from my past. I scouted physical and electronic spaces I had rarely frequented. My on-the-ground range was restricted due to health reasons, but luck was on my side. Numerous long lost buddies, relatives and teachers were found. A gratifying experience in its own right, it also revived my autobiographical memory, and corrected some misconceptions I had come to harbour about those days.

These reunions bear upon issues central to this book. As elsewhere, with a few exceptions, I omit the connections I developed after June 1968.

Teachers

A series of contacts landed me on a website with volumes of historic material on Lindi. At www.dewani.ca I was amazed to find, among other things, pictures of the Indian Public School students and teachers of the 1950s. Vatsalaben, the dreadful teacher who first channelled me into the world of numbers, was right there. The description of this lady I give in Chapter 1 was written before I saw her picture. While my recall of Lindi life was faulty in several instances, the image I had retained of her was accurate to ten decimal places. I guess she truly must have terrified me.

Mr Hirani, one of my two stellar maths teachers at the AKBS, had ceased teaching maths by 1970. He switched to accountancy and bookkeeping, subjects which were job-related and in demand at the time. I used to run into him from time to time during the 1970s. He was not too happy, particularly because the Aga Khan Education Board had not well appreciated his skills and contributions. Like most Ismailis, he and his family relocated to Canada. That was in 1993. Unfortunately, he acquired Alzheimer's disease and passed on in 2003. I learned of his demise in 2013. But I was able to contact his son and convey to him words of the heavy debt I owed to his father.

Fazli Datoo had been a student at the AKBS in the 1950s. He had a fine aptitude for maths from the outset. Yet, he had neglected the subject. Luckily, his potential was recognized by Mr Almeida. With encouragement from a guardian uncle and patient tutoring from this teacher, Fazli began to excel in maths. After his brief teaching stint at the AKBS, he went on to obtain a master's degree in maths and subsequently completed the professional actuarial science program at the University of Michigan.

He made the USA his home, though he worked in the UK as well. Distinguishing himself in his profession, he rose into the senior ranks in the corporate arena. In recognition of the reputation for excellence he had acquired over the years, he was invited by his alma mater to address the year 2005 actuarial science graduates. It is an inspiring speech, infused with pearls of wisdom. Reading it made me dream about the stupendous impact he could have made on his students had he gone on with teaching after completing university studies.

A year 2012 chance electronic encounter with Al-Noor Jiwan Hirji, a 1961 classmate and a distant relative, culminated in a pleasant electronic reunion with Mr Datoo. We connected with each other over the telephone in July 2013. I was elated to rehear the gentle voice of my wise teacher. And I found that excellence runs in the family. His daughter leads a non-profit organization that promotes nutritional products for humanitarian emergencies like those occurring in Africa, and has received high accolades for her work.

While I have no doubt that she has the best of intentions and plans, I remain sceptical towards all external initiatives taken to solve Africa's problems. Whatever their immediate benefit, in the long run, they create dependencies that weaken our resolve and ability to deal with our own problems. I have yet to find exceptions to this rule.

I tried to locate Mr Isaya and Mr Brooks, my favourite DTC teachers, but it was to no avail. No one currently at my former school and none of my DTC buddies knew what had become of the former. Contacting the US employer of the latter did not yield a positive result either. But I did not attempt to contact my Scandinavian teachers at Kibaha School – there are only twenty four hours in a day.

Lindi Friends

During the year 2013, I was able to get in touch with about twenty five people who were in Lindi or the surrounding areas during the years I was there. Many are in Dar es Salaam, but a number live in Canada or the UK. Several of them know my father and reminded me about aspects of Lindi life that I had forgotten.

The web site on Lindi noted above is maintained by Mustafa Pirmohamed. He joined the Indian Public School a few years after I did. It has been a pleasure to communicate with a person dedicated to the fast disappearing practice of maintaining historical memory.

Apart from Firoz Jadavji, I have not been able to locate my primary school classmates. We were together from standards one to three. He is now a sales manager in a wholesale firm. A mild mannered personality, he is well respected in the Ismaili community. His principal role at present is to organize recreational events for the elderly Ismailis of Dar es Salaam.

Gang Members

Four members of my Undali Street gang have passed away, one is in Canada and four remain in Dar es Salaam. Parvez Vira became an acclaimed cricketer and prospered in business. The two brothers Amilo Pipi and Shokat are working class persons facing major challenges in these strenuous times. For decades, both applied themselves most diligently to the task of making a living, but life did not deal them a fair hand.

Amilo worked aboard international sea-faring vessels for nearly fifteen years. Later he was a factory floor supervisor, and now is a delivery agent in an electronics firm in the city. Two years back, he experienced a painful, disfiguring attack of facial shingles. I am glad he got over it with minimal scarring. Riding a motor bike in his mid-sixties, he has maintained the physique he had in our gang days. He has one son. When the boy was in primary school, I gave him a chess set and instructed him at the game. Time has rushed by; the once young kid is a harried married man, and Amilo is a grandpa like me. Amilo comes home about once a month; we drink tea and have our usual long chat about the olden times. He likes to call me by my old title, captain.

Shokat went to Congo, mastered French and for years was a field supervisor on a large plantation. He too is married with a son. Upon returning home, he landed a similar job in Kibaha. However, the company relinquished its assets to another investor, thereby plunging him once more into that most frustrating pursuit: job hunting. Like his brother, he has too often faced the callousness of modern capitalism whereby the bosses underpay, overwork employees and display little regard for their welfare. Because of the rough and tough life he has led, he looks frailer and older than he is. Yet, he remains a calm person. I run into him fairly often in the city centre.

Amirali Bhanji is a saga unto himself. He went to the DTC in the late 1960s, and obtained a Diploma in Mechanical Engineering. For decades he worked as a boiler room engineer, first in state owned and later in Ismaili run factories. He put in extra time and effort wherever he worked. But even in the latter places, he was not paid well. He is by nature an honest and simple person. In our cut-throat era, when almost everyone is inclined to bluff, cheat and do a half-hearted job, he remained a steadfast exception.

The onset of neo-liberalism in the 1990s saw many local factories close down due to unfair competition from imports. Amirali found himself without a job and with zero prospects of landing a similar one. An Ismaili friend employed him as a sales person in a small toy shop, but the pay was minimal. And his heart was not into it. What he was eminently qualified for, what he enjoyed doing, he could not do. That catalysed the downhill spiral in his life.

He has little family support. On the contrary, he cared for a mentally disabled elder brother for decades. Though there was some financial and material assistance from the community, he bore the burden mostly on his own. His attachment to Firoz, a man of fine creative bent, was remarkable. When in a functional state, Firoz crafted wood carvings, decorative key chains and elegant wood toys for children. I used to purchase them for my grandkids.

As noted in Chapter 12, these years have been a time of insecurity and anxiety for the low income residents in Upanga. The NHC, in its headlong drive to build high rise structures, and in dubious alliances with local and foreign tycoons, has evicted tenants and owner occupants from places they have occupied for decades. Which building is the next one on the list is not known. Out of the blue, a notice lands on your doorstep: Pack your bags. Rumours saturate the air and create a vibrant climate of fear. With a ton of worries already on his mind, it was the last straw for this hitherto resilient man. Like his sibling, Amirali receded into an inward spiral of mental self-imprisonment. He talked to himself, moved about aimlessly, and missed work for days. Attempts by several persons, including myself, to turn him around failed to bear fruit.

And then came the final, tragic blow. His brother took his own life. In no time, Amirali lost his composure altogether, and was hospitalized for months. No one took care of his empty flat in the meanwhile. No one paid the bills and it was seized by the NHC. Now a homeless person, he has been put up in the Ismaili Welfare facility near the city centre JK. Elderly or otherwise dysfunctional persons who do not have sufficient family support are provided free room and board at this place. Two to three weekday mornings, the residents are brought to the JK compound, counselled, and guided in moderate exercise and spirit enhancing activities. I meet Amirali there once or twice a month. He is always happy to see me.

Medications for severe depression have strong side effects. Among other things, they induce twitching, tremors and extreme dryness of the mouth. They also distort personality, making the patient uncomfortable and edgy. It has been depressing to see the deterioration of this upright man. At one point, he had completely withdrawn into himself. Happily, recently he has shown signs of re-emergence; the side effects have diminished; he talks less about the bad guys harming him and more about normal issues, and goes out of his room frequently. I fervently hope that his progress continues, and my good friend will become his ebullient, active self once more.

DTC Buddies

I essentially lost contact with my DTC buddies after 1966. Between then and the year 2000, I met Ram Jogi and Abdul Karim but a couple of times. I heard a shocking story from Abdul Karim in 1994. On an unremarkable sunny day a few years back, his lovely seven year old daughter had as usual left home for school. But that day, she did not return. Presumed kidnapped, she never reappeared. His intense anguish was evident; I could not imagine what he and his family had endured. Had I experienced such a calamity, I would have fallen apart into a million pieces. I have not met him since then (Chapter 18).

Ram Jogi worked at a business college in Morogoro for many years. People tell me that he was as jovial as ever. One day, he did not report for work. The next day it was the same. No one had seen him leave his house. No signs of activity were observed. Concerned colleagues forced their way in, only to find him in a serene state of permanent sleep. His signature booming laugh had been silenced for ever.

Between 1980 and 2000, I spent most of my life in the US, first as a doctoral student, and later as a professor. I had come to deeply regret the fact of having lost touch with my DTC buddies. From the year 2005 onwards, I began an earnest search. But, no records existed. Internet searches were of no use. It was a job of asking from person to person, canvassing from door to door in a city that had grown almost tenfold in population, and had changed beyond recognition in locations. Each time I was in Kariakoo, I talked to shop keepers who had been in the area for decades. I gave a list of names to five taxi drivers whose stand is near my house, and requested them to conduct inquiries in the course of their trips. The sum of TSh 25,000 (about US $18) was promised for each person found. The amount exceeds what they usually earn in a day, but it was to no avail. Too much time had passed. No one knew anyone. I was dejected. After nearly a year, I ceased that type of search.

I was brooding about placing advertisements in the radio and newspapers, but had not got around to it. Work and home responsibilities had diverted my attention. It became moot on 17 August 2009 when an electronic thunderbolt struck my email box. The subject line read: *Greetings from Amer. Sec Tec. D'Salaam 1962/65*. I could not believe my eyes. It remains the most pleasant email I have received to date. Amer had been on the lookout for me for a number of years. His Internet explorations had finally hit the jackpot. Overjoyed, I responded at once.

Amer had moved to Oman in the late 1970s. By 2009, he held a senior managerial position in a large cement company. A flurry of emails ensued; a week later, we talked on the phone. We came face to face when he visited Dar es Salaam in August 2010. In the fine company of Jamila (his wife) and Farida, he and I chattered and laughed over a ton of matters while sipping cups of tea. The jubilant patter went on and on (Image 9: Appendix B).

Like me, he is a grandfather, faces health hurdles, and leads a life of steady retirement. We now dwell on issues quite unlike those of yesteryears. Instead of girls and engineering drawing assignments, we talk about our fabulous grandchildren, rickety joints and lingering ailments. The endless suffering of the people of Palestine and the ugly situation in Iraq is of concern to us both.

But he gave me sad news too. Not just Ram Jogi but a number of our DTC buddies including Nassoro are no longer with us. On the plus side, he put me in touch with Isaac Marande and Abdallah Abbasi. When I met Isaac, it was another merry occasion. He runs a farm in the outskirts of Dar es Salaam and has four children. In the DTC days, he was a happy go lucky, sporty boy. Now he has a mellow and steadfast persona. A decent man from head to toe, he devotes ample time to religious affairs. Once in a while, he brings us delicious sweet potatoes, papaya and oranges from his farm. In the typical spirit of our country folk, we lament health issues, water supply problems, the situation in our schools and the appalling state of our nation. Almost as a rule, we end with nostalgic reflections about the 60s. Last year I gave a large hard-bound book with colour photos and biographies of famous soccer players to this one-time local soccer star. It was a pleasure to see his face shine like a 500 watt bulb in instant delight (Image 9: Appendix B).

He too was struck by tragedy. His barely 16 year old second son, Abdulrahim, was doing so well in school, a happy contrast to many youngsters of today. He contracted severe malaria in early 2012 and passed away, just like that. I was aghast at the sad tidings. Why does life, and a blossoming one at that, remain so expendable in Africa? Most of the problems are preventable. Yet the horrible plight of our children persists. In my view, it is a real crime against humanity. Our greedy leaders, their Western funders, crooked businessmen and negligent professionals shoulder the responsibility for this state of affairs. It is they who maintain the inefficient, elitist government and institutions we have. Such tragedies derive from the ensuing mismanagement of our health and education services and other sectors of the economy. I think they need to be put on the dock.

On a happier note, Isaac's youngest son, Twaha, passed his Standard 7 exams in November 2013, and has joined a secondary school. A pleasantly mannered, inquisitive boy, he tells me, to my delight, that maths is his number one subject. I gave him several books to keep him occupied, telling him that whenever he is stuck, he should come to me. I hope to see him more often in the months ahead.

Abdallah Madenge was supposed to be somewhere in Dar es Salaam. I urged Isaac to find him through his contacts. Two months later, word came that Madenge had passed away. We had been two weeks too late. The chubby guy with whom I had tackled the arcane riddles of differential and integral calculus at the DTC had hastily embarked on a one-way interstellar voyage without even a word of goodbye. Our search for our other friends from that era continues.

Kibaha Friends

Two of my Asian friends from Kibaha, Salim Lalani and Badroo Molu are settled in Canada, and have done well in life. I am in sporadic contact with them by email. The fine basketball players Boniface Mwaiseje and Prof. Kaduri passed away too soon. Emmanuel Kigoni did exceptionally well in his medical training and joined the Muhimbili Hospital. As he treated me for a persistent cough in the 1970s, we often met each other. The last time I saw him was in Boston in 1985. He then vanished into thin air; his former colleagues at Muhimbili do not know where he is. I have no clue of the whereabouts of the jovial Titus Kamulali.

The Kibaha friend I most closely remained in touch with is Elias Kisamo, my fellow explorer of the realms of infinity. After studying physics, mathematics and education at the UDSM at the same time as I was there, he taught physics at the high school level. Eventually, he was appointed the head master of the famed Azania Secondary School in the city. During the late 1980s, my place of work was close to his. So I used to run into him occasionally. Over a cup of tea, we philosophized about the ups and downs of life, family, teaching, maths, recalling our Kibaha, Ruvu and UDSM days. Though grayed a bit, his knack for posing abstract, out of the ordinary enigmas persisted. As in the past, our verbal exchanges did not seem to have the sense of an ending, whether in place or time.

Of the scores of school teachers from my generation I have known, I count him as among the most dedicated and hardworking. Meeting this kind and wise soul, a man of unlimited patience and non-finite spirit of inquiry, always elated me. But ten years ago, I lost touch him. I assume he has retired from regular work. As he would put it, the finiteness of our world makes it probable that our paths will converge one day. I look forward to it.

It was by design that I met Salim Msoma, who was a year ahead of me, and by luck that I met Richard Mwakalinga, a classmate. Richard obtained a doctoral degree in economics and lectured at the UDSM for a long while. Salim graduated in Political Science from the UDSM and taught development studies at, of all places, my old school, the DTC. He rose to be the principal of the DTC. Student unrest during his tenure gained him some notoriety. Later he was a high official in the government. Salim and I were fellow student activists at the UDSM. He was one of the few brave students who visited the liberated areas of war torn Mozambique. It has been nice to engage with both about the vagaries of life and politics, past and present.

The other Kibaha classmates have been harder to locate. A number of my contemporaries or near contemporaries from Kibaha School became very senior officials and ministers in the government. One became the President of Tanzania. But apart from Salim Msoma, I have not been in contact with any of them of recent.

JK Buddies

Virtually all of my JK buddies of the 1960s are dispersed in Canada, the UK and USA. It has been decades since I last met them. However, we have email contact. Though my stubborn reluctance to join social media like Facebook has not helped in the retention of such contacts.

In 2010, there was a knock on my gate. Navroz stood there with a man I did not recognize at first. It was none other than Shiraz Jaffer, the person who had guided me into the world of classy English language cinema in the 1960s. I was happy to see him, but the first thing he said was that he was troubled by my emaciated appearance. A pleasant chat ensued. In a picture of the three of us recorded in his digital camera, I stand in the middle holding, at his insistence, the bulky text book on theoretical statistics I have written. He distributed the photo to our mutual friends.

After many years abroad like me, Navroz returned to Dar es Salaam in the 1990s. More than a JK buddy of the past, he has been a long standing partner in mathematical, scientific and related pursuits. Among the most dedicated of the Upanga JK volunteers, he secured the Best Volunteer Award in 1965. After a juncture in personal life prevented him from joining high school, he took the High School Certificate examination as a private candidate. I was happy to assist him. His good passes enabled him to register as an external candidate for the Bachelor's Degree in Mathematics of the University of Cambridge. A tough endeavour, to say the least, he was fortunate that Mr Patwekar of the AKBS agreed to be his local tutor. If an intricate problem arose along the way, he would approach me. I was a maths student at the UDSM at that time.

An outstanding performance in the first part of the BSc exam secured him a scholarship to Cambridge University. Eventually, he came to hold a master's degree in theoretical physics from the Imperial College. He subsequently worked for Bell Canada and then as a software engineer in the Middle East. He returned to Dar es Salaam in the early 2000s. A senior personality in the Ismaili community, currently he is with the Tanzania Office of the Aga Khan Development Network, and oversees their projects across East Africa. With his wife Yasmin, he ran a swimming club for young children in Dar es Salaam for many years. A universally beloved, chirpy person, she unbelievably passed away in 2010.

Navroz was among the few of my JK friends with a firm nationalistic spirit. He volunteered at the Kinondoni National Service Camp a year after I did. Our common interests made me cherish his company. Work and communal responsibilities keep him tied up these days, yet he takes time to come home. We dwell on a multitude of matters: education, nutrition, philosophy, the youth, mathematics and national and international politics. I get the latest news of our friends in Canada. There is always more to talk about than time permits. Though we have differences of opinion on secular and ethereal issues, we remain the best of buddies.

A Ruvu Camp Buddy

Shiraz Ramji and I were in the same platoon in the Ruvu Camp. At the university, we were active in student organizations that championed African liberation and socialism. Among the activist students, he was known as a man of the people, a title that reflected his exceptional knack for mingling with persons of diverse racial, religious and social backgrounds. Always smiling, he befriended the old and young, and was considerate towards everyone.

Upon graduation, he was assigned to the prestigious Mkwawa High School in Iringa. Besides teaching physics, he organized study groups on local, national and global issues. The range and quality of books and magazines in the school library improved in a marked way under the assistance he provided to the librarian. He set up self-help projects in which students went to assist nearby residents. He oversaw the production of a student magazine, invited scholars from the university and members of African liberation movements to give lectures on African history, local and global politics, and the relation between science and economic development.

On his feet from morning to evening, he also tended his backyard garden and poultry shed. Farida and I were at his place in Mkwawa for four days in 1973. Like most teachers, he had been allocated a low-rent but well-built house near the school. On the first day, he asked us if we wanted eggs for breakfast. We said yes, but the kitchen tray had only one egg. No big deal, he murmured as he stepped into the backyard, put his hand under three feisty hens, and came up with three good sized warm eggs. Taken with freshly baked bread and strongly brewed tea, it was one the most memorable breakfasts I have had in my life.

Shiraz is gentle and warm hearted. His empathetic stance endeared him to his students, a number of whom later became renowned scholars. Whenever I meet them, they remember teacher Shiraz with particular fondness.

Later he obtained a master's degree in applied mathematics and was a biostatistician at the UDSM and the Ministry of Health in Zimbabwe. In both places, he contributed to research, teaching and practical work relating to public health, nutrition, and to the welfare of the elderly and the refugees fleeing Portuguese army atrocities in Mozambique.

Strange as it may seem today, to Shiraz, brown skinned Asian that he was, service to his country of birth and Africa was a central purpose in his life. Though he stood out, he was not an exception. Mwalimu's inspiring, principled and honest persona and the socio-political atmosphere of the day planted the seeds of patriotism and national solidarity in the minds of the Tanzanian youth in general, including many Asian youth. At the university many of my African friends, like Henry Mapolu for example, went on to serve the nation in the same spirit of dedication after graduation.

Family troubles ultimately landed Shiraz in Canada in the 1990s. In Vancouver at present, he has qualified in geriatrics, and devotes time to the First Nation, Palestine and senior citizen support groups. An enduring humanist in outlook and practice, he has taken to crafting elegant, inspirational poems on issues of central concern to humanity. They have not only drawn the attention of civic groups in Canada, but have also been translated into several languages. The last I met him was in 1997. Still a man of the people, he remains concerned about Africa. Like me and a good number of our peers, he faces health hurdles that restrict his mobility.

Family

My brothers, Nazir and Munir are settled in Canada, and Rafik lives near Washington, DC, USA. My daughter Rosa, her husband and two lovely grandchildren are US citizens residing in Los Angeles. Some 90 percent of my relatives are in Canada. Those who remain are the ones who have not been able, due to economic circumstance or lack of a sponsor, to make it to the distant shores.

My parents were twice admitted into Canada as landed immigrants. First it was in 1984 and then in 1994. Unable to adapt to a new style of life, they voluntarily returned to Tanzania within a couple of years both times. Mother passed away in December 2003. Father, aged ninety five, stays with us in Dar es Salaam.

In sum, I sadly note that too many of my friends, acquaintances, teachers and relatives are no longer among the living. Of those who remain, a half are scattered all over the planet, and the rest in Dar es Salaam or elsewhere in Tanzania. Luck has enabled me to reconnect with a small but good number of them.

Race and Ability

My lifelong immersion in a universe of friends, relatives, teachers, elders, colleagues, shop keepers, workers, craftsmen, students and acquaintances has reinforced a key belief I had come to accept by the time I was at the Ruvu

National Service Camp: That race or colour of skin bears no relationship to outlook, ethic, ability, intelligence, educational achievement or economic advancement. If at times they seem to do so, that is only because of unaccounted factors like economic background, support network, social conditions, historic advantage or disadvantage, nature of official policy or just pure chance (see Chapter 9).

Race is a proxy explanatory factor. The intellectual and social tragedy of our times it that it is often thought to be, sometimes conveniently, a prime causative factor. Race and religion take the centre stage on the personal, social and international dimensions, and the resulting strife has consequences that are far from pleasant.

In colonial times, race was believed to be a determining force in educational attainment and business acumen. Yet, what was seen was a cumulative effect of colonial policies that for decades favoured one race over another. Advantage built on advantage and disadvantage reinforced disadvantage. Sociologists call this phenomenon, which operates in all hierarchal societies, the Matthew Effect (Rigney 2010).

Historic legacies of this type can be overcome only gradually, and that too in the wake of a fundamental transformation in the political and economic arenas. In the educational sphere, such an attempt was made after *Uhuru*. To a degree, there were positive results. But the central educational experiment was not implemented under a well thought out plan. Thereby, it did not go as far, and in some ways, backfired.

When I cast my net among my friends, who are from diverse racial and social backgrounds, I see no essential race-based differences in their life trajectories once I take into account other relevant factors. I have had smart and not-so smart, underachieving and overachieving, humanistic and thoughtless, gentle and rough, kind and mean friends and acquaintances of African, Asian and European/American origin. I have been instructed by excellent and bad teachers from all races. I have worked with competent and confused, kind and cruel, outstanding and mediocre, students and academics from all races. It has been a colour indifferent affair that has spanned fifty years across three continents.

As a seasoned statistician, I recognize the foolhardiness of drawing a broad conclusion from a personalized sample. But that is not my intent. I just say that my experience is in line with what the bulk of scientific investigations reveal. There is no gene for education achievement or economic advancement. The bell-curve type of claims based on distorted data have been discredited by meticulous research. Yet, in the common mind, the race-based myths and views persist. In fact, there is a reversal of sorts. For example, my African colleagues at Muhimbili University remark: 'What is it with these Asian students? They work hard and do so well.' The white man's stereotyping has become a self-denigrating black man's belief.

But that is not all. Despite their varied national, social, racial, religious, educational and economic dispositions, the perspectives on life and society my friends, relatives, co-workers and acquaintances express these days are more similar than different. Globalization has unified the outlooks of people across the world. Unfortunately, these shared views are too often of the undesirable, unsound, elitist variety. I discuss this point in Chapter 15.

Random Sampling   ❖   ❖   ❖   ❖   ❖   ❖   ❖

The allusion to selective sampling takes me back in time. During school vacations in the mid-60s, I used to go to Father's wholesale shop on Msimbazi Street to help out. A common scene: Upon entering the shop, a retailer takes the long, pointed metal plate rod with a shallow crevice running lengthwise kept near the door. He pokes it deeply into one or two places on a 100 Kg jute sack filled with beans, and closely examines the ten or so beans drawn. If satisfied, he buys that sack. Otherwise, he tries out another one.

The significance of this action dawned upon me only after I went to the university. The man wanted a sack containing fresh, good quality beans. But it could be filled so that the beans at the top or the side are good beans while the bottom or centre part has stale, shrivelled beans. Sampling beans from the interior was a means to avoid being short changed.

This practice and the tool came from the colonial era. The buyer sought protection from being cheated by the wholesaler. Those who purchased crops from farmers also used it if the crops were in a jute sack. A racial element operated here as well since wholesalers and crop purchasers were mostly Asians, and their customers were Africans.

In effect, the purchaser was drawing (random) representative samples from the population of beans. Random samples form the basis for drawing valid conclusions in science, health, agriculture, transportation and social studies. Samples obtained through other methods are generally biased and produce distorted conclusions. Ignoring this basic tenet is a key reason why people come to accept misleading, fanciful and harmful claims. Further, educational, health, agricultural and other policies and practices based on biased sampling or selective data can create problems more serious than the ones they intend to resolve.

Sampling was a pivotal topic in the medical statistics classes I taught at the University of California, Los Angeles and the Muhimbili University in Dar es Salaam. My post-graduate medical students grappled with the idea. They regarded clinical experience as an adequate basis for finding the cause of a disease, or the efficacy of a treatment. That unrepresentative samples can yield misleading conclusions was not appreciated. Only when I gave examples from the history of medicine about the pitfalls of relying on anecdotes or case studies did they begin to appreciate the point. Even then, their understanding left a lot to be desired.

Random sampling, on the other hand, was a crucial real life practice for the barely literate customers at my father's store. They seemed to have a better grasp of the idea than did my students with eighteen years of theory oriented formal education behind them.

Not only is the size of a sample important, but how it has been obtained is a critical matter too. Even for a large population, say ten million, a sample of 10,000 persons drawn in a random (representative) manner yields valid inferences to guide policy. That is a fascinating aspect of the science of statistics that people, despite years of education, do not appreciate. There is also much misuse of statistics and statistical methods in real life. While paying lip service to good science, most of the researchers and all the medical companies compromise scientific principles, conduct flawed studies and generate data and findings that promote commercial interests rather than public interest.

For over a period of four decades, I was directly connected with a large number of student and staff research projects at premier universities in the USA and Tanzania. I assessed about five percent of them as acceptable quality research. Cutting corners to secure rapid publication, academic advancement or future funding was too pervasive in both places. Use of non-representative samples was a frequent problem.

Of recent, the issue of sampling has generated much political heat and media headlines in Tanzania. This has occurred in the context of the process of developing a new constitution for the nation. The Warioba Commission, charged with the task producing an initial draft document, heard the views of some 300,000 people across the country. Its report firmly recommended that the current two-government union structure be replaced by a three-government federal structure. This was rejected outright by the ruling party. It said that a group of 300,000 cannot represent a nation of forty four million. The opposition parties held that since sampling was central to socio-political research, the recommendation had a valid scientific basis.

Both these stand points were misleading. By rejecting sampling off-hand, the ruling party displayed a tenth-century-BC-level ignorance of how reliable information can be obtained. On the other hand, by equating a self-selected, highly biased sample with a representative sample, the opposition parties showed a twenty first century knack for misusing statistical ideas for partisan politics. The Commission did not select random samples from the areas it visited, and many questions as to the nature of its sample remain. Sampling is an essential aspect of democratic governance, but a biased sample can be worse that pure guessing.

Yet, despite the sharply hostile political divide with potentially damaging consequences, this critical point has not emphatically been brought forth by our media pundits, scholars and political analysts. It is a reflection of both the timidity of our intellectual class and the major pitfalls of our education system.

Statistics is a common topic in school and college curricula. Yet, the public understanding of sampling and research is deficient because it is taught as number drudgery. It is not taught in lively and practical ways that show its relevance to our lives, demonstrate its centrality in technical and societal activities, uncover the regular misuse and abuse of data, or integrate critical thought with things that happen on a daily basis. It is not connected to real life. Without a thought-provoking and discussion-generating style, students do not internalize its concepts. Rather, they memorize a few formulas which are forgotten as soon as the exams are over.

An indispensable tool for processing information, which should be our lifelong companion along side the basic rules of grammar we internalize, lies by the wayside. This deficiency permits those who have a material interest in taking us for a ride, notably the multinational corporations, local business, the state and media, and cultural charlatans to have a field day. They present us with half-baked ideas and numbers, and make us part with our hard earned cash in return for deficient goods. Irrational beliefs and strange ideas dominate public and private discourse.

— 14 —

Spirals of Separation

As the world continually multiplies,
are we in a generation where people
are divided, or people are equal?
Anthony Liccione

❖ ❖ ❖ ❖ ❖ ❖ ❖

RACE WAS A SIGNAL feature of colonial society. Racial and economic divisions, both cemented by colonial policies, coincided in large measure. After *Uhuru,* the Asian business community throughout East Africa sought to retain its dominant economic status and the emergent African elite strove to step into its shoes. Only in Tanzania did vibrant socially unifying forces come into play. Under Mwalimu's leadership, valiant attempts were made at the outset to bring racial and religious groups together, and bridge the economic divide. There was a distinct potential at one stage that the emergent generation would more broadly support the causes of inter-racial harmony, religious tolerance and economic equality.

But it was not to be. The brown and black elite equally opposed and thwarted the policies promoting equality. Further, the policy of socialism and self-reliance was implemented by TANU under Mwalimu's leadership in a thoroughly incompetent manner. The basic sectors of the economy remained under the control of the West and the direction of the economy was determined by the global financial institutions. This combination served to convert *Ujamaa* into a farcical disaster whose calamitous consequences we still face. Instead of socialism, Tanzania now has spiraled down into a neo-liberal capitalist system that boasts an astronomical gap between the fabulously rich – brown and black – and the multitude of abysmally poor.

The question for now is: Given these conditions of inequality in the economy, where do we stand in terms of race relations?

Cricket

Let us begin with a positive sign. In the colonial era and well into the 1980s, not more than a handful of African faces graced the cricket teams in Tanzania. Cricket formed the jewel of the Asian sporting agenda. That was why our Undali Street gang had sought, through rather dubious means, quality cricket equipment. I did not play it thereafter only because it was not an option in my non-Asian dominated secondary and high schools.

Five decades on, cricket is still a minor sport in Tanzania, but with one major change. It now has a multi-racial face. Presently, cricket teams with African players in the majority exist. The web page www.demwani.ca/af/Features/agakhan_sports_club.htm has photos of the local cricket teams from the 1960s. All the faces are Asian. *The Citizen* of 10 March 2014 and 12 May 2014 respectively carry photos of happy faces from our national and Dar es Salaam junior cricket teams (Kazenga 2014a; 2014b). Only three out of the Dar es Salaam team of 12 players are Asian; the rest are African. The situation for the national team is similar. Though the senior national team has proportionately more Asian players, it features stellar African batsmen, bowlers and fielders. This is a picture of cricket that was unthinkable in the earlier era.

In my days, three to four school teams with only Asian players competed in the inter-school cricket tournament held annually in Dar es Salaam. The inter-school tournament organised by the Tanzania Cricket Association in 2012 stood a world apart. Here, a total 38 school teams took part, and the vast majority of the players were Africans (Kazenga 2012).

And in another scenario unimaginable in my days, women compete in cricket too. Thus, of the 38 school teams mentioned above, 18 teams were girls school teams. I gather that it is mostly, if not only, African girls and women who have taken up cricket. The race equation has thus been reversed, and Asian women have a ways to go on this front.

Overall, Asians still dominate the sport at the senior level. Complaints of racism are heard once in a while. The present broader interracial standing of the game emanates from years of diligent effort by Zully Rhemtulla, Taher Kitisa, Osman Bunda and others.

Unfortunately, the level of cricket play in Tanzania is sub-standard. The national men's team has shown lacklustre performance in international competitions. In 2013, it was in the 5th division of international cricket and faced relegation to the lowest division. But, our national women's cricket team has performed relatively better in regional tournaments. The long term requirement is to lay a sturdy foundation early on. The Tanzania Cricket Association has to provide more resources and support for school cricket and the junior teams. Without doing that, the prospects for raising Tanzania's rank in international cricket will remain bleak.

To get an introductory picture of cricket in Tanzania at present, see Jongo (2013a, 2013b, 2013c, 2013d, 2013e), Kazenga (2012, 2013a, 2013b, 2014a, 2014b) and Mkumbo (2013). For an overall history of the game in Tanzania until the 1980s, see Fazel (1992) and related articles on the same website.

Capitalism has invaded cricket as well, transforming the game in major ways in the past decade. Short games and fast play have risen to the fore.

Fabulous financial incentives now drive the global cricket agenda. The five day test match is in jeopardy. At the same time, different types of corrupt practices have reared their ugly heads in what was known as the gentleman's sport. The Indian Premier League, the most lucrative cricket tourney, features costly marketing campaigns by movie stars and business deals that border the boundary of legality. In recent years, prominent cricketers have been convicted of spot-fixing and other serious violations (Ali 2014; Astill 2013).

The poor state of cricket in Tanzania corresponds to the general decline in sports and games activities and standards across the nation. Up to the 1980s, we had a modicum of standing, at least in East Africa, and boasted a few exceptional players and teams in athletics, boxing and soccer. Now, we are stuck in the very back rows in all the sports. In schools, sports and games have, with a few exceptions, declined due to lack of funding, coaches and attention. Our modern day boxers, for example, are more famed for smuggling drugs and absconding after competing abroad than for claiming medals (Chambo 2013; Omary 2013).

A Muhindi

One day in 2009, I was shopping for vegetables in the overcrowded Kariakoo market. All of a sudden, two muggers accosted me in broad daylight. One faced me. Acting as if insane, he grabbed me by the shoulders, and made incoherent noises. Meanwhile, his accomplice was tugging at my cloth bag from behind. I sensed the move, and managed to hold on to the bag. Thereby, they had no option but to fast melt away into the crowd with nothing in their hands.

It was the first time I was mugged. Yet, it was not the attack as such but the reaction of the onlookers that made me – and you may wonder if that is possible – simultaneously breath a deep sigh of relief and squeeze my eyebrows in extreme annoyance.

Currently in this nation crime witnesses are ever ready to inflict deadly beatings on a petty thief. Reports of suspected petty criminals being stoned or hacked to death, or torched alive appear in the media regularly. People lack faith in the police and machinery of justice. Mob justice is a way of life; the authorities express mild displeasure occasionally, but do not act decisively to put a stop to it. Had I loudly screamed *mwizi, mwizi,* (thief, thief) the crowd would have been enraged sufficiently to affect the instant death penalty on my assailants. Keenly aware of the possibility, I held my tongue. In the end, I was glad I did not suffer any injury, retained my bag, and that the two desperate young fellows did not suffer grievous harm on my accord. On the last matter, I was actually quite relieved.

But I had expected someone to assist, in some way or another, an elderly man obviously in trouble. But no onlooker had batted an eye. On the contrary, a few had muttered gleefully in Swahili, *Muhindi anaibiwa, muhindi anaibiwa* (The Asian is being robbed, the Asian is being robbed). As the muggers fled, I angrily said to the bystanders, "Why did you not do anything?" They shrugged their shoulders and averted their eyes. I was but a *muhindi,* not one of them.

Crowd psychology is a curious entity. What normally would have elicited a violent response was here a spectacle to enjoy. Though, loud shouts on my part could have turned the tables on the young fellows. A more telling lesson on the current chasm between the races in Tanzania than this I could not have had.

A Tide of Intolerance

The incident is a sign of the times, a mirror on how people think and act. As I move among black and brown folk, among elites and ordinary people, I find racially couched language and ways of thought prevailing widely. African colleagues with PhD degrees at the university display that tendency as do my Asian acquaintances. Racialised thinking is a two-way street. Articles with an Asian subject in Swahili papers employ racially coded terms. For their part, Asians converse among each other about Africans in a plainly racist manner. That the Asians of my father's generation stick to their foul colonial era terminology one can perhaps understand, though not excuse. But their children and grandchildren are following in their footsteps. When an Asian exchange bureau owner is gunned down by armed robbers, it is seen by Asians as an anti-Asian attack. The story fast reaches the shores of Canada; it is taken as one more example of "the attacks against us." The known fact that senior African officials and rich Africans often experience similar attacks does not serve to place crime in context.

Consider some specific instances of how the two sides visualize each other:

Side IA: It was by chance that I caught a program on the Tanzania Broadcasting Corporation meter band focusing on reviving the game of badminton in our nation. The date was 8 February 2014. A young news lady interviewed an (African) Tanzanian enthusiastically leading the effort. Complaining that the game had virtually died in schools, he urged the authorities, public bodies and others with resources at hand to provide support. Further, he observed that only *wale wenye ngozi nyeupe* (those people with light skins) play badminton now. *Sisi wenye ngozi nyeusi* (We, the black skinned people) do not.

It was an observation with a basis in fact. Badminton is played, to an extent, not only along racial but also communal lines (Msyani 2013). Yet, I found the use of frank racially couched language on the premier public radio in the nation shocking. But they went on talking this way as if it was the normal way. Were they aware that in the 1960s and 1970s, expressions of that sort were taboo precisely on that particular radio station?

Side IB: One weekly local paper had a bold headline in February 2014: *Wahindi 'wateka' Bohari ya Dawa* (Asians 'hijack' the Medical Supplies Depot) (*Dira* 2014). The essence of the story was that a syndicate of Asian businessmen – from Tanzania and India – effectively control the main governmental medical supplies facility and are using it to import substandard medicines from India and peddle them at high prices. State coffers are being depleted and public health is endangered as these avaricious brown-skinned fellows reap loads of money.

I would not be surprised if there was some basis to the story. It is standard practice today for wealthy business people of all colours – black, brown, yellow and white – to concoct ghoulish schemes to cheat ordinary people, the public treasury and even one another. They often collude with national and local officials. Media report cases of African contractors who build substandard schools and dispensaries, violate school supply contracts and walk away with tens of millions of shillings. They may be owned by a Machaga, a Muhaya or another person. But you do not (and you should not) see a headline like: *Wachaga wanabomoa elimu.*

The *Dira* headline attacked a racial group. Most people cannot buy newspapers nowadays; most scan the headlines at the newsstands. When they see such a headline, it affirms their prejudices. Just around that time, a young Asian boy had knocked on our door, and had begged my wife for food, saying he was very hungry. Is he one of the *wahindis* who are pillaging the Medical Depot? For my part, I am outraged by such vile conduct; I want the culprits taken to court. Yet, that headline lumps me together with those crooks just because my skin colour is brown.

But the other side of the equation is equally repulsive.

Side IIA: In that same month, a relative emailed me an article from a Canadian magazine. Penned by an Asian-Canadian journalist originally from Tanzania, it was a comment on the year 2012 meeting between President Jakaya Kikwete and former Asian Tanzanians currently settled in Canada. Briefing them on the present economic opportunities in Tanzania, Mr Kikwete had appealed to them to invest in these projects. Noting the historic irony of the appeal, the writer dealt with the return of the properties of Asians nationalized during the *Ujamaa* era (Ladha 2012).

The article contained major distortions of history. With a racist tone, it contradicted what this journalist had written forty two years earlier (Ladha 1970). Nevertheless, many Asians who placed comments on the website praised it profusely, and added biased invectives of their own. According to them, Tanzania was in essence an ungrateful nation of thieves that even now cannot be trusted. Such essentially bigoted articles score frequent hits on the Internet.

Side IIB: One article making rounds among East African Asians is by Shamlal Puri, a famed journalist originating from Tanzania. Appearing in *The International Indian*, it asks whether Asians in Tanzania are 'saboteurs or saviours' (Puri 2013). For Puri, the answer is clear. He projects the thesis that Asians have been 'saviours' in the past and remain so today. Businessmen, statesmen and philanthropists of Asian descent have, in his view, rescued the nation from catastrophic governmental policies, and made significant contributions to the nation's advancement.

But he utilizes a skewed account of the economic situation in Tanzania, past and present. Presenting the perspective of the elites, his article is rife with inconsistencies. For example, while most problems are ascribed to Nyerere's socialism, Asian figures like Amir Jamal, Al-Noor Kassum and Andy Chande who played a prominent role in the socialist government and enterprises are cast in a purely positive light. Simple logic implies that they share the blame. But as the premise here is that Asians are good guys and Africans are bad guys, the basic rules of logic are suspended.

Take a clear flaw: It has a photo of rescuers at an accident site with the caption: *Tanzanian Indians (in yellow jackets) helped when this building collapsed [in] Dar es Salaam in March 2013.* The impression conveyed is that of altruistic Indians assisting others. What is left unsaid is that the collapse occurred in a mainly Asian business and residential area, next to an Asian prayer facility. The building under construction would have housed mostly, if not exclusively, Asian families. Owned by an Asian, it had Asian contractors. Apart from scores of African workers, bodies of six Asian kids were also under the rubble. The Asian owner and contractor and others associated with the scheme face serious criminal charges. None of that is brought to light. What seems good about Indians/Asians is highlighted, but what would cast their reputation in a bad light is pushed under the rug. Another instance: He lauds the philanthropic and civic activities of the Karimjee Jivanjee family. But what were the rates of malnutrition among the children of the workers on their sisal estates? Such matters, however, are not relevant to this article.

Under such a one-sided style, this article plays up numbers of dubious validity to bolster preconceived themes. Positing extremes – saviours or saboteurs – is an erroneous way of doing social analysis. In reality, they are both and they are neither. The question of who contributes how much and in what way to a nation's economic course is a race-neutral question. It is a complex venture that the author does not pursue; else the article would not have garnered the fame it has secured. People desire comfortable half-truths, not factual accounts that bring up unsettling realities. Such articles only reinforce mythologies.

Side IIC: Talk to Asians who left Tanzania in the 1970s and are settled in Canada now. Ask them why they left. One scholar who did so found one reason frequently stated: Asian women and girls had faced a grave risk of rape by Africans. The impression given was that such attacks were systematically and widely perpetrated against Asian females, and that racial hatred was the principal factor behind the attacks.

That depiction is utter nonsense. There are no data to back up claims of racially directed rape or any other serious crime. Apart from the handful of forced marriages that occurred in Zanzibar within a span of a few months and then were banned, there is no basis to the talk. If you ask them to state actual cases in mainland Tanzania, they cannot cite any. Perhaps there were a few; but rape is not an uncommon crime.

Women of Asian origin are raped every year in Canada too, even to this day. If you look at the data, over the past fifty years, far more crimes, assaults and murders with a clear racist motivation against Asian and other minorities have occurred in the UK than in Tanzania. The plague of racist violence against minorities has gathered more steam in the UK and Europe of recent. To give one example among hundreds: In mid-June 2014, a Saudi student was killed in a frenzied knife attack near Essex University in Britain. The police think she was targeted because she had put on her traditional Islamic dress (Peachy 2014).

Such attacks on racial, religious and national minorities have been an integral part of the histories of the UK, the USA, Europe and, to a lesser extent, even Canada in the past fifty years. They were rare in the Tanzania of the 1960s to the 1980s. Only in the past ten years has religious animosity been on the rise. But race based violence remains rare. Despite this fact, it is easy to find an Asian originating from Tanzania now residing in the West venting fury at the mythical rapes of Asian women in Tanzania while he or she remains non-plussed at the more horrific reality of his or her land of residence.

Side IID: An article by Moez Vassanji, the award winning Canadian-East African author, in the progressive magazine *New Internationalist* is of relevance here (Vassanji 2006). Focusing on the Tanzania of the 1960s, it mainly discusses the national service and education, and comments on the general socio-political situation. The clear and unmistakable messages it conveys are that the national service was rife with tribalism and favouritism; that the education system functioned in an erratic manner; and that the nation as a whole was a fertile ground for corruption. These pervasive maladies are ascribed to Nyerere's socialism which, in his view, was inspired by Maoism.

To make his case, Vassanji relies on anecdotes based on his personal experience and that of a few others. These incidents are no doubt real. Yet, simply relying on a few negative cases masks the fact that national service was a rewarding experience for the majority, Asians and Africans, and it taught them sound moral values and life practices as well. Many cases of Asian Tanzanians who gained from national service exist. A friend of mine from Lindi was, in 1966, in desperate economic circumstances. Having no avenue of support, he voluntarily joined the national service. With free room and board for two years, he learned skills from which he began life on a new footing. Now he is a prosperous retiree.

Vassanji criticizes the education system without regard to its history. Upon inheriting a racist system benefiting a minority, the nation had sought to rapidly build a fair, functional system for the majority. It was a huge task to be done with limited resources. Yet, much was accomplished. The problems he alludes to were minor glitches at that point in time. Like many fellow Asians, my brother Rafik and I gained from it, did the national service, learned about life, and went on to attain advanced degrees. This holds for many Asians and non-Asians; they had opportunities under Nyerere which were unthinkable under colonial rule. Children from poor Asian families, and Asian girls in particular, obtained free, quality education, and became competent professionals. Whatever the problems of the system, the good outweighed the bad.

Another key deficiency of this article is its obscurantist approach to the issue of corruption. That the rich initiate corruption is noted. But that rich Asians, by seeking special privileges for themselves and their families, played a central role in the promotion and entrenchment of corruption in Tanzania is not explicitly stated. As an Asian, Vassanji could seek the help of a rich businessman to change his national service placement. But could a village boy with a similarly serious ailment? How does his attempt to seek a dubious avenue to evade national service conform with the ethical tenets of his faith? Is it justified to cheat because you have a serious personal problem? Is that not how the initiators of corruption justify their action? And the strange thing is that his personal example shows that seeking the corrupt way out did not work!

At the end he undermines his own case by noting, though in an unclear way, that capitalist Kenya was as, if not more, corrupt. Most amazingly, he fails to state that under neo-liberal capitalism, corruption has become far more entrenched globally than ever before. Nations from the US to Brazil, China to India, Tanzania to Kenya and Uganda, exhibit corruption and bribery at levels and a scale a hundred times more than was the case in the 1960s. It is a form of corrupt, crony-capitalism inspired, funded, politically supported and championed by nations of the West – the US, the UK, European Union, and his own home country, Canada. Corruption in high circles enables multinational companies from these nations to drain the resources of and obtain enormous profits from Africa in general and Tanzania in particular. Part of those profits end up as taxes in those nations, and fund their health and education systems, from which Vassanji and his family benefit.

One expects an erudite author like Vassanji to lay bare such facts, and cry out as, if not more, loudly against them as he does against so-called Maoist Tanzania. But he maintains a discreet silence. Overall, he gives the readers a one-sided impression of Tanzania and Africa in the 1960s. Standard code words and a rigid mode of analysis of Africa, so typical in the West, have replaced a factual and logical approach. Like the article of Shamlal Puri, this article just reinforces the prejudices about Tanzania many Asians, especially in the diaspora, have come to harbour.

For other examples of one-sided, pro-Asian presentation of race issues in Tanzania, see Fazel (2011) and Kassum (2007).

A Reversal: The spiral of history has strangely turned the tables. In 2013, an African girl in Uganda was raped by two Asian men. As the ugly incident came to light, the local media became awash with scare stories about 'Pakistani rapists,' bent on assaulting African women, on the loose. The accused were judged not as individuals, but on the basis of skin colour and nationality. The media hysteria veered in the direction of deportation of all Pakistanis from Uganda. Ironically, it eventually transpired that the two men were from India, not Pakistan (Buwembo 2013). Of course, it does not mean that all Indian nationals in Uganda are potential rapists either.

Racist thinking remains as vibrant on both sides as it was in my childhood. Superficial words and actions apart, the colonial era ways have been resurrected. Each racial group sees itself as the sole possessor of righteousness and morality. And myths that bear little resemblance to historic or current reality sustain such a narrow-minded stance.

Balanced Visions

I recall an event when I was teaching at the National Institute of Transport (NIT). It was in 1978. The top administrators were not only inefficient, but had misused the budgeted funds as well. Cafeteria food quality and availability of class supplies deteriorated. Dormitories and general premises were poorly maintained. There were allegations of staff misconduct in the final exams for the Department of Motor Vehicle Mechanics. Angered as things went from bad to worse, one day the students staged a public, but peaceful protest.

I felt that their grievances were legitimate and supported them. This gave the senior bosses an excuse to employ the race-card. It would divert attention, derail the valid complaints put forward by the students and side-line me. Hence, they spread the story that this *muhindi* had selfish reasons for stoking the fire of student unrest. I was accused of turning molehills into mountains. But the students knew better, and did not buy into that line. They came to me by the dozen and frankly told me,

Mwalimu (Teacher), we know what they are saying is untrue; we realize that you have our interests at heart.

NIT Students

The students judged me by my actions, and not by the colour of my skin. This is what I have I found throughout my forty years of teaching in Tanzania; once students come to know you well, once they see that you are trying your best to teach them effectively, they judge you as person, and not by the stereotype. The higher ups, for their part, employ the race-card in an opportunistic manner when it serves their interests.

There are also voices in the Asian community who give a balanced view of the past. I give two cases:

An Accountant: Abdulrazak Fazel, born in Zanzibar, later moved with his family to the mainland. In the 1990s, he was a prominent journalist writing on cricket related news and issues. His memoirs appear on the web page Fazel (2008a). In it, he mentions that he was hired by the National Bank of Commerce as a management trainee in the 1960s. Then it was a state owned bank, and was the main commercial bank in the nation. He elaborates:

I owe a great deal to the National Bank of Commerce for grooming me into a caliber personnel. I was put on a vigorous training in accounts, on the job as well as at the Bank's Training Institute and the Institute of Finance Management where I attended several courses and seminars. Some of those who conducted the seminars were none other than President Nyerere's economic advisers like Dr [Reginald] Green and Dr John Loxley.

Being ethnic Indian the treatment accorded to us citizens at government and parastatal offices was worthy of praise. Tanzania is a beautiful country. . . .

Abdulrazak Fazel

Though Fazel takes issue with Mwalimu Nyerere's economic policies, he gives credit where it is due. He does not distort the past. In another article on the same website, he talks about the treatment of African servants by Asian employers (Fazel 2008b). His words are frank:

Not only are we [Asians] discriminatory but there is also meanness about us that is awful. We look down on our [African] houseboy, suspect him, humiliate him and subject him to harsh treatment. . . .

Abdulrazak Fazel

His stand is humanistic, not racial. It displays a level of integrity not common among Tanzania Asians, here or abroad. Elsewhere on this website, he talks of a protest over a move in the 1960s to terminate some bank employees who were of Asian origin. His words fail to distinguish between termination based on citizenship and that based on race. The move affected non-citizens only. The Asian employees who were citizens of Tanzania, like himself, held on to their positions. Further, more Tanzanians of Asian origin were later hired by the bank.

Two Activists: KL Jhaveri and Urmila Jhaveri, a husband-wife team of Asians, were active in the struggle for *Uhuru* and the establishment of the new nation (Jhaveri 1999). Among his many roles, KL Jhaveri was a president of the Tanzania Law Society for nearly fifteen years while Urmila stood in the forefront of the efforts to improve the status of women in Tanzania. As a senior official of *Umoja wa Wanawake of Tanzania* (National Union of Tanzania Women), she criss-crossed the nation to raise awareness about developmental and gender issues, being among a handful of Asian women who played a front-seat role in such activities.

In her beautifully crafted autobiography, *Dancing with Destiny*, Urmila Jhaveri narrates her eventful life in the local and international socio-political arenas (Jhaveri 2014). While she disagreed with the post-Arusha Declaration policies, her book gives a balanced presentation of race relations. She depicts the three-tier structure of the colonial era and shows the extent to which negative attitudes and practices from that time were carried over into the post-*Uhuru* period. She is among one of the few humanistic Asian voices from that era.

Race or Class?

Let us take up three societal problems in the colonial and early post-colonial eras that were said to have a racial basis, and investigate them further.

Weighing Scales: Under British rule, Asian traders were accused of shortchanging customers in various ways. Often, it was a valid accusation. They charged high prices for what they sold and paid low prices for what they bought. Rural African customers endured weighing scale fraud, African workers got extremely low wages, and African shopkeepers were excluded from opportunity generating networks and denied credit. It was no wonder that Africans viewed Asians as greedy, dishonest, aloof people. Public anger at such practices spurred the growth of the cooperative movement across the nation (Walji 1974, Aminzade 2013).

Now fast forward fifty years post-*Uhuru*. In July 2012, more than fifty weighing scales used in the purchase of cotton from farmers were seized in the Shinyanga Region by the inspection agent. Some scales showed the weight of a hundred kilogram cotton bag as seventy kilograms. The minuscule fines did little to discourage fraud (Felician 2012). Around the same time, it was reported that the farmers in Njombe district, a prime food producing area, had stopped selling their goods on the basis of weight. The scales are rarely calibrated or inspected. Hence, farmers sustain major losses. To safeguard their interests, they now sell produce in 20-liter containers which are tamper proof (Sanga 2012). An inspection of the butcheries in Dar es Salaam in July 2013 revealed that five of thirty two weighing scales had been tampered with (Mfuru 2013). Cashew nut farmers in southern Tanzania to this day face the problems of very low prices, delayed payments and weigh scale fraud (Editorial 2013a; Machira 2013). Grape farmers in Dodoma suffer from long delays in payment and farmers everywhere complain about substandard seeds, fertlisers and other basic supplies (Chibwete 2014). Currently, it is a race and ethnicity neutral affair in that the culprits are of all skin shades and regional origin.

The national weights and measures authority is understaffed, and has not operated as well as it should have. Customers, farmers and small sellers across the nation are susceptible to weights and measures fraud (*The Guardian Reporter* 2013). Moves proposed to deal with this longstanding problem include increasing the basic fine from TSh 10,000 to more than TSh 1,000,000. But whether the new rules will be effectively enforced is another question altogether.

Brain Drain: Tanzania experienced a major exodus of qualified professionals in the 1970s. Primarily of Asian origin, and mostly Ismailis, they had been trained at public expense, and held critical positions in various sectors including education. Even those who had not completed their contractual term of service broke their contracts. The loss of this vital human resource was a major blow to a poor nation trying to stand on its own feet.

Four decades later, focusing on the health sector, for example, we find a continued shortage of qualified doctors, especially in the smaller towns and rural areas. Yet a broad survey of doctors, almost all of whose education was paid by the government, found alarming results. About one out of eight doctors has sought and obtained work in other African nations or overseas. Among those who remain here, roughly forty percent cease practicing clinical medicine in a short while after graduation. And there was no race angle here. Doctors of Asian origin, in any case, form a minority of the medical staff in the nation. It was a race-neutral affair (Kisanga 2013; Msonsa 2013; Songa wa Songa 2013).

Foot Level Inequality: In Lindi of the 1950s, there were three highly skilled artisan shoe makers (*mochis*) from India. Starting from raw hide, they crafted sturdy but nice looking leather footwear. My father, brothers and I, like most Asians males, wore their shoes. The Africans by and large either went barefoot, or wore irregularly shaped rubber sandals made from discarded car and truck tires.

After Independence, the situation improved as local production of footwear using local input expanded. However, the neo-liberal policies from the 1990s on spelled a death knell for local factories. Imports took up the slack. Currently, a glut of footwear prevails. Street peddlers and shops sell plastic imports from the East, or discards from the USA and Europe. The low price enables most urbanites to put on shoes or sandals. But the quality is distinctly low. A pair easily falls apart after a few months of use. Most last barely a year.

The African and Asian elites put on designer US $100-dollar-a-pair variety from upscale city stores or abroad. The other day, I bought a used pair at the equivalent of US $4 near the Kariakoo market only to see a similar pair in a city centre store priced at US $45. An apparently race based difference of yesterday is a clear class based difference today. And dependency is back; we have reverted to the colonial mode of life where, mostly and for crucial items, we consume what we do not produce, and produce what we do not consume.

Where To?

Another equally grave contradiction to re-emerge is based on religion. As depicted in the next chapter, discord between Muslims and Christians is becoming more intense day by day. It hits the headlines now and then, but gathers momentum under the surface all the time.

The racial, religious, gender, regional and ethnic divisions stand upon a primary division, the astounding gap between the few haves and the millions of have-nots. This divide cuts across race, religious, ethnic and gender lines. On the one hand, a man spends two hundred thousand shillings for his family to have a single meal in a fancy restaurant; on the other hand, hundreds of thousands of men are lucky to earn that amount in a month. One earns millions with the stroke of a pen; another pulls a heavy cart for a mile for a putative three thousand shillings; one has regular medical check-ups in India and another cannot afford a malaria blood test for his feverish child.

That division between the rich and the poor transcends race, religion, ethnicity and gender. What in colonial times were seen as matters of race now are multiracial affairs. African as well as Arab, Asian and external firms cheat African farmers, and African, Asian and Arab customers. The driver then as now is unchecked greed, not skin colour. Africans now short change Africans with the same callousness as the *wahindis* did then and do now. African and Asian elites treat house and business workers in identical exploitative, abusive ways. Capitalism is the essential corrupter of modern human life.

But our politicians and religious leaders hardly attend to that reality. They mask it through diversionary ideologies. Instead of tackling the roots of the problems, Asians blame Africans and vice versa; Muslims battle Christians; men are pitted against women; farmers blame herders; ethnic groups form restrictive bonds; parents and teachers denounce each other; and so on. The main groups that benefit from the narrow divisions are the wealthy tycoons, foreign investors, senior bureaucrats and politicians. As ordinary people lunge at each other on the basis of a small difference they had hitherto shown ample tolerance towards, as they bicker and fight, the big fellows have a field day looting bare the national treasury and treasures.

The fundamental economic reality is kept in low profile by the scribes of the system – the local and foreign media, scholars, ruling and opposition politicians, state agencies and NGOs – who revel in, play up and stress other divisions, however small. That was how it was in the colonial era. Divide and rule it was then, divide and rule it is now. Instead of the colonial overlords, it is the power of money, state and foreign investors, political higher ups, local and Western media, and the Western governments that fragments us. It does so in indirect, subtle but effective ways. Our ways of thought are divisive in nature, producing greater and greater fragmentation and acrimony instead of unity and harmony. Extremists come to the fore in all corners, and, instead of being dismissed as the fanatics that they are, they are accorded respect as bearers of divine wisdom.

Only a few voices counter that ugly trend. One of them is Richa Nagar. Her recent article analyzes the historic and current trends in race relations in Tanzania using evidence from interviews and archival records (Nagar 2013). I regard it as an excellent summary of the main issues that also shows the linkage between race and social class. It critiques the false dichotomy that brands Asians as saviours or saboteurs and instead, lays out a balanced and fact-based analysis that deserves a wide audience.

Yet, it does not gain currency on the Internet. Reason is not central to a system that dilutes basic moral standards. This greed, money driven system makes ordinary people cease to regard their fellow human beings as human beings. They rely on race, religion, ethnicity and other identities as a psychological cover. The magnification of such differences discourages collective action to promote genuine change. Hatred and violence ensue. Conflicts of this nature have broken out on a large scale in Africa, Asia and the Middle East. While their intensity is now at a low level in Tanzania, the trends are headed that way.

But that is not the way. To solve our nation's multiple, serious problems, we need to focus on fundamental things: promoting economic justice and equality, reducing dependency on major capitalist powers, constructing a strong economy, building first class education and health systems, initiating internal and regional economic integration, instituting grass-roots democracy, adopting strictly accountable governance, and fostering respect for the basic rights of all the residents of our nation. Those ought to be the central items of our social and political discourse. If we instead devote most of our energies on racial, religious, regional and ethnic differences, and keep accusing each other over small transgressions, those who inordinately benefit from the current setup will benefit even more, and the majority who already suffer grievously, will suffer even more. Take a recent divisive issue: The central question is not that of having two or three governments in our union, but whether it is a people friendly or a tycoon friendly government.

Gigantic Numbers ✛ ✛ ✛ ✛ ✛ ✛ ✛

In the past, we attended to small numbers. One shilling gave me a loaf of bread; now I need TSh 1,000 for a loaf of the same size, but which lacks the aroma and crispy taste of the breads of the yesteryear.

While numbers have become a staple of social discourse, many are large numbers. A housing scheme costs billions of shillings; governmental budgets run in the trillions of shillings. A good grasp for social statistics is thus central to grasping our social reality. It is a tool against diversionary, irrational ideas.

When numbers exceed a billion, most of us enter a land of darkness. Take the tale of the flute player whose soothing melodies lifted a king out from a sustained bout of sadness. In gratitude, the king offered him any reward he desired. The boy said that seeing his king happy was sufficient for him. But the king insisted. Yielding, the boy took a chess board and stated his requirement:

Put one grain of rice on the first square, two grains on the second square, four grains in the third, and so on. At each step, double the amount in the previous square. When you reach the 64th square, combine all the rice and kindly give it to me.

Everyone was astonished. Instead of gold and diamonds, he wanted a few sacks of rice. The king asked his scribe to calculate the quantity of rice needed. The total number of grains is given by the geometric sum

$$R = a + ar + ar^2 + ar^3 + ar^4 + ar^5 \ldots + ar^n$$

where $a = 1, r = 2, n = 63$. Because $r > 1$, the terms in this series become larger and larger. Multiply both sides of this equation by r. Then

$$rR = ar + ar^2 + ar^3 + ar^4 + ar^5 + ar^6 \ldots + ar^{n+1}$$

Subtract the first expression from the second. Then we have

$$rR - R = R(r - 1) = a(r^{n+1} - 1)$$

Divide both sides of this by $r - 1$. Then we find that

$$R = \frac{a(r^{n+1} - 1)}{r - 1} = \frac{1 \times (2^{64} - 1)}{2 - 1} = 2^{64} - 1$$

This quantity approximately equals 2×10^{19} grains of rice. Assume that 1 kg of rice has $100,000 = 10^5$ grains. Thereby, one ton (1000 kg) of rice has 10^8 grains of rice. Therefore, the boy has to be given

$$\frac{2 \times 10^{19}}{10^8} = 2 \times 10^{11} \quad \text{tons of rice}$$

or

$$200,000 \quad \text{million tons of rice.}$$

The global output of rice in 2012 was around 750 million tons. Assuming that rate of production, the boy has to be given all the rice produced for the next 270 years! At the January 2013 international rice price of US \$500 per ton, its value is nearly $2 \times 10^{14} = 200,000,000,000,000 = 200$ trillion US dollars. The global economic output (total wealth generated) in 2013 is expected to be less than half this figure. In other words, the king must surrender all his possessions and more to cover what he owes to the boy.

My experience is that this tale never fails to amaze. When Nazir Virji – the lover of literature with an anti-mathematics bent – heard it, he too was taken in.

> *Karim, I never thought that your favourite subject has a fascinating face.*

Coming from him, it was a true compliment. This is another example of educative and exciting stories that can be woven into school maths lessons.

When our understanding of numbers – large and small, simple and elaborate, especially the numbers related to society and the economy – is sound, those who mislead us with superficial data and flawed reasoning will have a harder time defeating our critical faculties. We will be better able to identify our real problems and their sources, and will also have the tools to expose and respond to the irrationality of their claims.

— 15 —

Spirals of Despair

*I am afraid we must make the world
honest before we can honestly say to
our children that honesty is the best
policy.*

George Bernard Shaw

❖ ❖ ❖ ❖ ❖ ❖ ❖

THE JOURNEY OF LIFE is more than a movement in space and time. It is a migration across social relations, modes of thought and senses of being. Our intimate and external circles, guiding ideas, feelings and values form, evolve, ossify, dissolve and reform, perhaps times over.

The 1960s in Tanzania was a time of lofty expectations. Bigoted ideas of the past were on the wane. Our parents, community, religion, teachers and the socio-political atmosphere espoused values that generally reinforced each other. We, the youth, were implored to be honest, hardworking persons; to respect people of varied backgrounds and promote equality in human affairs; to be modest, spiritually inclined individuals, and not spendthrift, greedy individuals. We were guided to value the acquisition of knowledge and expand our mental vistas. Role models – black and brown – inspired us. A more tolerant and mutually respectful social order lay on the horizon.

It was in that atmosphere that my sense of being expanded from a purely familial, racial and communal one to a national and humanistic one. I strove to adhere to the messages of good conduct raining down on us, and from my schooling, acquired a lasting fondness for numbers and books.

Not that it was a smooth process. Facing stiff resistance from the conservative quarters, it was accompanied by contradictions, inconsistencies and social conflicts. And we were not angelic persons either; we had our share of wasteful, indulgent, morally wanting acts. In essence, we were not too different from teens of all space and time. But on the balance, we were entangled in a national transformational process that was unifying and uplifting in nature. And that process was occurring both on the mental and material planes.

Five decades on, I find that this laudable process has spiralled backwards in essential ways. The message the youth of today get from their parents, teachers and society, is, in real life terms, the opposite of what we got in those days. In this chapter, I touch on four aspects of that reversal, namely, deceptive behaviour, cynical thinking, intolerance and intellectual mediocrity.

Dualism

I revisit an aberrant segment of my early life. In upper primary school, I was an attentive, reserved student, falling under the spell of the ascetic morality of the Ismaili *ginans*. Concurrently, as the captain of the Undali Street gang, I was immersed in a fun-filled but shady mode of life after school. Our gang artfully appropriated what was not ours. One mitigating factor was that we did not engage in violence, and did not physically harm anyone. My knife cut sugar cane and fruits, or sliced through garden fences. That was it. Nevertheless, our actions contradicted the ethical principles taught to us by our elders.

Dualism denotes the maintenance, by the same person, of distinct ethical standards in different spheres of life. I had earlier thought that only a few people have dualistic tendencies; you are either good or bad, but not both at the same time. But I was mistaken. Dualism is a common occurrence. People often do not maintain ethical consistency in the different domains of their lives. A shopkeeper routinely lies to his customers, but at home, is a morally upright parent. A respected man contributes to charity, but cheats on his taxes and gives starvation level wages to his workers. A man goes to the JK daily, but at home inflicts physical abuse on his wife at the slightest transgression. A citizen of the USA loudly decries gun related deaths at home, but is as silent as a marble statue when it comes to the thousand of civilians killed by his president in Iraq and Afghanistan. Priests in Rwanda implored their congregations to follow Christian values, but also urged them to participate in the 1994 genocide.

Race related issues bring out a key form of dualism. Colonialism taught us to treat people of our own race differently from those of the other races. Our religion said that in the eyes of the Creator all humans were equals. Nothing in our sacred *ginans* condoned racism. Yet we practiced it, even at the premises of the JK. Neither my parents nor the two AKBS maths teachers whom I looked up to as model beings set an example on this central issue. It shows the power and internalized character of dualism. The outlook of the Asians was constrained by colonial ideology. In that broader framework, my dualism was not so much an aberration, but one instance of the general, wider rule.

As the gang captain, I did not see myself or my buddies as persons with bad intentions. We were peeved at the unfairness of society. Why should we miss out on the joys other children had? In correcting that deficit the way we did, we followed a Robin Hood mentality. Among ourselves, we considered unfairness, lies or insulting talk unacceptable. While we stole from and lied to others, it was taboo to do likewise to one of our own. As they say, there is honour among thieves.

Economic circumstance and childish proclivities had drawn me into that fishy dimension of life. But as I entered secondary school, I weaned myself from it. The gang fell apart as well. It was a passing phase. Interestingly, as moral beings, my gang members evolved into adulthood much like other children around us. I see decent and obnoxious persons in both groups. To put it in a technical jargon: The observed difference between the two groups is not statistically significant.

Life is never without internal and external contradictions, moral or practical, light or grave, wholesome or truly harmful. The central question then is which pole – the worthy or the unworthy – dominates. Are you mostly good and a little bit bad, or the other way around, and what is the nature of that goodness and badness? Today as yesterday, dualism is a fact of life. The main thing that has changed is that unlike in the past, the ugly facets of dualistic phenomena, deriving from the entrenchment of the neo-liberal, crony capitalist system, now overpower the edifying facets.

Deception

Today we live in a person eat person society where deceptive talk and behaviour are almost a reflexive practice, a daily routine.

One day, for example, I went to buy breakfast cereal. The elderly man at the counter was attired like and had the looks of a sage. Nearby lay a religious text he had been reading. I asked him if the box was from fresh stock.

I guarantee it; I never sell old stuff,

he asserted loudly as if I had offended him. I opened the box the next morning only to see lice-like bugs crawling out from within.

Another example among many: In May 2014, the main police training college in the nation had to expel 200 students because the documents they presented upon enrollment were discovered to be fake (Matowo and Lyimo 2014).

Holy or unholy; Muslim, Hindu, Christian or pagan; African, Asian or ex-patriate; Zanzibari or mainlander; teacher, mason, taxi driver or bureaucrat; student or parent – the capitalist ethic of money worship and deceptive modes of conduct taints us all. Unpleasant personal experiences have made people aware of that reality; they regularly talk and lament about it; but they always point the finger at others, not at themselves or their group.

Parents and teachers routinely lament that our children display dishonest, spendthrift and educationally irresponsible tendencies. We affirm that it was not so in our days. When I hear these charges, I ask the charger,

And how did you behave today? How many plainly false statements did you utter? How many questionable short cuts did you take? How many frivolous items do you buy every month? Do you practice your profession with integrity?

I further ask:

Do you set a good example of honesty, hard work and frugality to your children the way our parents, elders and teachers did?

Invariably, he/she keeps quiet.

My university colleagues complain that their students are lazy, do not read and cheat when they can in examinations. I ask the complainant:

Do you teach as well prepared classes as our lecturers did? Do you maintain high standards in the courses you teach? How can you

> *devote time to students when you perpetually seek and engage in*
> *dollar drenched consultancies?*

I further ask,

> *How many new books did you read last year? Do you read professional*
> *journals regularly? Do you take pains to ensure that the data collected*
> *by your research assistants are not compromised or invented?*

And they too keep quiet.

Duplicity, hypocrisy and craftiness have become as integral to our lives as eating. Posing as a morally elevated person is, however, the norm. That stand is sustained by self-deception and continuous deception of others.

Cynicism

Extensive double-dealing and hypocrisy have led overwhelming numbers of my country folk to adopt a cynical frame of mind. They feel that there is no one you can trust or depend on. Everyone in a position of responsibility or authority in the political, state, civic, business, education, health and even religious institutions appears unreliable or untruthful. Truth benders run the show. That is what people believe, and with good reason. Thereby, they behave likewise and justify their own socially irresponsible acts by saying that if they had not done that sort of thing, somebody else would have.

It is an atmosphere for breeding unhealthy tendencies: Everyone complains and condemns. The whole nation is rotten; only stories of doom and gloom prevail; the smallest problem raises intense antagonisms; a tiny episode of misbehaviour raises a nationwide tirade. For example, when 4 out of 500,000 pupils sitting for school exams are found cheating, hell breaks loose in the media and the public. No one praises the 499,996 who did not cheat. In particular, a rational, critical way of looking at issues is set aside in favour of a blind lashing out (see Chapter 9; Harrison 2013; Hirji 2012).

From the fruit vendor in Kariakoo, the elderly man on the street corner, and the barber to holders of PhD degrees, each person talks on a daily basis in the same boisterous, uniform way. The only song monotonously sung is *ufisadi, ufisadi, ufisadi* (corruption, corruption, corruption). If you point to relevant structural roots, international trends, global issues and basic long-term solutions, you are seen as a justifier of misdeeds, a lackey. Any attempt at social analysis is set aside; only pure, sanctimonious anger prevails. Wondrously, but not surprisingly, even the genuinely corrupt and obnoxious characters have the same song on their lips.

Money rules the day. Gross misconduct and greed at the top generate despair, cynicism and erratic behavior at the bottom. Anti-social conduct of extraordinary forms – like grizzly mob-justice, police brutality, sabotage of public works and projects, bribery and corruption, and bureaucratic profligacy – is ascendant (James 2011). Demoralization prevails as if the nation as a whole is in a state of acute depression. Only soccer and parochial loyalties provide some relief.

Intolerance

In the last chapter, I discussed the persistence and intensification of racist forms of thought and conduct. The level of religious tolerance in Tanzania has diminished in a serious way in several parts of the nation. Christians and Muslims are pitted against each other on matters they had previously accepted with equanimity. The spirit of mutual respect is being eviscerated and replaced by harsh words from both sides.

Small events generate intense or even violent confrontation. The other day, two twelve year old boys were arguing. Like boys everywhere, they were prone to wild behaviour. Thus the Christian boy defiled the Muslim boy's copy of the Koran. Word spread. Muslim hot-heads were enraged and went on a rampage; a Christian church was torched – all for the naughty action of a twelve year old.

The commercial slaughter of cows and goats has traditionally been done according to Islamic ritual and by a Muslim. This makes all the meat sold in the market *halal* and is purchased by Muslims and non-Muslims alike. In 2012, this decades old, universally accepted practice all of a sudden became a bone of extreme contention. The Christians in some areas demanded permits to set up their own slaughtering facilities. Riots and fights ensued. A truce prevails for now, but it can erupt again at any time. There are incidents of acid attacks on Muslim and Christian ministers. As extremists on both sides gain the upper hand, people cease to heed the voices of reason and respect.

Religious differences date back to the colonial era, and are expressed in the education and other sectors of society. After *Uhuru*, there were moves to heal those differences and bridge the social and economic disparities. But the small but palpable progress that was made has seen a major reversal. Young minds of various denominations are growing up in an atmosphere that preaches that their religion or denomination somehow accords them a superior spiritual status compared to the others. If these divisive trends are not halted, the nation faces rough times ahead.

Mediocrity

Another component of that scenario affects acquisition of knowledge, both of the general kind and of the specialized, in-depth variety. Modern youth learn the basic minimum needed to get a job or perform a task. Even then the tasks are not implemented as needed and the quality of the output is shoddy. The teachers, being a part of the problem, do not or cannot play their role in imparting the traits of devotion to learning and working for excellence to their wards.

Among the factors that detached me from the gang lifestyle was the influence of my three maths teachers: two at the AKBS and one at the DTC. They rescued me by drawing me into the mysterious world of ideas at a key juncture in my life. I found that this ethereal world was permeated with adventure and excitement as well. I engaged with mathematics, came to value knowledge, and fell in love with books. That influence eventually placed me on a successful academic life trajectory.

In *The Count of Monte Cristo*, an aged prisoner of the name Abbé Fariah, uplifts the spirits of the falsely imprisoned Edmond Dantès. The versed sage tutors Edmond in science and the arts. He is my favourite character. Mr Hirani of the AKBS possessed a broad-minded outlook on these two areas of knowledge. He was my Abbé Fariah, my liberator from mental myopia. The skillful, painless and entrancing manner by which he kindled a life long passion for both mathematics and general reading is worthy of emulation.

Books allow us to converse with varied human minds, past and present. We see facets of our grand human family that sparkle and facets that reveal its ugly features. We dive into an ocean that encompasses reality, fantasy and adventure; fun and games; astute intellectual rigor, shallow rambling and pure propaganda; science, religion and mysticism; and much more. We encounter ethically uplifting and morally degrading episodes. Books take us on a multidimensional trip whose scope defies easy description. They provide us the chance to exercise informed judgment on matters affecting the human race, to dwell on the rational and irrational, truth and deceit, beautiful and mundane, love and hate. Books also draw us into the mindless, morally dubious and repulsive facets of humanity. There are fine books, there are so, so books, and there are gross books. They are a double edged sword. But if we sharpen our wits as we tread through them, we develop the ability to make out the good edge from the bad.

What I observe today negates such possibilities. Instead of swimming in this vast arena of knowledge, our youth are being sucked into a tight embrace of electronic technology (cell phones, tablets and computers) in ways that are not intellectually edifying, and are being led away from reading books and acquiring in-depth knowledge.

Talkative Tanzanians: In a three month period of 2011, nearly 20 million Tanzanian phone subscribers racked up a total charge of TSh 555 billion in calls and text messages. This revenue went to seven companies, the principal ones being internationally based, and was slightly more than a third of the total governmental revenue in that period (Kamndaya 2011).

Let us conservatively put the quarterly expenditure on phones in 2014 to be TSh 600 billion. Then the annual per capita of mostly cell phone expenditure in Tanzania is in the region of

$$\frac{4 \times 600,000,000,000}{45,000,000} \approx 50,000 \, \text{Tsh} \quad \text{or nearly 35 US\$}$$

That is, on average, for every man, woman and child, we spend more money on what is but frivolous talk for the large part than the government spends for us on health and education. With the communication sector at about 12% and a fast rising percentage of the GDP, we seem to be bent on increasing our national wealth by spewing out words from our mouths instead of producing goods in factories and products in farms.

To add insult to injury, the stupendous profits generated by these companies that do not pay as much tax as they should be paying are, by and large, exported and not reinvested locally.

This is the context in which the habit of reading among the youth and adults in Tanzania has gone down precipitously. The results of school examinations, and the low level of language competency among university students and graduates attest to that fact. The majority of my classes of a hundred or so post-graduate students from varied health specialties at the Muhimbili University in the years

2006 to 2012 could not write a grammatical, appropriately structured paragraph in the English language. The bulk of their leisure time went to surfing the web and chatting on the phone. They did reasonably well in a test if only simple recall was needed. But if they had to analyse, interpret or discuss the results of a health research study, most students wrote stuff that was hard for me to decipher. In many cases, it was plain gibberish. Uninhibited plagiarizing, a universal and tolerated norm, was the only device that rescued many. I found the situation shocking, but nothing could be done about it.

In November 2012, I was at a book launching ceremony at the UDSM. Professor Geoffrey Mmari, a mathematical education specialist and distinguished academic (profiled in Chapter 16) was the guest of honour. During our chat, he raised a key question:

> *Karim, compared to your days here forty years ago, in what major way has this university changed?*
>
> Professor Mmari

I did not have to pause to answer that weighty query. I had thought about it the whole day as I had walked around the vast campus, visited seminar and lecture rooms, academic departments, the bookstore and student areas. I had talked with students and staff, sipped tea, read a book, savoured the cool breeze and observed the scene. One thing astonished me, which is what I conveyed to Professor Mmari. Below is the gist of what I said.

> *The number of students is perhaps ten times that in my days. Yet, in my wide exploration of the place today, I saw just a few students with a book in hand. Some carried papers, bound material and computers. In study areas in the library and across the campus, including the crowded cement desks under tree-shades, students were not reading books. They talked, read stapled papers, and worked on computers. But hardly a book was in sight.*
>
> *The university book store was a pathetic sight. Most of the books were secondary or primary school books. There was no section for any scientific discipline. Books were shelved at random and reflected the extraneous material from the West that is nowadays dumped on African nations. The shelves and books had a distinct layer of dust on them. I assessed that 90% of the books had not been touched for a while.*
>
> *I asked the manager where the mathematics section was. She asked, "What level?" "The university level, of course," I replied. She pointed to one book here and the other there; an assortment that bore no relation to the courses taught. I inquired why there were so few university level science books. The reply she gave, which I knew to be untrue, was that they had been bought up by the students.*
>
> *In the half an hour I spent in the bookstore, literally hundreds of students passed the doorway. Only two entered the store, spent a couple of minutes inside, but left without purchasing anything. Apart from one or two exceptions, it was clear that the academic staff did not utilize the store either. The manager and her clerk spent the time eating potato chips and chatting merrily away.*

Upon inquiring further, the manager said that if I needed university
level books on science, I should go to a store in Congo Street. This
street is a congested commercial zone brimming with scores of street
vendors. The place is filthy and so crowded that you struggle to go
from here to there. When I expressed surprise at how a decrepit store
in a chaotic area has better books than the bookshop at the premier
university in the nation, she smiled but said nothing.

In the sixties and seventies, the same store was stocked with the latest editions of
state-of-the-art books on most of the subjects taught at the university. Even with
the smaller student body, a decent bunch of students would be seen browsing
the shelves much of the time. At the start of the academic year, it would be
overcrowded. I do not think it now deserves to be called a university bookstore.
In my view, it is nothing but a pathetic show piece. That is what I reported to
Professor Mmari.

I have witnessed a miracle today; I have seen a university without
books.

That is most interesting.

was his sanguine comment. It is a common picture at the universities in
Tanzania. Even at the institution where he is the provost, the conditions likely
are not too different.

In the first two and a half decades after *Uhuru*, Tanzania experienced a mini
but worthy explosion of literary activities, both of the fictional and non-fictional
type, and in English as in Swahili. Today, almost all of those products of our own
intellectuals have been forgotten and cannot be found on the market. Today,
as writers from other nations in Africa make a mark on and win distinguished
prizes in the international arena, Tanzanian writers are missing from the action.

In 2010, I asked a leading Tanzanian intellectual and author of several books:
What books did you read in the past year? He scratched his head. There
were none he could recall. It took him more than six months to read a book
he borrowed from me. A new biography of a historic figure he was strongly
attached to, he would have read it from cover to cover within a week in the old
days. His daughter, a budding historian, gave a similar response. Other than
books directly related to a specific task, no time for reading a book for its own
sake existed.

Today excellent works of literature and the non-fiction genre, books on
science, law, history, in varied languages, books recent and old, are obtainable
in a number of formats, and free of charge from several web sites. One among
several is www.gutenberg.org. Yet, the students and intellectuals of Tanzania
do not make good use of such resources. It is not just that the electronic
medium has transplanted the paper based one. It is that intellectual and literary
expeditions in the format of book, a format that requires focus and reflection,
have lost currency.

The youth in Tanzania and Africa are adept at navigating the vast repository
of ideas and knowledge in the global digital realm. But they jump erratically
from X to Y to Z, taste one concept, then another and then another, acquire a
half-baked acquaintance, and end up with nothing solid to speak of. If utilized
in a measured, guided way, the Internet can yield a vast store of concentrated

and relevant information. For mathematics and the multiplicity of its branches, I am amazed at the number of quality old and new books, on-line courses, and lecture notes that are available for free download. Yet, our university teachers rarely use them, or point them out to their students. The students, for their part lack the motivation and guidance to find, study and reflect on such material. And that holds for most subjects.

The essence of underdevelopment, as Walter Rodney used to remind us, is the progressive loss of the ability to determine the direction of our own lives. Time and again, a technology said to liberate us is hoisted mindlessly from the West. It is adopted broadly, but is utilized so inappropriately that it undermines the little good that was built up over time. Books were a colonial era import, but they had acquired local roots. Once upon a time, academics at the UDSM produced a series of renowned books in a multiplicity of scientific and social science disciplines. They have vanished from the local scene but continue to be used in universities abroad. The new academic staff at the UDSM have no idea that such a body of work exists. They and their students are preoccupied in cell phone discourse or surfing the shallow and dubious segments of the Web, and exchanging tit-bits of chatter on social media.

I am not an anti-electronic technology person. I make use of computers and the Internet extensively. Much of the research and all the writing for this book has utilized them. But I know where to draw the line; I spend two to three hours a day reading physical books. My concern is that the youth of today lack the foundation to enable them to draw such lines in a responsible and measured way. They do not have positive role models, since the adults of my generation have abandoned books as well. So the modern youth twitter, text and chat, day and night. Thereby, as we become mired in shallow thought, our ability and desire to determine the direction of our own lives continues to be compromised.

The four negative tendencies – dishonesty, cynicism, intolerance and anti-intellectualism – occur in all cultures and across time. They were evident during my youth too. What is at issue is the extent to which they have come to dominate our lives. They are a product of the global neo-liberal capitalist system. These trends are also present in the technologically advanced nations, though to a different degree and in varied forms. In Tanzania, they are on the verge of reaching an extreme form.

Let me give one illustration of my claim. When Mwalimu took up the helm of the nation, he had a torch placed atop Mount Kilimanjaro which was to shine in perpetuity to foster hope, dignity and universal human bondage. It was a symbol of human goodness and decency.

On the 50th anniversary of the *Uhuru* day, 9 December 2011, a special team was sent to recreate that historic moment of placing the torch at the summit. And it was proudly announced by our political bosses that the job had been done. Yet, later we learned that it had not. Due to lack of planning and technical glitches, the team did not manage to make it to the top. The whole nation had been deceived. Cynical comments ensued; but no one was taken to task. Life went on as usual.

The Maze of Memory

In comparing the ethic of the youth of my days with that of modern youth, I mostly praise the former and criticize the latter. Is that assessment, in which my memory and experiences are the main basis of support, accurate or biased? I am drawn into the arena of memory.

This book stands and falls by the degree to which my memory is constricted or not, biased or impartial, hazy or precise. While writing, I found instances where my recall varied with what had transpired, and instances for which it was solidly accurate. Further, important things were missing from my memory. Reconnecting with people from my past, and documentary research enabled me to piece together the picture I have presented. Yet, it remains a subjective text, my vision of how life was in those days.

Memory, according to the Wikipedia, is '*the process in which information is encoded, stored, and retrieved.*' It is of several types: short-term and long-term memories, declarative memory (recall of facts), procedural memory (learning of skills), autobiographic memory, typographic memory and so on. Science has identified parts of the brain that are associated with different memory types and has made great strides in understanding the mechanisms and disorders of memory. Their diagnosis, prevention and treatment have been subjected to extensive research. In particular, age associated memory change has garnered central attention. Finding effective treatments of memory related ailments has, however, not been as successful.

However, memory is not just an innate feature, the product of biologic factors like genes, brain size and structure and nutrition. It is as well a psycho-social construct critically affected by social status, education, experiences, values, loyalties and relationships.

Memory is an integral aspect of our sense of self; it makes us who we are. What we think we are is a function of what we have been or think we have been. Loss of memory fractures our individuality. Likewise, a nation that forgets to record and authentically remember its history degrades its standing in the community of nations. Its status as a respected entity is compromised; its people act in a manner as aimless as that of an amnesiac.

I cannot talk about memory without thinking about my *Dadima*. She read hymn books, and once in a while, wrote a note or letter. But her roots lay in a time when family history was passed through generations by the oral medium. She was the only conscientious practitioner of that ancient art I have known. She enjoyed telling us long winded stories, but it also expressed a sense of responsibility. She had to pass on what she knew.

She began to exhibit symptoms of Alzheimer's disease in the mid-1980s. When Farida and I returned from the USA in 1988, she faced the gruelling final stages. Her body had shrivelled. Her brain had almost shut down. The shawl no more on her head, she slouched in a corner with a vacant stare, impervious to everything. She just mumbled a few words when she was hungry. In a couple of months, and without recognizing us, she passed away.

All who remember her talk of her fabulous memory. Yet, how things have changed. Now electronic gadgets remember for us. Our brains are used less and less for recall. 'Use it or lose it' is a basic tenet of biology. If we do not use our muscles, they atrophy. In the early day of the telephone, we knew many seven digit telephone numbers by heart. A young fellow today does not remember his own cell phone number. He does not need to. Is it the case that our memory related capabilities are heading towards substantive degradation?

In posing this question, we need to appreciate the heights the human mind can scale on the memory front. Consider the case of π, the ratio of the circumference to the diameter of a circle. In school we learn that $\pi = 22/7$ or, better, $\pi = 3.142$. But both are approximate values. If you write it in a decimal form, π goes on forever, and unlike $1/3 = 0.33333\ldots$, its digits do not exhibit a pattern. Stated to forty decimal points, it is

$$\pi = 3.1415926535\ 8979323846$$
$$2643383279\ 5028841971\ldots$$

In high school, I knew the first ten digits of π by heart. But that is a tiny feat. Many recall a hundred digits of π. Others reach up to thousands of the digits. The world record for reciting the digits of π at one sitting and from memory is held by Chao Lu of China, who, on 20 November 2005, correctly recited the first 67,890 digits of π. The feat took 24 hours and 4 minutes to complete. Next to him stands Krishan Chahal of India who, on 19 June 2006, took 5 hours and 21 minutes to accurately recite the first 43,000 digits of π.

Such stupendous feats are a product of millions of years of evolution. The structure, function, size and capabilities of our brains are what make us stand out among animals. While technology can improve human lives, if used blindly, without critical consideration and under corporate driven influences, it does more harm than good. That applies with a stronger force to electronic technologies. Premature introduction of computers to children may seriously compromise important educational characteristics like ability to focus and in-depth reflection. Similar problems arise from unchecked cell phone use (There is a large body of literature on this issue that I cannot go into here.).

I end my musings on memory with thoughts of how I failed my beloved *Dadima* when she was in sharply declining health. We had just returned to Tanzania. But right from the first day, I faced daunting problems, time consuming yet essential tasks, at home and work. My health, finances and family life suffered. Mohamed's schizophrenia exacted its price. The house was frequently in an uproar. Successions of sleepless nights exhausted me. Now and then, my brother would disappear for days. Father and I would scour the city from end to end to find him. Consequently, I was too tied up and did not take care of *Dadima* as well as I should have. But it was a transgression of epic proportions that gnaws me to this day. No excuse can justify my shameful conduct. She definitely deserved better. With tears in my eyes, I continue to say to her: I am so sorry.

Dadima's stories enthralled me; what she became in old age saddened me. What was behind her power of recall? A sense of responsibility? Daily practice? Leading an active life? Or, the handful of pepper corns she chewed daily? Why did it decline so precipitously? What can be done to prevent that type of regression of memory? I have many queries. And I have a reason to pose them: My ability to recall details that used to be at my finger-tips is now faltering.

But she has left an enduring lesson. In this era, when how, when, where and why we relate to family, friends, colleagues and society are recorded flawlessly, in vivid colour and virtual perpetuity, on a digital device or network, the significance of our memory is changing. Yes, it is a flawed human characteristic. But its flaws form a part of our essence. I guess human memory will be made superfluous once electronic media begin to record our entire lives in minute detail. Will our sense of self turn into a function of our interactions with electronic gadgetry? Will our grandkids need a *Dadima* with her long winded stories? Indeed, can you embed love and warmth in these electronic media? Or, will love, laughter, tears, warmth and hugs become superfluous as well?

A Touch of Elegance ❖ ❖ ❖ ❖ ❖ ❖ ❖

In a geometry class, the teacher draws a circle, and constructs a square (E-square) around it, and another square (I-square) inside it, as shown below. You have to prove that the area of the E-square is twice that of the I-square.

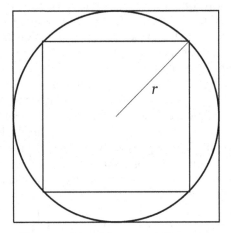

External and Internal Squares

Let the radius of the circle be r. Hence, each side of the E-square is $2r$. The Pythagoras theorem tells you that the side of the I-square is $\sqrt{2}r$. Therefore:

$$\text{Area of E-square} = (2r)^2 = 4r^2$$
$$\text{Area of I-square} = (\sqrt{2}r)^2 = 2r^2$$

This completes your proof. The teacher is happy, and you get the full score.

But your friend has a new method. She first rotates the I-square by 45 degrees, producing the diagram shown on the next page. No areas have changed. Then she joins the edges of the I-square by dashed lines, thus dividing the E-square into 4 small squares (S-squares). It is evident that the area of the E-square is four times the area of an S-square, and the area of the I-square is two times the area of an S-square. So the proposition is proved.

Your proof followed the mechanical style you had memorized from the geometry lessons; your friend has adopted a creative approach. Her proof is as valid as yours, and, in a way, it is more elegant. Will the teacher give her extra points, or will she be marked down for not using formulas?

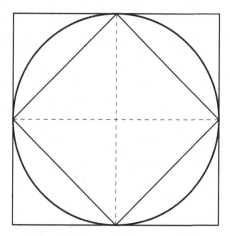

External and Rotated Internal Squares

Memory and Understanding: From the way maths and other subjects are taught and tested today, if you have a good memory, you can be deemed an excellent student. Over reliance on memory can, however, impede understanding. It only takes you thus far; and at some point, your poor grasp of basic ideas becomes a stumbling block for further educational advancement.

You read a book, and remember the details. Yet, you do not understand the essence and theme of the work. You can retell the story well, but are unable to evaluate it adequately.

Similarly, maths is not necessarily about fast calculation, recall of hundreds of digits of π, or similar feats. Some mathematicians have had an amazing power of recall; as there have been non-mathematicians with a similar ability. But most mathematicians have not had outstanding memories; what they displayed was a remarkable ability to focus, the ability to devise completely novel ways to attack intransigent conundrums, or formulate hitherto unknown tools and ideas.

The harsh methods of teaching maths in the colonial and early post-colonial days were effective, but they were for the majority of the students, mostly successful in terms of a memory based grasp of the subject. Multiplication tables, arithmetic sums, algebraic expressions and geometry exercises were reproduced as needed. Only minor variations were set. Problems needing creative effort were rare. The endeavour to introduce 'modern maths' went to the other extreme, and ditched drill and reproduction. Too abstract concepts were introduced too early. And that too did not fare well.

A good approach to learning maths, and indeed, most subjects, has to balance reliance on memory with conceptualization and development of deeper understanding. This cannot be done by force, but only by inspiring the students. Injection of recreational maths into the curriculum will, in my view, provide the fulcrum around which the two approaches can be integrated in an effective manner.

Our nation needs workers like clerks, nurses and journalists who can handle the basic numeric tasks; professionals like engineers, agronomists, transport planners, water development specialists, health and education researchers and the like, who can apply tools of advanced mathematics and statistics; maths teachers whose conceptual understanding is at a level that enables them to teach the subject in a creative, effective manner; people with a good training in basic statistics and data management in most major institutions; and theoretically attuned statisticians and mathematicians who can innovate and ensure that the edifices of these disciplines develop in directions that will benefit society and culture, and foster their own growth.

It also needs an environment in which mathematical and statistical ideas form a part of the common cultural edifice, and which are used to enhance creativity, provide entertainment, foster imagination, and enhance the spirit of inquiry and critical thought. Mathematical and statistical curricula, teaching and related activities need to be formulated with these broad objectives in mind.

My principal gripe with modern communications technology is that the manner in which it is being used by the youth in Tanzania and Africa (and perhaps everywhere) undermines both memory based skills and the ability to focus, conceptualize, inter-connect disparate ideas and critical thinking. Instead, it fosters shallow thinking based on recall of a few superfluous and questionable 'facts'. It promotes a shallow vision deriving from a short-cut approach to the realms of ideas, numbers and knowledge. And thus, it lays the foundation for a robotic existence that will ultimately undercut the moral and ethical codes the human family has developed over thousands of years.

Thereby, we need to exercise great caution in terms of when, how and to what extent we use electronic technology in the education system. We must ensure that the pencil, pen, paper, and physical books are available to all. In a poor nation like ours, I urge the return of the slate board in primary school. It will more effectively improve reading and writing skills than gadgets like smart phones and tablet computers. The latter will be damaged in no time and no replacements will be available. Above all, whatever the teaching tools, what a child absolutely needs is a nurturing, dedicated teacher. Direct human contact is indispensable for a sound education.

— 16 —

Spirals of Hope

*In all things it is better to hope
than to despair.*
                    J W von Goethe

❖ ❖ ❖ ❖ ❖ ❖ ❖

CYNICISM IS THE TWIN of despair. Both induce societal stagnation. Both promote what ails us. However dire the situation, we should seek explanations for why things are the way they are. The perpetrators of serious misdeeds must be held to account, and grave societal injustice has to be redressed. Having said that, we should realize that the pure blame mode of reasoning applied towards social groups only exacerbates the existing prejudices, divides and weakens us, and damages our resolve to work with each other. We have to avoid condemning whole social or ethnic groups, and instead concentrate on how we can together change things for the better.

Rational analysis of society and social change stimulates hope for the possibility of change. History has no shortage of examples to demonstrate that change can occur even under the most restrictive of conditions. Sound historic memory and recall of edifying role models are potent remedies for uplifting gloomy, cynical spirits. When the frequent societal mishaps of today lure me towards cynicism, I relive the moments when ordinary people joined hands to bring forth momentous change. I bring to mind exemplary persons of earlier generations, in Tanzania and across the world, who took a bold, principled stand; withstood adversity with courage and fortitude; or scaled Himalayan intellectual heights. They nourish my psyche. I say to myself, if it could be done then and there, it and better things can be done here, even if it will take time.

Previously, we have come across some exemplary persons I have known, including my fine teachers and friends – Elias Kisamo, Shiraz Ramji and Nazir Virji – who devoted themselves to teaching our children. I return to the youth of the 1960s, and then shine a light on three exemplary Tanzanians whose roots lie in those times. In the mathematical minuet, I look at four maths instructors from lands beyond our borders.

Room for Hope

A photo from the year 1966: Eight Ismaili youngsters stand with three African men and two African women (Image ?: Appendix B). Deftly clutching pick axes, hoes and spades, they smile in unison. I recognize my Upanga friends Nazir, Mamlo, Shiraz and Adil. It was taken by Fidu, also a JK buddy. They were in Buguruni, a suburb of Dar es Salaam, to work on the construction of a primary school. Upanga, where they lived, was an Asian enclave, and Buguruni, almost all African or Arab. I was a regular participant in these self-help activities, but am not in the picture because by then I had left for Kibaha School.

The month long service at the Kinondoni Camp which Amer, Ram, Nassoro, Abdul Karim, Saleh, Navroz and I performed returns to my mind. National service was not compulsory at that time. Unlike for the Standard 7 leavers, joining it did not affect our career goals. No financial incentive was involved. Students in the UK and USA do voluntary work to pad their CVs for education and job related reasons. High minded young fellows from the West fly in and fly out in a patronizing fashion to assist the poor and refugees in Third World nations. That their corporations and governments laid the foundation for these crises is not an issue for them.

Our service had no basis in such formalistic and self-serving charitable behaviour. No, there was none of that. We went to the camp because we felt it was the right thing to do. We had an internal desire to contribute to building our nation. It was like assisting your father on the family farm. At the end of the day, we felt happy and energized. And, believe me, that was a sufficient reward.

I recall my 1970s era students at the National Institute of Transport as enthusiastic and diligent. After getting their Diploma in Transport Management, many attempted to practice effective operational methods in the national and regional transport firms where they were posted. Most were frustrated by the old guard. The message was: Join us or else; Do not rock the boat. Still, a few persisted and tried hard to institute change. Predictably, they were ditched by the wayside.

Such memories symbolize the efforts of those youth to overcome past legacies and improve the social system. Their optimistic outlook and dedication to the common good promoted social harmony. It induced formation of inter-racial, inter-religious and inter-ethnic bonds. That the achievements were limited and mostly reversed later does not obliterate the real efforts that were done and the noticeable progress made. So I ask: If the youth could lead the way then, why can they not do it today?

Three Heroes

Many heroes – Tanzanian, African and global – inspire me. If they could scale such heights, can we not at least go half-way? In that spirit, I look at three of my home-grown heroes.

I. **Fundi Hamisi** is a gentle, tall man. Probably sixty years old, he has a no-nonsense bearing. His left leg is deformed from long standing filariasis. His arms, though, are muscular. In the year 2008 he accepted the task of making cabinets and work tables for our kitchen. We bought the wood, Formica sheets, glass panes, nails, glue and other stuff. It was to be a three-week job.

I saw him plan his work carefully, make measurements and keep short hand notes. He went on to implement his plan in a step-by-step, meticulous fashion. The cutting, drilling, nailing, smoothing and applying of glue were done exactly as if he was following a textbook. Adhering to rules of safety and not misplacing tools and supplies were built into his work style. Thus, as soon as he finished drilling, he shut off the power, and replaced the bit and key where they should be. After each step, he looked over what he had made. No irregularity was allowed. It was clear from the start that he was not a person who was content with a half-baked product.

When the job was done, we had elegant cabinets and tables with perfect fittings. They look like polished factory products. But unlike modern mass products, they are sturdy and have been built to last.

Fundi Hamisi stands head and shoulder above all other *fundis,* much younger than him, who have done varied jobs at my house in the past ten years. The young ones plunge into their tasks without a plan, are in a hurry, and have little regard for cost or waste. As they do not bear the cost of the material, their attitude is: Why care? Half the time, they chat on cell phones. And their output is considerably inferior.

Fundi Hamisi rises up to the stringent standards set by Mr Fredrick Isaya in our woodwork class at the DTC. Our teachers taught us to strive for excellence and avoid short cuts. This elderly man embodies that spirit of professionalism, a scarce trait now. He takes pride in what he does, and is not just a living instance of what Mwalimu Nyerere taught us: *Uhuru na kazi* (Freedom and work) but has also taken a step beyond it; *Uhuru ni kazi* (Freedom is work).

To the younger *fundis* of today, Mr Isaya would assign the grade 'D'. They have been seduced by effort saving devices, but their product is substandard. They are misled by superficial electronic communication. Virtually all sectors of the economy suffer from the malady of inattention to product quality. The fine professionalism of this self-taught skilled workman sharply contrasts the shallow, hurried, ill-planned research and teaching endeavours of my former colleagues at the Muhimbili University, most of whom held PhD degrees and some of whom had attained the rank of professor.

Our advanced degreed professionals earn millions while he barely gets 5% of that. Yet, in terms of genuine professionalism, striving for excellence and taking intrinsic pride in the product quality, he outshines them all.

II. Geoffrey V Mmari is a veteran educator who began teaching in secondary schools in 1958. Later, he joined the Institute of Education at the UDSM. He excelled, and went on to be a full Professor, the head of the Department of Education, and finally, the Vice Chancellor of the UDSM. During the past twenty five years, he has sat at the helm of three universities in the nation and is now the Rector for the Dar es Salaam campus of Tumaini University.

Professor Mmari was a founder of the Mathematics Association of Tanzania way back in 1966. He served the association in various capacities and was its president for over two decades. He was a principal driver of the move to introduce modern maths in Tanzanian schools. Though it had serious pitfalls, and was later abandoned, there is no doubt that he acted with the best of intentions. He has authored many academic and general papers on appropriate methods of teaching maths in schools.

Geoffrey Mmari was one of my teachers at the UDSM and I also had the occasion to work with him in the 1970s when he coordinated the national secondary school mathematics and statistics examinations. I set the Form VI statistics paper in those days. I recall the year 1975 exam marking session at Kibaha. Over a hundred teachers were present; there were thousands of scripts to grade. It was a major event needing a dedicated leader with good administrative skills. And that leader was Professor Mmari. He was on the move day and night, attending to one issue after another, be it personal, the quality of food at the canteen or misplacement of a script. Marking tasks and supportive activities were under control. He ensured accurate grading by spot checks. High standards and fair grading were his central priorities. The exercise occurred smoothly and efficiently. I was happy with his performance, and hold the view that the current leadership of the National Examination Council has much to learn from his example.

Professor Mmari spent more than fifty five years working to improve mathematics education and education in general in Tanzania. All who have come in touch with him praise his friendly and gentle demeanour, boundless energy, strict punctuality, devotion to detail and keen sense of responsibility. He is a simple man who does not favour the excessive pomp which characterizes academic life today. He does not beat about the bush, but speaks plainly and directly. In contrast to the bulk of present day academic and public figures, he is a genuinely respected and widely adored personality (Seka 2010).

If called for, he speaks his mind, even if it is to the displeasure of the authorities. It was his principled stand on important issues and refusal to be a yes-man that shortened his tenure as the Vice Chancellor of the UDSM. Tanzania needs educators and leaders like him at the helm to guide us out of our present morass. Well past the age of retirement and in a rather frail state, he keeps on serving the nation.

III. John Stephen Akhwari represented Tanzania at the Olympic games of 1968 held in Mexico City. He competed in the marathon race. A total of 74 runners were at the start line. Along the way, John fell down, sustaining deep cuts at his knee. The knee joint was partially dislocated. But he, unlike 17 other runners, did not give up. With majestic effort and under much pain, he ran on. He made it, but well after the sun had set and the stadium was mostly empty. His spirit and determination won global acclaim. While the gold medal was won by Mamo Wolde of Ethiopia, John earned the title: *A King Without a Crown.*

When he was asked why he did not quit, he replied:

> My country did not send me to 5,000 miles to Mexico City to start the race. They sent me 5,000 miles to finish the race.

(Note, 8,000 miles is a more accurate figure.) John Stephen Akhwari represented Tanzania for several more years. And he remains a symbol of courage in sports. Accordingly, he featured as an inspirational personality in the Sydney Olympic games of 2000 and the Beijing Olympic games of 2008.

John Stephen Akhwari inspired me first in 1968. The memory of his fine deed elevates my mood to this day. Our youth have forgotten his indomitable spirit. They are familiar with John F Kennedy and Abraham Lincoln, but not with outstanding Africans, in all the fields of human endeavour, of the past. They at best possess a passing acquaintance with the valiant struggles of the peoples of Africa, Asia and Latin America against injustice, humiliation, inequality and tyranny. Until they begin to take heed of history, their sense of self-worth will remain a dwarfed one, and they will remain susceptible to manipulation against their own interests.

Internationalism

This book has outlined my journey from the narrow parochialism of colonial times to broad-based patriotism, from an exclusive community based immersion among brown people into an existence in a multi-racial, nationwide arena. But the journey did not stop at this stage. After 1968, I moved on from plain nationalism to socialism, Pan Africanism and internationalism (The book *Cheche: Reminiscences of a Radical Magazine* covers a part of that story.). Consequently, while I remain a devoted Tanzanian, my primary identity stems from the sense of being a member of the single, planet wide human family.

I do not regard simple nationalism as a sound vision for life. I reject the mentality that says: my country, right or wrong. I am aware that such an outlook has serviced unjust wars and horrible atrocities. Imperial nationalism drove our colonial rulers. Today, the USA epitomizes that ideology. It considers itself an exceptional nation, the most civilized. Its people believe that launching atomic bombs on two cities and killing some two hundred thousand civilians was a justified act. They do not shed tears over the millions their bombs killed in Korea, Vietnam, Iraq or Afghanistan. In that land, a modern patriot launches deadly drones against distant villages he knows next to nothing about. If scores of civilians perish, he is not bothered. Having done his duty, he or she proudly goes home to teach his kids about the importance of nonviolent behaviour.

Blind nationalism is a particularly ugly face of modern dualism. But it is one among many. In one way or another, our social world injects many dualist tendencies into our lives. The key queries are: Are the ethical, mental and practical divides of that dualism extreme, frequent and consequential? Where do we draw the line? Which is the dominant tendency? Instead of denying or ignoring our dualistic feelings and acts, we need to be conscious of and talk about them. We need to fight against them, and control their negative aspects. Only then can we remain dignified, worthy members of the human family.

While we love our families, communities, culture and nation, we ought not be blind to their flaws. A consistent, honest perspective is essential for an ethical life. Mahatma Gandhi was asked: Which do you love more, India or the Truth? His answer came without hesitation, *"The Truth, of course."*

While I love my homeland, there have been times I have been ashamed of being a citizen of Tanzania. While I respect and honour the contributions of Mwalimu Nyerere to the liberation of Africa from colonial and racist domination, there were times when I was dismayed at his stand on African affairs. I was deeply appalled at our reaction to the gruesome genocide in Rwanda. As hundreds of thousands of our fellow human beings were being slaughtered next door, Tanzania stood by; Mwalimu Nyerere was mostly quiet. Our media reported the vile deeds, but the people or even the students did not take to the streets to demand action. Though no longer at the helm of the state, Mwalimu could have raised his voice plainly and loudly. Our troops should have rushed in. That was what was mandated by international law, basic sense of human solidarity, and the tenets of Pan Africanism. But, to our lasting shame, we became pure spectators.

We proudly and rightly claim to have decisively assisted the people of Uganda in deposing the dictator Idi Amin. Yet, our inaction on Rwanda has been forgotten. The least we can do is to pass a parliamentary resolution to convey an official apology from our president to the people of Rwanda. This question has nothing to do with the personalities in power. It is a fundamental issue of the relationship between people and people, an important requirement of good neighborliness.

Dreams

The type of solutions, resources, knowhow, manpower and tools for most of the serious or minor problems facing us are within reach. What we need are sound organization, effective planning and serious implementation. Above all, we need genuinely committed, honest, far sighted, incorruptible and thoughtful leaders. Only such leaders can mobilize the masses for undertaking the large scale, sustained collective actions that will arise in the process.

The cruel reality of neo-liberal policies, political charlatanism of our so-called leaders and blatant duplicity of the Western nations is increasingly apparent. The reality can only bite harder. The youth will sooner or later awaken, struggle, learn from past errors, lead and pave the way for a better world.

In these times, heroes abound, and are celebrated in the media. But I see them as glitzy, commercialized personalities often associated with lavishly funded NGOs or promoted by Western embassies. Some are ex-politicians or business personalities who seem to have amassed fortunes through questionable means but now donate funds for social causes.

I do not have them in mind; I am thinking of the potential John Stephen Akhwaris, Geoffrey Mmaris and *Fundi* Hamisis lurking in the shadows among our youth. I think till now they have been silent and subdued. But I suspect change is afoot. A few of them are beginning to show their mettle. *Fundi* Andrew, a young plumber, for example, shows the same devotion to excellence as Fundi Hamisi. I see a few school and university students taking learning seriously and probing deeper into socio-historic analysis. In varied walks of life, men and women, young and not so old, are embarking on creative endeavours to confront the obstacles of life.

A small start, but one that signifies a shiny spark that will ignite a prairie fire of awareness. I visualize a generation of honest, brave, caring and competent personalities emerging to serve the people. We will hear their voices of reason and witness their attempts to craft ingenuous actions. Others will take notice and emulate. Slowly, they will come together for long term effort to change social reality. Indeed, there is room for hope.

For all it is worth, I offer a few words of caution to the emergent youth. First, as I said before, despite its utility, do not place all your trust in modern electronic technology. It has to be deployed with care. Otherwise the bifurcated features of our times will intensify. The danger is greater in Africa, where extreme poverty and advanced technology coexist. Do we seek a future where each parent has a cell phone, yet malnutrition prevails? Do we want a future where we can communicate our predicaments in an efficient way but have damaged our capacity to tackle the major practical problems on our own? Do we want food, or the capability to text about our inability to feed our children?

To those who say that this is an artificial dichotomy, that technology is the solution to our problems, I say, prove it. The evidence before me says otherwise. I urge the youth not to put blind faith in fashionable pronouncements like a laptop or a tablet for each child or the wonders of genetically modified foods from experts, academics and corporate hacks. In their penchant for fancy technology, they follow self-serving interests. What Africa needs is for the people to place their feet on the ground, and tackle basic issues with the means that are at hand, means which we can produce ourselves, namely, the appropriate intermediate technology of the earlier times.

When I hear the calls from experts in health care for more funds for re-search, my response is: Take a basic text on public health from the 1960s, and implement what is stated in there. That will resolve more than 80% of our health problems. If research is needed, it should focus on finding out why the numerous well known, sound public health measures are not implemented.

While electronic social media and communication have a role, nothing can replace face to face contact, person to person action, intense study of books without interruption by phone beeps, and continual perspiration-generating, on-the-ground organizational and practical effort. To build a humane future and preserve our humanity at the same time, we must not lose sight of what makes us human. We must not surrender our remarkable capabilities to the machine. The master key to finding lasting solutions to our problems is not advanced technology but genuine human solidarity and elemental creativity.

Inspirational Teachers ✢ ✢ ✢ ✢ ✢ ✢ ✢

An ideal teacher informs and inspires, cajoles and entreats, pushes and makes us perspire, is understanding and critical, and is a friend but not a flatterer. She complements your own dedication and efforts, and fosters your creative powers and desire to excel. Good teachers at crucial junctures in my life made a world of a difference to my advancement in life.

Many examples, past and present, of outstanding teachers exist. Above I noted the case of Professor Mmari, a fabulous teacher, administrator and all-round person. Now I go beyond our borders for three cases of maths teachers in this category. I have not met any of them. To balance the picture, I give the case of a good math teacher who was led astray.

I. Louis Leithold had a long, distinguished career as a college level mathematics instructor. At the age of 72, he retired from that work in 1998. Among his achievements was a popular textbook for high school calculus courses. Over the years, he had led popular calculus workshops for high school maths teachers from across the USA.

Instead of spending his twilight years relaxing at the sunny beaches of California, he took a teaching position at the Malibu High School. His subjects were: Basic Calculus and Advance Placement Calculus. The former is at the level of Additional Mathematics I did at the DTC, and the latter is at the level of Form V mathematics.

At Malibu High, Leithold employed creative teaching aids to explain hard concepts, and had his students put in extra time, including weekends, into their studies. Every year, students from his class obtained high scores in the state examinations. While actively teaching, and just as his latest batch of students were to sit for these exams, he passed away in 2009.

Despite the setback, his students did not let him down. To honour him, they strove harder. And they excelled. Of the 16 candidates from that class, 14 secured the highest grade (5.0) and two, the next highest grade (4.0) (Woo 2009).

An energetic, popular eighty year old maths teacher who demonstrates keen dedication and exceptional effectiveness at his job, and one who moreover champions the subject matter as well – an astounding, moving and exemplary tale like no other.

II. Jaime Escalante was 33 years old when he moved from Bolivia to California in 1964. He educated himself and improved his English language skills while doing various blue collar jobs. After qualifying as a high school maths teacher, he joined Garfield High School in Los Angeles in 1974.

The American system of schooling remains a *defacto* segregated system with unequally endowed components. In areas like the Pacific Palisades, where Louis Leithold taught, and Santa Monica, where my grandchildren attend school, public schools are well administered, have sufficient resources and attract the best teachers. In contrast, in South Central and East Los Angeles, where the residents are predominantly Latino and African American, public schools present a major contrast. As in a Third World nation, you find extensive maladministration, deficient maintenance of the facilities, late procurement of necessary supplies likes books and stationary, too many unmotivated teachers, financial irregularities and wide spread disciplinary problems. Most schools in the former areas do well in the state examinations; a high proportion of their students proceed to university level studies. On the other hand, students in the latter areas get low scores in state exams, and rates of entry into well regarded higher education institutions are very low as well.

Jaime Escalante taught at a school of the latter kind. But he was not deterred. He devised novel, culturally fine-tuned strategies to attract and engage the students who traditionally neglected subjects like science and maths. Devoting extensive energies towards his class, he pushed them to the limit, and made them put in long hours into school work.

And it paid off. In the High School Advance Placement Calculus exam for the year 1982, his group of 14 students did exceptionally well, with some scoring the highest grade. But it was an unprecedented result; the conservative examination board refused to accept it, implying that the students had cheated somehow. In the ensuing imbroglio that was publicized by the media, 12 students retook the exam. And once more, to the astonishment of everyone, most secured the same high scores.

It was a turning point in the history of education in California. It showed that despite poverty and resource deficient conditions, Latino and African American students could excel in academic activities as well as the white kids. It made a dent in the prevalent racist stereotyping in education. This saga was the basis of the famed movie: *Stand and Deliver.*

Jaime Escalante was a pace-setter, a destroyer of myths, a teacher whose goals were as high as Mount Everest and whose love for his students was as deep as the Pacific Ocean. He influenced hundreds to follow in his wake. After retiring from teaching, he became an advisor for state education policy in California. Talking of his skills as a teacher, one former student called him a 'master artist'. He died in 2010 at the age of 79 (Adams 2010).

III. Abdul Malik has taught maths in a primary school in Kerala, India, for twenty years. From the day he started, he has faced a big problem. Though his school is not too far from his house, it is separated by a river. The distance between the riverbanks and the depth vary according to season. The former can be fifty meters or more, and the latter ranges from knee deep to well above his height. There is no bridge nearby. Thus, he had to travel a long distance to get to the school.

Initially, he boarded a bus that crossed the river some kilometres down. A second bus took him back towards the school. In all, he still walked two kilometres. With the two-hour journey, he was tired and occasionally late to work. That did not put him in good standing with the headmaster. Additionally, the bus fares consumed a decent sum from his modest salary.

A year on the job, he took a bold step. One day, he crossed the river directly. In summer, he can wade across. During the rainy season, he swims with the help of a rubber tube. Either way, he holds his work clothes and lunch in a plastic bag above his head. From that day, he has never been late, and has not missed a single day of work.

At the outset, family and friends discouraged him and he became an object of ridicule. Over time, his dedication and spirit earned him wide admiration. He is so punctual that the locals set time by the moment he steps into the river. Having enjoyed swimming since childhood, he now offers lessons in swimming to children during his spare time (Naha 2013; Shaju 2013).

IV. Matthias Vheru, in contrast to these admirable teachers, is an anti-hero. Hailing from Zimbabwe, he taught maths for 20 years in schools in the low income areas of Los Angeles. Like Jaime Escalante, he faced the tough job of teaching algebra and geometry to disadvantaged, unmotivated kids. But he seems to have met the challenge well. He also wrote and published school level textbooks in these two subjects. After facing the blackboard for a decade or so, he joined the administration and later was promoted to be the Interim Director of Mathematics in the Unified Los Angeles school district.

And that is where things began to unravel. Apparently, as the director, he made decisions that were not in the best interest of the students. He set up a company to distribute his books and circumvented the required procedures to influence the district to order 46,000 copies of the books. It earned him nearly US$ 1 million in 2009. Unfortunately for him, this was uncovered during an audit, and he was charged with fraud and misrepresentation. The last time I read about him, he sounded regretful as he awaited the verdict of his case in a Los Angeles area court (Lozano 2009).

The teacher is the centre of gravity of any education system; it fails or succeeds according to the quality and quantity of effort she expends. The teacher guides, inspires and informs. Her influence moulds young persons into either exemplary or unsavoury human beings; into intellectually able and skilled persons, or ignorant and dysfunctional characters. If we want to improve the performance in maths we have to foremost devise ways of generating able, dedicated, creative and inspiring maths teachers (Kilasi 2011). There is no short cut.

In particular, no purely technological or computer based option like one-laptop-per-child or mobile-learning can save the day. Influential voices in our nation proclaim hi-tech to be the solution for all manners of problems in our education system (Editorial 2014a). I disagree. For example, while this editorial posits use of computer data bases to resolve the problems of non-enrollment and truancy, it has been found that providing porridge to students can go a long way towards tackling them. Also, the Internet based programme with giant screens instead of teachers is, to put it bluntly, pure nonsense. Africa has been subjected to too many external, corporate driven initiatives over the past fifty years; these hi-tech ones are just the latest. All the previous ones have led us into a blind alley; and the now fashionable ones will do likewise (Winters 2013).

Without good teachers, our education system will fall apart. Its output will be half-backed in theory and practice. Lack of appropriate role models will drive this mis-educated youth away from excellence and public service. We need to devise and implement policies that will help produce effective and inspiring teachers. And teachers have to be involved in the design of education programmes. At present they are abandoned. It is not easy for them to function in the rough economic waters of the present times. We have to accord them respect and cater adequately for their welfare. But they, in turn, have to give their best. Ultimately, it is only they who can propel our children towards, and equip them for, productive, relevant and morally uplifting careers for the benefit of our nation and the human race as a whole.

As I write these words, vivid images from more than fifty years back float before my eyes. There is the fearsome Vatsalaben, who almost drew me away from maths; Mr Fazli Datoo and Mr Mehrali Hirani, who magically enticed me back into the fold; and Mr Calvin Brooks, whose cool stories and magnificent style firmly cemented my feet in that mysterious arena of real and unreal numbers, arcane equations, mysterious curves lines and shapes, and, above all, uncompromising logic. To me personally, and I suspect to many others, they and their counterparts embody the quantified aphorism:

2 teach is 2 touch lives 4 ever.
Unknown Author

Spirals of Song

*The whole universe is based on
rhythms. Everything happens
in circles, in spirals.*
John Hartford

❖ ❖ ❖ ❖ ❖ ❖ ❖

OUR HOME HAS BEEN graced by a radio from as far back as I can recall. In colonial Lind, a typical Asian household resonated with shortwave music or news broadcasts from India and the BBC. In African homes, it was a rare sight. I got my first set – actually a cassette player and radio in one – upon joining the UDSM in 1968.

The radio audience expanded significantly after *Uhuru* due to the availability of cheaper, locally assembled radio sets, a stronger Radio Tanzania signal, culturally relevant programming and enhanced socio-political awareness. In large measure, it was accessed collectively. People congregated in the *pombe* (local brew) drinking areas, bars or near homes with sets on at a high volume. There was radio time in boarding schools, places of work, national service and other institutions. Town market area loudspeakers blared Radio Tanzania programs from dawn to dusk. Families, friends and neighbors assembled for a popular show, a speech by Mwalimu, the annual budget speech or a soccer match. It was a national ritual to tune into *Tarifa ya Habari* (News Bulletin) and *Mazungumzo Bada ya Habari* (News Commentary) daily at 8 pm. Listening to these news programmes came to be seen as the trade mark of a bona-fide Tanzanian. The informational program *Majira* was heard by many. Children knew the drum beats and musical score introducing main popular programs.

Mass Medium

Despite major transformations in communications and media over the past fifty years, the radio remains the medium of the masses in Tanzania, their primary source of news, views and music. For most rural residents, it is still the sole source. People nowadays deploy their cell phones as radio sets too. Hence, the reach of the audio signal, and possibly its impact, are greater.

Yet, much has changed. What is heard on the radio, and the social setting in which it occurs have changed. Collective access persists, but to a lower extent, and more as TV viewing. A Simba/Yanga or a UK soccer game with the top teams draws a large crowd. The societal significance is smaller. With cell phone access, it is more of a personal experience.

The contents have been transformed, in essence and style. The end of state monopoly has increased choices. But the apparent progress belies retrogression in key aspects. The music and songs are generally of a mind numbing, Western-based variety. Traditional songs, music and tunes of the past are infrequent. News and commentary on local affairs feature shallow politicking. Foreign news in both private and public radio stations are couched in language that brings a smile to the public relations officers from the US, UK and European embassies. Religion based stations have a dominating presence. And you will encounter priests, imams and charlatans promising miracle cures for a bundle of ailments.

Imaginative entertainment programs, science based sessions, or literary programs – Swahili or English – are few and of poor quality. Sound educational programs on public health and critical issues are too few, too donor driven and not reflective of our societal priorities. But you do get a stock of sensationalized stories that capture the public imagination. To cap it all, health messages aired on public and private radio stations that demean our national dignity appear on a daily basis.

With my radio, I hear local and external programs. But the biased content and unappealing music make me do it less and less. The Internet gives me the news and information I need. However, I do not view videos of any kind on my computer.

With no TV at home, I watch it only once in a blue moon. TV viewing forces you to sit at one place, and do little else. For desk bound workers, it adds a couple or more hours of sedentary time. It is a health hazard that also interferes with intra-family dialog. Moreover, it is inundated with unedifying but tantalizing, escapist fare. The radio allows me to brush my teeth, shave, arrange my stuff, prepare my food, eat or play with our kittens in the front yard while listening to news, discussion and songs. I hardly watch movies, though once upon a time, I was embedded in that medium. My leisure time is for books and music. My library of books from a range of genres and authors keeps me busy two to four hours daily. When I complete a book, I am as edified as if I have consumed a sumptuous meal.

A Dream: I dream of a local radio channel where a major book from local, African or global literature features in a regular hour-long session. Forty five minutes are for actual reading, and the rest, for discussion. Contemporary and classic English and Swahili books – entertaining, imaginative, edifying and informative – are on stage. There are no commercials, the sessions are serialized, and as one book ends, another takes off. Young and old listeners and teachers participate in selecting the featured books. And I visualize that it is a popular program. For high school students, it is a required part of their civics or general paper studies.

Patriotic Songs

What I miss particularly are the patriotic and culturally edifying songs and music of the 1960s and 1970s. A staple in our times, they occur irregularly now; you hear one by pure luck. The other day, I happened to catch a rendition of *Tanzania, Tanzania*. Its first stanza is shown below.

Tanzania, Tanzania

Tanzania, Tanzania	Tanzania, Tanzania
Nakupenda kwa moyo wote	I love you with all my heart
Nchi yangu Tanzania	My country Tanzania
Jina lako ni tamu sana	Your name is so sweet
Nilalapo nakuota wewe	Asleep, you enter my dreams
Niamkapo ni heri mama we	Awake, you are still with me
Tanzania, Tanzania	Tanzania, Tanzania
Nakupenda kwa moyo wote	I love you with all my heart

Instantly, I was transported back to the morning of 12 January 1965, my last day at the Kinondoni Camp. We, the enlistees, saluted our flag, moodily bade farewell and, in a loud voice, sang the lyrical ballad *Tanzania Nakupenda Sana* (Chapter 5).

Nakupenda Sana

Tanzania nakupenda sana	Tanzania, I love you a lot
Na jina lako ni tamu sana	And your name is so sweet
Nafurahisha moyoni	Happiness engulfs my heart
Nakuota	You pervade my dreams

This song seeded its essence into my bone marrow to the extent that from then on my blood cells had the label Made In Tanzania etched into their nuclei.

While the former song is known, no trace of the latter exists. The lyrics and audio files of *Tanzania, Tanzania,* as rendered by several artists, appear on the web. But not of the other. Yet, both songs are equally evocative. Their captivating melodies deserve frequent presence on the airwaves. In these cynical times, they will likely sooth the sour minds of the old, calm the hectic persona of the working folk, and inspire our easy-going, sluggish youth.

I keep the smaller ballad alive in a way by singing it, at home of course, on my own and to my grandkids. I make variations by placing their names in the song. If I am with Samir, the first line changes from *Tanzania nakupenda sana* to *Samir, Samir mtoto mzuri sana,* (Samir, Samir is a very good boy), and the second stanza begins as *Emma, Emma dada mzuri sana,* (Emma, Emma is a very good sister).

Mtoto Mzuri Sana

Samir, Samir mtoto mzuri sana	*Emma, Emma dada mzuri sana*
Na jina lako ni tamu sana	*Na jina lake ni tamu sana*
Nafurahisha moyoni	*Nafurahisha moyoni*
Nakuota	*Nakuota*

Names of friends, parents, relatives and pets add more stanzas. In a loud voice, we carol till one of us tires. But as they reside in the USA, I get this chance only once every eighteen months or so. And, it is one of the rare times they are exposed to a Swahili song.

As I revive my musical memories, I remember my sweet grandkids in a distant land, and think of the beautiful children of Tanzania and the world. I remember Dawood *chacha, Dadima,* and old friends, here and in the heavens. I am simultaneously happy, sad, sentimental and worried.

But I see that the time for dreaming is up. My bedridden father is getting restless. I observe him swinging his arms as if striking down a demon. It is time he heard two or three Ismaili hymns. When I sing the *ginans* that were recited by my *Dadima* – his mother – he reacts as if given a potent tranquilizer. He calms down and is attentive. I need to pick up my Gujarati script version of the hymns and sit near him.

Later in the evening, as we savour homemade rosella juice, Farida and I treat ourselves to Mukesh and Lata Mangeshkar. Yesterday, it was Harry Belafonte, and the day before, Jim Reeves. It is a daily ritual enacted before calling it a day.

A Fragmented Fabric

While I immerse myself in a multi-cultural, multi-racial, internationalist mental atmosphere, the reality around is otherwise. By 2012, the global human family was divided among 195 sovereign states, and more than 50 dependent or disputed areas. A typical nation has its own ethnic and religious groups. There are divisions within divisions; divides within, across and between nations, religions, cultures. These subdivisions, which increase by the day, serve less to promote harmony. Commonly, they enhance tensions and confrontations.

Yet, there is a paradox here. International capitalism has economically unified the entire globe. Should that not promote global peace and harmony? But it ceases to be a paradox when you realize that the economic unification has taken place not on terms that benefit the vast majority of the planetary population, but on terms that benefit a few in the rich and poor nations. The process has created historically unprecedented inequalities. In early 2014, it was reported by OXFAM that the 85 wealthiest persons in the world had as much wealth as the bottom half of humankind, that is, 3.5 billion people. Seen in a different light, the top 1% owned assets worth US $110tn, an amount which was 65 times what was owned by the poorest 50% (Wearden 2014).

The stark inequalities are reproduced at the local, communal and national levels. The haves and have-nots live in parallel universes. That is what I observe in front of my eyes in Dar es Salaam. At one end, we have near-billionaires and tycoons, and at the other, burgeoning numbers of destitute children harassing motorists for a hand-out. In India and Africa, you have the co-development of an obesity epidemic combined with the persistence of high levels of malnutrition and stunting. Official policy today unashamedly serves the super-rich and multinational firms, but pays volumes of lip service to the welfare of the common person.

While making unrestrained greed and selfishness normal modes of conduct, globalization shatters societies. Extreme inequality and rampant misery breed despair, endanger political stability and fuel social strife. Governments, in poor and rich nations, spend enormous sums on military and security sectors, but have minimal resources for the pressing needs of their peoples. Hypocrisy runs the world. Major media mislead and dumb down the masses in this so-called age of information. In this technologically adept era, people bask in half-backed, trite, unscientific, emotion-infused modes of thinking that elevate one's own societal group and denigrate the others. Social turbulence makes nations, races, ethnicities, localities and religions mistrust one other. Antipathy intensifies by the day. One incident of discord leads to another; tensions pile up until the boiling point is reached. Once blood is spilt, a return to harmony appears almost impossible.

As the American minds are conquered by blind patriotism, we see US might laying to rubble one nation after another. We see the horrific killings of Christians by Muslims and of Muslims by Christians in the Central African Republic (CAR). Numbers run in the thousands; legions are driven off their abodes. Massacres in the name of religion and broad attacks on civilians by the military typify the Nigeria of today. Sudan just broke up into two parts, yet is headed towards further divisions. Shias and Sunnis lunge at each other in the Middle East and Pakistan. In Myanmar, Buddhists unleash violent pogroms against Muslims. Elections in Kenya generate inter-ethnic carnage. As anti-Muslim, anti-immigrant rhetoric pervades the politics, skin head gangs and fascist parties gain following in the West. These are the signs of our times. Powerful hidden and overt hands of Western economic, military and political imperialism underlie most of these conflicts. Other major powers are joining the fray as well (see, for example, Duodu 2014).

The increasing strife between Muslims and Christians in Tanzania is a manifestation of that global tendency (Chapter 15). As I lie in bed, the radio informs me about another episode in Zanzibar of a priest being attacked with acid by unknown assailants. We have religious riots within our borders. Is Tanzania driving towards the CAR scenario? Will our future feature extensive exploitation of oil, gas and mineral deposits coexisting with rampant poverty, malnutrition and disease, and complicated with intense animosity along religious, racial or regional lines?

My thoughts once more revert to the past. I recall the wisdom of Mahatma Gandhi on the question of religious tolerance. Prior to and after its partition, that subcontinent experienced gruesome massacres of Muslims by Hindus and of Hindus by Muslims. Migration of millions and immense agonies for the very young and old unfolded. Gandhi had worked tirelessly to prevent inter-communal strife and uphold the rights of all communities within the framework of a united India. Yet, his voice was lost in the wind. After the conflagrations had taken their dismal toll, in a matchlessly noble move, he urged Hindu families to adopt orphaned Muslim kids and bring them up as Muslims; and vice versa.

In that context, I recall Yash Chopra, a celebrated director of Indian cinema, with several award winning, block-buster films to his credit. Some of his exquisitely crafted romantic movies, thrillers and social dramas gained global recognition. Aspiring actors and actresses from his early movies later became top stars. But one key fact has been forgotten: His first two films squarely addressed the issue of religious conflict in a Gandhian spirit. *Dhool ka Phool* (Flower of Discord), followed the consequences of a Muslim raising a Hindu child, and *Dharmputra* (Child of Faith) was a harrowing story of a Hindu bringing up a Muslim child. Expression of religious fanaticism formed the backdrop to both. These films boldly espoused the Gandhian philosophy of tolerance as tinged by Jawaharlal Nehru's secularism (Wikipedia 2014a; 2014b; 2014c).

They garnered critical acclaim and awards, but did not do well at the box office. The public was not in a mood for the moderation and compassion they championed. In fact, the second film faced attacks from Hindu groups. Yash Chopra abandoned that theme for nearly four and a half decades. And most major Indian movie directors did likewise, or raised it in a toned down manner.

As a young man, I was enamoured of Gandhi's philosophy of tolerance. Take one instance: He was a strict vegetarian. The slaughter of cows and eating cow meat was an unholy anathema to him. Once a reporter asked him how he viewed the Muslims who did these things. He said he would explain his own beliefs to them, but would also respect their beliefs and practices. Despite being deeply aggrieved by the killing of creatures held to be holy by his faith, he would not, under any circumstances, confront Muslims in a hostile or violent manner.

Not Hindu & Not Muslim

Tu hindu banega na musalamaan banega	Neither Hindu nor Muslim will you be
Insaan ki aulaad hai, insaan banega	Born of a human, a human you will be
......	......
Maalik ne har insaanko insaan banaya	The good Lord made us all human
Hum ne use hindu ya musalaman banaya	We brand ourselves as Hindu or Muslim
Kudrat ne to hume baksi thi ek hi dharti	Nature blessed us with the one planet Earth
Humne kahi bharat kahi iran banaya	And we turned it into India, Iran and the like

Gandhi's humanism was the inspiration for a song from *Dhool Ka Phool* composed by Sahir Ludhiyaanvi and superbly serenaded by Mohamed Rafi under the musical directorship of N Dutta. A Hindu caring for an abandoned Muslim child croons the number: *Na Hindu na Musalmaan* (Neither Hindu nor Muslim). This song is a song of genuine globalization; an expression of unity among the human family; of authentic mutual respect among all faiths and nations; a song of unshakable tolerance and intrinsic harmony among people of varied cultures. A personal favourite then and today, it reflects a fundamental tenet of my philosophy on life. A few of its memorable lines appear above.

Mahatma Gandhi, Martin Luther King, Mwalimu Nyerere and Ernesto Che Guevara had the audacity to envision a just, equal and harmonious existence for humanity. Mwalimu Nyerere, for his part, stood for tolerance and respect between religions, races and ethnic groups in a way that was consistent with the Gandhian philosophy. The words of Aga Khan III and Aga Khan IV I was exposed to as a child projected the same outlook. Though, as I look back, I assess that their words did not match the profundity of Gandhian humanism.

Further, what I imbibed through daily social practice within my own faith and community was a view that cast us as a specially endowed group. While many faiths proclaim a special exclusive linkage to the Almighty, I doubt if a philosophy of that bent can sustain genuine harmony and unity among human beings. Unless we consider all humans equal in every essential respect – secular and spiritual – in the eyes of God, Allah, Vishnu or nature, there can be no peaceful future for the human race.

No one needs to discard his or her unique culture. Diversity is to be celebrated. But diverse cultures have to be posited harmoniously within the global family of cultures. It is a matter of the relationship between the whole and the parts. The morally profound question is: Can you be firmly rooted in one part, but primarily identify with the whole? Or, do deep roots in one part set you far from and in conflict with the other parts? Is there a way to peacefully exist with the local and the global at the same time?

Divisive Arithmetic ❖ ❖ ❖ ❖ ❖ ❖ ❖

Biologically, humanity is divided into two principal parts: female and male. Historically, the former has generally been dominated by the latter. Struggle for gender equality is thereby a fundamental aspect of any striving for a just society.

Education is one arena where males have traditionally had greater and better opportunities than females. That was the case in colonial Tanzania. In my co-educational primary school, for example, boys outnumbered girls. In that respect the relationship between the colonial officials and the Agakhan III was a paradoxical one. On the one hand, there was tension between them on the issue of an integrated system of education for all Asian communities. The Agakhan had a more narrow-minded stand. But on the question of promoting education for girls, he was far ahead of all sectors of the colonial society. Ismaili girls went to school in relatively and absolutely larger numbers compared to other communities, and adopted Western style dressing and cultural habits earlier. My mother, who became a primary school teacher in the 1940s, was a testament to that state of affairs. Dar es Salaam had separate Agakhan secondary schools for boys and girls. Subjects like domestic arts and needlework were offered only at the girls' school.

Education for girls in Tanzania made noticeable strides after *Uhuru*. At the UDSM in 1968, girls were about a fourth of the student body. A fair number pursued the traditionally male dominated science subjects. Yet, progress to date has been slow, with ups and downs, and to this day, unfair treatment of girls and women persists in the Tanzanian society. Gender equality remains a distant goal.

This issue is, however, often conceptualized in a restricted way. Consider a story in a local daily with the headline *'Only 31 pct of girls enroll at universities'* (Protace 2013). A speech by a deputy minister at a school in Bagamoyo was the basis of the story. The minister was promoting education for girls.

Let us probe the issue. Of the nearly 44 million people in Tanzania, say some 3 million were youth of university age (19 to 26 years), with half male and half female (These figure are not exact but serve to make the point.). If 31% of the age-eligible females were in the universities, the number of females at these institutions was $1,500,000 \times 0.31 = 465,000$. A pretty large number, I told myself. Under a most optimistic scenario, the 1970 female university students were at most 1,500, out of a total of at most 5,000 students. Thus, while the population in the nation has tripled, the female university student number has risen by more than 300 times. This is a remarkable feat for a poor nation. There is not much to complain about, I concluded.

The news story stated that the minister had alluded to *'strategic plans to ensure by 2015 the ration [sic] of female students is reached 50:50 with male students.'* I took this unclear phrase to indicate a goal of reaching a 50:50 male to female ratio within two years. It was implied that the ratio in 2013 was 31:69. In that case, the number of male university students was $465000/0.31 = 1,500,000$. In other words, all age-eligible male students in Tanzania were at one university or another. If so, that would be a global first in the entire community of nations. We have to be truly proud, at least by one criterion.

The numbers and percentages implied by this story are (roughly) depicted below.

Scenario I: University Enrolment by Gender

Gender	Enrolled	Not Enrolled	Total
Female	465,000 (31%)	1,035,000 (69%)	1,500,000
Male	1,500,000 (100%)	0 (0%)	1,500,000
Overall	1,965,000 (65.5%)	1,035,000 (34.5%)	3,000,000

Note: Percentages are calculated row-wise.

Even a cursory familiarity with education in Tanzania tells us that this cannot be. But it is what is implied by how the story and information are presented.

Scenario II: University Enrolment by Gender

Gender	Enrolled	Not Enrolled	Total
Female	62,000 (4.1%)	1,438,000 (95.9%)	1,500,000
Male	138,000 (9.2%)	1,362,000 (90.8%)	1,500,000
Overall	200,000 (6.7%)	2,800,000 (93.3%)	3,000,000

Note: Percentages are calculated row-wise.

The number of university students in the nation does not exceed 200,000. If 31% are female, then $200,000 \times (1.0 - 0.31) = 138,000$ are male. A more realistic scenario then is depicted above.

The key message from Scenario II is that of the 3 million age-wise eligible youth, about 93% do not make it to the university. Gender wise, some 96% of females, and 91% of males, fail to do so. Educational opportunity is the real problem that affects the bulk of the males and the bulk of the females. Gender imbalance is a part, but not the dominant part, of the problem. Recent estimates indicate that Tanzania sends about four percent of its age eligible youth to universities, and about five percent more to other college level institutions (Ubwani 2014).

A percentage has two components, the numerator and the denominator. The former is a part of the latter, the whole. Citing a percentage without clearly stating the relevant whole creates confusion. That is what this newspaper story did. The headline and initial paragraph implied that the whole was the population of university age females, but the latter sections implied that it was the total number of university students.

Garbled numbers and ungrammatical, illogical writing are common in the print media, English or Swahili, in Tanzania (Hirji 2012). Journalists and editors cannot handle simple numbers or express their social meaning with clarity.

The report took at face value the deputy minister's assertion that a strategic plan will ensure perfect gender balance in two years. How can such a major goal be reached so rapidly? One way to achieve that is to reduce male enrolees and increase female enrolees without regard to academic eligibility. But would that constitute progress? To our neo-colonial overlords, the external financiers, gender balance is the primary issue. For us the objective should be to raise overall student numbers and promote gender equality in the context of solid plans for job creation. Otherwise, we just worsen the problem of high youth unemployment.

The frequency of such flawed reports in the media reports demonstrate that in our schools:

⇒ Teaching of mathematics is far from satisfactory.
⇒ Teaching of English is far from satisfactory.
⇒ Training in critical thinking is virtually non-existent.
⇒ Both depth and breadth of knowledge are limited.

Journalists are thereby unable to provide accurate reports that clearly say what they mean, or probe beneath the surface. Instead, they conveniently sing tunes favoured by the donors, but in ways so odd that they embarrass the latter. Instead of uniting boys and girls into a common movement to improve education and society, the media needlessly foment antagonism between these two important parts of our society.

A simple focus on a single antagonism makes us set aside the common struggle to analyse and transform the whole. It allows the academics, NGOs, media and politicians to score points with the 'donors' and keep funds flowing. But the consequences can be deadly. Parts battle parts; the whole is lost sight of. Social groups fight one another, spill blood, and the nation disintegrates.

Relating wholes to parts is a central problem in mathematics, logic and science. It is also a fundamental problem for individuals, social groups, nations and the world. Striking a stable, ethical balance between parts and wholes has been a major theme of my life and of the history of my nation too. It underlies the major dualities and dilemmas facing humankind today. How we resolve them will determine the continued existence of life on this planet. Believe me, I am not exaggerating.

Our society needs astute persons and movements that will seek ways of analysing issues in scientific and holistic terms and unite us to confront common problems. The usual style in the social sciences, public health and development related disciplines focuses on one thing at a time; say, gender-wise inequity, disability rights, problems of the elderly, youth issues, HIV, malaria and so on. This is understandable, but if it, at the same time, does not take the whole picture into account, and is not framed within a general analysis of the social system as a whole, it can mislead and generate partial, temporary solutions at best. Presently, this NGO fuelled, single issue based approach is also underpinned by financial incentives that are ethically dubious and call into question the integrity of the people involved.

— 18 —

Spirals of Self

*Integrity simply means a willingness
not to violate one's identity.*
                    Erich Fromm

❖ ❖ ❖ ❖ ❖ ❖ ❖

AS I FACED THE MIRROR this morning, I was taken aback. I was looking for the athletic, handsome guy of the Ruvu National Service days. Instead there was a skinny skeleton with an almost bald head, scrawny-face and sunken-eyes. Who is this strange buffoon? Is it me? Who am I? The more I stared at him, the more ridiculous he looked. I started to laugh; he did the same. Farida wondered why I was cackling by myself. Had I gone bonkers? Perhaps: I was amused at myself, life and the unpredictable days ahead (Image 9: Appendix B).

Our identity transforms over time. From a child and a student, I became a husband, father, uncle and grandparent. I was a teacher at colleges and universities in Tanzania and abroad; my fields being mathematics and statistics, as applied to transport, medicine and public health. I did research, and published scientific papers and books. I was a political activist of the left-wing persuasion. And I have been a resident of Lindi, Dar es Salaam, Boston and Los Angeles. And more.

Such compartmentalized micro-identities rest upon a fundamental sense of self: Who are you, truly? Which is that whole being that is greater than the simple sum of its parts? And does that change too?

But it is not just me. Images in the mirror of life show that people, places and institutions, while retaining the same name, are not what they were. Some are reshaped to the extent that practically they are the opposite of their original versions. So what are they now, truly?

The two are interlinked: As people and places around us change, so do we and our sense of self. On the personal and societal fronts, the search for self is an ever flowing quest. When entire social groups or nations face a transformation of their identity generating essence, it can be an uplifting process, or it can be a demoralising one that can portend grave dangers and instability ahead.

Disjointed Existence

In my childhood, there were three overarching influences that strove to shape my sense of being: the colonial/imperial, Asian/cultural and family/communal influences. By the end of primary school, the last one prevailed: I was a son of the Hirji family, but with firm roots in the Ismaili community. The attainment of *Uhuru* brought forth a different set of influences. Consequently, by the time high school and national service ended, a significant change had occurred: By then, I saw myself as a loyal citizen of Tanzania of Asian heritage, still rooted in the Ismaili community. And today my primary identity transcends cultural and political borders. My internally embedded passport, which will expire the day I leave this planet, now bears the stamp of the grand human species even as I retain unshakable roots in the soil of Tanzania. Above all, I see myself as a member of the grand human family with billions of brothers and sisters.

Yet, as the society around me and I continue to change, the question of identity confronts me on a regular basis. Uncertainties cloud the answer. For one thing, my language skills lack firm, authentic roots (Chapter 9). I mostly converse in English and Swahili. With some, my talk is in Kutchi or Gujarati. I tune into radio programs and read newspapers in English and Swahili. I read three to four books a month, but all are English books. I write exclusively in English, but am trying to improve my Swahili and Gujarati proficiency.

My poor grasp notwithstanding, I view Hindi and Gujarati as the most poetic and expressive of the tongues I know. The music and songs I most often turn to are from old Hindi movies. Though I have a secular disposition now, I still like to recite Ismaili *ginans* since they revive pleasant childhood memories, and their melody and moral values continue to enchant me. The Swahili songs I prefer are *taarab* songs and songs with a social or nationalistic theme.

Adrift in a multi-national and varied linguistic, musical, culinary, cultural, professional and intellectual oceans without firm mooring towards any particular shoreline, and having spent nearly two decades in the USA, and further with my daughter and grandchildren living in that distant land, I find myself posing the key question: Where is the place, if there is one, that I can call home? To just say that planet Earth is my home is not an entirely satisfactory answer.

Go Home

That weighty question makes me recall two rather unpleasant but revealing experiences.

America to Africa: I sat with a group of people in Los Angeles. A close relative and I discussed politics; others listened. Unlike the usual citizen of that land, she is an open minded, liberal person who moreover has lived in and knows Tanzania and Africa well. I talked about episodes deriving from the US foreign policy in central and south America in the 1970s and 1980s. In my view, it was a plainly barbaric policy that funded and armed death-squad regimes which attacked teachers, priests and journalists. My words reflected the public record. That same week, an editorial in the *Los Angeles Times*, a major US daily, had presented some of the shocking episodes. Four years hence, President Bill Clinton was to formally apologize to the people of Guatemala for the US role in the mass murders of and atrocities against the indigenous people of that nation.

Yet, my words were too forthright, and importantly, they came from an outsider. It was a combination unacceptable to a patriotic American. Quite unexpectedly, she rose abruptly, angrily yelled at me,

Why don't you go home?

and swiftly walked away. I was dumbstruck. At UCLA, where I taught, a number of academics reacted similarly when I took issue with the state of their nation. Contrary to perceptions abroad, unless you toe the mainstream line, the USA is a singularly intolerant society. If you express critical views, you will not be locked up, but will soon find one door of opportunity and interaction after another closed for you.

Africa to America: After completing my doctoral degree in biostatistics and working at UCLA for three years, I joined the Faculty of Medicine at the UDSM. Two years later, in 1990, I wrote an article for the magazine of the university academic staff union. My topic was the impact of foreign links on the university activities. I argued that the level of external dependence was excessive, to the extent that it undermined the primary mission of the university (Hirji 1990). Writing critical papers has been my forte since the late 1960s. It was precisely for that reason that I was summarily dispatched from UDSM to Sumbawanga in 1974 (Hirji 1973).

I write as a patriotic Tanzanian concerned about the problems we face. In this instance, my aim was to stimulate debate among the academic staff and explore ways to confront the negative effects on teaching quality of that dependency. But not everyone was pleased. For some, quite generous benefits were at stake. At least one professor was highly offended. In a meeting at which I was not present, he referred to my article and indignantly stated:

If he does not like it here, why does he not simply go back to where he came from?

In the US, I was told to return to Tanzania; in Tanzania, I was told to go back to the US (I assume this as it was the place from which I had recently returned after an eight year stay. But maybe he meant India!).

In both these instances of being told to go home, instead of addressing the substance of what I presented, my minority status in society was the basis of the attack. In the US, I was being treated as an immigrant who had no right to talk about 'internal matters,' even if they were true. In Tanzania, the fact that I was a brown-skinned *muhindi* was taken to disparage my intentions and doubt my patriotism. As they say, if you do not like the message, shoot the messenger.

With my universalistic stand point which regards all humans as equals and respects all cultures, you would think I am a popular person, befriended by many. You would think I am invited where narrow minded characters are not. That, as the above incidents indicate, is hardly the case. We live in a time where insular loyalties dominate social life, be it in the US or Tanzania. Educated, hitherto enlightened persons have sunk into circumscribed, closed circles that speak their own language and have their own modes of operation. According to this mode, it is OK to deal with 'others' in public life; but the inner life is with one's own type. If you are by chance invited into a closed circle, the instant you utter a contrary word, silence creeps in. Though no one says anything, you know that you are no longer welcome.

Consider my critique, given in Chapter 14, of the article by the famed author Moez Vassanji (Vassanji 2006). The main points I raise have nothing to do with him as a person. I take issue with the bias projected by his article and its serious inaccuracies. But because he is of Asian heritage and is celebrated by Asians in and from East Africa, my motives will come under scrutiny. I will be dismissed as 'Nyerere's stooge' or 'a communist.' Others will wonder, 'Why do you have strong words for a major star of your own community?' By adopting a non-communal, universal perspective, I end up neither here nor there, but as secluded as ever.

To be a broad minded, forward looking person nowadays is to seek social isolation. To have respect for the truth is a recipe for loneliness and ridicule. It matters little that at a one-to-one personal level, you treat people in a considerate way. You will be formally respected but otherwise shunned. People will wonder why you are not with 'one of your kind.' Perhaps something is wrong with you upstairs, as we used to say back then. Or, you are a trouble maker, or have a secret money-making agenda. Behind your back, they call you names; they laugh at you; they curse you; they fear you will mislead their children with bad ideas. The pressures to bring you back into the fold are unceasing and immense. They operate directly or through close relatives. If you are not morally firm and intellectually resilient, and given the lack of alternatives, you soon succumb, especially as you see one after another of your former buddies adopting inward looking, narrow-minded ideas and practices. As old age creeps up and the jitters of immobility and death become concrete, you cast a rationalist outlook aside and search for a beyond life insurance policy. And, if you have long-standing health issues that restrict your mobility like I have, unless you persistently take innovative steps, your social seclusion will have no bounds.

Tolerance for different points of view has become a rare commodity. As the cowboy George Bush put it, either you are with us or you are against us. That is how people – Asian, Arab or African, Muslim or Christian or Hindu, mainlander or Zanzibari, Tanzanian or American – think at present. Respect for facts, logic and humanistic principles, and genuine human solidarity have become as exotic as a unicorn.

Japanese Shoes

To repeat: As a devout believer in human equality in all its essence, and given my infirm cultural roots, I am a lonely guy. Thereby, the identity question still gnaws me. Once more I ask: Do I have a real home, a place where I can comfortably, naturally interact with others as I did with my brothers when I was seven years old? Or do I have to drift along a barren social desert like a perpetual outsider, only occasionally encountering a traveller who briefly says hello and then coolly takes off?

These thoughts make me recall the cherished song of Dawood *chacha* from the Lindi days: *Mera juta hai Japani* (My shoes are Japanese; Chapter 1). It seems to me that a reasonable and emotionally calming answer to my predicament may emerge from engaging with the spirit of this song. I am thus drawn to harmonise it with these modern times, and render it in Swahili:

Chinese Shoes

Viatu vyangu vya Chinani	My shoes are Chinese
Sura yangu ni Banyani	My appearance is Indian
Elimu nayo wa Marekani	After an American education
Roho bado ni Bongomani	My heart remains Tanzanian
Viatu vyangu ...	My shoes ...

Bongoland is the popular, somewhat sarcastic, name we give to our homeland these days. I am a third generation resident of Bongoland. Looking back on what I have done in a life of sixty five years thus far, why I did it and my experiences, and in the spirit of this song, I arrive at an unshakable conclusion: My atypical cultural or other tendencies do not make me less of a Tanzanian than say, an *Mgogo* from Dodoma, a *Muhaya* from Bukoba, a *Makonde* from the South or an *Mpemba* from Pemba. Each locale has its dialect, traditions, songs, foods and culture. A man from the north has no clue when the fellow from the south talks in his own tongue. Tanzanians are of varied cultural, mental, religious, physical and behavioural dispositions. Yet, we sail in the same boat, and under the same flag, national language and anthem. We brave the same perilous seas to bring up, love and care for our children – all our children. We work, haggle and compete with each other, celebrate life together, and face the obstacles confronting our people in unison. We fondly remember and respect Mwalimu Nyerere.

No, no matter as to who says what: Dar es Salaam is my home; it is the only place where I can have my hair cut by the smiling Kantibhai, as he did fifty five years ago; where I can sit and laugh with Isaac Marande, my DTC buddy, and so many others. It is the only place with strong memories, familiar sounds and sights. It is only here that I can visit the grave sites of *Dadima*, Mother, relatives and friends who presently reside in the skies, and commune with them. Despite the unwelcome transformations in people and places, and the multiplicity of problems of daily life, so many familiar and heart-warming things remain in this fine city. It is the only place where my heart beats at a normal pace, where my soul is at ease and where I can go to bed and wake up with that feeling of homeliness that I had when I was a young boy. Yes, this is my home, even as I regard the entire human family as my real family.

A Nation Adrift

Were it just a personal identity crisis, a saga of an individual. But a far graver trend is afoot. Our unified national family itself appears to be in danger of facing a gradual, or perhaps an abrupt, break up. I have pointed to the multiplicity of warning signs in the previous chapters.

The fundamental cause, I reiterate, is the astounding gap between the few rich, who are the prime influential entities in the seats of state power, and the enormous mass at the bottom, who are stuck in desperate poverty and despair. The latter have no opportunity to make any fundamental societal changes that can turn their lives around. At best, they can participate in a fishy, donor-driven process that selects every five years who is to rule over them on behalf the local and external wealthy entities.

One sign of the changed circumstance is that Tanzania has become a favoured guest in the economic and state power centres of London, Paris, Brussels and Washington, DC. Our leaders are feted, praised and showered with prizes (Mugarula 2014). International financial bodies give highly positive ratings to Tanzania. External investments and so-called foreign 'aid' keep pouring in. The discovery of oil, gas, uranium, gold and other minerals is the main attraction for the corporations. International retail giants and gas, oil and mining firms, for example, place Tanzania high on the list of growth markets (Banks 2014; Chacha 2014; *The African* 2014; *The Citizen* Correspondent 2014). Economic and strategic rivalry with China is intense: as soon as the Chinese president pays a visit, Barack Obama is obliged to make his presence felt here as well.

In addition, military and security ties between Tanzania and the Western powers are getting stronger by the day. The minute lucrative energy contracts were signed with the UK, it was announced that elite British forces would begin training missions on our soil, and Tanzanian commandos would be sent to the UK for training. Ties with the AFRICOM, the US military command centre for Africa, have strengthened over the past few years. Of the three regional AFRICOM led military exercises of 2012, two were held in Tanzania. The Tanzanian defence forces have had historic ties with China; the Western nations earnestly seek to displace it (Mande 2014; Warner 2014).

In the colonial times, the West said they had come to civilise us. After Independence, they said they wanted to save us from communism and bring development. Then they said they wanted to protect Africa from drug trade and pirates. Now they say they want to protect us from terrorism, and teach us good governance and human rights. These are silly lies that only one with no knowledge of recent and past history, and of the economic realities can stomach. All this time, their eyes have been on our resources and wealth, on our potential for markets and profit for their companies, and on exercising control over our future. That is the verifiable truth; anything else is plain hogwash. Even when they fund our soldiers for peace keeping missions, what they are doing is to further their long term agendas (Turse 2013).

But what is amazing (no perhaps it is to be expected) is that our political class (the ruling and oppositions parties), our media (government owned and private), our academics, thinkers and scientists, and the bulk of the educated youth too, have accepted such propaganda in its entirety. They see the West as the noble saviour of Tanzania and Africa from the corrupt leaders, but forget that the West funds and arms these corrupt leaders and their regimes in the first place.

While such sell-out tendencies prevail at the top, superficially measured economic growth rates rise, and investments boom, discontentment and hopelessness take root among the people. Ordinary people experience joblessness, exorbitant prices for basic goods, deficient but costly services such as health care, deadening rural poverty, an avalanche of land-grabs, child malnutrition, schools where no learning occurs, nightmarish transportation log-jams and the like. As rural to urban migration gathers steam, urban congestion and ghetto type living expand with rapidity.

People tire of hypocritical and empty speeches. Elections give them no other options but to select one among the despised or unpopular personalities. They have no sense of direction, no real understanding of the causes of societal trends and maladies. This is an atmosphere ripe for narrow, divisive, blame casting ideologies to take root. Varied inward looking and extremist visions dominate people's minds. The highly educated professionals also fall prey to such backward modes of thought.

These are global trends; the specific manifestations vary from place to place. Tanzania is also caught up in this unrelenting onslaught of capitalism, corporate globalisation and the US and Western promoted militarism.

What is particular about Tanzania is that in the 1960s, under the fine leadership of Mwalimu Nyerere, it stood at the forefront of opposing such trends. It championed the right to self-determination; liberation of Africa from external domination; ethnic, racial and religious harmony; cooperative mode of social advancement; social justice and economic equality. There were problems of unsound planning and implementation in the past. Yet, these were essential tenets that retain their critical relevance to this day. But now our nation is in the forefront of discarding them wholesale and blindly adopting dubious recipes from the very entities that have dominated and exploited us not for decades but for centuries. Within the group of the five nations comprising the East African community, Tanzania is regarded as the most pro-American, a situation unthinkable in Mwalimu's time.

If you take a look behind the curtain, you find that they effectively rule us. They determine the economic path our nation takes. Our politicians squabble about superfluous matters. The people tussle among themselves. At the same time, the foreign multinationals, the local wealthy classes and the senior personalities in power grab the national treasures.

As things go from bad to worse, the deprived majority at the bottom becomes angry and unruly by the day. People lose their traditional poise and lash out at any perceived wrong-doer or foe. Social violence becomes the norm, not an exception. Every day, alleged witch doctors and elderly people are killed. Mob justice is routine. Suspects are stoned, hacked or burnt to death. Some recent cases: Three alleged cattle rustlers and a butchery owner were swiftly put to death by a mob of 1,000 (Freddy 2014); suspects were buried alive (Editorial 2013b); the preventive death penalty (killing of persons who may be intending to commit a crime) was applied (Kiama 2014); the home of the suspect, with him inside, was set alight (Magashi 2014). These are not once-in-a-blue-moon cases, but a regular feature of the rural and urban life of our nation today. Some of these horrors are sparked off by a transgression as small as stealing a chicken.

We are mired in a sea of economic, political, cultural and actual violence. At the surface, superficial calm prevails. But underneath strong tensions are brewing. They erupt now and then, and can spread far with a tiny catalyzing spark. Tanzania, the nation of tranquillity and peace, is now a myth. It is on a path of joining other nations of Africa and the world where divisiveness and internal strife brought forth by a heavy dose of neo-liberal economics, imperial intervention and cultural animosities have wreaked havoc. It is on the fast track to be a classic banana republic.

In the Western world, neo-fascist, anti-immigrant, racist, insular and religiously extreme parties and politicians are on an upswing. In an irony of ironies, the land of Mahatma Gandhi is led by a person accused of fomenting religious strife and communal violence. Yet, he is simultaneously supported by the educated and unemployed youth, and by the nation's billionaires.

These are the multiplying manifestations of global capitalism in crisis. As the extremely rich frolic in unparalleled luxury and the masses experience stark misery, Tanzania, Africa and the world are descending into a vicious spiral of instability, mistrust, civil conflict and war.

Hope or Despair?

A surprising event, seemingly bucking the negative trends of the day, occurred in April 2014. In one sporting activity, Tanzania out-performed all the nations participating in a global competition. Our boys won the 2014 Street Child Soccer World Cup competition held in Rio de Janeiro, Brazil. In a remarkable feat, they demonstrated superb skills. In the semi-final, Team Tanzania trounced the USA 6 to 1; in the finals, it beat Burundi 3 to 1 (Street Child World Cup 2014). It was received by President Kikwete and the nation celebrated (Editorial 2014b). People said that if these disadvantaged kids could scale such a majestic height, there was no reason why we cannot reach as high goals in other arenas.

But I did not celebrate. These days you see so many kids who beg from passers by or wipe wind screens of vehicles for a few shillings. Most are skinny and under nourished. Some have skin scratches, eye sores and open wounds. Are these our soccer stars? Is it the case we have such a large pool of street children that world champions lurk among them? That is the law of large numbers. Is it that those who eventually became soccer stars were housed, fed well, treated for health problems, and trained thoroughly over a long period? Are they still street children? I note that among the industrialized nations, only the USA had a boys team, and only England had a girls team, in this competition.

I am drawn to hypothesize that perhaps we can produce a world champion soccer team of street kids because we are near the top of the world in terms of the percentage or absolute number of kids in roaming on our streets. According to a recent estimate, Tanzania has over 400,000 children who are effectively homeless (Aman 2014). Is that a thing to boast about? I would rather have a Tanzania that cannot send a team to such a competition because it has hardly any kids for whom bed means the pavement. The competition where my nation should lead the world should be that of truly catering for the welfare of its children.

NGOs claiming to further social causes have mushroomed by the hundreds. Some promote gender equality; some foster the rights of the handicapped persons or the Albinos; some cater for HIV afflicted persons; some seek to reduce maternal deaths; and so on. They use the bulk of their funds for meetings in glitzy hotels, travel and personal expenses for the officials. They shy away from the root causes, and promote short-term, surface level solutions.

In their decorative reports, they show major accomplishments even though the reality they deal with has hardly changed. In this make-believe world, several NGOs claim to serve homeless street children in our urban and rural areas. But they function like a regular NGO: a lot of talk, little meaningful, effective action. To me they are not a solution but a big part of the problem.

The number of street children in the nation is rising (Aman 2014). The reality is hidden by the municipal authorities who brutally round them up and herd them off like cattle to god knows where. We mask social maladies with forceful measures. Such things make me weep and be angry. It dampens my pride in my nation. What is the point of celebrating when our precious kids do show that they are real human beings too? I see it as sheer hypocrisy. Our fundamental goal should be to house, feed, clothe, educate and take good care of each and every child within our borders. It should not be to produce prize winning teams from the innocent victims of a dog-eat-dog capitalist system.

Parting Thoughts

We are child or adult; man or woman; Christian, Muslim, Hindu, Pagan or what not; but of one family. Like all families, sometimes we tussle among ourselves, but they are temporary rifts that heal. There are ordinary, good and rotten apples in our midst. Some deserve high praise; some need to be locked up. Nonetheless, each of us is an authentic Tanzanian. We must protect and build on this historic foundation.

It is a strong, vibrant and admirable foundation; I feel it in my bones and heart every day. Whether at home or in the streets of Dar es Salaam, whether encountering friends, trades people, or those just going about, I continue to sense the spirit of a unified nation. Despite all the changes, the sights, sounds and smell of that authentic Tanzania persist everywhere. The enticing aspects of our culture envelope you even after two decades of neo-liberal onslaught. There is laughter, excitement together with loud, contentious but friendly talk in all corners of the city. People argue about issues of life and national politics and continually complain about a host of things, but they do as those who are sailing in the same boat on the same rough seas.

Yet, as I have indicated throughout these pages, gradually that goodness is in the process of being undone. The trends are worrying. Our social and economic divisions are headed towards an unacceptable level. In the glitzy brochures produced for the tourists, I see astounding places of luxury where 95% of the city-folk are totally shut out except as servants. It is a barrier as effective as the racial barrier of the colonial era. Day by day, Dar es Salaam is turning into a city less and less for ordinary Tanzanians. We better be on guard. Intense, mass frustration only makes the myopic, divisive, dogmatic forces gain momentum. Large cracks in our hitherto unified edifice are slowly but surely appearing.

Unprecedented inequality is piercing our nation's moral fabric. The ethic of mutual concern and social responsibility is on the wane. From parent to child; brother to brother; teacher to student; manager to worker; doctor to patient; farmer to official; and national, communal or religious leader to the ordinary person; there flow untruth, distrust and discord. There is no lasting remedy but to reorganize society on the basis of economic equality and social justice, real and routine participation of the people in governance, mutual respect, social harmony, a meticulous sense of personal responsibility, and a strong tradition of dialog. The modern outlook that leans towards exhibitionism, possessiveness, consumerism, intellectual superficiality, wasteful living and moral dualism has to be countered. And it is most imperative that we celebrate our panoramic cultural, linguistic, religious, ethnic and regional diversities.

Else, our lives will become entangled in an unstable, injurious dog-eat-dog system. If we do not take heed in a timely manner, we will fall faster than a house of cards does in a breeze.

A dire sign of the times is that the fabulous snow cap of Mount Kilimanjaro is receding fast, and may soon vanish. Will that torch placed atop the mountain as Mwalimu took up the helm of the nation, and which was meant to shine in perpetuity to foster hope, dignity and human unity, will that symbol of goodness and decency fade away? In this age of deception, cynicism, intolerance, mediocrity, inequality, strife, violence and unparalleled greed, who is paying attention? I hope some are, but I cannot see them. As I age and witness the unwholesome changes within and around me, my sense of self remains in a state of conflict. Simultaneously, I see my nation acquiring features that are weakening the essence of its authenticity, dignity, unity and identity. I can come to terms with my personal predicament, but the national trends make me profoundly unhappy.

On that rather dismal note, I thank you, my patient reader, for accompanying me on this convoluted sojourn along memory lane, and for allowing me to share my recollections and ramblings with you.

Expect the Unexpected

I add these lines at the last minute: The file has to go the printer. Amer is visiting from Oman after some eighteen months. He, Isaac and I trample the city streets, sip cups of tea and chatter on. We place an ad in a daily paper to locate our DTC sec-tec peers.

The phone rings. Amer is on the line: 'Karim, someone wants to talk to you.' And it is none other than Abdul Karim, the guy we have sought earnestly for six years. The last I met him was some twenty five years ago. Two days on, we hug at my place. He has grayed, walks guardedly with a limp, but remains active as an inspector of heavy duty earth-moving and construction equipment. And he has fourteen grandchildren. In a merry spirit, we recall our struggles with Additional Maths at the DTC in 1965, the days of thrill and fun, and how we have fared in life since then.

My dear reader: Thus far, I have presented you optimistic as well as despairing messages, the latter more often than the former. What were to be my last words projected a distinctly downcast vision. But my friends have turned me around. We concur on how things were and are. Yet, their gentle humanity, warm smiles, calm persona and elemental wisdom convey a radiant future. They impress upon me that with the intellectual and moral power of the seven and a quarter billion of our brothers, sisters, sons, daughters, and elders on this planet, it is foolish to loose hope. No matter how grotesque the conditions capricious capitalism, drone-led militarism and fervent fanaticism unleash in the near future, our family will find a way around. Mohamed Rafi and Asha Bhosle's vocalization of Sahir Ludhiavni's stirring poetic call *Saathi haath bahraanaa* (Compatriots join hands) is on my lips. Let us act as one for humanity to survive, prosper and head to the stars. Then the creeds of universal love, logical thinking and environmental sanity will triumph. Every human will have a decent, dignified life, and child poverty and misery will be history. Those, my friend, are my parting sentiments.

Fibonacci Farewell ❖ ❖ ❖ ❖ ❖ ❖ ❖

Talking of unity and division, wholes and parts, is an occasion to revisit Fibonacci numbers (Chapter 12):

{ 1, 1, 2, 3, 5, 8, 13, 21, 34, 55, 89, 144, 233, 377, 610, . . . }

Take any four successive numbers from this series, say, 3, 5, 8 and 13. We form a grid using the third number, namely, an 8×8 grid. Divide this grid into four areas, **A**, **B**, **C** and **D**, as done in the diagram below.

A + **B** form an 8×3 rectangle, and **C** + **D** form an 8×5 rectangle. The area of the grid, 8×8 = 64 square units, is also the sum of the areas **A**, **B**, **C** and **D**.

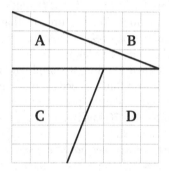

Fibonacci Square

Now look at the 13×5 rectangle below, and divide it again into four areas **A**, **B**, **C** and **D**. These are just like the earlier areas with the same symbols.

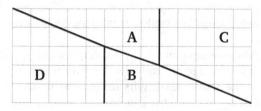

Fibonacci Rectangle

The total area of the previous grid is 64 square units. But the total area of the rearranged rectangular grid is 5×13 = 65 square units.

Question: Where did the extra square unit area come from?

The same four parts, arranged in two different ways, seem to give different total areas. Is the whole not the sum of its parts? Recall Hotel Infinity (Chapter 7), where we found an entity equivalent to one of its parts?

Let us now consider a numerical paradox concerned with gender rights. A front page news story announced: *Tanzania nosedives in gender balance* (Mosoba and Mwalimu 2013). The reader learns that on multiple criteria of gender equity – educational, health and economic – the position of Tanzania had declined dramatically over the past six years. Thus, in the Global Gender Gap for economic participation, Tanzania went from No. 1 rank in 2006 to No. 70 in 2013. It was similar for several other criteria. Overall, in 2013, Tanzania ranked 66 out of the 133 nations surveyed. By any reckoning, the fall was astonishing.

The essence of this scenario is the relationship between two parts (male and female) in a whole (human society). Either the whole can deteriorate, with one part going down faster than the other; or the whole can progress, but with one part climbing up faster than the other. In either case, the relative gap widens. Or it can be that one part falls and the other ascends; one becomes poorer as the other is enriched; then the gap widens in relative and absolute terms.

This news story did not pursue such possibilities, but cited the international survey basically verbatim. Interviews of two female governmental ministers produced superficial explanations. They assured us that new measures to make the country '*quickly pick up in the rankings*' were being undertaken.

It does not require rocket science to know that females and males in Tanzania face serious problems in education, health, employment, income, life security and social wellbeing. No drastic shift has occurred on any front over the past six years. No practical change to make the position of women in society nosedive from No. 1 in the world to No. 70 has been seen. And it is not the case that other nations have made major strides in gender equity while we have been left behind. The media report simply does not make sense.

Most likely, the data on which the report is based are unreliable. Either the No. 1 ranking or the No. 70 ranking or both deviate from the truth. Both cannot simultaneously reflect the reality of the years they refer to.

Many of the donor funded research projects in Africa are of abysmal quality, and fail to meet the essential scientific criteria. Often done in haste, their final glossy report is not worth the paper it is printed on. But they are the big guys who hold the purse strings. So we locals take their words as if they emanate from the heavens.

Steeped in a donor-worship mentality; dealing with a topic that is favoured by the 'donors'; not versed in critically dealing with numbers; rushed at work; easily swayed by the small, small gifts dished out by the 'donors'; lacking patriotic commitment; and with the penchant for sensationalist headlines; our media and reporters are not surprisingly prone to churning out such stories on a regular basis. One day it is this; the next, the opposite. The public is confused, and ceases to pay attention, and the grave problems of national life persist.

The square root of -1, or $\sqrt{-1} = i$, is an imaginary number. Imaginary data and bogus numbers also lurk in the least expected corners of social statistics. A sound judgment and careful scrutiny are required to separate the wheat from the chaff.

The Good, Bad and Ugly: I bring up one aspect of maths (and statistics) that we regularly avoid, especially with students. Even qualified, competent teachers of the subject do not venture into it.

Students are told that in essence, mathematics is a logic driven discipline, that it has many applications in the real world and connects to most aspects of our lives: scientific medicine; economics and linguistics; engineering, transportation, agriculture and industry; detection of crime; governance and economic planning; and even sports, music, poetry and folklore. Famous people associated with it are praised. Not only is it a supreme intellectual product, but it also serves the human race.

This is quite true, and it forms a solid basis for my attachment to maths. But what also holds is that it has faces that go from good to the ugly. It can produce not just benefits, but considerable harm as well. Misuse of numbers in the media, of which we saw one example, is one aspect of this phenomenon.

Like most products of human endeavour, it has a worthy side and a debased side. A knife is a kitchen tool, but is also used in murder; religion provides solace, but also generates blood spilling animosities. Maths, for its part, facilitates building construction and agriculture, but is also used to produce weapons of mass destruction. It has tools for critical thinking, but is also used in deceptive advertising. It is of value in economic planning, but sophisticated mathematical models also underpin the predatory practices of global banks. These dualities – utilitarian and recreational, laudatory and evil – make maths what it is.

Instead of a one-sided view, students have to be exposed to the good uses as well as to the misuse of maths so that they can discern one from the other, and develop an ethically sensitive relationship to the subject. It is for this reason that I cited the case of the deviant teacher Matthias Vheru (Chapter 16). Mathematicians are humans: some are worthy and some are repulsive. In the technologically advanced nations, too many mathematicians and statisticians serve major corporations and banks, security agencies, weapon makers and the military in activities that harm human welfare. While this has been seen throughout history, today it has reached new heights. The infamous US National Security Agency is the largest employer of mathematicians in the US at present (Beilinson 2013; Leinster 2014; NSA 2014).

Students should learn about mathematicians engaged in worthy endeavours. But adopting a dreamy view is self-defeating. We need to convey the reality so that our gifted children do not unwarily fall into the trap of being used for purposes that benefit a few and harm many.

What is truly troubling is that it is a wide phenomenon. Many of the supreme possessions of humanity are being utilized to ravage humanity. Instead of jointly fostering human benefit, mathematics, science, religion and the arts are being hijacked to serve the economic and military overlords of this planet. As maths is deployed in the US to create barbaric weapons, religion is employed in the Central African Republic to foment intense hate. Xenophobic or extremist religious political parties gain momentum in Europe, India, Africa and elsewhere at the same time as cell phones become a common possession. What should facilitate communication and understanding now spread falsehood and spite. In this age of information, the public and thinkers of Tanzania, for example, have been brainwashed by the Western media to an astonishing degree. These are not unrelated things, but are the complementary faces of the irrational global capitalist system. This joint abuse and misuse of the most elevated components of human culture can generate an explosion far greater than that created by dividing One with Zero. It can lead to a transition into an infinite oblivion.

Maths and human life are linked conceptually as well. The numeric identities Zero and One resemble human identities. In arithmetic, operating with an identity leaves the original entity unchanged. Likewise, if you cling blindly to a single human group, you remain stagnant in outlook and behavior. Deficient experience floods your mind with stereotypical images. As arithmetical identities lead to negative and inverse numbers, excessive inward identification generates its opposite. Sour feelings arise from sweet ones, hate emanates from love, and intolerance from tolerance. What is rational becomes irrational.

While the real number system based on maths identities is a logical system, it has irrational and imaginary numbers as well. Mathematicians constructed the field of complex numbers in which negative numbers have a square root to counter key hurdles. And that imaginative venture now underpins the basic formulas used in electrical and electronic engineering.

On the social front, avoiding conflicts caused by narrow loyalties requires initiatives that are more imaginative than those of the mathematicians. We need a bold vision wide enough to encompass, in practice and morality, not just humans, but all life bearing creatures. A creative, collective, long-term effort by humanity as a whole is essential. Otherwise, there is little hope of redressing the myriad of social complexities, environmental challenges and historic conflicts we face. And this effort cannot succeed other than by appropriate use of science and mathematics, together with focusing on the unifying, edifying aspects of our rich religious, literary, artistic, linguistic and cultural diversities.

The kernel of the paradox between human wholes and parts is: What are the consequences when humanity functions mostly as a collection of discrete, competing entities and when it functions primarily as a cooperative unit? Do the two scenarios portend a similar future? The usual compartmentalized approach of most scholars cannot fathom these issues. We need to revive and expand the multi-disciplinary integrated approach that eminent minds of the sixties had began to develop.

Years of immersion into maths led me to the subtleties of the real number system. That life journey has also propelled me towards the necessity of being a global citizen. In both cases it was a matter of transcending the insularities of the past, and reciprocating towards the potentialities of the future.

It is in that combined persona of a global citizen and an aficionado of maths that I have, in a brotherly mood and with a few juicy *zambarau* in hand, placed a multiplicity of human and mathematical conundrums in front of you. When we got stuck in a maths exercise, Mr Hirani would fondly nudge us: '*Think, think, think.*' In that hopeful spirit, I urge you to do likewise and bid you a good day.

❖   ❖   ❖   ❖   ❖   ❖   ❖
❖   ❖   ❖   ❖   ❖   ❖   ❖

Appendix A
Recreational Mathematics

*Mathematics is the music of
reason.*
James J Sylvester

A BRIEF EXPLANATION of the term recreational mathematics (RM) was given in
Chapter 11. Let us develop it further by noting key areas of RM.

RM #1: Limericks, songs and poems relating to mathematics and mathematical
structures rendered in a poetic form. The mnemonic for the digits of π shown
in Chapter 3 is a relevant example.

RM #2: Humor, word play, catchy definitions with a mathematical bent, content
or linkage.

RM #3: Historic tales, sagas and anecdotes, including biographies, about maths,
science, mathematicians and scientists. There are many books and articles of
this sort and which originate from Africa, Asia, Europe and the Americas. Many
feature inspiring life stories.

RM #4: Attractive, intricate, beguiling, complex, colourful graphs, computer
graphics, pictures and patterns with an underlying mathematical essence.

RM #5: Investigation and presentation of curious features of objects like
numbers, circles, pentagons, cubes, the Mobius strip and so on. The number
patterns of chapters 1, 2, 3 and 6, the golden spiral and Fibonacci numbers
(Chapter 12) are a few examples.

The readable booklet by the Mozambican mathematician Paulus Gerdes,
Drawings from Angola: Living Mathematics has Africa-derived material (Gerdes
2007). Based on the art of the Cokwe people in Angola, it is designed for
children of ages 8 to 14. Impressive patterns constructed from dots and lines
depict life and nature, illustrate geometrical and arithmetical ideas, and introduce logical thinking. One pattern incorporates the numbers addition method
normally attributed to the European mathematician Carl F Gauss (Chapter 4).
We learn from this book that two very different cultures independently came up
with a similar mathematical technique.

RM #6: Simple and complex puzzles and paradoxes based on maths and logic. These may be stated directly or as perplexing and amusing tales. Examples are the story of Hotel Infinity (Chapter 7), Zeno's paradox (Chapter 8), lottery schemes based on infinite sums (Chapter 8), and vanishing area (Chapter 18). **RM #7:** Long form novels that contain maths or allusions to maths ideas. This type of material, described in Chapter 10, includes books like *Flatland* and *The Man Who Counted*. Production of such material has expanded of recent. One well-written book is: *Conned Again, Dr Watson!* (Chapter 10).

A primary component of the effort to improve school mathematics is to produce appropriate teaching material and make it available in our public schools. This task is not as onerous as it first seems. The resources are at hand. Much material is freely available on the Internet. It can be used as is, or adapted to suit our purposes and translated into Swahili. Relevant new material can be created. The onus is on the educational authorities, experts, teacher training colleges and teachers to embark on these activities in a planned manner. It can, for example, be started as a series of projects by students doing a second degree in maths education.

In this sub-section, I list a few books and websites dealing with recreational mathematics. My aim is to provide a taste of what is available, and a first step for wider exploration into the field. I start with books.

Books

Book 1: Abbott EA (1992) *Flatland: A Romance of Many Dimensions*, Dover Publications, New York (First published in 1884). Free download in several formats can be done at `www.gutenberg.org/ebooks/97`. See Chapter 10.

Book 2: Posamentier AS (2003) *Maths Wonders to Inspire Teachers and Students*, Association for Supervision and Curriculum Development, New York. Free pdf format download available at `www.ebooks-share.net/math-wonders-to-inspire-teachers-and-students/`. Some of my examples come from this illuminating book.

Book 3: Zaslavsky C (1988) *Math Games and Activities From Around the World*, Chicago Review Press, Inc., Chicago, is a broad based accessible book with a multi-cultural perspective.

Book 4: Pickover CA (2002) *The Mathematics of Oz: Mental Gymnastics from Beyond the Edge*, Cambridge University Press, Cambridge, is authored by one of the giants in this field. A wide range of mathematical diversions and snippets, from the simple to complex, appear in the book.

Book 5: Pickover CA (2000) *Wonders of Numbers: Adventures in Math, Mind, and Meaning*, Oxford University Press, Oxford, is another exemplary work among the more than thirty popular mathematics books by this author.

Book 6: Gerdes P (1999) *Geometry from Africa: Mathematical and Educational Explorations*, The Mathematical Association of America; Washington DC. This book displays a fascinating variety of geometrical patterns from different parts of Africa. It is of high relevance to secondary school maths teachers and students.

Internet Material

There is an extensive, mind-boggling amount of relevant material on the Internet. I note only a few of these sources.

Web Material 1: Burkard Polster and Marty Ross, two Australian mathematicians, have written a mathematically oriented column for *The Age* since July 2007. More than a hundred in number, they are freely available at www.qedcat.com/archive/index.html. The mostly short columns have stories, illustrations, mathematical twisters, educational commentaries relating to maths. Many will appeal to high school teachers and students. Swahili translations of appropriate columns would widen their appeal.

Web Material 2: The web page www.mathematics-magic.com/5th-main. html contains recreational mathematical material suitable for primary school kids in fifth to seventh grades.

Web Material 3: Cindy Donaldson shows that a set of twenty four tooth picks and a coin can be source of fun geometry puzzles for upper primary school grade. The web page is www.education.com/print/Toothpick_Math/. Other relevant puzzles and entries are accessible from the home page.

Web Material 4: The site www.vickiblackwell.com/math.html is a gateway to popular and technical mathematical websites. These include sites suitable for maths teachers and students.

Web Material 5: Mr R's World of Math and Science has hundreds of poems, stories and lessons relating to school maths. A number of them have been constructed by school students. See the page mathstory.com/index.html.

Web Material 6: The unique properties of numbers ranging from 0 to 9999 are found at www2.stetson.edu/~efriedma/numbers.html. I have made use of this site in Chapter 6. The home page has links to topics on mathematics including puzzles in algebra, geometry and arithmetic that are suitable for teachers and students in secondary school.

Web Material 7: For entry into the history of maths and biographies of mathematicians, the web page www.dcs.warwick.ac.uk/bshm/resources.html is an outstanding portal.

Web Material 8: Information on mathematics and mathematicians of Africa and the African Diaspora is well documented at www.math.buffalo.edu/mad/. It also links to related sites.

Web Material 9: The site www.plus.maths.org is the home of the *PLUS Magazine,* a great resource for secondary school students and teachers for articles and illustrations on mathematical topics. Advanced ideas in maths are presented in a well illustrated, simplified manner. It has a section on maths puzzles as well.

Web Material 10: scholarship.claremont.edu/jhm is the home of the *Journal of Humanistic Mathematics.* This is an outstanding journal exploring the relationship between culture, society, literature and poetry on the one hand and mathematics on the other. It is suitable for graduate maths teachers and post-Form IV maths students.

Web Material 11: mathematicalpoetry.blogspot.com is a recommended gateway into different varieties of mathematical poetry.

I learned from Web Material 8 that the first person from Africa to obtain a PhD in mathematics was Ali Mostafa Mosharafa of Egypt. He obtained it in the year 1923. There was also information about mathematicians from Kenya and Uganda here, but there was not a line about maths in Tanzania.

The Internet, available even in small towns of Africa, can be accessed with selectivity for a wealth of free material for class use. Visiting the web sites noted above will begin your exploration.

Class Projects

Class projects, involving physical and mental activities, are a crucial part of the effort to improve maths education. A few simple examples are:

Class Project 1: Construct Swahili limericks and mnemonics for the first six, ten, twenty, or more digits of π. Extend this exercise to constants like $\sqrt{2} \approx 1.4142\ldots$, the square root of two.

Class Project 2: Inform students about amazing feats like the memorization of thousands of digits of π and begin a memorization drive. Hold within class and school wide competitions for that activity.

Class Project 3: Encourage students to write poems, sentences and phrases with a mathematical element. Math based poems suitable for primary and secondary schools are plentiful (see above). Our teachers and high school students should be encouraged to both translate them, and write original Swahili poems and stories with a mathematical and/or scientific flavour.

Class Project 4: Extract puzzles from books and web sources and challenge your students to solve them.

Class Project 5: Children in many nations celebrate March 14th, namely 3/14, as π-day each year. The Tanzania Mathematics Association has recently begun to involve primary and secondary school teachers and children in celebrating this day. Mathematical competitions, song performances, marches and exhibitions are held for the occasion. Enroll your students in this activity.

Class Project 6: Search the web for different graphical proofs of the Pythagoras Theorem. Ask students to study and present them in class. Devise relevant experiments that involve use of graph paper.

Class Project 7: Involve students in estimation of the heights of tall trees and structures near the school using the method of Thales.

Class Project 8: Bring sea shells to class or take students to the beach to collect sea shells. Study their patterns; explain the origin and function of the shells; and look into the mathematical basis of the patterns (see Chapter 12).

Appendix B
Images of A Life

Image 1: Father, Mother, Author, Mohamed
Lindi: 1951

Image 2: Author   Image 3: Dawood Uncle
    Lindi: 1953   Lindi: 1956

Image 4: Dadima, Dar es Salaam: 1970

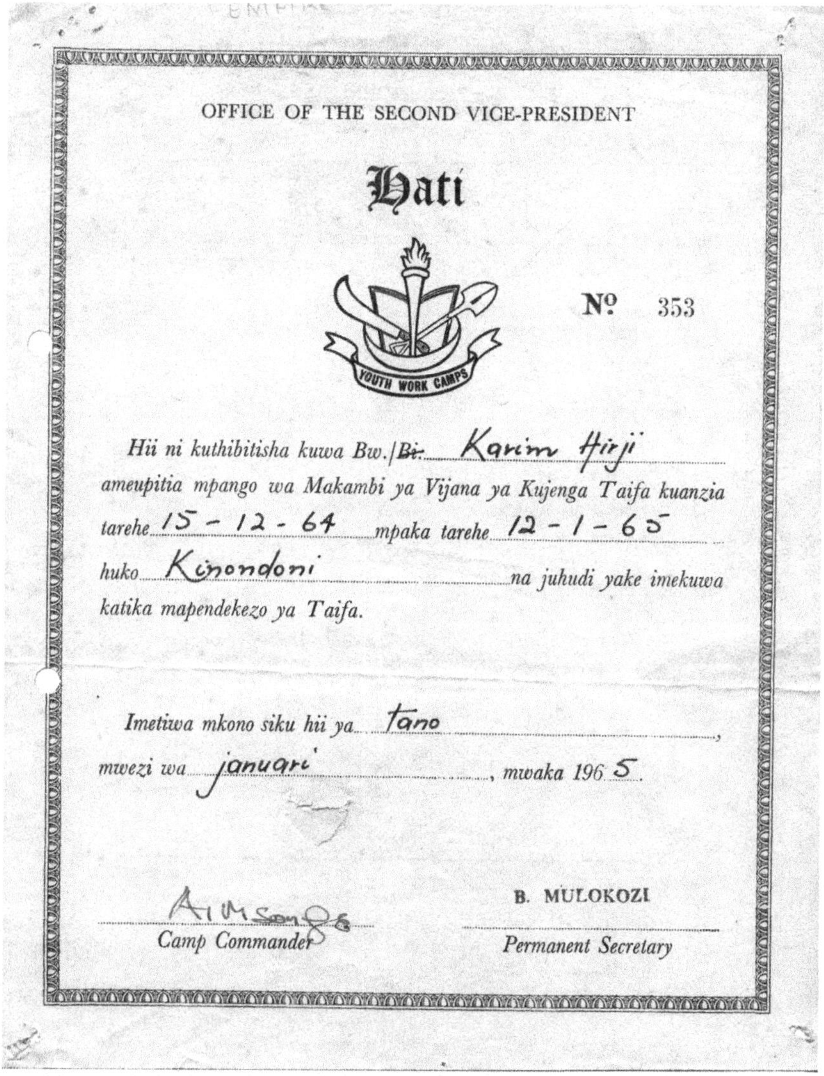

OFFICE OF THE SECOND VICE-PRESIDENT

Hati

№ 353

Hii ni kuthibitisha kuwa Bw./Bi. *Karim Hirji* ameupitia mpango wa Makambi ya Vijana ya Kujenga Taifa kuanzia tarehe *15 - 12 - 64* mpaka tarehe *12 - 1 - 65* huko *Kinondoni* na juhudi yake imekuwa katika mapendekezo ya Taifa.

Imetiwa mkono siku hii ya *tano*, mwezi wa *januari*, mwaka 196 *5*.

A. M. Songa
Camp Commander

B. MULOKOZI
Permanent Secretary

Image 5: National Service, Kinondoni: 1964

KIBAHA SECONDARY SCHOOL

Tel: (School Office)   **SCHOOL REPORT**   P.O. KIBAHA
Kibaha 215   Dar es Salaam

Name: HIRJI Karim _____   Form VI ɪ   Term I   1967.

Subject	Marks	Order	Ability	EFF Remarks
SWAHILI				
ENGLISH				
GENERAL PAPER	60	2	B	C
FRENCH / GERMAN				
HISTORY				
GEOGRAPHY				
ECONOMIC & PUBLIC AFFAIRS				
MATHEMATICS	85	1	B	A
„ PURE / SUBSIDIARY				
„ APPLIED / ADDITIONAL	100	1	A	A
STATISTICS				
PHYSICS / GENERAL SCIENCE	80	1	A	B
CHEMISTRY	86	1	A	A
BIOLOGY / BOTANY				
ZOOLOGY				
ART				
PHYSICAL TRAINING				

GENERAL CONDUCT: D.

Date: 13-6-1967

                                                        Headmaster.

(A: very good;   B: above average;   C: average;   D: below average;   E: unsatisfactory)

Image 6: Kibaha School Report: 1967

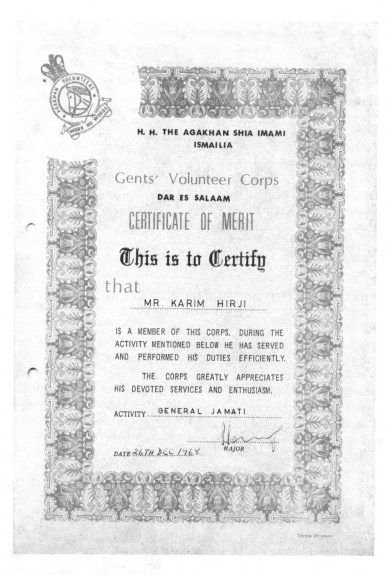

Image 7: Jamat Khana Volunteer: 1963 – 1968

Image 8: Ismaili Youths and Local Residents,
Buguruni: 1966

Image 9: DTC Buddies: 1962 – 2014
Isaac Marande, Karim Hirji, Amer Mohamed

Acknowledgments and Notes

In order to have friends, you
must first be one.
Elbert Hubbard

❖ ❖ ❖ ❖ ❖ ❖ ❖

I HAVE BENEFITED from numerous helpful contacts with friends, relatives, writers and others, in person, by telephone or by email. I located long lost persons, and consulted the records and diaries I had kept. I was blessed to find new material and firsthand witnesses. Gaps in my memory and records were filled, and errors were rectified. Below I list the persons who assisted me according to subject and location.

Family Affairs: Rafik Hirji, Rosa Hirji, Farida Hirji, Rumina Sunderji, A K Shah, Shera Aunty, Firoz Mitha, Mehdi Mitha, Razia Mitha, Parin Jetha, Yasmin Sharrif, Nurbanu Kassam, Shiraz Kassam, Nizar Rhemtulla.
Lindi & Southern Tanzania: Abdul Dossa, Firoz Jadavji, Mustafa Pirmohamed, Kanubhai, Jayantibhai Patel, Shiraz Ladhu Jaffer, Mohamed Kam, Ahmed Sumar, Gulamabbas Gangji, Gulamabbas Dhirani, Navroz Kassam, Ashok Sanghvi, Akber Jetha, Library Assistant at the Bureau of Statistics Library, Adrian Roden.
Agakhan Boys School: Fazli Datoo, Nizar Visram, Nizar Fazel, Issa Shivji, Navroz Lakhani, Al-Noor Jiwan-Hirji.
Dar es Salaam Technical College: Amer Mohamed, Isaac Marande, Salim Msoma.
Upanga Life: Nazir Nensi, Navroz Lakhani, Mohamed Budhani, Shiraz Ramji, Fidahussein Moledina, Issa Shivji, Farida Hirji, Firoz Kanji.
National Service: Amilo Pipi, Suresh Bhatt.
Kibaha High School: Richard Mwakalinga, Salim Msoma, Salim Lalani.
History of Ismailis and Tanzania: Nizar Fazel, Nizar Visram, Issa Shivji, Aly Kassam-Remtulla, Navroz Lakhani.

Comments on Draft Chapter(s): Rosa Hirji, Rafik Hirji, Rahim Dawood, Navroz Lakhani, Rumina Sunderji, Amer Mohamed, Isaac Marande, Shiraz Ramji, Johnson John, Morten Fagerland, Omme Rahemtulla, Farida Hirji, Zarina Patel. **Editing, Cover Design, and Support:** Lisa María B Noudéhou, Mkuki Bgoya, Walter Bgoya, Tapiwa Muchecherewa.

Nizar Fazel provided many potential names and sources of historic material, and discussions with him served to sharpen my thoughts.

Last but not least, Farida patiently endured my mood swings while I was engrossed in writing. Rosa fondly encouraged me to pursue this work and gave frequent comments. I have been blessed to have them in my life.

To all these persons, I extend my heartfelt thanks. And sincere apologies to any one whose name I have inadvertently left out. The views expressed herein are my own, and I bear the sole responsibility for the misconceptions and errors that undoubtedly remain.

Notes

Note 1: Notwithstanding my external sources and records, my primary source is my memory. Despite a sustained effort to cross check what I wrote, I do not claim to have overcome the limitations of a memory based narrative. This book is not a social analysis but a subjective story of my early life, as seen from my present location, and a collection of my own views on important social issues.

Note 2: Even when my recall is broadly factual, it may not be precise. Say, in Chapter 1, I mention my sole early childhood interaction with children who were not of my race. Yet, it is possible that I had five interactions. Nevertheless, they would remain but a tiny portion of the hundreds of dealings I had with children of my race. That my early life was strictly restricted by racial boundaries remains valid. When I paint an event as a dialog, the words reflect the essence of what went on.

Note 3: Our memories magnify our praiseworthy deeds, and downplay those which taint our image. You may thus come across statements you may feel as one-sided, or of dubious validity. Even if your judgment is valid, such bias is what makes me human. It allows you to see where I stand. What I say is that I did strive to uphold the tenets of logic and fact to the best of my ability.

Note 4: I generally use the term 'mainland Tanzania' instead of the historic name Tanganyika.

Note 5: When a Swahili, Gujarati, or Hindi word or phrase occurs for the first time in the text, the English equivalent is, in most cases, given in the adjacent brackets.

Note 6: All direct quotes in this book fall within the fair use clauses of copyright laws and rules. The quotes by prominent personalities are found in numerous Internet websites. The websites that served as my sources are listed in the last part of References and Readings.

References and Readings

- Additional readings are listed separately.
- Selected author publications are listed separately.
- Items marked ++ are particularly recommended.
- More sources on recreational mathematics are in Appendix A.
- Websites for quotations appear after the reference list.
- Websites for hymns, songs and anthems are listed thereafter.
- For all audio renditions other than the Tanzania National Anthem, only a few lines of the lyrics are quoted.
- External photo and image credits are indicated.
- All other images belong to or are produced by the author.

References

Abbott EA (1992;1884) *Flatland: A Romance of Many Dimensions*, Dover Publications, New York.++

Abdallah F (2013) Wazazi wacharaza viboko walimu, *Habari Leo Jumapili*, 17 February 2013.

Abualy M (1967) Spotlight on boxing, *Volunteer* (Dar es Salaam), 11 July 1967:11–15.

Adams G (2010) 'Stand and Deliver' maths teacher dies, aged 79, *The Independent*, 1 April 2010.

Aga Khan III (1954) *The Memoirs of the Aga Khan: World Enough and Time*, Simon & Schuster, New York.++

Aga Khan IV (1957) Speech at *Takht Nashini* ceremony, Kampala, Uganda, 25 October 1957, www.ismaili.net/speech/s571025.html.

Ahearn ST (2005) Tolstoy's integration metaphor from *War and Peace*, *The American Mathematical Monthly*, 112:631–638.

Ali T (2014) Short cuts, *London Review of Books*, 36(9), 8 May 2014, www.lrb.co.uk/v36/n09/tarq-ali/short-cuts.html.

Ally E (2014) Mwalimu mmoja afundisha shule mwenyewe, aelemewa, *Majira*, 20 March 2014.

Aman F (2014) S'wanga grapples street children problem, *The Guardian* (Tanzania), 7 June 2014.

Aminzade R (2013) *Race, Nation, and Citizenship in Post-Colonial Africa: The Case of Tanzania*, Cambridge University Press, Cambridge, UK.

Astill J (2013) *The Great Tamasha: Cricket, Corruption, and the Turbulent Rise of Modern India*, Bloomsbury USA, New York.

Bakari R (2013) Mwanafunzi apata ulemavu kwa kipigo, *Uhuru*, 25 October 2013.

Banks JP (2014) Key sub-Saharan energy trends and their importance to the US, *The East African*, 3–9 May 2014.

Beilinson A (2013) AMS should sever ties to NSA (letter), Notices of the AMS, 60(11):1432.

Bello W, Cunningham S and Rau B (1999) *Dark Victory: The United States and Global Poverty*, Food First Books, San Francisco.

Braithwaite ER (1977;1959) *To Sir With Love*, Penguin Books, New York.

Brennan JR (2007) Between segregation and gentrification: Africans, Indians, and the struggle for housing in Dar es Salaam, 1920–1950, in JR Brennan, A Burton and Y Lawi (editors) (2007): 118–135.

Brennan JR, Burton A and Lawi Y (editors) (2007) *Dar es Salaam: Histories From an Emerging African Metropolis*, Mkuki na Nyota Publishers, Dar es Salaam.++

Bruce C (2001) *Conned Again, Watson! Cautionary Tales of Logic, Math, and Probability*, Perseus Publishing, Cambridge, MA.

Buwembo J (2013) Rape, racism and how we became a nation of pathetic xeno-phobics, *The East African*, 26 October – 1 November, 2013.

Cameron J and Dodd WA (1970) *Society, Schools & Progress in Tanzania*, Pergamon Press, Oxford.

Carroll L (1981;1865) *Alice in Wonderland*, Puffin Books, Harmondsworth, UK.++

Carroll L (1981;1871) *Through the Looking Glass*, Puffin Books, Harmondsworth, UK.++

Census (1957) *Report on the Census of the Non-African Population Taken on the Night of 20th/21st February 1957*, Government Printers, Dar es Salaam, 1957.

Chacha C (2014) Why retail giants may head to Dar, *The Citizen*, 19 March 2014.

Chambo T (2013) Miaka 52 ya Uhuru inaendana na mafanikio michezoni? *Tanzania Daima*, 9 December 2013.

Chibwete R (2014) Wine making firm owes grape farmers Sh85m, *The Citizen*, 19 March 2014.

Cliffe L and Saul JS (editors) (1973) *Socialism in Tanzania: A Reader*, Volumes I & II, East African Literature Bureau, Nairobi.++

Coulson A (2013;1982) *Tanzania: A Political Economy*, 2nd edition, Clarendon Press, Oxford.++

Daily News (2013) This strange world: Man dies after eating 28 eggs in a row for a bet, *Daily News*, 1 January 2013.

Danaher K (1994) *50 Years Is Enough: The Case Against the World Bank and the International Monetary Fund*, South End Press, Brooklyn, MA.

Dharas SG (1973) *Development of Southern Tanganyika & the Ismailis*, Mimeo-graphed Report, Ismaili Provincial Council, Mtwara.

Dira (2014) Wahindi 'wateka' Bohari ya Dawa, *Dira ya Mtanzania*, 17–23 February 2014.

Duodu C (2014) Halting the Central African Republic's descent into hell, *Pambazuka News*, Issue 668, 5 March 2014, pambazuka.org/en/category/comment/90844.

Editorial (2013a) Give cotton farmers their [due], *The Citizen*, 6 November 2013.

Editorial (2013b) Another live burial: A very disturbing trend, *The Citizen*, 17 November 2013.

Editorial (2014a) Education needs a hi-tech boost, *The Citizen*, 6 May 2014.

Editorial (2014b) Emulate winners to attain endeavours, *The Citizen*, 10 May 2014.

Editorial (2014c) Save Dar, keep it clean, *The Citizen*, 20 May 2014.

Edwards AR (2011) *The Slope of Kongwa Hill: A Boy's Tale of Africa*, Agio Publishing House, Canada.

Faustine A (2012) Dkt. Bilal azindua ujenzi wa nyumba za NHC mjini Mpanda, *Majira*, 25 November 2012.

Fazel AS (1992) Agakhan Sports Club, *The Express*, 21 May 1992, www.demwani.ca/af/Features/agakhan_sports_club.htm.

Fazel AS (2008a) *Memoirs*, www.dewani.ca/af/memoirs.

Fazel AS (2008b) Typical Indian mentality, www.dewani.ca/af/Forum/typicalindianmentality.htm.

Fazel N (2011) Uzawa: Ruffling feathers in Tanzania, *The African*, 2 November 2011.

Felician S (2012) Farmers massively cheated – inspector, *The Citizen*, 24 July 2012.

Freddy A (2014) 4 suspected rustlers lynched, *The Citizen*, 19 March 2014.

Gandhi MK (2008;1927) *My Experiments with Truth: An Autobiography*, Jaico Books, Mumbai, India.++

Gerdes P (2007) *Drawings from Angola: Living Mathematics*, Research Center for Culture, Mathematics and Education, Maputo, Mozambique.++

Germanos A (2014) Ocean acidification dissolving shells of key marine creature, *Common Dreams*, 1 May 2014, www.commondreams.org/headline/2014/05/01-9.html.

Greenwall HJ (1952) *His Highness The Aga Khan, Imam of the Ismailis*, The Cresset Press, London.

Grossman D (2009) *On Killing: The Psychological Cost of Learning to Kill in War and Society*, 2nd edition, Black Bay Books, New York.

Harrison GP (2013) *Think: Why You Should Question Everything*, Prometheus Books, New York.++

Hayter T (1971) *Aid as Imperialism*, Penguin Books, UK.

Henle J (2011) Is (some) mathematics poetry? *Journal of Humanistic Mathematics*, 1(1):94–100.

Hood J (2012) Jack London's *The Iron Heel*: An enduring classic, *World Socialist Web Site*, 8 March 2012, www.wsws.org/en/articles/2012/03/iron-m08.html.

Irwin A, Kim JY, Gershman J and Millen JV (2002) *Dying For Growth: Global Inequality and the Health of the Poor*, Common Courage Press, Monroe, Maine, USA.++

Ivaska A (2011) *Cultured States: Youth, Gender, and Modern Style in the 1960s Dar es Salaam*, Duke University Press, Durham and London.

Jalee P (1968) *The Pillage of the Third World*, Monthly Review Press, New York.

James B (2011) Agony, frustration as anti-social behavior rampant in Tanzania, *The Citizen*, 19 June 2011.

James CLR (2011;1993) *Beyond A Boundary*, Duke University Press, Durham.++

Jhaveri KL (1999) *Marching with Nyerere*, B R Publishing Corporation, New Delhi.

Jhaveri U (2014) *Dancing with Destiny*, Partridge Publishing, India.

Jongo S (2013a) Excitement engulfs cricket fraternity as APL nears, *The Citizen*, 21 January 2013.

Jongo S (2013b) Cricketers fly to Kampala for ICC tourney, *The Citizen*, 22 February 2013.

Jongo S (2013c) Zully: The man behind cricket development, *The Citizen*, 6 May 2013.

Jongo S (2013d) Tanzania cricketers in high spirits, *The Citizen*, 7 November 2013.

Jongo S (2013e) Dar girls defeat Mozambique in Twenty20 match, *The Citizen*, 9 December 2013.

Kahangwa G (2014) Kwa nini wamalize shule wakiwa mbumbumbu? *Mwananchi*, 20 May 2014.

Kaigarula W (2013) The 'nondo' dose kept division zero far away, *The Citizen*, 10 March 2013.

Kamndaya S (2011) Tanzanians spend Sh555bn on phone calls in 3 months, *The Citizen*, 17 January 2011.

Kassum A (2007) *Africa's Winds of Change: Memoirs of an International Tanzanian*, I. B. Tauris, London.

Kazenga J (2012) Dar schools set to battle it out in cricket league, *The Citizen*, 21 April 2014.

Kazenga J (2013a) ICC tourney an acid test for Dar as season unfolds, *The Citizen*, 4 February 2013.

Kazenga J (2013b) More push needed for women's cricket to grow, *The Citizen*, 4 November 2013.

Kazenga J (2014a) Junior cricket tourneys deserve more attention, *The Citizen*, 10 March 2014.

Kazenga J (2014b) Time for U19 side to prove worth, *The Citizen*, 12 May 2014.

Kiama H (2014) Mob lynches two suspected robbers in Kisarawe, *Daily News*, 4 June 2014.

Kilasi D (2011) Learning mathematics in the Tanzania classroom: Efforts and challenges, *Tanzania Journal of Education*, 1(1):1–19.

Kimboy F (2014) Only 70pc of radar change books issued, says report, *The Citizen*, 20 May 2014.

Kisanga D (2013) Where are the doctors? *The Guardian* (Tanzania), 18 November 2013.

Kubegeya M (2014) Gwiji wa taarabu Juma Bhalo hatunaye, *Mwananchi*, 12 April 2014.

Ladha M (1970) Islam - The most multi-racial faith: An interview with His Highness Aga Khan IV, *The Standard* (Tanzania), 1 November 1970. www.ismaili.net/heritage/node/27547.

Ladha M (2012) President here to woo Tanzania diaspora, *The Anchor Weekly*, 22 November 2012, www.theanchor.ca/2012/president-here-to-woo-tanzania-diaspora/.

Leinster T (2014) Maths spying: The quandary of working for the spooks, *New Scientist*, 23 April 2014, www.newscientist.com/article/mg22229660.200-maths-spying-quandary-of-working-for-spooks.html.

Leys C (1975) *Underdevelopment in Kenya: The Political Economy of Neo-Colonialism, 1964–1971*, University of California Press, New York.

Liganga L (2014) Hostile environment in schools: The past meets the present, *The Citizen*, 23 May 2014.

London J (1908) *The Iron Heel*, Macmillan, London.

Lozano A (2009) Math teacher awaits verdict in fraud trial, *Los Angeles Times*, 16 February 2009. www.latimes.com/news/local/la-me-mathteacher16-2009feb16,0,3630986.story.

Lusugga Kironde JM (2007) Race, class and housing in Dar es Salaam: The colonial impact on land use structure, in JR Brennan, A Burton and Y Lawi (editors) (2007): 97–117.++

Macha F (2013) Suala la adhabu ya uchapaji viboko kwa wanafunzi, *Mwananchi*, 5 May 2013.

Machira P (2013) Low prices worry cashew farmers, *The Citizen*, 6 November 2013.

Magashi E (2014) Auawa kwa kudaiwa kuiba jogo, *Mwananchi*, 17 June 2014.

Magdoff H (2003;1969) *Imperialism Without Colonies*, 2nd edition, Monthly Review Press, New York.

Major A (2013) Zeno's Paradox, in Sarah Glaz (editor) *Bridges 2013 Poetry Anthology*, www.math.uconn.edu/~glaz.

Mande M (2014) UK armed forces to train in Tanzania, *The African*, 21–27 April 2014.

Mapolu H (editor) (1979) *Workers and Management in Tanzania*, Tanzania Publishing House, Dar es Salaam.

Maregesi C (2014) Two charged with assaulting headmaster, *The Citizen*, 19 March 2014.

Matowo R and Lyimo F (2014) 200 cheats kicked out of police college, *The Citizen*, 10 May 2014.

Maumba F (2013) DC akemea wananchi wanaochafua shule, *Mtanzania*, 14 March 2013.

Mfuru J (2013) Mizania ya mabucha Dar wizi mtupu, *Nipashe*, 17 July 2013.

Mgamba R (2014) From Mokehouse to pamphlets: How education quality crashed, *The Citizen*, 20 May 2014.

Mjema D (2014) Atakayekacha mafunzo JKT kushtakiwa, *Mwananchi*, 14 May 2014.

Mkumbo V (2013) Osman Bairu: Mwanaharakati wa Kriketi mwenye ndoto lukuki. Apiga vita ubaguzi wa rangi kwa viongozi wa Kriketi nchini, *Majira*, 9 February 2013.

Mosoba T and Mwalimu S (2013) Tanzania nosedives in gender balance, *The Citizen*, 16 November 2013.

Msonsa F (2013) Where TZ doctors go for greener pastures, *The Citizen*, 18 November 2013.

Msyani B (2013) Dar team claims Nanak crown, *The Citizen*, 18 November 2013.

Mugarula F (2014) JK dedicates Africa Award to Tanzanians, *The Citizen*, 18 April 2014.

Mwakyusa A (2014) 700m/= job plan to create 6,400 jobs, *Daily News*, 21 January 2014.

Mwananchi (2013) Hapa na pale wiki hii, *Mwananchi*, 17 February 2013.

Mwaria CB, Silvia Federici S and McLaren J (2000) *African Visions: Literary Images, Political Change, and Social Struggle in Contemporary Africa*, Praeger, New York.

Mwinyi M (2013) Wanafunzi 200 wasomea chumba kimoja, *Uhuru*, 19 November 2013.

Mwita S (2014) Caning is harmful to young children, *Daily News*, 21 January 2014.

Nagar R (2013) Saboteurs? Or saviours? *Samar Magazine*, Issue 13, samarmagazine.org/archives/articles/10.

Naha AL (2013) Swim to school in fine fettle, *The Hindu*, 23 October 2013, www.thehindu.com/todays-paper/tp-national/tp-kerala/swim-to-school-in-fine-fettle.html.

Nkrumah K (1966) *Neo-Colonialism: The Last Stage of Imperialism*, International Publishers, London.

NSA (2014) Technology transfer – advanced mathematics, www.nsa.gov/research/tech_transfer/adv_math/.

Nyerere JK (1966) *Freedom and Unity: A Selection of Writings and Speeches, 1952–1965*, Oxford University Press, Dar es Salaam & Oxford.

Nyerere JK (1967) *Education for Self-Reliance*, in JK Nyerere (1968), pp. 267–290.++

Nyerere JK (1968) *Freedom and Socialism: A Selection of Writings and Speeches, 1965–1967*, Oxford University Press, Dar es Salaam & Oxford.

Omary M (2013) Dar boxer goes missing in Australia, *The Citizen*, 19 November 2013.

Paroo A (2012) *Aga Khan III and the British Empire: The Ismailis in Tanganyika, 1920–1957*, PhD Thesis, Graduate Program in History, York University, Toronto, Canada.

Peachey P (2014) Saudi student may have been murdered because she was wearing a hijab, *The Independent*, 19 June 2014, www.independent.co.uk/news/uk/crime/saudi-student-may-have-been-murdered-because-she-was-wearing-a-hijab.

Perkins J (2005) *Confessions of an Economic Hit Man*, Plume, New York.

Prashad V (2008) *The Darker Nations: A People's History of the Third World*, The New Press, New York.

Protace Y (2013) Only 31 pct of girls enrol at universities, *The Guardian* (Tanzania), 25 October 2013.

Puri S (2013) Asians in Tanzania: Saboteurs or saviours? *The International Indian*, ?? 2013:77–82.

Qorro E (2013) Did the Deputy Minister for Education get it right? *The Citizen*, 16 April 2013.

Raizada L (2011) Maths and punishment, *Gulf News* (Dubai), 13 September 2011.

Redlin L, Viet N and Watson S (2000) Thales' shadow, *Mathematics Magazine*, 73:347–353, www.csulb.edu/~saleem/Publications/Thales.pdf.

Reiss T (2012) *The Black Count: Glory, Revolution, Betrayal, and the Real Count of Monte Cristo*, Crown Publishers, New York.

Resnick IN (editor) (1968) *Tanzania: Revolution by Education*, Longmans of Tanzania, Arusha.

Rigney D (2010) *The Matthew Effect: How Advantage Begets Further Advantage*, Columbia University Press, New York.

Roden A (2012) *A Tanganyika Adventure: 1950–1956*, Wise Old Owl Publishing Company, Australia.

Rodney W (1972) *How Europe Underdeveloped Africa*, Bogle-L'Ouverture and Tanzania Publishing House, Dar es Salaam.

Rowden R (2013) The ghosts of user fees past: Exploring accountability for victims of a 30-year economic policy mistake, *Health and Human Rights*, 15(1), www.hhrjournal.org/archives/.

Rweyemamu JF (1973) *Underdevelopment and Industrialization in Tanzania: A Study of Perverse Capitalist Industrial Development*, Oxford University Press, Nairobi.

Sadallah M (2013) Shamuhuna: Tunasaka adhabu mbadala ya viboko kwa wanafunzi, *Nipashe*, 19 July 2013.

Sanga F (2012) No checks for Njombe crop traders, *The Citizen*, ?? July 2012.

Saul H (2013) Grandfather used pen knife to free himself from nine-tonne tractor, *The Independent*, 3 October 2013, www.independent.co.uk/news/world/grandfather-used-pen-knife-to-free-himself-from-nine-tonne-tractor.html.

Seka B (2010) Rekodi ya pekee ya Profesa Mmari, *Mwananchi*, 13 January 2010.

Semdoe H (2013) Ofisa elimu awaua madaraka walimu 50, *Mwananchi*, 6 March 2013.

Shaju P (2013) Kerala teacher swims to school to save time, *The Indian Express*, 6 September 2006, www.indianexpress.com/story-print/1165299.

Songa wa Songa (2013) Scholars show why doctors flee TZ, *The Citizen*, 20 November 2013.

Street Child World Cup (2014) Street Child World Cup, 2014, streetchildworldcup.org/rio-2014/

Sylvester R (2014) Wilaya ya Nyangw'ale yawekeza ziadi ya millioni 228 sekta ya elimu, *Mwananchi*, 12 May 2014.

Tahan M (1993;1938) *The Man Who Counted: A Collection of Mathematical Adventures*, WW Norton & Company, New York.

Tammet D (2012) What I am thinking about . . . Tolstoy and maths, *The Guardian* (UK), 23 August 2012, www.guardian.co.uk/books/booksblog/2012/aug/23/tolstoy-maths-daniel-tammet.html.

TANU (1967) *The Arusha Declaration and TANU's Policy of Socialism and Self-Reliance*, TANU Publicity Section, Dar es Salaam.++

The African (2014) Dar inks multi-billion dollar LNG deal, *The African*, 21–27 April 2014.

The Citizen (2014) Ugandan pupils worst at counting and reading in EA, *The Citizen*, 10 May 2014.

The Citizen Correspondent (2014) Oil, gas executives inspire UK alumni, *The Citizen*, 19 March 2014.

The Guardian Reporter (2013) Govt: Weights and measures must benefit rural producers, *The Guardian*, 24 June 2013.

Thomas DL (2012) *Globetrotting: African American Athletes and Cold War Politics*, University of Illinois Press, Illinois.

Torrie J (editor) (1986) *Banking on Poverty: The Impact of the IMF and World Bank*, Institute for Food and Development Policy, San Francisco.

Toussaint E (2007) *The World Bank: A Critical Primer*, Pluto Press, London.

Turse N (2013) AFRICOM's gigantic "Small Footprint," *Tom Dispatch*, 5 September 2013, www.tomdispatch.com/blog/175743/.

Ubwani Z (2014) EA sends to varsity only 4pc of youth, *The Citizen*, 20 May 2014.

Vassanji MG (2006) I was a city boy, a soft Asian, *New Internationalist*, Issue 396, 1 December 2006, www.newint.org/features/2006/12/01/psychology.

von Eschen PM (2004) *Satchmo Blows Up the World: Jazz Ambassadors Play the Cold War*, Harvard University Press, Cambridge, MA.

von Freyhold M (1979) *Ujamaa Villages in Tanzania: Analysis of a Social Experiment*, Monthly Review Press, New York.

Walji SRA (1974) *A History of the Ismaili Community in Tanzania*, PhD Dissertation, Department of History, University of Madison, Wisconsin.

Warner LA (2014) Why Africa should remain a priority for America, *The East African*, 3-9 May 2014.

Wearden G (2014) 85 richest people as wealthy as poorest half of the world, *The Guardian* (UK), 20 January 2014, www.guardian.co.uk.

Wikipedia (2013a) Muhammad Ali, *Wikipedia*, en.wikipedia.org/w/index.php?oldid=538916997.

Wikipedia (2013b) Pumpkin, *Wikipedia*, en.wikipedia.org/w/index.php?oldid=540116127.

Wikipedia (2014a) *Dhool ka Phool*, *Wikipedia*, en.wikipedia.org/w/index.php?oldid=587270216.

Wikipedia (2014b) *Dharmputra*, *Wikipedia*, en.wikipedia.org/w/index.php?oldid=587270216.

Wikipedia (2014c) Yash Chopra, *Wikipedia*, en.wikipedia.org/w/index.php?oldid=596906613.

Wikipedia (2014d) Chess-Boxing, *Wikipedia*, en.wikipedia.org/w/index.php?oldid=591290700.

Winters N (2013) How teachers in Africa are failed by mobile learning, *Science Development Network*, July 2013, www.scidev.net/global/education/opinion/how-teachers-in-africa-are-failed-by-mobile-learning.html.

Woo E (2009) Fitting tribute to math teacher, *Los Angeles Times*, 18 September 2009.

Yussuf I (2014) Zanzibar school feeding scheme now re-introduced, *Daily News*, 4 June 2014.

Additional Readings

Aga Khan IV (1964) *Speeches of Mowlana Hazar Imam, His Highness the Aga Khan, Part II, 1958–1963*, Shia Imami Ismailia Association for Africa, Kenya.

Alibhai-Brown Y (1997) *No Place Like Home: An Autobiography*, Virago Press, London.++

Blatner D (1997) *The Joy of* π, Walker and Company, New York.++

Bocock RJ (1971) The Ismailis in Tanzania: A Weberian analysis, *British Journal of Sociology*, 22: 365–380.

Callaway E (2013) Number games, *Nature*, 493:150–153.

Carr D (2008) *The Night of the Gun: A Reporter Investigates the Darkest Story of His Life*, Simon & Schuster, New York.++

Chomsky N and Herman ES (1979) *The Washington Connection and Third World Facism*, South End Press, Brooklyn, MA.++

Damji JS (2006) *Oyster Bay & Other Short Stories*, Author House, Bloomington, Indiana, USA.++

Enzesberger HM (1996) *The Number Devil: A Mathematical Adventure*, Metropolitan Books, New York.++

Gumede W (2010) Wealth for Africa, not from Africa, *Pambazuka News*, Issue 447, 10 September 2009, www.pambazuka.org/en/category/features/58601.

Harrison GP (2009) *Race and Reality*, Prometheus Books, New York.++

Kaniki MHY (editor) (1980) *Tanzania Under Colonial Rule*, Longmans, London.++

Kassam-Remtulla A (1999) *(Dis)placing Khojas: Forging Identities, Revitalizing Islam and Crafting Global Ismailism*, MA Thesis, Department of Anthropology, Stanford University.

Katz V (editor) (2000) *Using History to Teach Mathematics*, Mathematical Association of America, Washington, DC.++

Lowenstein R (2010) *The End of Wall Street*, The Penguin Press, New York.

Madsen W (1999) *Genocide and Covert Operations in Africa: 1993–1999*, Edwin Mellen Press, Lewinstone, New York.

Saunders FS (2001) *The Cultural Cold War: The CIA and the World of Arts and Letters*, New Press, New York.

Trivers R (2011) *The Folly of Fools: The Logic of Deceit and Self-Deception in Human Life*, Basic Books, New York.

Vassanji MG (1992) *Uhuru Street*, McClelland & Stewart Inc., Toronto, Canada.++

Wagner A (2009) *Paradoxical Life: Meaning, Matter and the Power of Human Choice*, Yale University Press, New Haven.

Zirin D (2005) *What's My Name, Fool? Sports and Resistance in the United States*, Haymarket Books, San Francisco.

Zirin D and Carlos JW (2011) *The John Carlos Story: The Sports Moment That Changed the World*, Haymarket Books, San Francisco.

Author Publications – Selected

Hirji KF (1973) School education and underdevelopment in Tanzania, *MajiMaji*, No. 12:1–23.

Hirji KF (1990) Academic pursuits under the link, *CODESRIA Bulletin* (Senegal), No. 2:9–16. (New version in CB Mwaria, S Federici and J McLaren (editors) (2000), Chapter 6.)

Hirji KF (2006) *Exact Analysis of Discrete Data*, Chapman & Hall/CRC Press, Boca Raton.

Hirji KF (2008a) Asians in Tanzania: Two contrasting fictionalized portraits, *Awaaz Magazine*, 5(2):49–51, www.awaazmagazine.com.

Hirji KF (2008b) Book review of Kassam (2007), *Awaaz Magazine*, Issue 2, July 2008, www.awaazmagazine.com.

Hirji KF (2009a) Liberating Africa with laughter: Ahmed Gora Ebrahim at the University of Dar es Salaam, *Awaaz Magazine*, 6(1):26–27, www.awaazmagazine.com.

Hirji KF (2009b) Books, bytes and higher miseducation, *ChemChemi: Fountain of Ideas* (University of Dar es Salaam), April 2009, Issue 1:13–20, with rejoinder by Justinian Galabawa, *ChemChemi*, Issue 1:20–22.

Hirji KF (2009c) No short-cut in assessing trial quality: A case study, *Trials*, 10:1 (with additional files), (highly accessed paper with editorial commentary: Gotzsche (2009) *Trials*, 10:2), www.trialsjournal.com.

Hirji KF and Premji Z (2011) Pre-referral rectal artesunate in severe malaria: A flawed trial, *Trials*, 12:188 (highly accessed paper), www.trialsjournal.com.

Hirji KF (2011) *Cheche: Reminiscences of a Radical Magazine*, Mkuki na Nyota Publishers, Dar es Salaam.++

Hirji KF (2012) *Statistics in the Media: Learning from Practice*, Media Council of Tanzania, Dar es Salaam.++

Websites for Quotations

math.furman.edu/~mwoodard/mquot.html

quotes.dictionary.com

www.beachquotes.net

www.brainyquote.com

www.famousquotesabout.com

www.finestquotes.com

www.goodreads.com

www.mrlsmath.com

www.quotegarden.com

www.quoteland.com

www.quotesdaddy.com

www.searchquotes.com

www.todayinsci.com

www.wisdomquotes.com

Websites for Hymns and Songs

Hindi Songs: www.indiamp3.com/music/
Ismaili Hymns: ismaili.net and ginans.net
English Songs: en.wikipedia.org
Swahili Songs: Google Search
National Anthems: national-anthems.net

Photo and Image Credits

Image 1: Mohamed Kassam
Image 4: Rumina Sunderji
Image 8: Fidahussein Moledina
Image 9: Karim Hirji, Amer Mohamed, Isaac Marande
Sunflower Floret Pattern (Chapter 12): *Wikipedia*, Sunflower, en.wikipedia.
org/wiki/File:SunflowerModel.svg#filelinks

Author Profile

Karim F Hirji holds BSc (First Class, Mathematics and Education, University of Dar es Salaam, 1971), MSc (Operations Research, University of London, 1972), and SM and DSc (Biostatistics, Harvard University, 1982 and 1986) degrees, and has taught at the University of Dar es Salaam, the National Institute of Transport, and the University of California at Los Angeles. Once a visiting professor at the University of California, San Francisco, he has taught short courses at the University of Bergen and the University of Oslo.

He was founding editor of *Cheche*, a renowned progressive student magazine at the University of Dar es Salaam (1969–1970); the initiator and staff patron of *The Transporter* at the National Institute of Transport, Tanzania (1977–1979); and an associate editor of the international biostatistics journal *Statistics in Medicine* (1994–2004).

He is the author of *Exact Analysis of Discrete Data* (Chapman and Hall/CRC Press, Boca Raton, 2005) and *Statistics in the Media: Learning from Practice* (Media Council of Tanzania, Dar es Salaam, 2012). He also edited and is the main author of *Cheche: Reminiscences of a Radical Magazine* (Mkuki na Nyota Publishers, Dar es Salaam, 2010).

A recognized authority on methods for statistical analysis of small sample discrete data, the author of the only book on the subject, he received the Snedecor Prize for Best Publication in Biometry from the American Statistical Association and International Biometrics Society for the year 1989.

He has published many papers and book chapters in the areas of statistical methodology, applied biomedical research, the history and practice of education in Tanzania, and written numerous essays, commentaries and book reviews on varied topics for the mass media and popular magazines.

He retired from his position of Professor of Medical Statistics at the Muhimbili University of Health and Allied Sciences in 2012. Currently a Fellow of the Tanzania Academy of Sciences, he walks, talks, reads, writes and dreams in the friendly but congested, fume-filled, expensive environs of Dar es Salaam. He may be contacted at kfhirji@aol.com.